HYDRODYNAMICS OF LAKES

DEVELOPMENTS IN WATER SCIENCE, 11

advisory editor

VEN TE CHOW

Professor of Civil and Hydrosystems Engineering
Hydrosystems Laboratory
University of Illinois
Urbana, Ill., U.S.A.

OTHER TITLES IN THIS SERIES

HYDRODYNAMICS OF LAKES

PROCEEDINGS OF A SYMPOSIUM 12–13 OCTOBER, 1978
LAUSANNE, SWITZERLAND

EDITED BY

WALTER H. GRAF

Laboratoire d'hydraulique, Ecole Polytechnique Fédérale, Lausanne,
Switzerland

and

CLIFFORD H. MORTIMER

Center for Great Lakes Studies, University of Wisconsin, Milwaukee, U.S.A.

ELSEVIER SCIENTIFIC PUBLISHING COMPANY
Amsterdam–Oxford–New York   1979

ELSEVIER SCIENTIFIC PUBLISHING COMPANY
335 Jan van Galenstraat
P.O. Box 211, 1000 AE Amsterdam, The Netherlands

Distributors for the United States and Canada:

ELSEVIER/NORTH-HOLLAND INC.
52, Vanderbilt Avenue
New York, N.Y. 10017

Library of Congress Cataloging in Publication Data
Main entry under title:

Hydrodynamics of lakes.

    (Developments in water science ; 11)
    Bibliography: p.
    Includes index.
    1. Lakes--Congresses. 2. Hydrodynamics--Congresses.
3. Lakes--Europe--Congresses. I. Graf, Walter Hans,
1936-   II. Mortimer, Clifford Hiley. III. Series.
GB1601.2.H89   551.4'82   79-17492
ISBN 0-444-41827-X

ISBN 0-444-41827-X (Vol. 11)
ISBN 0-444-41669-2 (Series)

Printed in The Netherlands

FOREWORD

The Symposium, of which this volume constitutes the Proceedings, was organized as part of the 50th anniversary celebration of the founding of the Hydraulics Laboratory (LHYDREP, *Laboratoire d'hydraulique* of the Ecole Polytechnique Fédéral de Lausanne).

The earliest documentary evidence of the name *Laboratoire d'hydraulique* was a receipt dated October 1928 acknowledging the purchase of a hydraulic flume. The year 1928 is therefore taken to mark the establishment of the laboratory as a distinct unit by Prof. Alfred Stucky.

The research of the laboratory, while varied, has always been linked to the needs of the civil engineering profession. Although the majority of the activity was directed towards hydro-electric engineering of major national and international importance, the laboratory has always maintained a certain capacity for problems of coastal engineering.

Obviously for an educational laboratory of the size of LHYDREP it became increasingly impossible to cover the entire field of hydraulics. Thus in recent years, the research activities have been focused mainly in four directions: "Two Phase Flow", "Hydrodynamics of Lakes", "Extreme Value Hydrology", and "Model Techniques".

Intensive research on hydraulic problems encountered in and around lakes was begun at LHYDREP in the fall of 1975, in the belief that this *new* activity would add to the better understanding of lakes, which are an important part of our national water resources. In 1976, the significance of lake research was recognized officially in Switzerland, when the "Swiss National Science Foundation (FNSRS)" announced a closely related topic as one of its first national programs.

Thus the symposium on the "Hydrodynamics of Lakes" represents a continuing activity of the laboratory. The international response - researchers from eleven countries submitted papers - provided evidence of the immediate and timely importance of the topic; thus the symposium was a memorable event celebrating the first 50 years of progress in the Laboratoire d'hydraulique of the Ecole Polytechnique de Lausanne.

The symposium consisted of four sessions. Together with the four general lectures, which opened each session, 21 papers cover the inter-related experimental and theoretical aspects of lake hydrodynamics.

The session MATHEMATICAL MODELLING (p. 1 - 122) discusses the problems arising in the formulation of the basic equations (especially with respect to turbulence), numerical algorithms and their mathematical properties, as well as verification of models. The session MEASURING TECHNIQUES (p. 123 - 182) focuses on field problems, measuring instruments, data collection and physical modelling. In the session DATA ANALYSIS (p. 183 - 276) strategies for coupling field data and mathematical and/or physical models is discussed. The session AIR-WATER INTERFACE (p. 277 - 356) is devoted to the principal mechanisms which are responsible for water movement in lakes.

As is the case with many symposium proceedings, this one suffers from some lack of coherence and from incompleteness in coverage of the session topics. Nevertheless the editors hope that physical limnologists and oceanographers, as well as general readers, will find much to interest them in this volume, viewing it as a conspectus of some recent advances as well as historical trends in this field. The papers are reproduced largely in the form in which they were presented. Editorial changes have, by deliberate choice,been minor and made only in the interest of clarity.

The Hydraulics Laboratory (LHYDREP) expresses its gratitude to all who made this celebratory symposium possible, in particular to those who presented papers, also to Clifford H. Mortimer FRS for his assistance as co-editor, to the LHYDREP staff, especially Sebastian W. Bauer, Jean-Patrick Prost, and Perrinjaquet for their enthusiastic help in the organization.

Walter H. Graf

CONTENTS

AIR-WATER INTERFACE

General Lecture

Papers

NUMERICAL MODELLING OF CIRCULATION IN LAKES

J. SÜNDERMANN

Institut für Meereskunde, Universität Hamburg, Hamburg (Fed. Rep. of Germany)

ABSTRACT

This paper surveys the present stage of numerical modelling of circulation in lakes. Problems concerning the formulation of the basic equations, especially with respect to turbulence, numerical algorithms, and their mathematical properties, as well as the verification of models by Hansen-Huber, Bauer-Graf, and Hollan-Simons are discussed in detail.
In the final part, recommendations for further research work are given.

INTRODUCTION

This very special topic - at least for a non-expert - has been chosen as one of the four main papers of this Symposium for a number of reasons.

In the first place, studying the circulation in lakes must be sufficiently interesting and important for close study. This is undoubtedly a fact. From a scientific viewpoint, it is complicated enough, so that we are far from having solved all problems. At the same time it is so specific that the approaches of the further advanced marine hydrodynamics cannot simply be transferred to it.

In recent times, economic arguments have been increasingly used in connection with scientific problems, in the hope of persuading politicians to make funds available. Circulation in lakes is closely related to questions of environmental protection, water supply, and ecology. An analysis and, if possible, a prognosis of these processes is, therefore, of economic interest as well.

A primary requirement for numerical modelling of circulation in lakes is an understanding of the basic physical processes which must be sufficiently understood for formulation in strict laws. Generally, use is made of the fundamental conservation laws of mechanics and hydrodynamics. They can be formulated as integral or differential equations. Although the corresponding fundamentals are available, their application to specific situations in natural waters with their non-linear and turbulent behaviour presents some difficulties.

The basic equations cannot be solved analytically in a closed form. Therefore, they must be treated by approximation with the help of the discretization methods which have been developed in numerical mathematics. This leads to new problems originating from mathematics. Some of these can be dealt with, but a larger portion has not yet been sufficiently studied, particularly in the case of non-linear equation systems.

The actual solution of a numerical algorithm is not possible without the existence and suitable programming of large electronic computers. The influence of this aspect on the original scientific problem should not be underestimated. Available computer capacities are already influencing the formulation of the basic equations, and even the formulation of the hydrodynamic problem itself.

Considerable progress has been made in this direction within the last decade. This is proved by a large number of successful investigations; as in the field of lake research, it is generally agreed that systematic research work is hardly possible without the use of mathematical models. This short survey of the problems incurred also indicates the flexibility and capability required of the numerical modeller. In the following, I will spotlight individual fields.

It is not possible to give a thorough review. I present a survey of the existing model classes, problems of parametrization, numerics, and verification. This survey is not fully systematic but emphasizes certain aspects. Finally I shall deal in detail with three representative models: Hansen-Huber, Bauer-Graf, Hollan-Simons.

For extensive studies, I call attention to the work of F.M. Boyce, 1974; C.H. Mortimer, 1974, and R.T. Cheng, T.M. Powell, T.M. Dillon, 1976.

BASIC HYDRODYNAMICS OF LAKES

Characteristic properties

Hydrodynamics of lakes is certainly closely related to hydrodynamics of the sea. Consequently, the corresponding sciences are closely related to each other in content as well methods; and both can draw profit from each other. Which, however, are the specific properties of lakes?

Boyce, 1974, has listed four characterizing properties for the Great Lakes. They do, however, not apply to all lakes. In general, the following three statements may be made:

1) Lakes are closed basins.

   This geometric behaviour characterizes, to a large degree, the hydrodynamic behaviour. The influences of lateral boundary conditions are insignificant, the main boundary condition being exercised by the surface. The mechanical energy introduced into the system is also dissipated within it.

2) The water volume of lakes is considerably smaller than that of the ocean. Consequently, the astronomical tides are negligibly small. On the other hand, the water volume can be large enough for the Coriolis force to become an important influence.

3) Wind is the principal source of mechanical energy. This follows from 1)
and 2). Moreover, in baroclinically stratified lakes, circulations may
also be induced by density gradients. Furthermore, the system can gain
or lose energy through inflows and outflow.

The formation of stratified water masses by seasonal heating of the upper boundary
layer is not a typical property of lakes alone, since it occurs in the sea as well.

A lake as well as the ocean can be considered as a system which reacts with a
corresponding output to certain external inputs. Thus the dynamical processes in
a lake are essentially responses to the wind's influence. These processes take
place on different scales, as Boyce, 1974, has explained in detail.

As in the ocean, a lake is more or less a nonlinear system, which means that
the different scales of the motion spectrum interact with each other, and therefore,
cannot in principle be treated separately. This fundamental property, and the task
of parametrization connected with it, also pose problems for the modelling of lake
hydrodynamics, as noted below.

Fundamental equations

The physical state of a lake can be completely described by seven macroscopic
quantities, all of them expressed as functions of space and time:

v_i (i = 1, 2, 3)   velocity vector
p   pressure
T   temperature
S   salinity
ρ density

Seven equations are required for determining these seven variables. They are obtained from the conservation laws of mechanics and thermodynamics (Krauss, 1973).

Equation of motion (Navier-Stokes):

$$\frac{\partial v_i}{\partial t} + v_j \frac{\partial v_i}{\partial x_j} = \frac{1}{\rho}\left(k_i - \frac{\partial p}{\partial x_i}\right) + \nu \frac{\partial^2 v_i}{\partial x_j \partial x_j} \tag{1}$$

where k_i is the resultant of the external forces and ν the (molecular) kinematic
viscosity. x_i are the co-ordinates in space and t in time.

Equation of continuity :

$$\frac{\partial \rho}{\partial t} + \frac{\partial}{\partial x_j} (\rho v_j) = 0 \tag{2}$$

Equation of heat conduction:

$$\frac{\partial T}{\partial t} + v_j \frac{\partial T}{\partial x_j} = \beta^{(T)} \frac{\partial^2 T}{\partial x_j \partial x_j} \tag{3}$$

$\beta^{(T)}$ denotes the (molecular) thermo-diffusion coefficient.

Equation of diffusion :

$$\frac{\partial S}{\partial t} + v_j \frac{\partial S}{\partial x_j} = \beta^{(S)} \frac{\partial^2 S}{\partial x_j \partial x_j} \tag{4}$$

where $\beta^{(S)}$ is the (molecular) salinity diffusion coefficient.

Equation of state :

$$\rho = F (p, T, S) \tag{5}$$

F is an empirical function.

Parametrization of turbulence

The set of equations (1) to (5) exactly describes the physics of a lake. The coefficients involved are material properties.

Simple estimation shows that the Reynolds number associated with most motions in lakes is large. Therefore, the flow is dominantly turbulent. The turbulence occurs on different scales with respect to space and time, interacting with each other. This means that even the "mean motion", in which the limnologist is mainly interested, is also determined by microscale processes. For economical reasons, however, a simultaneous treatment of all interacting scales is impossible, although their interaction cannot be ignored physically. In this situation normally the short wave part of the motion spectrum is cut at a certain abscissa, and the "subgrid turbulence" is parametricized.

If $q (x_i, t)$ is a physical quantity of the fluid, it is split up into a mean and a fluctuating part

$$q (x_i, t) = \bar{q} (x_i) + q'(x_i, t) \tag{6}$$

where the mean part is defined as an averaged value over a characteristic period
of the scale considered.

The application of (6) to the basic set of equations (1) to (5) results in the
fundamental equations in terms of the mean quantities in which we are mainly
interested. There remain, however, non-vanishing correlations of the turbulent
fluctuations, such as

$$\overline{v_i' v_j'} \quad , \quad \overline{v_j' T'}$$

These quantities act as additional stresses or diffusion, much greater than the
molecular ones. Their elimination represents the closure problem of turbulence.

Normally, the Boussinesq approximation is used for parametricizing turbulence
by means of eddy viscosity or diffusion coefficients, A and K:

$$- \overline{v_i' v_j'} = A \left(\frac{\partial \overline{v_i}}{\partial x_j} + \frac{\partial \overline{v_j}}{\partial x_i} \right) \tag{7}$$

$$- \overline{v_j' T'} = K \frac{\partial \overline{T}}{\partial x_j} \tag{8}$$

In most cases, A and K are determined by calibration of the hydrodynamical model
against field data. In doing so, analytical approaches such as Prandtl's mixing
length hypothesis, or the dependency on the Richardson number are of some help.

Recently mathematical models of turbulence have also been increasingly used.
Here the eddy coefficients are related to characteristic quantities of the turbulence, e.g. the kinetic energy k and the dissipation ε.

$$A = c_o \frac{k^2}{\varepsilon}$$

The unknowns k and ε are determined by means of additional equations (Launder and
Spalding, 1972).

$$\rho \left(\frac{\partial k}{\partial t} + \overline{v_j} \frac{\partial k}{\partial x_j} \right) = \frac{\partial}{\partial x_j} \left(\frac{A}{\sigma_k} \frac{\partial k}{\partial x_j} \right) + A \left(\frac{\partial \overline{v_i}}{\partial x_j} + \frac{\partial \overline{v_j}}{\partial x_i} \right) \frac{\partial \overline{v_i}}{\partial x_j} - \varepsilon$$

$$\rho \left(\frac{\partial \varepsilon}{\partial t} + \overline{v_j} \frac{\partial \varepsilon}{\partial x_j} \right) = \frac{\partial}{\partial x_j} \left(\frac{A}{\sigma_\varepsilon} \frac{\partial \varepsilon}{\partial x_j} \right) + c_1 A \frac{\varepsilon}{k} \left(\frac{\partial \overline{v_i}}{\partial x_j} + \frac{\partial \overline{v_j}}{\partial x_i} \right) \frac{\partial \overline{v_i}}{\partial x_j} - c_2 \frac{\varepsilon^2}{k}$$

The empirical constants c_o, c_1, c_2, σ_k, σ_ε change very little, even in varying
applications.

Finally, the turbulent fluctuation q' can be simulated directly by choosing it from a statistical distribution F. Assume, for instance,

$$v_i' = \frac{dx_i'}{dt} \qquad \text{with} \qquad dx_i' \in F(dx_i')$$

Then the corresponding isotropic eddy coefficient can be expressed as (Einstein, 1905):

$$A = \frac{1}{2T} \int_{-\infty}^{+\infty} x_j' x_j' \; F(dx_i') \; dx_i' \Bigg/ \int_{-\infty}^{+\infty} F(dx_i') \; dx_i'$$

where T is a time period. This form allows to apply the Monte Carlo technique.

Specifying conditions

When applying the basic equations (1) to (8) to natural lakes, their specific geometrical and physical conditions allow a number of simplifications. These "specifying conditions" are:

1) The water is incompressible.
   Density variations are of importance only for buoyancy forces.

2) Vertical accelerations can be neglected.

3) The flow is quasi-hydrostatic.

4) The only external force is gravity.

5) Salinity can be taken as constant.

On the other hand, for larger lakes, the Coriolis force must additionally be taken into account, commonly in a simplified form.

By means of these specifying conditions, the following equations are obtained:

$$\frac{\partial \bar{u}}{\partial t} + \bar{u}\frac{\partial \bar{u}}{\partial x} + \bar{v}\frac{\partial \bar{u}}{\partial y} + \bar{w}\frac{\partial \bar{u}}{\partial z} - f\bar{v} = -\frac{1}{\rho}\frac{\partial \bar{p}}{\partial x} + \frac{\partial}{\partial x}(A_h\frac{\partial \bar{u}}{\partial x}) + \frac{\partial}{\partial y}(A_h\frac{\partial \bar{u}}{\partial y}) + \frac{\partial}{\partial z}(A_v\frac{\partial \bar{u}}{\partial z}) \quad (9)$$

$$\frac{\partial \bar{v}}{\partial t} + \bar{u}\frac{\partial \bar{v}}{\partial x} + \bar{v}\frac{\partial \bar{v}}{\partial y} + \bar{w}\frac{\partial \bar{v}}{\partial z} + f\bar{u} = -\frac{1}{\rho}\frac{\partial \bar{p}}{\partial y} + \frac{\partial}{\partial x}(A_h\frac{\partial \bar{v}}{\partial x}) + \frac{\partial}{\partial y}(A_h\frac{\partial \bar{v}}{\partial y}) + \frac{\partial}{\partial z}(A_v\frac{\partial \bar{v}}{\partial z}) \quad (10)$$

$$\frac{\partial \bar{u}}{\partial x} + \frac{\partial \bar{v}}{\partial y} + \frac{\partial \bar{w}}{\partial z} = 0 \qquad (11)$$

$$\frac{\partial \overline{T}}{\partial t} + \overline{u}\,\frac{\partial \overline{T}}{\partial x} + \overline{v}\,\frac{\partial \overline{T}}{\partial y} + \overline{w}\,\frac{\partial \overline{T}}{\partial z} = \frac{\partial}{\partial x}\left(K_h\,\frac{\partial \overline{T}}{\partial x}\right) + \frac{\partial}{\partial y}\left(K_h\,\frac{\partial \overline{T}}{\partial y}\right) + \frac{\partial}{\partial z}\left(K_v\,\frac{\partial \overline{T}}{\partial z}\right) \tag{12}$$

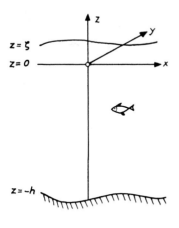

Here $\overline{u}$, $\overline{v}$, $\overline{w}$ are the components of the velocity vector in the x, y, z directions of a Cartesian co-ordinate system (Fig. 1); f is the (constant) Coriolis parameter. The indices h and v refer to the horizontal and the vertical direction, respectively.

The assumption of a hydrostatic equilibrium leads to the following expression for the pressure:

Fig. 1. Cartesian co-ordinates

$$p = p_s + g\left(\rho_o\zeta + \int_z^\zeta \Delta\rho\,dz\right) \tag{13}$$

where p_s denotes the atmospheric pressure, g the acceleration of gravity, ζ the surface elevation, ρ_o the mean water density, and $\Delta\rho$ the density anomaly.

These equations are sometimes linearized by neglecting the convective terms. For steady conditions, the time derivatives can be set equal to zero.

If, due to the geometrical shape of a lake, the motions in certain co-ordinate directions are obviously dominating, a mean value can be introduced for these components by integration over the other space co-ordinate. In this manner, for instance, plane models with vertically integrated velocities

$$\overline{\overline{u}} = \frac{1}{z_1 - z_2}\int_{z_2}^{z_1}\overline{u}\,dz\,,\qquad \overline{\overline{v}} = \frac{1}{z_1 - z_2}\int_{z_2}^{z_1}\overline{v}\,dz \tag{14}$$

are obtained. The water body can be discretized into a number of vertically stratified layers, with averaged horizontal flows. As a limiting case, a single layer model is obtained when integrating over the whole depth.

In a similar way (for an elongated lake) an integration over the width can be carried out, leading to a water discharge formulation. Any such space-averaging reduces the computational effort, but it results - by analogy with the introduction of turbulence - in "dispersion coefficients" to be determined empirically.

Boundary conditions

In order to integrate the partial differential equations (9) to (12), forming a hyperbolic system of the second order, boundary conditions must be prescribed at the geometrical borders of the lake. They represent the fluxes of momentum and heat through the free surface and the bottom, as well as the kinematic conditions.
Normally they are chosen as follows:

Free surface s:

$$\rho A_v \frac{\partial \overline{u}}{\partial z}\bigg|_s = \tau_{sx} \quad , \quad \rho A_v \frac{\partial \overline{v}}{\partial z}\bigg|_s = \tau_{sy} \tag{15}$$

$$c_p \rho K_v \frac{\partial \overline{T}}{\partial z}\bigg|_s = q_s \qquad \frac{\partial \zeta}{\partial t} + \overline{u}_s \frac{\partial \zeta}{\partial x} + \overline{v}_s \frac{\partial \zeta}{\partial y} - w_s = 0$$

Bottom b:

$$\rho A_v \frac{\partial \overline{u}}{\partial z}\bigg|_b = \tau_{bx} \quad , \qquad \rho A_v \frac{\partial \overline{v}}{\partial z}\bigg|_b = \tau_{by} \tag{16}$$

$$\overline{u}_b \frac{\partial h}{\partial x} + \overline{v}_b \frac{\partial h}{\partial y} + \overline{w}_b = 0 \quad , \qquad \frac{\partial \overline{T}}{\partial z}\bigg|_b = 0$$

Lateral boundaries:

$$\overline{u} = \overline{v} = \overline{w} = 0 \qquad \text{(non slip)} \tag{17}$$

Sometimes this condition is used also at the bottom. The socalled radiation boundary condition used for open boundaries is of no relevance for the hydrodynamics of lakes.

Here τ_s and τ_b denote the stresses at the surface and the bottom due to wind and friction, respectively, q_s the downward heat flux, and c_p the heat capacity.

For the stresses the following empirical relationships are commonly chosen:

$$\tau_{sx} = \lambda \sqrt{U^2 + V^2} \ U \tag{18}$$

$$\tau_{sy} = \lambda \sqrt{U^2 + V^2} \ V$$

where U and V are wind velocities in the x and y directions respectively and

$$\tau_{bx} = r \ \sqrt{\overline{u^2} + \overline{v^2}} \ \ \overline{u}$$

$$\tau_{by} = r \ \sqrt{\overline{u^2} + \overline{v^2}} \ \ \overline{v}$$

(19)

where λ is the drag coefficient and r is the bottom friction factor.

NUMERICAL MODELS OF THE CIRCULATION IN LAKES

Because of the non-linear behaviour and irregular geometry of natural lakes, equations (9) to (12) cannot be solved analytically, and they must therefore be treated numerically. Many very powerful methods for approximate solution of non-linear partial differential equations are now available from numerical mathematics. These methods, however, involve some mathematical problems, such as stability, convergence, consistency, which are by no means completely solved. These questions are mentioned here, but not treated in detail.

Classification of models

Nearly all models used for the simulation of circulation in lakes can be equally applied to the ocean or to coastal waters, and vice versa. They were developed in the fields of physical oceanography and coastal engineering. A review of the different models has been published by Cheng, Powell and Dillon, 1976. Their classification partially coincides with the one presented here.

The grouping of numerical models can be guided by
- the form of the basic equations (including the parametrization),
- the method of numerical solution used.
In the following, the most important variants, including a few representative examples, are compiled. This compilation cannot claim completeness.

Concerning the basic equations

The numerical solution of the basic equations in the general form (9) to (12) requires a three-dimensional discretization of the water body which is to be in-vestigated. Normally the region is covered by a spatial Eulerian grid (Fig. 2). The unknown state quantities are computed at the nodal points for successive time steps. These most comprehensive models, which involve a high computational effort, are called baroclinic multilevel models. The successive numerical integration of the equations with respect to time is known as time-stepping.

The most advanced models of physical oceanography and coastal engineering can be found in this group, e.g. the models of Bryan, 1969, Marchuk and Zalesny, 1974, Simons, 1974, 1975, Leendertse and Liu, 1975, as well as the model of Hollan and

Simons, 1978, which will be discussed later.

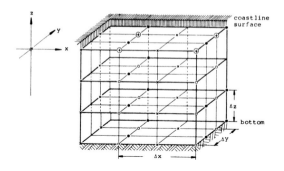

Three dimensional computational grid. The unknowns are calculated in the following points

+ ζ x u   • v   ∘ w   ⊕ ζ and w

Fig. 2. Multi-level grid

In these models the surface response, the non-linear inertial terms, the buoyancy forces, and variable viscosities in the horizontal and the vertical directions are included. If the density is assumed to be constant, which is a very rough approximation for lake dynamics, a barotropic <u>multi-level</u> model is obtained. Equation (13) then yields

$$p = p_s + g\rho_o \, (\zeta - z)$$

which states that the pressure is dependent only on the atmospheric pressure and on the distance from the water surface. Such a model was investigated by Sündermann, 1974 and Tsvetova, 1974. Equation (12) for the temperature is separated from the remaining system.

If the basic equations (9), (10), (11), (13) are further simplified and linearized by neglecting the inertia terms, they can be partially treated analytically. Heaps, 1973, has designed a three-dimensional barotropic model, which approximates the vertical structure of the currents by an analytical expansion into eigenfunctions. In the horizontal directions and in the time domain the equations are integrated numerically.

The simplest multi-level model takes only the balance of Coriolis force, pressure gradient, and vertical momentum exchange from equations (9) and (10). It is therefore called an <u>Ekman-type model</u>. In that case the vertical structure of the currents can also be determined analytically. The horizontal velocity field can be calculated numerically by means of the stream function. Applications of this method have been carried out by Liggett and Hadjitheodorou, 1969, and Bauer and Graf, 1978.

Those models, which are based on piecewise vertical integration of equations (9) to (12), according to (14), differ principally from the multi-level models. In such models the water body is divided into a number of vertically stratified layers, each with constant density, and with only horizontally varying state

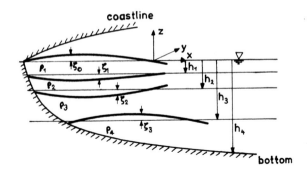

Fig. 3. Multi-layer model

quantities. Those models use a fixed Eulerian grid only in the horizontal plane,
whereas the interfacial boundaries in the vertical are free-moving (Fig. 3).
They are called multi-layer models. A main difficulty of these models is presented
in the formulation of suitable boundary conditions at the interior interfaces.
The model developed by Simons, 1973, for the Great Lakes is referred to as an
example. As a limiting case, the vertically integrated barotropic models also
belong to this class (Hansen and Huber, 1966).

Concerning the numerical technique

For the numerical solution of the governing equations the finite difference method
(FDM) or the finite element method (FEM) are mostly used. They are formulated in
various versions, with different behaviour with respect to stability and convergence.

Recently also the Monte Carlo technique has been applied to solve the heat
transport equation.

Computational techniques

Many different numerical methods exist at present in mathematical hydrodynamics.
It is impossible to give a complete review of them within the scope of this article.
For a more detailed study, reference is made to the books of Richtmyer-Morton,
1967, Roache, 1972, Zienkiewicz, 1972, and Marchuk, 1977. Again, in what follows,
only certain classes of computational techniques are discussed.

Time integration

Considering the time derivatives alone, the systems (9) to (12) can be represented by the following matrix equation

$$\frac{dq_i \ (x_i, \ t)}{dt} = L_{ij} \ q_j \ (x_i, \ t) \tag{20}$$

with the initial condition

$$q_i \ (x_i, \ 0) = q_i^{\ o} \ (x_i)$$

L_{ij} is a linear operator. The discretization of the time domain T by finite time steps Δt transforms (20) into a finite difference equation. The special form depends on how many successive time levels are considered and what type of differences are used. Forward differences are most commonly used, leading to an explicit procedure:

$$q_i^{n+1} = L_{ij}^{*} \ (\Delta t) \ q_j^{n} \tag{21}$$

where L_{ij}^{*} is a linear difference operator and n denotes the time step. It is required of any time integration scheme that L_{ij}^{*} is a consistent, convergent, and stable approximation of L_{ij}; mass, energy, momentum, and vorticity have to be conserved.

There are several stability criteria which are based on the necessary condition of von Neumann:

$$|\lambda_m| < 1 + O \ (\Delta t) \tag{22}$$

where λ_m (m = 1,...,M) are the eigenvalues of L_{ij}^{*} (Δt).

Applying criterion (22) to the basic equations (9) to (12) and (13), depending on the instantaneous balance of the acceleration term with one of the other terms, a set of stability criteria is obtained which must be simultaneously satisfied:

$$Cr = \frac{\Delta t}{\Delta x} \ (|\overline{u^2} + \overline{v^2}|^{1/2} + |2gh|^{1/2}) \leqq 1 \tag{23}$$

$$\frac{2A_h \Delta t}{\Delta^2 x} \leqq 1 \ , \qquad \frac{2A_v \Delta t}{\Delta^2 z} \leqq 1 \tag{24}$$

$$|w| \frac{\Delta t}{\Delta z} \leq 1 \qquad\qquad (25)$$

Here $\Delta x = \Delta y$ is the horizontal, Δz the vertical grid distance; and (23) is the wellknown stability criterion of Courant-Friedrichs-Lewy. Cr denotes the Courant number.

From (12) we obtain

$$\frac{2K_h \Delta t}{\Delta^2 x} \leq 1 \; , \qquad \frac{2K_v \Delta t}{\Delta^2 z} \leq 1 \qquad\qquad (26)$$

Conditions (23) to (26) can impose a very severe restriction on the time step. For instance with a grid distance of $\Delta x = 1$ km, and a maximum depth of 200 m, which may be typical of a lake, a time step of 20 seconds is obtained. This requires a very large computational effort. Moreover, the above conditions are only necessary, and there is no guarantee of a stable solution.

We find frequently in numerical computations that condition (22) is sufficient for stability by means of an automatically-acting dissipative mechanism, the "numerical diffusion". In some cases, such "dissipative interfaces" (Abbott, 1974) are specially introduced in order to achieve stability.

A dissipative interface acts as a filter, which substitutes q_i by a quantity q_i^* (q_i) with

$$\| q_i^{*n} \| < \| q_i^n \| \qquad\qquad (27)$$

$\| \cdot \|$ is commonly chosen as the "energy norm".

Frequently according to (27) the so-called α-algorithm is used:

$$q_i^{*n} = \alpha q_i^{n+1} + (1-\alpha) \; q_i^n \; , \qquad 0 \leq \alpha \leq 1 \qquad\qquad (28)$$

The dissipative operator (28) requires for $\alpha = 0$ (fully explicit) the satisfaction of the Courant condition (23); for $0 < \alpha < 1/2$ the procedure is conditionally, and for $1/2 \leq \alpha < 1$ it is unconditionally stable. It was shown by Crank-Nicholson, 1947, that the highest accuracy is given by $\alpha = 1/2$. For increasing α the improved stability is paid for by a loss of accuracy. Therefore, Courant numbers of about 5 should not in general be exceeded.

The application of implicit methods to three-dimensional problems leads to large equation systems and, hence, to a great computational effort. This can be reduced considerably by dividing the whole numerical procedure by means of a "partitioning" algorithm into a series of one-dimensional implicit and explicit procedures, which can be solved very effectively by the double sweep technique. This work was pioneered in hydrodynamics by the alternating direction implicit method (ADI) of Leendertse, 1967.

It has been shown by Yanenko, 1967, and Marchuk, 1978, that the ADI is a special case of their "splitting-up" method. Concerning the three-dimensional difference operator L_{ij}^* of (21), it has been proved that it can be split into three one-dimensional operators

$$L_{ij}^* = L_{ij}^{*(1)} + L_{ij}^{*(2)} + L_{ij}^{*(3)}$$

They can be applied successively to the vector q_j^n of unknowns. That means that the three-dimensional implicit scheme is transferred to those one-dimensional ones, which can be solved very economically. The stability of this procedure has been proved. Up till now, this powerful method is used practically in the Soviet Union only.

There remains a further type of numerical instability, which is caused by the non-linear inertia terms and is therefore called "non-linear instability". It is generated by an energy transfer from the lower to the higher modes in the wave spectrum. It results, finally, in a concentration of wave energy in the smallest resolvable mode, that means a wave length of twice the grid distance. The solution may then become unstable, or it may oscillate unphysically. The non-linear instabilities can be filtered out by weighted dissipative interfaces damping specially the higher wave modes, see Abbott, 1974.

The numerical diffusion, improving the stability behaviour of the method, at the same time makes the convergence worse. In the mass - momentum equations (9) to (11) this error remains in the order of the truncation error. For the heat-transport equation (12), however, the second law of thermodynamics can be gravely violated.

Space integration by finite difference method (FDM)

By means of the Eulerian computational grid, which discretizes the water body, the spatial derivatives in the system (9) to (12) are substituted by quotients of finite differences. Due to the structure of the equation system, the staggered grid of Hansen, 1956, is in most general use (figs. 2 and 4). Here the gradients can be very easily replaced by central differences. The boundary conditions (17) can be also immediately realized when approximating the solid boundary by a polygon with the corresponding computational points.

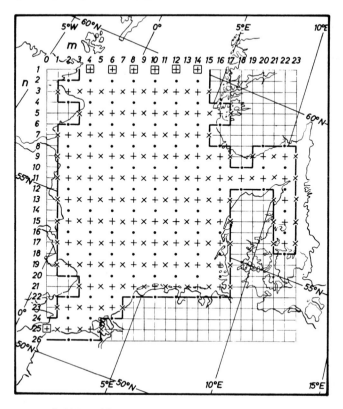

Fig. 4. Staggered FDM grid

In order to explain the principal problems of spatial differencing, we may consider only the balance of acceleration terms and horizontal gradients in the x-direction from the system (9) to (12). We obtain, instead of (20), the matrix equation

$$\frac{\partial q_i}{\partial t} = B_{ij} \frac{\partial q_j}{\partial x} \tag{29}$$

where B_{ij} should be a linearized operator. The most simple difference representation for (29) is given by the explicit scheme of Hansen, 1956

$$\frac{1}{\Delta t} [(q_i)_m^{n+1} - (q_i)_m^n] - \frac{B_{ij}}{\Delta x} [(q_j)_{m+1/2}^n - (q_j)_{m-1/2}^n] = 0 \tag{30}$$

The indices n, m denote grid points in time and space, respectively.

For a stable solution of the procedure (30), it is necessary to satisfy the

Courant-Friedrichs-Lewy condition (23). Introducing the α-algorithm

$$(q_i^*)_m = \frac{\alpha}{2} (q_i)_{m+1/2} + (1-\alpha)(q_i)_m + \frac{\alpha}{2}(q_i)_{m-1/2} , \qquad 0 \leqq \alpha \leqq 1 \qquad (31)$$

The algorithm (30) can be made unconditionally stable.

For instance, $\alpha = 1$ yields the wellknown stable scheme of Lax, 1954:

$$\frac{1}{\Delta t} [(q_i)_m^{n+1} - \frac{1}{2}((q_i)_{m+1/2}^n + (q_i)_{m-1/2}^n)] - \frac{B_{ij}}{\Delta x}[(q_j)_{m+1/2}^n - (q_j)_{m-1/2}^n] = 0$$

The application of (31) functions physically as a horizontal viscosity with a horizontal eddy coefficient of

$$A_h = \frac{\alpha}{2} \frac{\Delta^2 x}{\Delta t}$$

It turns out that, in case of an unproper relation of Δx and Δt, this coefficient may become unphysically large, with the consequence of very strong numerical damping.

Space integration by the finite element method (FEM)

When using the FEM, the water body to be considered is discretized into a finite number of finite elements. Many different types of elements, one-, two-, and three-dimensional, with different shapes, have been investigated. In most cases, triangular elements are chosen, because of their easy adaptation of the computational grid to a given topography (Fig. 5). The unknowns are computed at the nodal points.

In the FEM, the state quantities q_i within an element are obtained from the nodal values q_i^k by means of given functions

$$q_i(x_i, t) = \varphi^k(x_i, t) q_i^k , \qquad k = 1, \ldots, K \qquad (32)$$

The discretization of the time domain can be included into (32), formulating a "space - time - element".

The finite system of equations for the evaluation of nodal quantities q_i can be achieved by a physically-founded functional, originating from the basic conservation laws of hydromechanics. Mostly, however, this functional is substituted by an error minimization principle applied to the governing differential equations (9) to (12). This is commonly carried out by the method of weighted residuals, which, in a special case, coincides with the well-known Galerkin procedure. For equation (29), this leads to

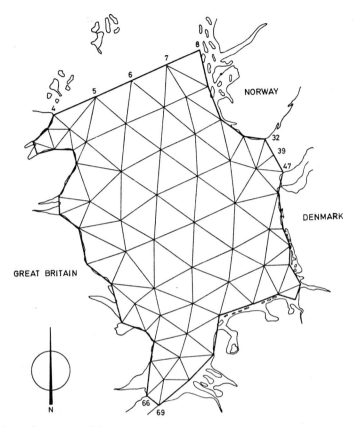

Fig. 5. Triangular FEM grid

$$\int_d \int_{\Delta t} (\frac{\partial \varphi^k}{\partial t} q_i^k - B_{ij} \frac{\partial \varphi^k}{\partial x} q_j^k)\ \varphi^1\ dt\ dx = 0 \tag{33}$$

where d is the extension of the domain in x-direction and $1 = 1, \ldots, K$.

As in the case of FDM, the stability behaviour of the FEM depends on the special type of time discretization, and the corresponding dissipative interface. For a linear approach in the time domain, considering two successive time levels, the FEM leads to a difference equation similar to (21) with the α-algorithm (28). The Galerkin method (33) yields $\alpha = 2/3$, and, therefore, stable solutions, but with a relatively high numerical diffusion.

Gärtner, 1977, has developed a generalized sub-domain collocation technique - called the "support method" - which avoids the non-uniform weighting of the Galerkin technique. Here all adjacent elements of a nodal point with the same constant weight are considered for error minimization. This method gives an arbitrarily small numerical damping.

The vertical dimension in the FEM can be resolved either by a "stratification" of elements or by the use of higher shape functions, approximating the natural current profiles. As an example, Fig. 6. shows the vertical extension of a horizontal element by a cubic element approach (Ebeling, 1977).

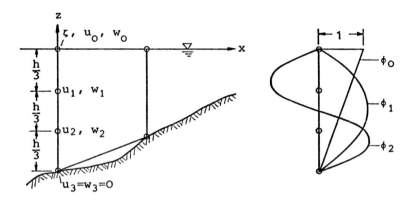

Fig. 6. Vertical discretization and cubic approximation FEM

The often-raised question, wether the FDM or the FEM is superior in hydrodynamics, seems to be reduced to the question of the computational effort required. All the other often-mentioned advantages or disadvantages of FDM or FEM involve no substantial differences. In the presently known models, the computational effort is significantly smaller for the FDM.

The crucial point is that there generally exists an overall connection between all nodes in the FEM, and this influences the band width of the system matrix. This means that the computational effort per node increases with the size of the global system. In the FDM, for both explicit and implicit procedures - using a splitting-up scheme - the computational effort per grid-point can be expressed in absolute working units, not dependant on the size of the system considered. Thus, the larger the grid system, the more economic does FDM become. Weare, 1976, has shown that the required computational work can differ by orders of magnitude. But this is not the final stage. There are world-wide investigations underway to further improve the efficiency of FEM. The most encouraging approaches are explicit and hybrid formulations (Herrling, 1977) and iterative solution techniques.

Application of the Monte Carlo technique

In a survey of Eulerian and Lagrangian FDM for solving the convection - diffusion equation, Maier-Reimer, 1973, concluded that most of them violate the fundamental laws of thermodynamics, because of high numerical diffusion. A Monte Carlo method

was presented in the same paper, avoiding all these disadvantages. Referring to
equation (3), the basic idea is to treat the pure convection equation instead:

$$\frac{\partial \overline{T}}{\partial t} + v_j \frac{\partial \overline{T}}{\partial v_j} = 0$$

assuming that v_j is the superposition of a mean flow $\overline{v}_j$ and a turbulent fluctuation
v_j', according to (6). This fluctuation causes the turbulent diffusion.

In the computation, this fluctuation is simulated by a random number generator
prescribing a certain statistical distribution. Then the path of a finite number
of particles with a fixed amount of heat under the influence of the mean currents
and a super-imposed random walk is calculated. After a certain time the particles
just present in a certain horizontal grid element are counted. Their common thermal
energy gives the actual temperature. In the two-dimensional case the following
formula holds (Bork and Maier-Reimer, 1978):

$$\overline{T}(x, y, t) = \frac{N\ W}{\Delta x\ \Delta y\ h\ \rho\ c_p}$$

where N is the number of particles in the grid element (x, y) with the volume
$\Delta x\ \Delta y\ h$. W is the energy density at the heat source.

Verification

Let us assume that for a given hydrodynamical problem a mathematical model has
been formulated, a solution algorithm has been chosen and realized on a computer by
means of a program. The computer will then produce results in the form of numbers,
tables and graphical plots. But by no means guarantees that the output reproduces
nature: the model must be verified.

At first, the process of verification is preceeded by the process of calibration.
The basic equations (9) to (12) contain a number of empirical constants, which
reflect the parametrization of subscale processes in the time and space domains.
These constants cannot be determined from theory alone but must be tuned by means
of a proper field data set (in most cases in a large number of computer runs) in
such a way that agreement between the model and the prototype is sufficiently
"satisfactory". (Unfortunately, at this point arguments on the quality of a model
are only qualitative and quasi - philosophical). It is important to define clearly
a "quality measure", e.g. a least square principle, in order to develop an efficient calibration strategy, and to judge the relative merits of model versions by
quantitative criteria.

There certainly exist different measures of quality, depending on the given
system. Verification can be carried out by means of histograms, spatial distribu-

tions, wave spectra, etc. Emphasis on the comparison can be directed to different state quatities such as water level, current velocities, or temperature profiles. In general, different system parameters will be determined for different quality measures. A correctly computed water level, for instance, is by no means a guarantee for proper simulation of the circulation pattern.

On the other hand, a model successfully calibrated by observations is not automatically verified in general. It must also be demonstrated that the chosen constants are fairly universal, which means that further data sets can be simulated as well as the original one. Only after a long period of verification can a numerical model proceed from the diagnosis of field data to a forecast of future events. In this connection, sensitivity analysis is always very useful, showing how strongly a state quantity reacts on the variation of system parameters.

Besides tuning the empirical constants, a reformulation of the basic equations, and, hence, of the mathematical model, must also be taken into account. If the basic model is not adapted to the real physical processes in a given lake, the calibration procedure makes practically no sense. Thus a barotropic model is unsuitable, when buoyancy effects are important.

Finally, the field data must always be treated with some scepticism. They are frequently incorrect, incomplete, and not representative. It is absolutely necessary to compress them by an appropriate filtering procedure into a reliable data set, which corresponds to the accuracy and the resolution of the model. Any verification by means of unsuitable data leads to a bad model, even if its original design was fairly good.

Selected examples

As has already been mentioned, it is impossible to demonstrate in this brief survey, all specific lake models derived from the above-described general classes by application to a given natural area. In order to give some practical ideas, only three very different examples representing typical models are discussed in more detail. They are

- the little-known barotropic one-layer model of Lake Constance by
  Hansen and Huber, 1966,

- the better known barotropic Ekman-type model of Lake Geneva by
  Bauer and Graf, 1978,

- the as yet unpublished baroclinic multi-level model of Lake Constance
  by Hollan and Simons.

Barotropic model of Lake Constance (Hansen-Huber)

This model is a very rough representation of natural conditions in Lake Constance and permits, therefore, only some qualitative statements on the circulation field.

It is assumed that the density is constant. Hence, no baroclinic effects are considered, and the temperature acts only as a tracer for the velocity field. In the next step, equations (9) to (11) are integrated from the bottom to the surface, introducing mean horizontal velocities $\bar{\bar{u}}$ and $\bar{\bar{v}}$, or transports, according to (14). By the boundary conditions (16), the tangential stresses at the bottom and at the surface then enter the equation of motion. The inertia and the horizontal viscosity terms are omitted. The pressure gradients are determined only by the slope of the surface. The following equations are then obtained:

$$\frac{\partial \bar{\bar{u}}}{\partial t} - f\bar{\bar{v}} = -g \frac{\partial \zeta}{\partial x} - \frac{r}{h+\zeta} \sqrt{\bar{\bar{u}}^2 + \bar{\bar{v}}^2} \ \bar{\bar{u}} + \frac{\lambda}{h+\zeta} \sqrt{U^2 + V^2} \ U$$

$$\frac{\partial \bar{\bar{v}}}{\partial t} + f\bar{\bar{u}} = -g \frac{\partial \zeta}{\partial y} - \frac{r}{h+\zeta} \sqrt{\bar{\bar{u}}^2 + \bar{\bar{v}}^2} \ \bar{\bar{v}} + \frac{\lambda}{h+\zeta} \sqrt{U^2 + V^2} \ V \qquad (34)$$

$$\frac{\partial \zeta}{\partial t} + \frac{\partial}{\partial x} ((h+\zeta) \ \bar{\bar{u}}) + \frac{\partial}{\partial y} ((h+\zeta) \ \bar{\bar{v}}) = 0$$

The lake, with a length of about 60 km and a maximum width of nearly 15 km is represented by a staggered two-dimensional grid (Fig. 4) with a grid spacing of $\Delta x = \Delta y = 375$ m. For the numerical solution of (34), the explicit Hansen scheme (30) is used. The Courant criterion then requires a time step of $\Delta t = 5$ s for a maximum depth of 252 m. The remaining constants are chosen as: $r = 0.003$, $\lambda = 3.2 \cdot 10^{-6}$, $f = 1.07 \cdot 10^{-4}$ s^{-1}. A weak α-algorithm has been used in the space domain for improving stability according to (31) with $\alpha = 0.01$.

Two situations have been investigated:

- a westerly wind with a speed of 6 m/s, which represents the
  main energy input into the system,

- a superposition of the wind's action and the river Rhine, which
  flows through the main part of the lake. At the inflow and the
  outflow sections a velocity of 80 cm/s is prescribed.

The stationary transport fields are shown in Fig. 7. They are explained mainly by the influence of the bottom topography. The essential pattern is a flow in the wind direction in the shallow Northern and Southern parts of the lake, compensated by a reverse flow in the deeper central trough. This current system can be easily explained by means of the equation system (34). The wind stress terms in the equation of motion show that a given constant wind has a greater effect in the shallow nearshore region. A reverse flow is required by the continuity equation. These flows drive two large gyres in the Northern and the Southern bay. The flow of the river Rhine passes the central trough of the lake in the same direction as the wind driven transport does, thus intensifying the existing circulation system.

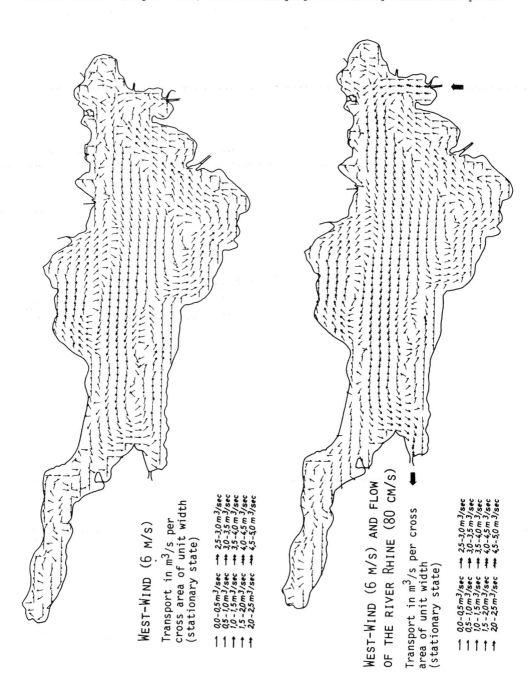

Fig. 7. Mass transport in Lake Constance due to wind and the Rhine river

We all know, of course, that the wind-driven circulation has a distinct vertical structure, often including a reverse flow in deeper layers. Moreover, in the case of seasonal thermal stratification of Lake Constance, baroclinic effects certainly play a role in the momentum budget. The results from a barotropic one-layer model here presented have, therefore, some significance only for the global mass transport in the lake. No attempt has been made to verify the model. Only the computed period of the main seiche (57 minutes) coincides fairly well with the observed one.

Application of an implicit FDM could reduce computer time remarkably.

Barotropic model of Lake Geneva (Bauer-Graf)

The model has been designed for the simulation of the steady wind-driven three-dimensional circulation in Lake Geneva, neglecting baroclinic effects. Accordingly, the basic equations (9) to (11) and (13) have been simplified to a large degree. The inertia as well as the horizontal viscosity terms have been omitted. The vertical exchange coefficient has been assumed to be constant. The equations then have the form

$$- f\bar{v} = - \frac{1}{\rho} \frac{\partial \bar{p}}{\partial x} + A_v \frac{\partial^2 \bar{u}}{\partial z^2}$$

$$f\bar{u} = - \frac{1}{\rho} \frac{\partial \bar{p}}{\partial y} + A_v \frac{\partial^2 \bar{v}}{\partial z^2}$$

$$0 = - \frac{1}{\rho} \frac{\partial \bar{p}}{\partial z} - g$$

$$\frac{\partial \bar{u}}{\partial x} + \frac{\partial \bar{v}}{\partial y} + \frac{\partial \bar{w}}{\partial z} = 0$$

This set of equations leads to a barotropic Ekman-type model, which can be treated in a combined analytical-numerical way. First, an exact integration is carried out in the vertical direction of the equation of motion, resulting in the well-known Ekman spiral for the velocities $\bar{u}(z)$ and $\bar{v}(z)$. Then, by ingrating from the bottom to the surface, according to (14), mean horizontal velocities $\bar{\bar{u}}(x,y)$ and $\bar{\bar{v}}(x,y)$ are introduced, leading to a barotropic one-layer model. This is treated numerically after the definition of a stream function ψ with

$$\bar{\bar{u}} = \frac{1}{h} \frac{\partial \psi}{\partial y} \quad , \qquad \bar{\bar{v}} = - \frac{1}{h} \frac{\partial \psi}{\partial x}$$

by means of the FEM. The authors make use of a computer program by Liggett and Hadjitheodorou (1969).

The lake with a length of about 70 km, a width of nearly 15 km, and a maximum depth of 310 m was discretized by 1 025 triangular horizontal elements with 579 nodal points. The Coriolis factor was taken as f = $1.05 \cdot 10^{-4}$ s^{-1}.

The calibration of the model was effected by two 36 hours' measuring campaigns with steadily blowing winds from the North-East (9.1 m/s) and the South-West (6.4 m/s), which are the most typical ones in this area. The only coefficients to be tuned were the vertical eddy viscosity A_V and the drag coefficient λ. By comparison of calculated and measured velocities in different depths they were determined as

$$A_V = 460 \text{ cm}^2/\text{s} \quad \text{and}$$

$$\lambda = 4.8 \cdot 10^{-6}$$

With these values the few field data could be approximated reasonably well, with the exception of some records of the South-West wind event.

The calculated three-dimensional circulation field is governed by a uniform surface flow with a right-hand declination from the wind's direction, as follows from Ekman's theory. In the deeper layers, there is a continuous rotation and a weakening of the flow, according to the Ekman spiral. The spoon-shaped topography causes an anti-clockwise circulation in the central trough. Although we obtain an insight into the three-dimensional structure of the wind-driven circulation, this Ekman-type model is not essentially different from the one-layer model by Hansen and Huber described above. The same information on the vertical velocity profile could be obtained for the latter from the mean currents, using Ekman's theory in a subsequent run. This is also indicated by the fact that in both models only two constants can be tuned in a calibration procedure: the drag coefficient λ and some friction coefficient, A_V or r. There is a need for further field observations to verify the model.

Baroclinic model of Lake Constance (Hollan-Simons)

This model was developed for the simulation of the wind-driven three-dimensional circulation under the influence of a thermal stratification. Special emphasis was directed to the question of how closely an approximately parametricized two-dimensional vertical model does already reproduce the essential dynamical features. Calibration has been carried out by means of an extensive measuring campaign with a duration of several weeks. Mainly temperature data were considered.

The numerical model was based on the basic equations (9) to (13). The following relationship was assumed as equation of state (5) (Simons, 1973):

$$\frac{\Delta \rho}{\rho_o} = -6.8 \cdot 10^{-6} \, (\overline{T} - 4^0)^2$$

where $\overline{T}$ is given in degrees centigrade.

As Boyce, 1974, has explained in detail, the motions occuring in lakes have very different time and space scales. Although all these motions, from a theoretical point of view, depend on each other, certain modes practically do not interact. It has been proved by Hollan and Simons by examining the data that exists (with a typical horizontal length scale of 10 m and a time scale of 1 s) no influence of surface gravity waves is exerted on the internal waves and up- and down-welling processes (with a length scale of 10 km and a time scale of 1 day). The investigation was focussed on currents and temperature. As a consequence, the surface waves could be neglected in the model. So it was possible to use large time steps in favour of the efficiency of the model.

In order to study the necessary spatial resolution of a multi-level model, the authors designed three different types:

- A three-dimensional model with a staggered grid. A horizontal mesh size of $\Delta x = 1$ km and 8 levels in the vertical have been used with variable distances ($\Delta z = 10, 10, 10, 10, 10, 20, 30, 100$ m).

- A quasi-two-dimensional model in a longitudinal vertical plane with $\Delta x = 1$ km, and 20 vertical levels with $\Delta z = 10$ m. This model includes the Coriolis effect.

- A two-dimensional model in a transverse vertical plane with $\Delta x = 250$ m and 20 vertical levels with $\Delta z = 10$ m.

With these three models, a one-week period in Autumn 1972 was investigated. That period included a 4 days' storm event and corresponding up- and down-welling. The calibration and verification was carried out by comparing the observed to the computed temperature histories at 5 different sites, each with 4 measuring levels in the vertical.

It turned out that, for the nearshore regions, the two-dimensional models, especially the longitudinal one, were in excellent agreement with observations (Fig. 8). In these models, the drag coefficient was set equal to $1.6 \cdot 10^{-6}$. The vertical eddy viscosity coefficient varied from 50 cm^2/s at the surface to 10 cm^2/s at the thermocline.

In the interior region, however, the three-dimensional model gave better results. Due to the different degree of parametrization, the physical constants had to be readjusted, and a drag coefficient of $\lambda = 2.4 \cdot 10^{-6}$ was determined.

For both model types, a sensitivity analysis was carried out with respect to the grid size and the eddy viscosity. It was found that a refinement of the vertical mesh as well as an enlargement of the eddy coefficient by a factor of 2 did not significantly change the temperature distribution. At the same time it became evident that the wind input exerted a dominant influence on the distribution of isotherms. This model should be verified by further storm events.

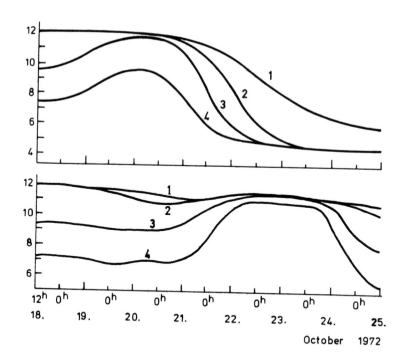

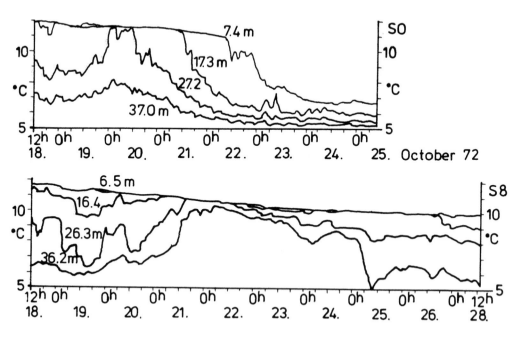

Fig. 8. Computed (upper group) and observed (lower group) temperature
histograms at sites 0 and 8 for four vertical levels

CONCLUSIONS

Summarizing, it can be stated that remarkable progress has been achieved in limnology by numerical modelling of circulation in lakes. The models, in principle enable us to understand the complex causal dependencies of the atmospheric input and the hydrodynamical – thermodynamical responses of the system under the influence of a given topography, and even to forecast them to a certain extent. For further research, three-dimensional multi-level models and properly parametricized two-dimensional vertical models seem to be equally useful, both incorporating baroclinic forces.

One of the main future tasks remains the verification of the models. This means, in the first place, the availability of reliable field data, which are sufficiently representative to be compared with numerical results. This includes, furthermore, the definition of a fairly objective verification strategy, which gives a quantitative measure of quality of a model.

Certainly this verification cannot be achieved only by tuning the system parameters. Sensitivity analysis must prove what the parameters' influence is and where the possibilities of verification are exhausted. In this case, the basic equations may need reformulation in order to adjust them more closely to the physics of the lake. In this connection, deterministic models of turbulence, which involve a parametrization on a higher level, and contain, therefore, more "universal" constants, are of increasing importance.

REFERENCES

Abbott, M.B., 1974. Continuous flows, discontinuous flows, and numerical analysis. J. Hydr. Res., 12, 4

Bauer, S.W. and Graf, W.H., 1978. Wind-induced water circulation of Lake Geneva. Proc. 10th Int. Liège Coll. Oc. Hydr., Liège (in press)

Bork, I. and Maier-Reimer, E., 1978. On the spreading of power plant cooling water in a tidal river applied to the river Elbe. Adv. Wat. Res. 1, 3

Boyce, F.M., 1974. Some aspects of Great Lakes physics of importance to biological and chemical processes. J. Fish. Res. Board Can., 31, 5

Bryan, K., 1969. A numerical method for the study of ocean circulation. J. Comp. Phys., 4

Cheng, R.T., Powell, T.M. and Dillon, T.M., 1976. Numerical models of wind-driven circulation in lakes. Appl. Math. Modelling, 1, 3

Crank, J. and Nicholson, P., 1947. A practical method for numerical integration of solutions of partial differential equations of heat conduction type. Proc. Cambr. Phil. Soc., 43

Ebeling, H., 1977. Berechnung der Vertikalstruktur wind- und gezeitenerzeugter Strömungen nach der Methode der finiten Elemente. Fortschritt-Berichte FDI-Zeitschrn., Reihe 4, 32

Einstein, A., 1905. Über die von der molekularkinetischen Theorie der Wärme geforderte Bewegung von in ruhenden Flüssigkeiten suspendierten Teilchen. Ann. Phys. 4, Folge 17

Gärtner, S., 1977. Zur Berechnung von Flachwasserwellen und instationären Transportprozessen mit der Methode der finiten Elemente. Fortschritt-Berichte FDI-Zeitschrn., Reihe 4, 30

Hansen, W., 1956. Theorie zur Errechnung des Wasserstandes und der Strömungen in Randmeeren nebst Anwendungen. Tellus 8

Hansen, W. (Ed.), 1966. Die Reproduktion der Bewegungsvorgänge im Meere mit Hilfe hydrodynamisch-numerischer Verfahren. Mitt. Inst. Meereskd. Univ. Hamburg, 5

Heaps, N., 1973. Three-dimensional numerical model of the Irish Sea. Geophys. J. R. astr. Soc., 35

Herrling, B., 1977. Eine hybride Formulierung in Wasserständen zur Berechnung von Flachwasserwellen mit der Methode finiter Elemente. Fortschritt-Berichte FDI-Zeitschrn., Reihe 4, 37

Hollan, E. and Simons, T.J., 1978. Wind-induced changes of temperature and currents in Lake Constance. Arch. Met. Geophys. Biokl., Ser. A (in press)

Krauss, W., 1973. Methods and results of theoretical oceanography. Vol. 1, Gebr. Bornträger

Launder, B.E. and Spalding, D.B., 1972. Mathematical models of turbulence. Academic Press

Lax, P.D., 1954. Weak solutions of nonlinear hyperbolic equations and their numerical applications. Comm. Pure Appl. Math., 7

Leendertse, J.J., 1967. Aspects of the computational model for long-period water wave propagation. Rand Memorandum 5294

Leendertse, J.J. and Liu, S.K., 1975. A three-dimensional model for estuaries and coastal seas. Vol. II, Aspects of computation, Rand Corp., Santa Monica, R - 1764 - OWRT

Liggett, J.A. and Hadjitheodorou, C., 1969. Circulation in shallow homogeneous lakes. Proc. Am. Soc. Civ. Engs., 95, Hy2

Maier-Reimer, E., 1973. Hydrodynamisch-numerische Untersuchungen zu horizontalen Ausbreitungs- und Transportvorgängen in der Nordsee. Mitt. Inst. Meereskd. Univ. Hamburg, 21

Marchuk, G.I. and Zalesny, V.B., 1974. Numerical model of the global ocean circulation (in Russian), Siberian Branch, USSR Academy of Sciences

Marchuk, G.I., 1977. Methods of numerical mathematics (in Russian), Nauka Press

Mortimer, C.H., 1974. Lake hydrodynamics. Mitt. Int. Ver. Limn., 20

Richtmyer, R.D. and Morton, K.W., 1967. Difference methods for initial value problems. Interscience Publishers

Roache, P.T., 1972. Computational fluid dynamics. Hermosa

Simons, T.J., 1973. Development of three-dimensional numerical models of Great Lakes. Scient. Ser. 12, Can. Centre Inl. Wat., Burlington

Simons, T.J., 1974. Verification of numerical models of Lake Ontario. Part I, Circulation in spring and early summer. J. Phys. Oc., 4

Simons, T.J., 1975. Verification of numerical models of Lake Ontario. Part II, Stratified circulation and temperature changes. J. Phys. Oc., 5

Sündermann, J., 1974. A three-dimensional model of a homogeneous estuary. Proc. 14th Coast. Eng. Conf., Copenhagen

Tsvetova, E.A., 1974. Non-stationary wind-driven currents in Lake Baikal (in Russian), Siberian Branch, USSR Academy of Sciences

Weare, T.J., 1976. Finite element or finite difference methods for the two-dimensional shallow water equations. Comp. Meth. Appl. Mech. Eng., 7, 3

Yanenko, N.N., 1967. The splitting-up method for the solution of multi-dimensional problems in mathematical physics (in Russian), Nauka Press

Zienkiewicz, D.C., 1972. The finite element method in engineering and science. McGraw-Hill

APPLICATIONS OF A TRANSIENT MATHEMATICAL MODEL TO LAKE KÖSEN

J. WITTMISS

Department of Water Resources Enginerring, University of Lund,
(Sweden)

ABSTRACT

This report contains a verification of a multi-layer hydrodynamic
model for wind-driven lake circulation. Current measurements were
carried out in Lake Kösen for different situations in May 1977. The
results of the model simulation for five of those situations were
compared to field measurements. Lake Kösen was homogeneous during
the measurement period.

With a suitable set of model parameters the correspondence between
model results and observations is satisfactory for most of the comparisons.

INTRODUCTION

The applications described in this report were made with a three-
dimensional, transient model developed by J. Simons at Canada Centre
for Inland Waters. The model is of the so called multilayer type,
with the layers separated by rigid permeable interfaces. The calculations were made for Lake KÖSEN in the south of Sweden. Different
coefficients were used for the vertical and horizontal turbulent
exchange of momentum. Also different values of the coefficient for
wind stress were used. By comparisons to field measurements the most
suitable set of these coefficients for this specific lake has been
determined.

OUTLINE OF THE MODEL

The model is three-dimensional, but only the two momentum equations for the horizontal velocities are solved. The vertical velocity component is obtained from the continuity equation. In order to
calculate the transports in the different layers a system of vertically integrated equations are solved. Then the velocity differences between the layers are calculated. From the total transport
and the velocity differences the transport in each layer is easily
obtained.

The following assumptions are made for the general equations of in-compressible, turbulent flow:

1. The effect of laminar viscosity is negligible.
2. Turbulent diffusion can be described by turbulent exchange coefficients.
3. Hydrostatic pressure distribution.
4. Boussinesq's approsimation is valid.
5. The effect of the earth's rotation can be taken into account by the Coriolis parameter f.
6. The convective terms can be neglected in the equations of motion.

With these assumptions the equations take the following form.

$$\frac{\partial u}{\partial t} = f \cdot v - \frac{1}{\rho_0} \frac{\partial P}{\partial x} + \frac{\partial}{\partial x} \left(A_H \frac{\partial u}{\partial x}\right) + \frac{\partial}{\partial y} \left(A_H \frac{\partial u}{\partial y}\right) + \frac{\partial}{\partial z} \left(A_v \frac{\partial u}{\partial z}\right)$$

$$\frac{\partial v}{\partial t} = f \cdot u - \frac{1}{\rho_0} \frac{\partial P}{\partial y} + \frac{\partial}{\partial x} \left(A_H \frac{\partial v}{\partial x}\right) + \frac{\partial}{\partial y} \left(A_H \frac{\partial v}{\partial y}\right) + \frac{\partial}{\partial z} \left(A_v \frac{\partial v}{\partial z}\right)$$

$$\frac{\partial T}{\partial t} + \frac{\partial}{\partial y} (vT) + \frac{\partial}{\partial x} (uT) + \frac{\partial}{\partial z} (wT) = \frac{\partial}{\partial x} \left(K_H \frac{\partial T}{\partial x}\right) + \frac{\partial}{\partial y} \left(K_H \frac{\partial T}{\partial y}\right) +$$

$$+ \frac{\partial}{\partial z} \left(K_v \frac{\partial T}{\partial z}\right)$$

$$\frac{\partial u}{\partial x} + \frac{\partial v}{\partial y} + \frac{\partial w}{\partial z} = 0$$

$$p (x,y,z) = \int\limits_{z}^{x, \, y-surface} \rho \, g \, dz$$

Numerical solutions of the above equations are obtained by finite difference methods, with the different variables being distributed on a staggered grid.

A more detailed discussion of the physical and numerical approximations employed in the model, has been presented by Simons (1).

DESCRIPTION OF LAKE KÖSEN

Lake Kösen near Ljungby in the south of Sweden, has a maximum depth of 27 m. Large areas of shallow water are situated in the south and along the eastern coast. A lot of islands are contained in the lake especially in the shallow parts. The area is about 11 km² with a maximum length of 7 km.

All field measurements took place in May 1977. During this period
the vertical temperature distribution was rather homogeneous. All
current measurements were carried out with drogues. Fig. 1 shows
the vertical temperature distribution at the beginning and at the
end of the field measurement period.

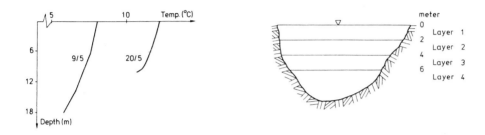

Fig. 1. Vertical temperature distri-   Fig. 2. Simulated layers of
       bution in Lake Kösen   Lake Kösen

CALCULATIONS

Lake Kösen was for computational reasons divided into four layers
as shown in Fig. 2.

The computational grid system has a horizontal resolution of
200 m. In order to get the best correspondence between measured and
calculated velocities, the same wind situations were calculated with
different drag coefficients for the wind stress and different vertical and horizontal turbulent exchange coefficients for momentum.
It was then possible to determine the most suitable set of coefficients for this specific lake.

The wind stress (τ) is proportional to the square of the wind
speed (W).

$$\tau = \rho_{air} \cdot C_D \cdot W^2 \tag{1}$$

According to Bengtsson (2), the drag coefficient C_D for enclosed
waters was found to average about $1.0 \cdot 10^{-3}$. However, this value
can very a great deal.

The vertical exchange coefficient (A_v) for the eddy viscosity is
proportional to the wind speed, Bengtsson (3).

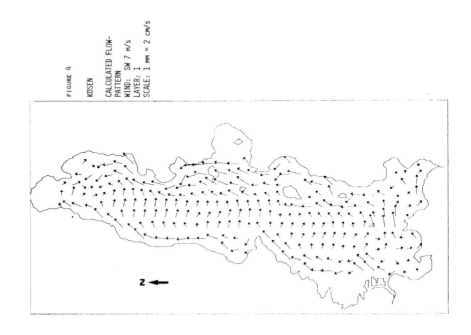

FIGURE 4

KOSEN

CALCULATED FLOW-
PATTERN
WIND: SW 7 M/S
LAYER: 1
SCALE: 1 MM = 2 CM/S

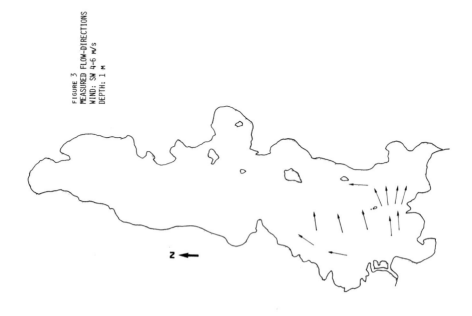

FIGURE 3
MEASURED FLOW-DIRECTIONS
WIND: SW 4-6 M/S
DEPTH: 1 M

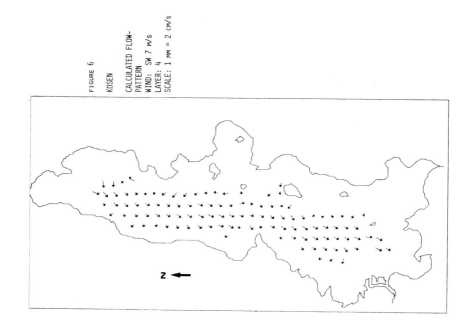

FIGURE 6

KÖSEN

CALCULATED FLOW-
PATTERN
WIND: SW 7 M/S
LAYER: 4
SCALE: 1 MM = 2 CM/S

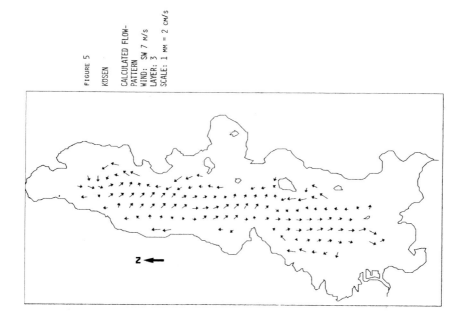

FIGURE 5

KÖSEN

CALCULATED FLOW-
PATTERN
WIND: SW 7 M/S
LAYER: 3
SCALE: 1 MM = 2 CM/S

$$A_V = c \cdot h \cdot W \quad cm^2/s \qquad\qquad (2)$$

h = average depth

c = constant; $2 \cdot 10^{-5}$

During the field measurement period the wind was blowing from two main directions SW and NE. Fig. 3 summarize the measured flowpatterns at a depth of one meter for winds blowing from SW. Fig. 4 shows the the corresponding calculated velocities in the upper layer for the whole lake area. Figs. 5 and 6 illustrate the calculated flowpattern for one intermediate layer and the bottom layer for winds blowing from SW.

Figs. 7-12 shows the correspondence between measured and computed velocities for some windsituations. The wind-drag coefficient and the exchange coefficients for momentum are the same for all calculations shown in these figures. For more detailed information see Wittmiss (4).

CONCLUSIONS

The possibility of simulating the hydrodynamics of Lake Kösen, using a numerical model has been demonstrated. With a careful calibration of the different coefficients the model is able to predict the flow pattern with sufficient accuracy. Provided a suitable combination of coefficients is used, the calculated and measured velocities are in good agreement for the upper layer and the bottom layer. In the intermediate layers, however, the correspondence in the direction of the velocities is not good. The transports in these layers are often very small. Therefore the directions of the calculated velocities easily become erroneous. As just one measurement of the intermediate and bottom layers is represented, it is not possible to draw any further conclusions. There is a trend that the calculations result in too high velocities near the shoreline. This could be eliminated by the introduction of an upper layer with a depth of 0.5 m. As all depths in this application are greater than 1 m, this allows the development of a return current at the bottom for all gridpoints close to the shore. Presumably the velocities parallel to the shoreline will be reduced.

The two most important coefficients for calibration purposes are the wind drag coefficient C_D and the vertical exchange coefficient (or the eddy viscosity) A_V. The corresponding horizontal exchange

37

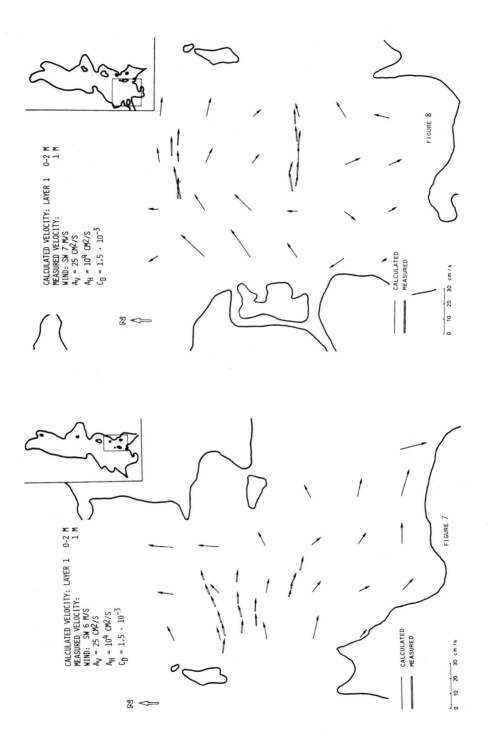

CALCULATED VELOCITY: LAYER 1   0-2 M
MEASURED VELOCITY: 1 M
WIND: SW 7 M/S
$A_V = 25$ CM2/S
$A_H = 10^4$ CM2/S
$C_D = 1.5 \cdot 10^{-3}$

N ⇐

CALCULATED
MEASURED

0 10 20 30 cm/s

FIGURE 8

CALCULATED VELOCITY: LAYER 1   0-2 M
MEASURED VELOCITY: 1 M
WIND: SW 6 M/S
$A_V = 25$ CM2/S
$A_H = 10^4$ CM2/S
$C_D = 1.5 \cdot 10^{-3}$

N ⇐

CALCULATED
MEASURED

0 10 20 30 cm/s

FIGURE 7

38

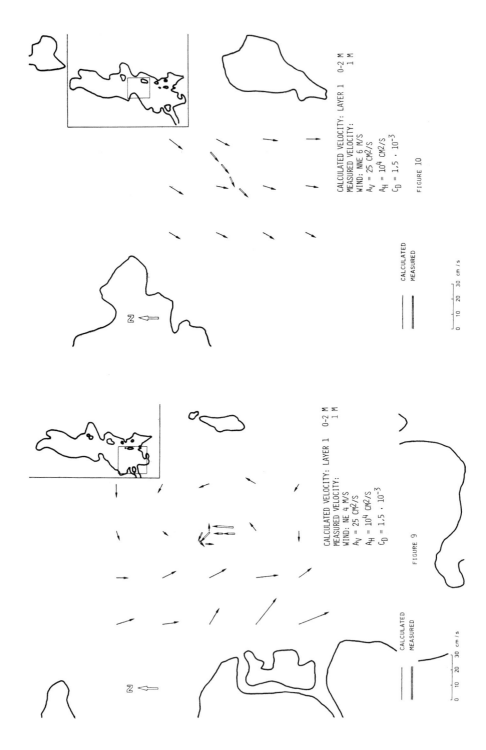

CALCULATED VELOCITY: LAYER 1   0-2 M   1 M
MEASURED VELOCITY:
WIND: NNE 6 M/S
$A_V = 25$ CM2/S
$A_H = 10^4$ CM2/S
$C_D = 1,5 \cdot 10^{-3}$

FIGURE 10

CALCULATED
MEASURED

0 10 20 30 cm/s

CALCULATED VELOCITY: LAYER 1   0-2 M   1 M
MEASURED VELOCITY:
WIND: NE 4 M/S
$A_V = 25$ CM2/S
$A_H = 10^4$ CM2/S
$C_D = 1,5 \cdot 10^{-3}$

FIGURE 9

CALCULATED
MEASURED

0 10 20 30 cm/s

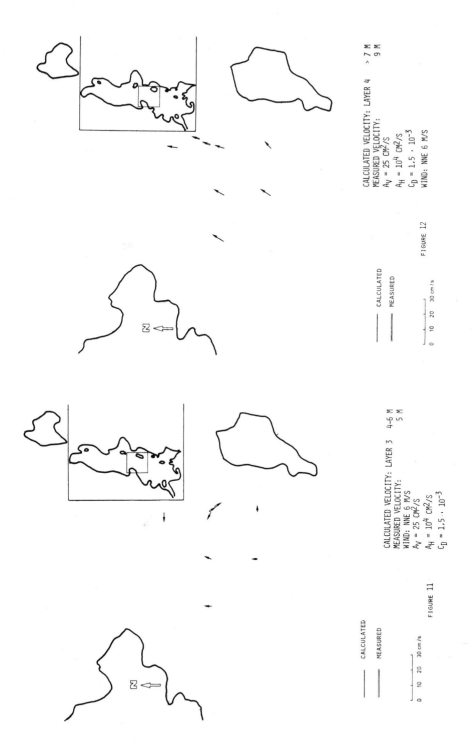

CALCULATED VELOCITY: LAYER 4   > 7 M
MEASURED VELOCITY: 9 M
$A_V = 25$ CM²/S
$A_H = 10^4$ CM²/S
$C_D = 1.5 \cdot 10^{-3}$
WIND: NNE 6 M/S

—— CALCULATED
══ MEASURED

0 10 20 30 cm/s

FIGURE 12

CALCULATED VELOCITY: LAYER 3   4-6 M
MEASURED VELOCITY: 5 M
WIND: NNE 6 M/S
$A_V = 25$ CM²/S
$A_H = 10^4$ CM²/S
$C_D = 1.5 \cdot 10^{-3}$

—— CALCULATED
══ MEASURED

0 10 20 30 cm/s

FIGURE 11

coefficient A_H has a minor influence on the calculated flowpattern in the off shore parts of the lake. Along the shore line, however, this influence becomes more significant. The most convenient combination of coefficients seems to be $C_D = 1.3 \cdot 10^{-3}$ and $A_V = 25$ cm²/s.

NOTATION

The following symbols are used in this report:

A_H = horizontal eddy viscosity
A_V = vertical eddy viscosity
C_D = drag coefficient for windstress
f = Coriolis parameter
h = depth
K_H = horizontal turbulent heat diffusivity
K_V = vertical turbulent heat diffusivity
p = pressure
t = time
u = velocity in the x-direction
v = velocity in the y-direction
w = velocity in the z-direction
W = wind speed
x,y = horizontal coordinates
z = vertical coordinate
ρ = density of the water
ρ_{air} = density of the air
τ = shear stress of the wind
T = temperature
p = pressure

REFERENCES

1. Simons, T.J., 1973. Development of three-dimensional numerical models of the great Lakes. Scientific Series No. 12 Inland Waters Directorate, Canada Centre for Inland Waters, Burlington, Ontario.
2. Bengtsson, L. Models of wind generated circulation in lakes – comparison with measurements. University of Luleå, Sweden, page 6.
3. Bengtsson, L., 1973. Conclusions about turbulent exchange coefficients from model studies. International Symposium Hydrology of Lakes, Helsinki, IAHS Publ. No. 109, p 306-312.
4. Wittmiss, J. Applications of a transient mathematical model to Lake Kösen in Modelling of dynamic phenomena in Lakes. Report from the Swedish IHP research group on Lake Hydrology. Division of Water Resources Engineering, University of Luleå. Editor: Lars Bengtsson.

APPLICATION OF A MATHEMATICAL HYDRODYNAMIC MODEL TO LAKE MJØSA

TORULV TJOMSLAND

Norwegian Institute for Water Research, Oslo (Norway)

ABSTRACT

   A three-dimensional model was used to compute current and temperature distribution in Lake Mjøsa. The model was not calibrated for this specific lake. The
values for the model parameters were obtained from the literature. The results
show a good accordance with temperature observations in the field.

INTRODUCTION

   Lake Mjøsa, Norway's largest and Europe's fourth deepest lake, has been the subject of extensive limnological investigations, in part because of concern regarding
recent eutrophication of the lake. In an attempt to understand more about the hydrodynamics of this fjord-like lake, the 3-dimensional, transient, numerical model developed by J. Simons of the Canada Centre for Inland Waters was used to predict temperature and current fields (Simons 1973a).

   Mjøsa is located in southeastern Norway. The lake's surface area is 365 km^2, length
is 110 km, and the greatest width is 14 km (Fig. 1). The mean depth is 153 m. The
lake is divided into two basins. The northern basin is less than 100 m deep. The larger
central and southern basin has a maximum depth of 450 m. The surrounding landscape
slopes gently up to a height several hundred meters above the lake.

   Simons' model consists of the two momentum equations for the horizontal velocity
components without the advective terms, one equation for the temperature, and one
equation for the conservation of mass (continuity equation). In addition there are
equations for the hydrostatic law and the relationship between density and temperature.

   The model is three-dimensional but only the two momentum equations for the horizontal velocity are solved. The vertical component is obtained from the continuity
equation. First the equations are integrated vertically. Then the velocity differences between the layers are calculated. From the vertically-integrated velocity
and the velocity differences, the velocity in each layer is obtained. A detailed
discussion of the physical and numerical approximations in the model is given by
Simons (1973a).

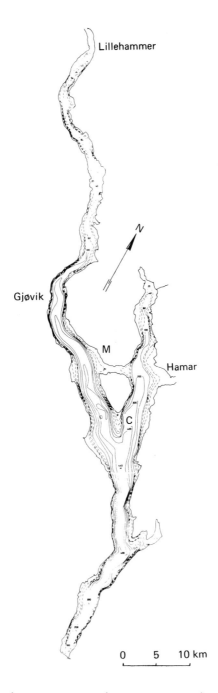

Fig. 1. Bathymetric map of Lake Mjøsa.

APPLICATION OF THE MODEL

Initial values and model parameters

The lake was divided into 4 layers, 0-4 m depth, 4-12 m, 12-25 m and greater than
25 m. A horizontal grid of 1 x 1 km was chosen. Initial temperatures for the 4 layers
were taken at $9.7^{o}C$, $9.5^{o}C$, $9.2^{o}C$ and $6.0^{o}C$, respectively, which correspond to temperatures measured in a profile taken in the center of the lake in September 1977 (Fig. 5).
All current velocities were assumed to be zero. In the north of the lake the discharge
of the major inflowing river was 200 m^{3}/s with a water temperature of $8^{o}C$. The outlet
discharge in the southern end was 100 m^{3}/s.

Values for some parameters should ideally come from calibration of the model using
measurements in the field for the lake of interest. Relevant data for Lake Mjøsa were
not available, however, so instead values obtained from investigations of the North
American Great Lakes were used (Simons 1973b, 1974, 1975). All sub-grid-scale diffu-
sive fluxes were computed on the basis of the classical gradient diffusion concept.
In the momentum equations horizontal and vertical eddy viscosities were $2 \cdot 10^{5}$ cm/s
and 20 cm^{2}/s, respectively. Horizontal and vertical heat-diffusion coefficients were
$2 \cdot 10^{4}$ cm^{2}/s and 1 cm^{2}/s. A 24-hour period with steady wind from the SE at 6 m/s at
10 m above the lake surface was chosen for trial of the model. The wind data came
from a meteorological station near the end of the peninsula dividing the lake (M on
Fig. 1). The wind stress was calculated using the quadratic stress law ($\tau = \rho_{air} \cdot C_{D} \cdot W^{2}$)
with a drag coefficient (C_{D}) of 1.4 $\cdot 10^{-3}$.

Data obtained from two automatic current meters located near the center of the
lake (C on Fig. 1) at 8 and 40 m depths, and from a series of temperature measurements were used to evaluate the success of the model.

Results

The model predicts that after 24 hours of steady wind from the SE water in the two
surface layers would generally move in a direction to the right of the wind (Fig. 2).
Horizontal current velocities would be as high as 20 cm/s. In the bottom layer the
current would be to the south (against the wind) with velocities less than 2 cm/s
(Fig. 3). Data from the automatic current samplers indicate that actual currents
were indeed in the directions as predicted by the model but observed velocities were
higher.

The model predicted downwelling generally at the northern and eastern ends of the
lake (Fig. 4) and upwelling at the opposite end with the greatest vertical velocities along the shores. The simulated temperature distribution followed the vertical
current system in such a way that cold water was associated with upwelling areas and

44

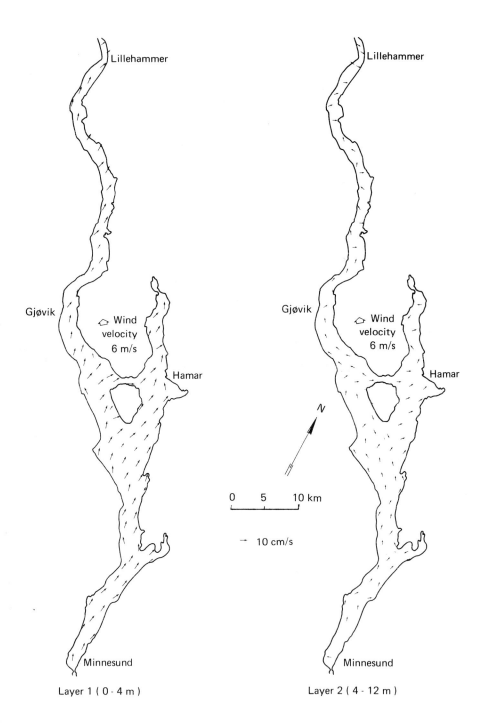

Fig. 2. Simulated horizontal velocities.

45

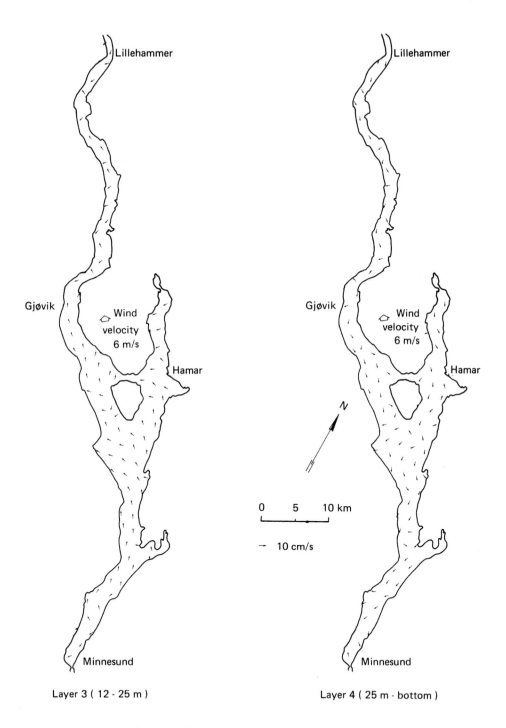

Fig. 3. Simulated horizontal velocities.

46

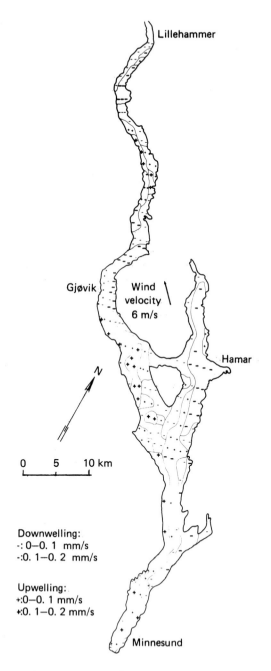

Fig. 4. Simulated vertical velocities.

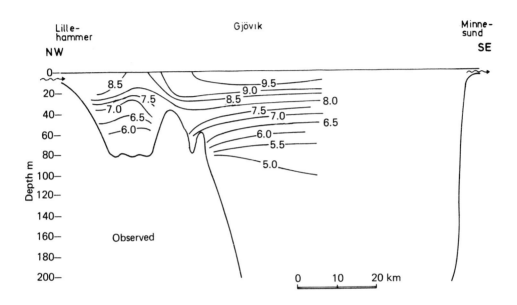

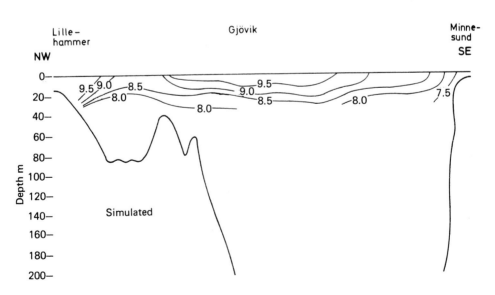

Fig. 5. Observed and simulated temperatures.

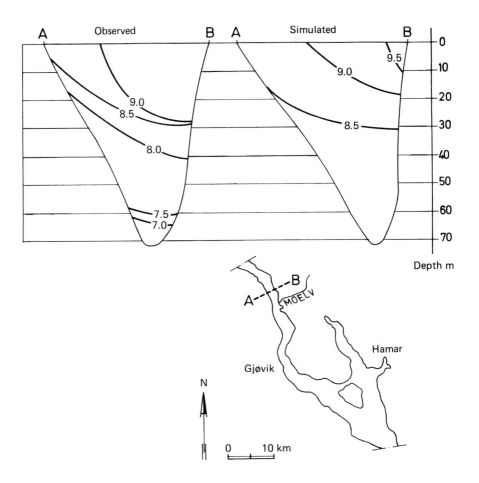

Fig. 6. Observed and simulated temperatures.

warm water with downwelling. Simulated and observed temperatures showed good accordance (Figs. 5 and 6).

In the shallow area between the two basins of the lake the simulation showed a marked upwelling zone associated with low temperatures (Figs. 4 and 5); observed temperatures also showed this distribution. This may be related to the bottom topography.

The results might be improved if sufficient data were available to calibrate the model by varying the model parameters. Simulated temperatures were lower than the observed; the observed currents may include a residual component that originates from wind stress prior to the onset of the simulation period. This uncertainty might be overcome by running the simulations over longer time periods.

REFERENCES

Simons, T.J., 1973a. Development of three-dimensional numerical models of the Great Lakes. Sci. Ser. No. 12, Canada Centre for Inland Waters, Burlington, pp. 26.
Simons, T.J., 1973b. Comparison of observed and computed currents in Lake Ontario during Hurricane Agnes, June 1972. Intern. Assoc. Great Lakes Res. Ann. Arbor, 831-844.
Simons, T.J., 1974. Verification of numerical models of Lake Ontario, Part 1: Circulation in spring and early summer. J. Phys. Oceanogr., 4: 507-523.
Simons, T.J., 1975. Verification of numerical models of Lake Ontario, Part 2: Stratified circulations and temperature changes. J. Phys. Oceanogr., 5: 98-110.

THREE-DIMENSIONAL SIMULATION OF TIME-DEPENDENT ELEVATIONS AND CURRENTS IN A HOMO-
GENEOUS LAKE OF ARBITRARY SHAPE USING AN IRREGULAR-GRID FINITE-DIFFERENCE MODEL

S.W. BAUER

Laboratoire d'Hydraulique (LHYDREP), Ecole Polytechnique Fédérale, Lausanne,
Switzerland

ABSTRACT

   Combining the neat representation of boundary geometry of finite-element models
with the advantage of fast numerical solution of finite-difference models, an irregular-grid finite-difference scheme was used to solve the hydrodynamic equations
of motion in a three-dimensional homogeneous lake. The model was applied to a
test lake of arbitrary shape using vertically integrated equations in one- and
three-layer formulations for which the outputs are compared and interpreted.

INTRODUCTION

   The purpose of the present mathematical model is to simulate time dependent

lake circulation. Due to the fact that repetative calculations for the simulation

of unsteady flow are necessary, it is highly desirable to develop an algorithm,

which requires the least possible amount of numerical operations. Generally two

methods for solving the hydrodynamic equations describing flows in shallow bodies

of water are available, i.e. the finite difference method and the finite element

method. Thacker (1977b) found, comparing the two methods, that the computational

requirements for the finite element method are about one order of magnitude larger

than those for the finite difference method.

   Comparing however finite element models with conventional, i.e. rectangular,

finite difference models, a major disadvantage of finite difference models is found

to be their rather inelegant way of representing the boundary lines of a given

geometry. This can become a serious problem, if one is required to simulate flow

situations in bodies of water such as estuaries, where there is the large, relative

uniform sea, which could well be represented by a rather coarse grid and an often

very distorted shore line, which can be represented properly only by a rather fine

grid. One way of handling such a situation has been suggested by Ramming (1973),

whereby rectangular grids of different mesh size are combined. In a series of ap-

plications, Ramming (1976, 1978a, 1978b) demonstrates the workability of such an

approach. With finite element models, problems of representing geometry normally
do not occur since a completely irregular grid can be selected and thus any complicated geometry can readily be represented.

Combining the advantages of a smooth geometrical representation of finite element models with the advantages of fast execution of finite difference models,
Thacker (1977a) proposed an irregular grid finite difference model. Thacker demonstrated successfully the power of his technique by applying it to one- (Thacker
1978b) and two-dimensional (Thacker 1977a, 1978c), linearized shallow water wave
equations. In a further article, Thacker (1978a) applied his method to the full
hydrodynamic, nonlinear, two-dimensional and vertically averaged equations governing
a storm surge.

In the present paper, the Thacker finite difference method is applied to the
equations governing the motions in a shallow, homogeneous lake. The model has been
developed such that it can be run either for a lake represented by one layer only,
as in Thacker's (1978a) model, or for a lake which has been subdivided into several horizontal layers.

DESCRIPTION OF THE MATHEMATICAL MODEL

The equations describing the motion in a homogeneous, shallow lake on a large
scale may be simplified to read as follows:

$$\rho\left(\frac{\partial u}{\partial t} - fv\right) = -\frac{\partial p}{\partial x} + \eta\,\frac{\partial^2 u}{\partial z^2} \tag{1}$$

$$\rho\left(\frac{\partial v}{\partial t} + fu\right) = -\frac{\partial p}{\partial y} + \eta\,\frac{\partial^2 v}{\partial z^2} \tag{2}$$

$$\rho g = -\frac{\partial p}{\partial z} \tag{3}$$

$$\frac{\partial u}{\partial x} + \frac{\partial v}{\partial y} + \frac{\partial w}{\partial z} = 0 \tag{4}$$

where

u, v and w are the velocity components in the x, y and z directions respectively
   with x being positive towards east,
       y being positive towards north and
       z being positive upwards,
t is the time,
f is the Coriolis parameter
ρ is the density of the water,
p is the local pressure,
η is the eddy viscosity and
g is the acceleration of gravity.

Equations 1-4, used in the present model, may be solved numerically by first integrating them vertically and then expressing them in finite differences for a lake
that has been subdivided into horizontal layers. The dynamic boundary conditions

on the lake surface and lake bottom as well as on the layer interfaces are given by the frictional forces existing at these surfaces. The geometric boundary condition is that there must be no flow across the lake boundaries.

While, in a conventional rectangular finite difference scheme the approximation of horizontal gradients is straightforward, some thought must be given to the horizontal gradient approximation in an irregular difference scheme as shown in Fig. 1. Thacker (1977a) suggested a scheme in which the x and y gradients of a

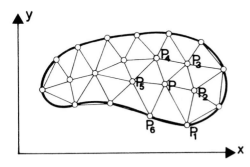

Fig. 1. Irregular finite difference grid.

function, f, at a point P(x,y) are approximated by the weighted means of the slopes of the planes in the x and y directions, defined by the functions at the vertices of the triangles adjacent to the point P. The weight of each slope is given by the area of the corresponding triangle. If a point P(x,y) is surrounded by N points $P_i(x_i,y_i)$ where the surrounding points, P_i, are indexed counterclockwise about P, the gradients in the x and y directions are respectively given by

$$\frac{\partial f}{\partial x} \approx \sum_{i=1}^{N} f_i(y_{i+1} - y_{i-1}) / \sum_{i=1}^{N} x_i(y_{i+1} - y_{i-1}) \tag{5}$$

$$\frac{\partial f}{\partial y} \approx - \sum_{i=1}^{N} f_i(x_{i+1} - x_{i-1}) / \sum_{i=1}^{N} x_i(y_{i+1} - y_{i-1}) \tag{6}$$

where the summation is cyclic, modulo N. When the point P is situated on a lake boundary, it is simply included as one of the surrounding points of equations 5-6. Thacker (1977a) has also shown that equations 5-6 satisfy Green's lemma and thus the total volume of water remains constant as long as there is no flow across the boundaries.

APPLICATION OF MATHEMATICAL MODEL TO HYPOTHETICAL TEST LAKE

The operation of the mathematical model developed will be demonstrated with the aid of a hypothetical test lake described by Figs. 2-7. The water surface of the test lake is $4,54\cdot10^8$ m^2, its volume is $1,5\cdot10^{10}$ m^3 and its mean depth is thus 33 m.

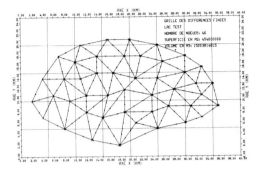

Fig. 2. Planview of irregular finite difference grid of test lake.

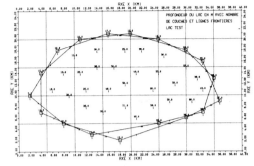

Fig. 3. Depth and number of layers of one-layer test lake including boundary tangents.

As can be seen in Fig. 2, the irregular finite difference grid strongly re-sembles a conventional finite element grid. Figs. 3-4 show the depth of the lake and the number of layers at each point together with the "boundary tangents" for each layer. While in Fig. 3 the number of layers and the boundary tangents are shown for the lake represented by one layer, Fig. 4 shows them for the lake re-presented by three layers. In Fig. 5 the irregular finite difference grid is dis-played in three dimensions. The position of points 4, 21 and 41 marked in Fig. 5 is for later reference. In Figs. 6-7 the parameters used in the model execution

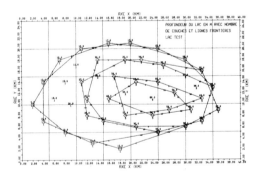

Fig. 4. Depth and number of layers of three-layer test lake including boundary tangents.

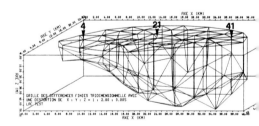

Fig. 5. Three-dimensional grid of test lake.

are listed. Comparing Figs. 6-7 with Fig. 5, one finds that the "box" of Figs. 6-7 corresponds exactly to the box of Fig. 5 containing the three-dimensional irregular finite difference grid. Thus, the boxes of Figs. 6-7 may be used to visualize the position in space of the lake, the ellipses indicating the mean positions of the layers. The scales shown within those ellipses refer to the water velocity vectors

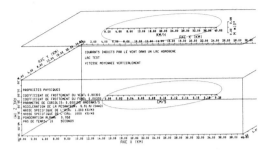

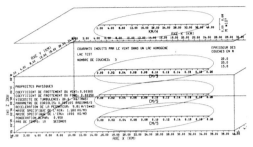

Fig. 6. Scales and list of parameters
for one-layer formulation

Fig. 7. Scales and list of parameters
for three-layer formulation

which will be computed in model runs. In the model simulation to be presented, the
displacement of the water surface will also be shown. To avoid visual confusion
with the vectors presented within the box, the lid of the box containing the water
surface of the lake has been moved upwards, as can be seen in Figs. 6-7. The
velocity scale, also shown in the lid of Figs. 6-7 is for the wind velocity vector.
The vertical scales shown in the "lids" of Figs. 6-7 are for the displacement of
the water levels. It should be noted that in Figs. 6-7, all parameters and all
scales are the same. The simulation will be performed for 2000 time steps of 10 seconds each with an easterly wind of 10 km/h followed by another 2000 time steps
without wind showing the return of the lake to its starting condition.

DISCUSSION OF SIMULATION RESULTS FOR THREE POINTS

The results of the simulation using the one-layer formulation for the points 4,
21 and 41 as indicated on Fig. 5 are shown in Fig. 8. The time axis is horizontal
with the date indicated each 300 steps, starting at step 300. Proceeding from top
to bottom, the first two bands on which the data are plotted contain the x and y
components of the wind. The water levels and the x and y velocity components of
the points 4, 21 and 41 follow respectively. When the data exceed the band width
of one band, their trace is continued over the next band whereby the original
scale is maintained.

In Fig. 5, it can be seen that the points 4 and 41 are situated near the western
and eastern boundaries of the lake respectively, point 21 is located near the center
of the lake. Investigating first the output from the one-layer formulation in
Fig. 8, one finds that the geographical situations of points 4, 21 and 41 are
clearly reflected in their behaviour. The easterly wind produces a rise of the
water level at the western end of the lake (band 4:H) and a fall of the water
level at the eastern end of the lake (band 41:H). The water level near the center

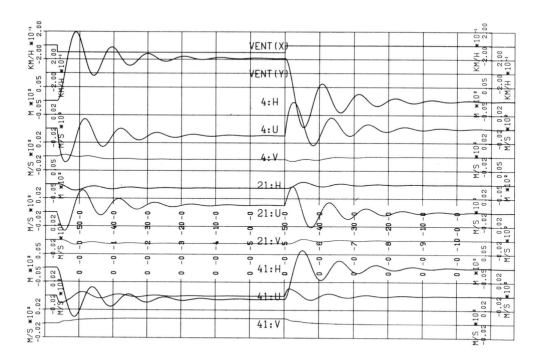

Fig. 8. Simulation for test lake with the one-layer formulation (drawing produced by program TRACE, Bauer and Perrinjaquet, 1979).

of the lake (band 21:H) appears to be little affected. Considering the velocities, one finds that the x components of the velocities (bands 4:U, 21:U and 41:U) react much more strongly than the y components (bands 4:V, 21:V and 41:V). This is to be expected, since firstly the wind blows in the x direction and, secondly, the dimensions of the lake in the x direction are larger than those in the y direction. Most notable however, are the seiches (see for example Forel, 1895) created by the sudden wind which starts blowing with a force of 10 km/h without any slow build-up. Similarly, when the wind suddenly stops, the equilibrium between all forces that has been established is suddenly disturbed and the lake approaches its starting position, again displaying the phenomenon of seiches. One finds, from Fig. 8, that the period of the seiches is about 3200 seconds. Calculating the period, T, of a longitudinal seiche with the simplified formula of Merian (Forel, 1895),

$$T = \frac{2B}{\sqrt{g\bar{D}}} \tag{7}$$

where $\underline{B}$ is a mean length of the lake   and
         $\underline{D}$ is the mean depth of the lake,

one obtains with B = 2,9.10^4 m and with $\overline{D}$ = 33 m a period of T = 3224 s which agrees well with the observed value of 3200 s. It should be noted that the period of the water surface and the velocity fluctuations is the same, even though the optical impression might be different. Only in the beginning of the y velocity components at the two extremities of the lake (bands 4:V and 41:V), does it appear that there is a secondary period of about T = 2200 s which is probably due to a transverse seiche in the corners of the lake.

In Fig. 9, the simulation for the test lake with a three-layer formulation is shown. Thus, while point 4 has again only one layer, points 21 and 41 have three layers. This is also reflected by Fig. 9, where the point 4 has only one U and V band, and where the points 21 and 41 have three U and V bands respectively. The

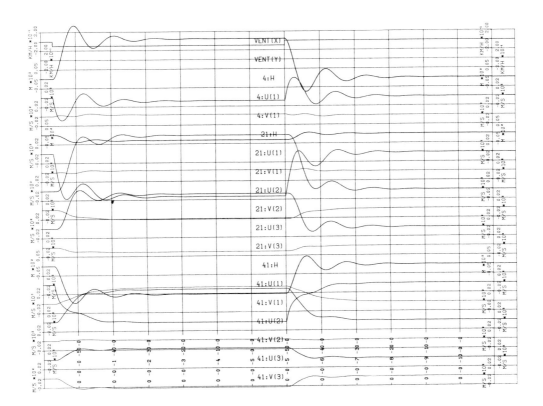

Fig. 9. Simulation for test lake with the three-layer formulation (drawing produced by program TRACE, Bauer and Perrinjaquet, 1979).

scales relative to the band width in Fig. 9 are the same as those of Fig. 8. Comparing now the simulation results of the one-layer formulation, Fig. 8, with those of the three-layer formulation, Fig. 9, one finds that the principal tendencies have remained the same. However, the amplitudes of the surface fluctuations have been increased by about one tenth and damping is more rapid in the three-layer formulation than in the one-layer formulation. The increase in damping is attributed to the additional internal friction between the layers, as it is introduced in the present model.

DISCUSSION OF SIMULATION RESULTS FOR ENTIRE LAKE

In Fig. 10 the entire vector fields together with the water surfaces are shown every 100 time steps. To save space the simulation sequence has been shortened by omitting the first 100 "idle" steps and by cutting the following two 2000 step sequences to 1000 steps each*.

In Fig. 10, the left side shows the simulation of the one-layer formulation, the right side, the simulation of·the three-layer formulation. The time is indicated in days, hours, minutes and seconds in the lower, left corner of each image. Underneath, the number of time steps is shown. The wind velocity vectors are shown in the upper right corner of the "lid". Water velocity vectors are shown within the box.

As can be seen on the first two images of the one- and the three-layer formulation, the lake surface is, at the outset of simulation, horizontal and there are no currents. Considering first the simulation of the one-layer formulation of the lake, one finds that at image 100, all vectors point westwards, resulting in a water level rising at the western extremity of the lake and falling at its eastern extremity. At image 200, the vectors appear to be turning; however, the vectors at the northern and southwestern boundaries remain pointing westwards. At image 300, a return current covering the central part and the southeastern boundaries is well established, resulting a tendency for the water level elevations to reverse. The vectors at the southwestern boundary have been strongly reduced. At image 400, the water level in the west has nearly reached its lowest position. The vectors have again turned indicating a new reversal of trends of the water surface. This oscillatory phenomenon repeats itself until, at image 1000, the equilibrium situation has become almost established. The special behaviour of the boundary points corroborates, to some extent, earlier applications of a stationary model to the Lake of Geneva (Bauer et al., 1977; Bauer and Graf, 1979). A similar oscillatory pattern can be observed after cessation of the easterly wind (images

---

* A computer drawn film showing every time step for the "unshortened" sequence of Figs. 8-9 has been produced as well.

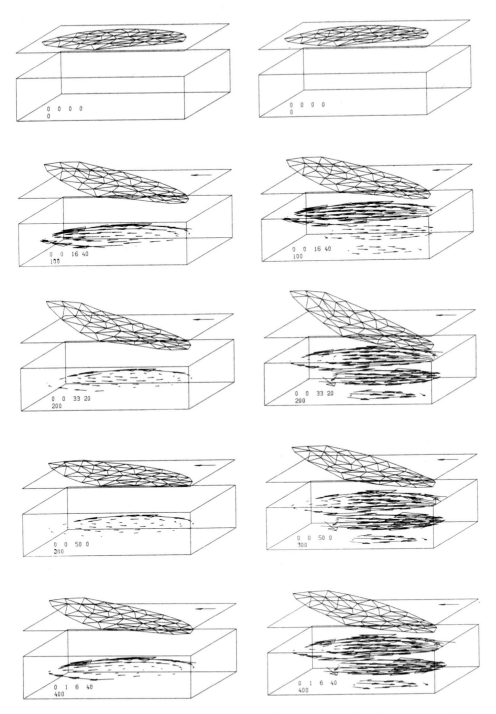

Fig. 10. Simulation of wind-induced, unsteady currents in a homogeneous lake (note that images 1500-1900 have not been reproduced).

60

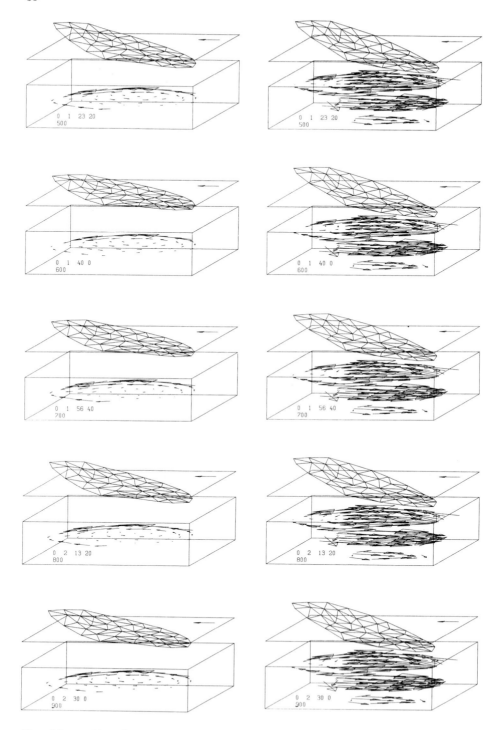

Fig. 10. continued

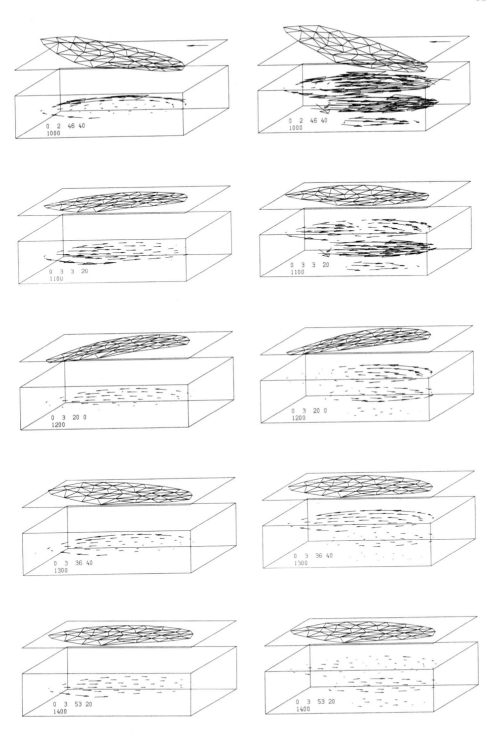

Fig. 10. continued

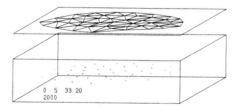 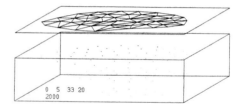

(a) one-layer formulation   (b) three-layer formulation

Fig. 10. continued

1100-2000). Now however, the boundary points no longer display a behaviour distinctly different from that of the center points (note that images 1500-1900 have not been reproduced).

Turning now to the simulation of the three-layer formulation, it can be seen that the behaviour of the water surface of the three-layer simulation is very similar to that of the one-layer formulation. Considering the velocities in the two lower layers, one finds that a return current has established itself. This current, although fluctuating in magnitude, changes very little in direction. The vector field of the first layer behaves similarly to the one-layer mean vectors: at image 100, all vectors pointing westwards result in a rise of the water level. In the following images, one finds that the first-layer vectors change their directions in the western extremity of the lake only. Also, velocities in the three-layer formulation are generally higher than those of the one-layer formulation. In image 1000, equilibrium between all forces is almost obtained. At the cessation of the wind, the vector fields of all three layers change their directions periodically, and the velocities decrease slowly.

Comparing the results of the one- and the three-layer formulations, one finds that their behaviour is in principle similar. As might be expected, the three-layer formulation allows visualization of the velocity fields in grater detail. The fact that damping is more pronounced in the three-layer simulation is probably due to internal friction between the layers, which in the one-layer formulation cannot be taken into consideration.

ACKNOWLEDGEMENTS

This article would not have been written, had the author not met Dr. W.C. Thacker at the 1978 Liège Colloquium on Ocean Hydrodynamics. The author gratefully acknowledges the discussions and subsequent extensive correspondence with him as well as the constructive comments and suggestions by Professors C.H. Mortimer and W.H.

Graf. This work was partially sponsored by the Swiss National Science Foundation (FNSRS) under its special program "Fundamental problems of the water cycle in Switzerland".

REFERENCES

Bauer, S.W., Graf, W.H. and Tischer, E., 1977. Les courants dans le Léman en saison froide. Une simulation mathématique. Bull. Techn. Suisse Romande, Vol. 103, No 19.

Bauer, S.W. and Graf, W.H., 1979. Wind induced water circulation of Lake Geneva. In: Marine Forecasting, ed. J.C.J. Nihoul, Elsevier Scientific Publishing Company, Amsterdam.

Bauer, S.W. and Perrinjaquet, C., 1979. Data bank and -visualization for sequential data with special reference to Lake Geneva. In: Hydrodynamics of Lakes, ed. W.H. Graf and C.H. Mortimer, Elsevier Scientific Publishing Company, Amsterdam.

Forel, F.A., 1895. Le Léman, Monographie Limnologique, Tome second. Slatkine Reprints, Genève, 1969.

Ramming, H.G., 1973. Reproduktion physikalischer Prozesse in Küstengebieten. Die Küste, Heft 22.

Ramming, H.G., 1976. A nested North Sea model with fine resolution in shallow coastal rivers. Mém. Soc. Roy. Sc. de Liège, 6e série, tome X, 9-26.

Ramming, H.G., 1978a. Numerical investigations of the influence of coastal structures upon the dynamic offshore process by application of a nested tidal model. Hydrodynamics of Estuaries and Fjords, ed. J.C.J. Nihoul, Elsevier Scientific Publishing Company, Amsterdam.

Ramming, H.G., 1978b. The influence of river normalization on the distribution of tidal currents in the river Elbe. Recent results of a numerical model. Proc., International Harbor Congress, Vol. 2, Antwerp.

Thacker, W.C., 1977a. Irregular grid finite difference techniques: simulations of oscillations in shallow circular basins. J. Physical Oceanography, Vol. 7, No 2.

Thacker, W.C., 1977b. Reply to a discussion of Thacker (1977a). J. Physical Oceanography, Vol. 7, No 6.

Thacker, W.C., 1978a. Irregular-grid finite-difference techniques for storm surge calculations for curving coastlines. In: Marine Forecasting, ed. J.C.J. Nihoul, Elsevier Scientific Publishing Company, Amsterdam.

Thacker, W.C., 1978b. Comparison on finite-element and finite-difference schemes, Part 1: one-dimensional wave motion. J. Physical Oceanography, Vol. 8, No 4.

Thacker, W.C., 1978c. Comparison of finite-element and finite-difference schemes, Part 2: two-dimensional wave motion. J. Physical Oceanography, Vol. 8, No 4.

THE DYNAMICS OF SHALLOW LAKES SUBJECT TO WIND
AN APPLICATION TO LAKE NEUSIEDL, AUSTRIA

H.-G.RAMMING
Institut für Meereskunde der Universität Hamburg

INTRODUCTION

Lake Neusiedl (Fig.1),situated south-east from Vienna,is the only prairie lake in Europe.It has many pecularities and owing to this it has been the subject of various scientific investigations.

For example,there exist many publications on this lake in the fields of geography,biology,geology,meteorology and water-supply,so that one can speek about a body of knowledge on Lake Neusiedl.It seems remarkable that there are only general descriptions of the hydrology and that detailed studies particularly of the motion processes have not been carried out.However records of observations and corresponding publications are unknown to the author.In any case publications of this kind were not available to the author for his own investigations.

Exact information about the time- and space-dependent alterations of the wind-generated circulation are of great importance for the biological and limnological research on Lake Neusiedl.Results of a numerical model and measurements could be very important to unify results and to understand processes which arise in various scientific fields.

The results of the submitted numerical model of Lake Neusiedl could not be compared with measurements and observations.Thus this publication of the model should be regarded as a first step.The aim of this investigation could be only

a) to reproduce the dynamics of the extreme shallow areas by numerical methods including the control of mass conservation which could be violated,

b) to apply some ideas on how to reproduce the motion processes in the reed area and the advection between the reed area and the free lake,

c) to obtain a general insight in the wind generated circulation.

LAKE NEUSIEDL

The free lake has a surface of 174 km^2.Especially in the northern,

southern and western parts of the lake the free surface is marked off
by a reed area of varying width.The area of reeds,11o-12o km^2,is not
always clearly marked at the lakeside (Löffler,1974).The length is
35 km and the breadth is 12 km.Without the consideration of the reeds
the length amounts to 3o km and the breadth to 7.5 km.Pichler (1969)
gives the whole surface of Lake Neusiedl as 3oo km^2 and its volume as
2oo-25o . 1o^{6}m^3.

Measurements of depths (Löffler 1971,1974) came to the following
results :   southern part of the lake   1.75 - 2.oo m

northern part mostly on average   1.5o m

reed area   o.5o m.

1951 the average depth of the lake is given as 1.31 m.

It must be noted that measurements of depths in some parts of the
lake can be very difficult because of the varying thickness of the mud
(between 1o and 6o cm).Strong currents can transport the mud under specified circumstances to other regions especially to the south,because
there an increase of mud is observed (Löffler 1971,1974).The main problem of the lake is its water balance.In long term periods there are
strong deviations which cause an increase and decrease of the mean water level.

Averaged over short time,one can consider Lake Neusiedl as a closed
basin,because one can neglect the evaporation and the precipitation.
The inflow (Wulka) and the outflow (Einser Kanal) are of the same range
(6o x 1o^{6}m^3/a = 2 m^3/sec).

The circulation in the lake is generated by winds,which blow mostly
from the south-east and the north-west.Other wind directions are very
exceptional (Felkel 1972,Dobesch/Neuwirth 1974,Löffler 1974).

Wind velocities of 6 m/sec in spring and of 3 m/sec in autumn are
very frequent (Löffler 1974).It is remarkable that the wind can rise
very suddenly from north-west or south-east with velocities from
18 m/sec up to 22 m/sec.These conditions may last up for 3 hours.The
system of currents which is created by this wind and the vertical and
horizontal motion afterwards is only partly known.A great number of
instruments - working silmutaneously - must be mounted to obtain an
adequat synopsis.According to Löffler (1974) two counter-rotating
eddies occur in the northern part of the lake.

THE PROBLEM

The reason for developing a numerical model with a high resolution of
Lake Neusiedl was the insufficient knowledge about the hydrodynamics
of the lake.With the aid of the numerical results and the results of a
program of measurements it should be possible to obtain not only a

better insight into the velocity field but also to understand the other complicated processes (sediment transport,biological phenomena, pollution) in connection with the dynamics.The simulation of the circulation shown in Fig.2 can only be very rough because the distances between the points are not small enough to resolve these small-scale processes.The reed area and the drying banks are not taken into account.

In connection with the development of this model the following problems have to be dealt with :

a) The reed area is very shallow and the mass transport is partially stopped there as a consequence of the reed itself.How can this matter be simulated in the numerical model ? It seems inappropiate to the author to use another dimensionless coefficient of the bottom friction other than r = o.oo25.During the numerical treatment it was supposed that 25% of the surface is covered with reed.The discharge for this area at the border between the reed and the free lake was reduced to 75% : a tentative,provisional and very simple treatment.

b) The windstress on the water surface within the reed area is not the same as on the free lake.Here the question arises too,of how to simulate this occurance.In this case it was supposed that the wind velocity in the reed is a quarter of the wind on the free surface (w_{reed}= o.25 $w_{free\ lake}$).

c) Lake Neusiedl is very shallow.If we have a sufficient duration of wind,some areas will not be covered by water (drying banks).The author has developed some models of the coastal regions of the German Bight where tides occur.A special approach for handling the difference equations to simulate the drying banks - problem of moving boundary - was applied with success (Ramming 197o,1978). In tidal areas with open boundaries it is only possible to check the conservation of mass by some restrictions.In this model of a closed lake the simulation of the shallow water dynamic system and the conservation of mass can be checked.This is very necessary because in the first approximation it is conceivable that the conservation of mass can be violated by application of the shallow water dynamic system.

d) The last question is,if the numerical model can reproduce the eddies at the border between the reed and the free lake.Such eddies can be expected because of the strong gradient of velocities in this region.In shallow water areas one can not neglect the advection terms in the equations.

68

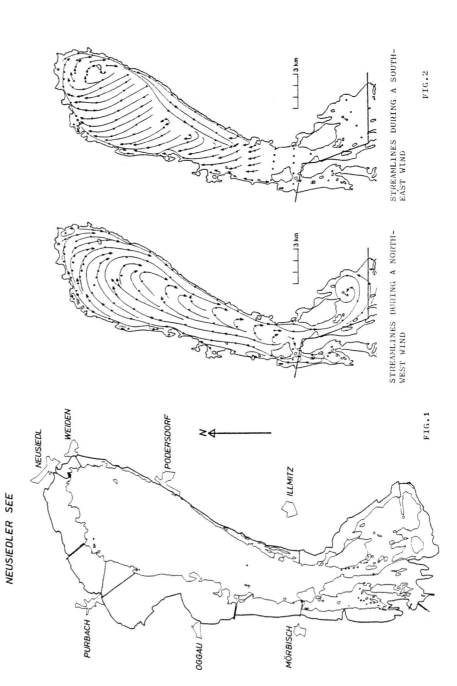

NEUSIEDLER SEE

NEUSIEDL

WEIDEN

PODERSDORF

ILLMITZ

PURBACH

OGGAU

MÖRBISCH

N

FIG. 1

STREAMLINES DURING A NORTH-
WEST WIND

3 km

STREAMLINES DURING A SOUTH-
EAST WIND

3 km

FIG. 2

THE MODEL

The following vertically integrated partial differential equations of momentum and continuity were applied :

$$u_t + R^{(x)} - fv + uu_x + vu_y + g\zeta_x = W^{(x)} \tag{1}$$

$$v_t + R^{(y)} + fu + vv_y + uv_x + g\zeta_y = W^{(y)} \tag{2}$$

$$\zeta_t + (Hu)_x + (Hv)_y = 0 \tag{3}$$

Nomenclature :

g	acceleration of gravity	H	total water depth $(h+\zeta)$
u,v	components of the velocities	x,y	space coordinates
t	time coordinate	f	Coriolis parameter
$R^{(x)}$, $R^{(y)}$	components of the bottom friction force	$W^{(x)}$, $W^{(y)}$	components of the windstress

The approach developed by Hansen (1956) and well-established in the past years and modified under consideration of special methods for the shallow water dynamics (Ramming 1970,1978) was applied. The numerical model of the Lake Neusiedl has approximately 4.800 triples of points.The constant distance between points of the same kind (ζ,u,v) amounts to 250 m,the time step is 15 sec.The bottom topography is approximated by depth values in the ζ-,u- and v-points. By using this method the time- and space-dependant distribution of the water levels and currents comes out.It is possible to determine those areas which are not covered by water (H less than 5 cm) during the corresponding weather conditions.A set of tests based on physically meaningful questions within the computer program was developed.By this means one can determine the water-line as a moving boundary, which depends on the bottom topography,on the water depth and on the time.

THE RESULTS

The following investigations were carried out :

a) homogenous south east wind , w = 14 m/sec , without consideration of the reed bank,

b) homogenous north west wind , w = 14 m/sec , without consideration of the reed bank.

Three hours after the beginning of the wind the surface has the well-known sloping position.A great area in the south and in the north of the lake is not covered with water.Strong currents occur in the northern part when the wind blows from the south east.When the wind blows from the north west strong currents also occur in the small channel between the reed and the southern part.There are no eddies at the bor-

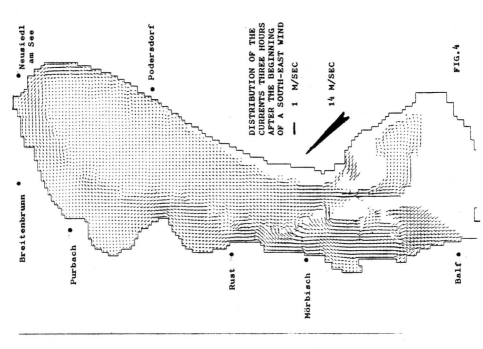

DISTRIBUTION OF THE
CURRENTS THREE HOURS
AFTER THE BEGINNING
OF A SOUTH-EAST WIND

— 1 M/SEC

14 M/SEC

Neusiedl
am See

Podersdorf

Breitenbrunn

Purbach

Rust

Mörbisch

Balf

FIG.4

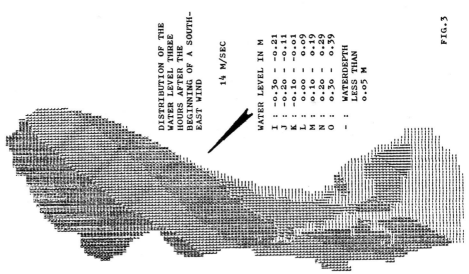

DISTRIBUTION OF THE
WATER LEVEL THREE
HOURS AFTER THE
BEGINNING OF A SOUTH-
EAST WIND

14 M/SEC

WATER LEVEL IN M

I : -0.30 - -0.21
J : -0.20 - -0.11
K : -0.10 - -0.01
L : 0.00 - 0.09
M : 0.10 - 0.19
N : 0.20 - 0.29
O : 0.30 - 0.39

- : WATERDEPTH
    LESS THAN
    0.05 M

FIG.3

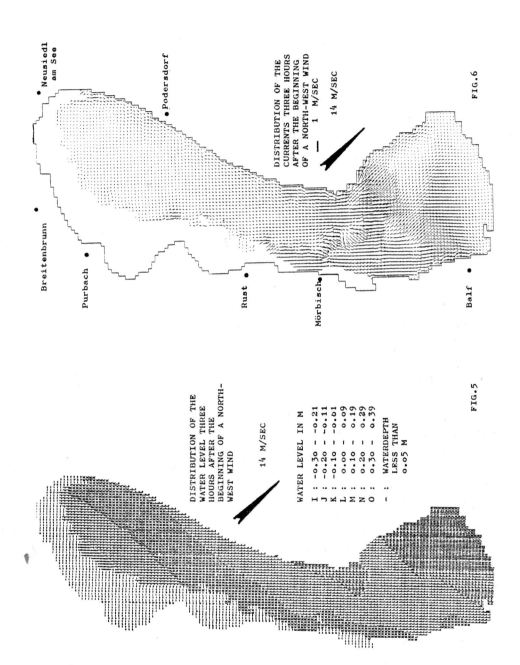

Neusiedl am See

Podersdorf

Breitenbrunn

Purbach

Rust

Mörbisch

Balf

DISTRIBUTION OF THE
CURRENTS THREE HOURS
AFTER THE BEGINNING
OF A NORTH-WEST WIND

1 M/SEC

14 M/SEC

FIG.6

DISTRIBUTION OF THE
WATER LEVEL THREE
HOURS AFTER THE
BEGINNING OF A NORTH-
WEST WIND

14 M/SEC

WATER LEVEL IN M

I : -0.30 - -0.21
J : -0.20 - -0.11
K : -0.10 - -0.01
L : 0.00 - 0.09
M : 0.10 - 0.19
N : 0.20 - 0.29
O : 0.30 - 0.39

- : WATERDEPTH
LESS THAN
0.05 M

FIG.5

der between the reed and the free lake.

c) homogenous south east wind , w = 2o m/sec , with the reed bank
   taken into consideration,

d) homogenous north west wind , w = 2o m/sec , with the reed bank
   taken into consideration.

The sloping position of the surface is stronger than in the two cases
before,as one could expect.The distribution of currents is more com-
plex.Some eddies occur at the border between the reed and the free
lake as a consequence of the numerical approach.

THE CONSERVATION OF MASS

   The over all total of the computed water levels of all 4,8oo points
of the model amounts to o.12 m instead of o.oo m after a duration of
the wind of 12 hours or 2,88o time steps of 15 sec.That means an error
of o.o24 mm per point or an increase of 1.5 m^3/12 h over a volume of
62,5oo m^3.Of course it is very easy to bring the mass into line at
each time step,but this should not be the task in this study.For the
time being this result is satisfactory and one can conclude that the
simulation of the shallow water dynamics is within permissible accuracy.

THE SEICHE

   Merian's formula for the seiche period in a closed basin

$T_1 = \dfrac{2 \cdot L}{\sqrt{gh}}$ can be modified in this special case of the Lake

Neusiedl to $T_1 = \dfrac{2.73 \cdot L_2}{\sqrt{gh_2}}$. On the assumption that the mean water

depth h_1 in the reed area is to the mean water depth h_2 in the free
lake as 1 : 4 and the corresponding lengths L_1 and L_2 have the same
rate a period of T_1 = 22o75 sec comes out.Because one has to consider
that the bottom friction has a great influence on the eigen-oscilla-
tion of Lake Neusiedl with its small depth the following formula is
valid :

$$T_f = T_1 \left(1 + \frac{ß^2 \cdot T_1^2}{32\, h^2} \ldots\ldots \right).$$

Let us take into account a linear bottom friction ß = o.oo1 m^{-1}
then we have a period of the seiche T_f = 5516o sec = 15.6 hours.
In the literature (Löffler 1974) it is stated that periods of about
2o hours occur.It seems to me that the system of oscillations is very
complicated and also that an analysis of observed water levels can
only give an partial answer.

73

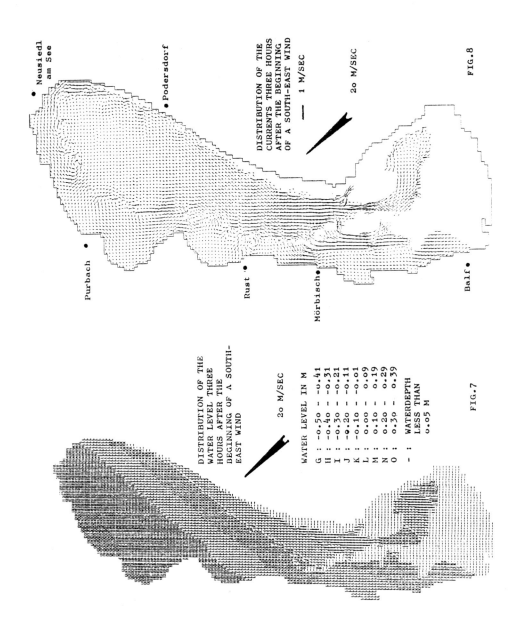

Neusiedl am See

Podersdorf

Purbach

Rust

Mörbisch

Balf

DISTRIBUTION OF THE
CURRENTS THREE HOURS
AFTER THE BEGINNING
OF A SOUTH-EAST WIND

— 1 M/SEC

2o M/SEC

FIG.8

DISTRIBUTION OF THE
WATER LEVEL THREE
HOURS AFTER THE
BEGINNING OF A SOUTH-
EAST WIND

2o M/SEC

WATER LEVEL IN M

G : -o.5o - -o.41
H :: -o.4o - -o.31
I :: -o.3o - -o.21
J :: -o.2o - -o.11
K :: -o.1o - -o.o1
L :: o.oo - o.o9
M :: o.1o - o.19
N :: o.2o - o.29
O :: o.3o - o.39

- : WATERDEPTH
LESS THAN
o.o5 M

FIG.7

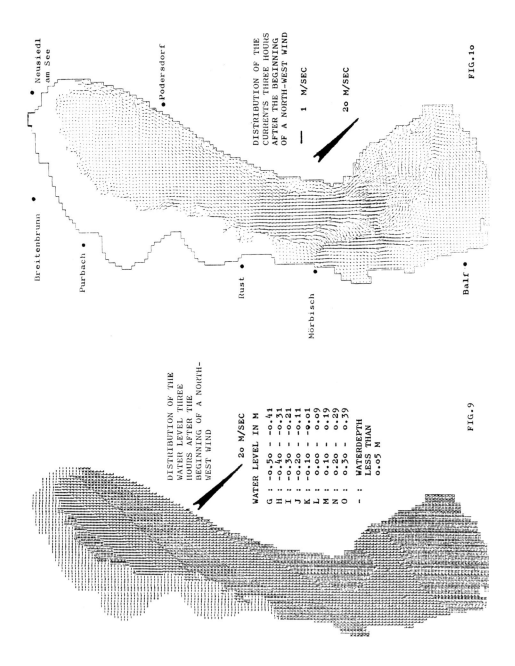

DISTRIBUTION OF THE
CURRENTS THREE HOURS
AFTER THE BEGINNING
OF A NORTH-WEST WIND

— 1 M/SEC

2o M/SEC

FIG.1o

DISTRIBUTION OF THE
WATER LEVEL THREE
HOURS AFTER THE
BEGINNING OF A NORTH-
WEST WIND

2o M/SEC

WATER LEVEL IN M

G : : -o.5o - -o.41
H : : -o.4o - -o.31
I : : -o.3o - -o.21
J : : -o.2o - -o.11
K : : -o.1o - -o.o1
L : : o.oo - o.o9
M : : o.1o - o.19
N : : o.2o - o.29
O : : o.3o - o.39

- : WATERDEPTH
LESS THAN
o.o5 M

FIG.9

Neusiedl
am See

Podersdorf

Breitenbrunn

Purbach

Rust

Mörbisch

Balf

REFERENCES

Dobesch,H.,Neuwirth,F.,1975. Kleinräumige Unterschiede des Windfeldes im Südteil des Neusiedler Sees.Wetter und Leben,Jahrgang 27, 9:38-46.

Felkel,H.,1972. Stürme in Podersdorf am Neusiedler See.Wetter und Leben,Jahrgang 24,1o:198-2o7.

Hansen,W.,1956. Theorie zur Errechnung des Wasserstandes und Strömungen in Randmeeren nebst Anwendungen.Tellus VIII.

Löffler,H.1971. Beitrag zur Kenntnis der Neusiedler See Sedimente. Aus den Sitzungsberichten der Österr.Akademie der Wissenschaften, Math.-naturw.Kl.,Abt.I,179.Bd.,8.-1o.Heft.

Löffler,H.1974. Der Neusiedler See - Naturgeschichte eines Steppensees.Verlag Fritz Molden,Wien-München-Zürich.

Pichler,J.,1969. Entwicklung und Forschung des Neusiedler Sees und seiner Umgebung.Hidrólogiaia Közlöny 7,12:289-3oo.

Ramming,H.-G.,197o. Investigations of Motion Processes in Shallow Waters.Proceedings of the Symposium on Coastal Geodesy,München, 14:439-452.

Ramming,H.-G.,1978. Numerical Investigations of the Influences of Coastal Structures upon the Dynamic Off-shore Process by Application of a Nested Tidal Model.Hydrodynamics of Estuaries and Fjords.Elsevier Scientific Publishing Company,Amsterdam, 34:315-348.

APPLICATION OF A THREE-DIMENSIONAL STORM SURGE MODEL

DONALD C. RANEY[1], DONALD L. DURHAM[2] and H. LEE BUTLER[3]

[1]Professor of Engineering Mechanics, The University of Alabama, University, AL 35486

[2]Oceanographer, Naval Ocean Research and Development Activity, NSTL Station, MS 39529

[3]Research Physicist, U.S. Army Engineer Waterways Experiment Station, Vicksburg, MS 39180

ABSTRACT

An integral part of the feasibility assessment of a proposed offshore jetport site near Cleveland Harbor was an investigation of effects of the structure on Lake Erie hydrodynamics. As a part of this analysis, the U.S. Army Engineer Waterways Experiment Station (WES) conducted a model feasibility investigation. To study effects of the jetport structure on lake hydrodynamics during storms, a three-dimensional numerical storm surge model was applied to Lake Erie. The model was applied with and without the jetport structure providing an estimate of the changes in lake hydrodynamics which would be expected if the jetport were constructed.

INTRODUCTION

The basic governing differential equations for the storm surge model are the three-dimensional momentum equations and the continuity equation of fluid mechanics. The general equations are, however, considerably simplified by assumptions consistent with the intended application. The major assumptions are:
a. The lake is considered to be homogeneous.
b. The nonlinear inertial forces are assumed to be small in comparison with the Coriolis force.
c. The effects of the horizontal internal friction of the fluid are ignored.
d. The pressure is assumed to be hydrostatic as a result of neglecting vertical acceleration and velocity terms.
e. The turbulence in the lake is modeled by a constant vertical eddy diffusivity.
f. The displacement of the lake surface is assumed to be small in comparison with the depth of the lake.

Under the assumptions listed, the governing equations are reduced to a linear system. A free surface condition is imposed in order that details of the transient behavior are simulated. These equations are nondimensionalized as follows:

$$x^* = \frac{x}{L} \ , \ y^* = \frac{y}{L} \ , \ z^* = \frac{z}{H}$$

$$u^* = \frac{u}{U_R} \ , \ v^* = \frac{v}{U_R} \ , \ w^* = \frac{Lw}{HU_R}$$

$$p^* = \frac{p}{\rho f U_R L} \ , \ \zeta^* = \frac{g\zeta}{f U_R L} \ , \ t^* = ft \tag{1}$$

$$\tau_x^* = \frac{\tau_{wx}}{\tau_R} \ , \ \tau_y^* = \frac{\tau_{wy}}{\tau_R} \ , \ \tau_R^* = \frac{\rho A_V U_R}{H}$$

where L = characteristic horizontal length scale, U_R = characteristic velocity, H = characteristic vertical dimension, f = Coriolis parameter, and A_V = vertical eddy diffusivity.

To insure no loss of accuracy in the numerical computation for the shallow regions of the lake, a more convenient coordinate system is introduced. The desired transformation maps the bottom of the lake onto a constant σ surface where σ is a transformed vertical coordinate given by

$$\sigma = 1 + \frac{z}{h(x,y)} \ . \tag{2}$$

After integrating the hydrostatic equation and the continuity equation over the lake depth, the governing equations can be written as

$$\frac{\partial u}{\partial t} - v = - \frac{\partial \zeta}{\partial x} + \frac{E_V}{h^2} \frac{\partial^2 u}{\partial \sigma^2} \tag{3}$$

$$\frac{\partial v}{\partial t} + u = - \frac{\partial \zeta}{\partial y} + \frac{E_V}{h^2} \frac{\partial^2 v}{\partial \sigma^2} \tag{4}$$

$$\frac{\partial \zeta}{\partial t} + \beta \ (\frac{\partial U}{\partial x} + \frac{\partial V}{\partial y}) = 0 \tag{5}$$

where

$$\beta = \frac{gH}{L^2 f^2} \ , \ E_V = \frac{A_V}{fH^2}$$

and the horizontal mass fluxes U and V are defined by

$$U = h(x,y) \ \int_o^1 u \ d \ \sigma \tag{6}$$

$$V = h(x,y) \ \int_o^1 v \ d \ \sigma \tag{7}$$

In these equations, the asterisk notation has been dropped for convenience. The boundary conditions are

$$u = v = 0 \quad \text{at } \sigma = 0$$

$$\frac{\partial u}{\partial \sigma} = h\tau_x \quad \text{at } \sigma = 1 \tag{8}$$

$$\frac{\partial v}{\partial \sigma} = h\tau_y \quad \text{at } \sigma = 1$$

and $\overline{V}_n = 0$ at the shoreline where $\overline{V}_n$ is velocity normal to shoreline.

The finite difference grid uses constant grid spacings Δx, Δy, and $\Delta \sigma$ with variables defined as shown in Figure 1. The staggering of variables simplifies representation of required derivatives. Values for variables needed at points at which they are not defined are obtained by linearly interpolating from the values immediately adjacent to the point under consideration.

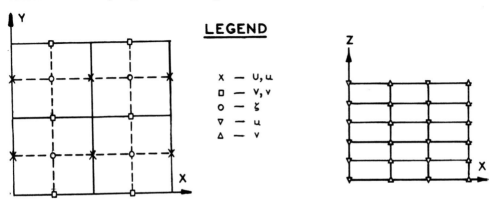

Fig. 1. Arrangement of Variables in Grid System

Equations 3-5 are written in an explicit finite difference form using forward time and centered space differences with a modified DuFort-Frankel scheme for the vertical diffusion terms. In addition, the mass fluxes U and V are evaluated by numerically integrating Equations 6 and 7 using Simpson's rule. The system stability is found to be limited by the well-known limitation on surface gravity waves. In order to conserve computer time, three grids are used in the surge calculations. An 8-mile grid was applied to the Eastern Basin of Lake Erie where the maximum depth occurs. A 4-mile grid was applied to the rest of the lake. For the Cleveland nearshore region, where a finer resolution was required, a 1-mile grid was used. The three grids are dynamically coupled during application of the model. The model was originally developed at Case Western Reserve University (Haq, Lick and Sheng, 1974) with modifications introduced at WES (Durham, Butler, and Raney, 1976).

MODEL APPLICATIONS

The study consisted of running storm surge simulations for three storms: a severe storm occurring in April 1973 for which prototype data were available to partially verify the surge model for existing conditions and two additional storms for which extreme wind conditions occurred. The first of the very severe storms occurred in November 1913 with peak winds crossing Lake Erie along its minor axis from north to south. The second storm occurred in November 1950 with strong winds crossing the lake along its major axis from east to west during a portion of the storm. In order to apply land-station wind data to the numerical model, the data must be transformed to provide reliable, unbiased estimates of wind over water. The procedure for transforming the winds was developed at WES (Resio and Vincent, 1976) and the wind shear stress was calculated by standard techniques (Wilson, 1960). For a spatially varying and time-varying wind stress, the stress at any point in the lake is obtained by interpolating from the known value at a few velocity-measuring stations around the lake (Platzman, 1963).

MODEL VERIFICATION

The storm of 8-9 April 1973 was chosen to verify the application of the three-dimensional storm surge model to Lake Erie. For this storm, wind data from six land stations were used to interpret the wind field over the lake. In general, good agreement exists between surface and geostrophic winds from synoptic weather charts and the interpreted wind fields over the lake. Surge elevation data from five lake-level gages were available for comparison of prototype observations of storm surge with numerical computations. The results of this verification are shown in Figure 2. Time histories of the prototype and model storm surge elevations for 0100 April 8 - 0000 April 10, 1973 agree within 0.5 ft at all lake-level gages except for those at the west end of Lake Erie, where agreement is within 1.0 ft. The difference in surge comparisons for the west end of the lake may be associated with the topographical representation of the islands in the Western Basin of Lake Erie. The good agreement in the vicinity of Cleveland, Ohio and Erie, Pennsylvania increases one's confidence in the numerical model and assures reasonably good results in determining relative effects of a proposed jetport island on the storm surge in the area of major importance. However, a full calibration and/or complete verification of the application of this numerical storm surge model to Lake Erie was not within the scope of this feasibility study.

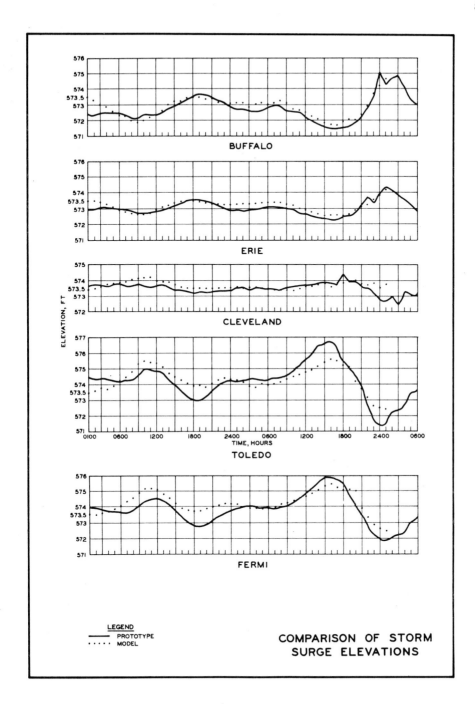

Fig. 2. Comparison of Storm Surge Elevations for 1973 Storm

RESULTS

Surge Elevations-Full Lake

For each of the three storms, surge elevations over the full lake were computed and contoured at 4-hour intervals throughout the storm duration. A representative contour plot is presented in Figure 3. For all three storms, comparison between the surge contours and the wind field over the lake vividly demonstrates the spatial and temporal coupling between the wind stress and the storm surge over the entire lake. During most of the duration of the April 1973 storm, the maximum surge setup is located in the western end of Lake Erie while east/northeasterly winds dominate. During the last 8 hours of the storm, the wind field changed dramatically to southwesterly winds with the surge rapidly migrating eastwardly along the southern shoreline to Buffalo, New York.

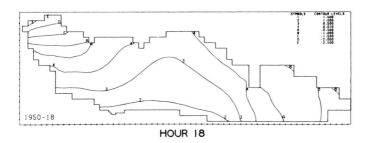

HOUR 18

Fig. 3.   Contours of Storm Surge Elevations for Full Lake
         18 Hours Into Storm of 1700 April 24 - 1000 April 26, 1950

For the November 1950 storm simulation, the surge initially set up on the southern shoreline of Lake Erie near Erie, Pennsylvania, slowly migrated westward as the wind field changed its predominate direction from NNW to N to ENE and increased, with maximum surge occurring approximately 26 hours (1800 EST 25 November 1950) after initial wind field was applied. During the last 12 hours of the storm, the wind is predominantly from the E to ESE with maximum surge setup located in the western end of the lake at Toledo, Ohio. For the November 1913 storm simulation, the initial setup of the storm surge occurred along the southern shoreline with maximum surge located near Sandusky, Ohio. As the predominate wind direction changed from NW to W, the maximum setup slowly moved eastward along the shoreline, reaching Buffalo about 28 hours (0300 EST 10 November 1913) after the beginning of storm simulation. West to southwest winds dominated the wind field over the lake during the last 24 hours of the storm simulation. Although these wind directions persisted during the remainder of the storm, the wind velocity over the lake as a whole decreased significantly. These SW winds along the major axis of the lake sustain relatively large (>5 ft) surge setup between Buffalo and Toledo.

However, the peak setup of 10 ft occurred around 0700 EST 10 November 1913 or about 32 hours after starting storm simulation. This peak setup occurred about 12 hours after occurrence of peak winds at 1950 EST on 9 November 1913. The predominate direction associated with the peak wind field was from the NW. Crossing the minor axis of the lake, these peak winds produced a smaller surge setup than the later SW winds which crossed the major axis of Lake Erie. However, these peak winds did create a relatively large surge setup of 6.5 ft between Cleveland and Toledo, Ohio.

Surge Elevations-Nearshore Region

The surge elevation contour plots for the entire lake do not have sufficient resolution to indicate the relatively local effects of a jetport island offshore of Cleveland, Ohio. To define such local effects, a nearshore region of 15 miles along shore and 15 miles offshore of Cleveland, Ohio was selected. In this region a one-mile grid was used.

For each of the three storms of interest, contours of storm surge elevations in the nearshore region with and without a jetport island were determined. The surge elevations were contoured at 4-hour intervals through the duration of each storm. In addition to surge contours in the nearshore region with and without a jetport, a contour of the difference in surge elevations in the nearshore region with and without a jetport was determined at each 4-hour interval throughout the storm duration. The nearshore results with the jetport in place are illustrated in Figure 4. Time histories of surge elevation at selected locations in the nearshore region and full lake are also determined.

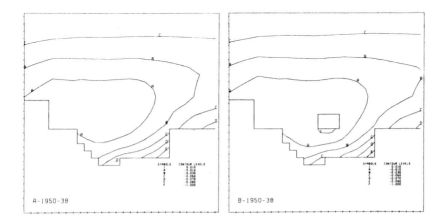

Fig. 4.   Contours of Storm Surge Elevations for Nearshore Region 38 Hours
           Into Storm of 1700 April 24 - 1000 April 26, 1950

The maximum increase in surge elevations due to the jetport occurred during the 1913 storm and was an increase of 0.12 feet (6 percent) both near the jetport and along the shoreline. The maximum decrease in surge elevation due to the jetport also occurred during the 1913 storm and was a decrease of 0.06 feet (15 percent) near the jetport and 0.04 feet (25 percent) along the shoreline. The maximum effects of the jetport on surge elevations along the shoreline for the other two storms (1950 and 1973) are less than one-half of the jetport's effects on surge elevations for the 1913 storm. In all cases the maximum change in surge elevations associated with the jetport is less than 0.15 feet. This maximum change, for the 1913 storm, occurred for one of the severest storms recorded on Lake Erie. This storm produced in the vicinity of Cleveland, Ohio significant and maximum wave heights which are larger than wave heights expected to occur once in 50 years to 75 years.

A careful analysis of results indicates that effects of the jetport on surge elevations are very local with the largest effects normally being within two to three miles of the jetport. Maximum effects occasionally reach the shoreline near Cleveland, Ohio, as in the case of the 1913 storm at 0000 EST 10 November 1913. For all practical purposes and engineering applications, effects of the jetport on storm surge elevations are contained within the 15-mile-by-15-mile nearshore region. Differences in surge elevations diminish to 0.01 feet or less as the boundaries of the nearshore region are approached. From results of this study, storm surge along Lake Erie shoreline SW of Cleveland from Rocky River to Lorain and NE of Cleveland from Euclid Creek to Fairport, Ohio can be considered unaffected by the jetport.

Nearshore Horizontal Velocity Field

Typical plots of horizontal velocity vectors with and without a jetport island are shown in Figure 5. Figure 5 indicates the velocity distribution at the 30-ft depth in the water column. Similar velocity plots were generated at 4-hour intervals throughout the duration of each storm at selected depths in the water column. Major effects of the jetport on the horizontal velocity for the 1913 storm are confined within 1 to 2 miles of the jetport. Smaller velocity variations extend to the shoreline during the 25th hour of this storm. During peak wind conditions of the 1913 storm, the horizontal velocities at all depth levels between jetport and shoreline have maximum increases in magnitude of approximately 25 percent near the jetport and 10 percent along the shoreline with 18° and 4° maximum changes in direction, respectively. There are areas of relatively strong upwelling and downwelling existing along the perimeter of the jetport. Along the shoreline, percent changes in magnitude vary from 0.5-10 percent. Around the jetport and along the shoreline, maximum velocity changes occur nominally at mid-depths of the water column.

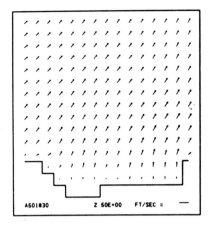 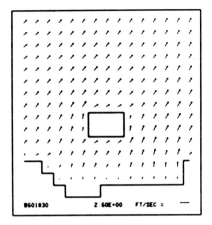

Fig. 5. Velocity in Nearshore Region at 30 ft Depth in Water Column at
Hour 18 of 1950 Storm

Maximum velocity differences occur around the third hour for the 1950 storm
with 27 percent and 16° changes near the jetport and 22 percent and 33° changes
along the shoreline. For the 1950 storm, velocity differences are greatest at
mid-depths of the water column. Maximum velocity differences occur around 44
hours for the 1973 storm with 160 percent and 46° changes near the jetport and
47 percent and 23° changes along the shoreline. These large percent changes in
velocity magnitudes for this storm are associated with relatively small absolute
changes of 0.14 ft/sec and 0.12 ft/sec, respectively, near the lake bottom. Dis-
regarding velocity changes near the lake bottom where absolute velocity values
are quite small for this storm, all changes in velocity magnitudes and directions
are less than 35 percent and 30°, respectively. For this storm, the jetport effects on velocity magnitudes increase with depth in water column.

Since the jetport basically influences the net mass transport in the nearshore
region, the jetport effects at each depth level is dependent upon the magnitude
and direction of the current in each level and the spatial location relative to
the jetport structure. The horizontal mass transport is primarily generated by
the wind stress associated with the wind field of the storm over the lake; therefore, the horizontal velocity regime and perturbations in this regime due to the
jetport can vary immensely from storm to storm as well as during the duration of
any one storm.

CONCLUSIONS

Numerical simulations of storm surges and horizontal velocity fields associated with three specific storms of 8-9 April 1973, 25-27 November 1950 and
7-10 November 1913 were performed during an investigation of the effects of a

jetport island located approximately four miles offshore of Cleveland, Ohio. The jetport island effect on the storm surge in Lake Erie was investigated particularly along the shoreline between Lorain and Fairport, Ohio.

Based on the results from this study, it is concluded that a 2-mile by 3-mile jetport island located in Lake Erie at least four miles offshore of Cleveland, Ohio will have minimal effects on storm surge in Lake Erie. All local effects of engineering interest will occur within 2 miles of the jetport island with smaller effects extending shoreward and occurring along approximately 10 miles of shoreline in the immediate vicinity of Cleveland, Ohio. Estimates of jetport effects on the horizontal velocity regime are more subject to error than storm surge estimates; however, relative comparisons of numerical results indicate major changes in horizontal velocity are confined within 2 miles of jetport island with some changes extending to the shoreline.

ACKNOWLEDGEMENTS

The work upon which this paper is based was performed while the first writer was working as a research engineer with the U.S. Army Waterways Experiment Station (WES), Vicksburg, Mississippi under terms of the Intergovernmental Personnel Exchange Act. Funds for this investigation were authorized by the Lake Erie Regional Transportation Authority (LERTA).

REFERENCES

Durham, D.L., Butler, H.L., and Raney, D.C., 1976, "Lake Erie International Jetport Model Feasibility Investigation; Results of Numerical Time-Dependent Three-Dimensional, Storm Surge Analysis," Miscellaneous Paper H-76-3, Report 17-8, U.S. Army Engineer Waterways Experiment Station, CE, Vicksburg, Miss.

Haq, A., Lick, W., and Sheng, U.P., 1974, "The Time-Dependent Flow in Large Lakes with Applications to Lake Erie," Report of FTAS Department and Earth Sciences Department, Case Western Reserve University, Cleveland, Ohio.

Platzman, G.W., 1963, "The Dynamical Prediction of Wind Tides on Lake Erie," Meteorological Monographs, Vol. 4, No. 26, pp. 1-44.

Resio, D.T. and Vincent, C.L., 1976, "The Estimation of Winds Over the Great Lakes," Miscellaneous Paper H-76-12, U.S. Army Engineer Waterways Experiment Station, CE, Vicksburg, Miss.

Wilson, B.W., 1960, "Note of Surface Wind Stress Over Water at Low and High Wind Speeds," Journal of Geophysical Research, Vol. 65, No. 10, pp. 3377-3382.

DIFFUSION IN A LAKE, COMPARISON OF MATHEMATICAL MODELS

JUERG TROESCH

Laboratory of Hydraulics, Hydrology and Glaciology annexed to the Federal
Institute of Technology Zürich

ABSTRACT

Trösch, J., 1978. Diffusion in a Lake, Comparison of Mathematical Models. Proceedings
of the Symposium on Hydrodynamics of Lakes, Lausanne.

The 3-D diffusion equation of a tracer in a turbulent fluid medium is discretized
using the finite element method. Taking Baldeggersee (in central Switzerland) as
an example, it is shown that the finite element results are of comparable accuracy
as those which were already derived by well known finite difference techniques.
The differences of the two methods lie primarily in the adaptivity to a given geometry, in the respective computing times and in the aquisition of data and exploitation of the results. The weight, naturally individually assigned to these facts,
decides in the end what technique should be used in an individual case.

INTRODUCTION

To understand the mass balance and its transport in a lake requires knowledge
of the turbulent diffusion processes in the entire 3-D domain a lake is situated
in. Such overall knowledge can be tested and extended by mathematical models,
whereby in-situ measurements must obviously serve as means to calibrate and verify
these models.

The numerical procedures known today to solve partial differential equations
are finite difference techniques and the finite element method. The differences
of the two methods do not lie so much in their accuracy, but rather in their adaptivity to an arbitrary geometry, the necessary computer time and the work involved to prepare the data and to exploit the results.

Using "Baldeggersee" (central Switzerland) as an example various aspects can
be compared, because this lake was already subject to field experiments, and because
D. Imboden did already apply a finite difference technique to it. Therefore, our
finite element model can be tested against another independent finite difference
model, which was established by a different author.

BASIC EQUATIONS

The 3-D diffusion equation for turbulent flow of a medium filling the 3-D domain V is

$$C_{,t} + u_i C_{,i} = (D_{ij} C_{,j})_{,i} + J - \lambda C \tag{1}$$

The symbols in this equation have the following meaning

x_i	Cartesian coordinate system	$i = 1, 2, 3 \quad [\,L\,]$
t	Time	$[\,T\,]$
C	Concentration of tracer	$[\,kg/L^3\,]$
D_{ij}	Turbulent diffusivities	$[\,L^2/T\,]$

($D_{ij} = 0$, if $i \neq j$, provided that the principle diffusion axes coincide with the coordinate axes)

J	Production	$[\,kg/L^3 T\,]$
λ	Reaction rate	$[\,1/T\,]$
u_i	Components of the velocity vector,	$i = 1, 2, 3 \quad [\,L/T\,]$

We adopt the summation convention, according to which summation over doubly repeated indices is understood,

$$a_{ii} = \sum_{i=1}^{3} a_{ii} \qquad \text{respectively} \qquad a_i b_i = \sum_{i=1}^{3} a_i b_i$$

and we write for spatial derivatives

$$a_{,i} = \frac{\partial a}{\partial x_i} .$$

The boundary conditions on the boundary set ∂V_1 are

$$C(x_i, t) = \hat{C}(x_i, t) \tag{2}$$

and on the remaining boundary set ∂V_2 they are

$$\frac{\partial C(x_i, t)}{\partial x_i} \cdot n_i = \hat{q}(x_i, t) , \tag{3}$$

where $\hat{C}(x_i, t)$ is a function of space and time which denotes a prescribed concentration, whereas $\hat{q}(x_i, t)$ is a prescribed flux density.

Moreover, the initial conditions

$$C(x_i, 0) = C^*(x_i) \tag{4}$$

must be prescribed in V as well as the advective velocities $u_i(x_i, t)$.

MATHEMATICAL MODELS

The schemes to be compared are a finite difference model and a finite element model.

The finite difference model was established by D. Imboden and B. Eid (1977). They also provided the data and results as obtained for Baldeggersee.

The finite element model is based on the Galerkin procedure. In this method the true concentration C is replaced by the approximation

$$C(x_i, t) \cong \sum_{\alpha=1}^{n} N_\alpha(x_i) \cdot c_\alpha(t) = N_\alpha c_\alpha \qquad (5)$$

N_α are so called shape functions, and c_α are the concentration in n discrete points. In what follows the summation sign will be deleted, whereby the occurance of doubly repeated Greek indices means summation over all n points.

Substituting equation (5) into equation (1) yields the approximation

$$N_\alpha c_{\alpha't} + u_i N_{\alpha'i} c_\alpha - (D_{ij} N_{\alpha'j} c_\alpha)_{,i} = R . \qquad (6)$$

According to the Galerkin method the error R is minimized if the weighted error vanishes in the n different points; to this end the shape functions N_α are used as weighting functions. This gives

$$\int_V N_\beta \cdot R dv = \int_V N_\beta (N_\alpha c_{\alpha't} + u_i N_{\alpha'i} c_\alpha - (D_{ij} N_{\alpha'j} c_\alpha)_{,i}) dv = 0 \qquad (7)$$

$$\beta = 1, 2 \ldots n$$

The third term is integrated by parts; consequently equation (7) becomes

$$\int_V (N_\beta N_\alpha c_{\alpha't} + u_i N_\beta N_{\alpha'i} c_\alpha - D_{ij} N_{\beta'j} N_{\alpha'i} c_\alpha) dv - \oint_{\partial V} N_\beta N_{\alpha'i} n_i c_\alpha da = 0 \qquad (8)$$

$$\beta = 1, 2 \ldots n .$$

The surface integral corresponds to the boundary condition (3), as can easily be seen if (5) is substituted into (3). Therefore, this term must only be calculated for $q \neq 0$.

The discretization of the time is achieved by an implicit finite difference approximation with time step Δt,

$$c_{\alpha't} = (c_\alpha^{t+\Delta t} - c_\alpha^t)/\Delta t \qquad (9)$$

The solution of the linear system of equations

$$\int_V \{N_\alpha N_\beta (c_\alpha{}^{t+\Delta t} - c_\alpha{}^t)/\Delta t + u_i N_\beta N_\alpha{}_{,i} c_\alpha{}^{t+\Delta t} + D_{ij} N_\beta{}_{,i} N_\alpha{}_{,j} c_\alpha{}^{t+\Delta t}\} dv = 0 \qquad (10)$$

$$\beta = 1, 2 \ldots n$$

for the n unknown yields the desired values for c_α. It is to be noted that the matrix of this system is non-symmetric owing to the fact that convection terms have been taken into account.

EXAMPLE: BALDEGGERSEE

Baldeggersee covers a surface of 1.5 x 4.5 km and has a maximal depth of 60 m. The topography is given in figure 1.

We calculate the distribution of ^{222}Rn. This is a naturally occurring tracer decaying from ^{226}Ra. The spatial and temporal ^{222}Rn-concentration can be used to evaluate the turbulent diffusion coefficients (Imboden and Emerson, 1978). The investigation of the ^{222}Rn-concentration is, in particular, interesting during the summer month period, when rapid vertical mixing is hampered by the vertical tempe-rature stratification. The ^{222}Rn-distribution is in this period influenced by the following facts:

(i)   In the epilimnion a large ^{222}Rn-concentration exists, because it is brought in from rivers.

(ii) The sediments at the lake bottom continuously emit ^{222}Rn

(iii) Because of the radioactive decay the ^{222}Rn-concentration in the water is continuously diminished (decay time 3.83 days).

The resulting system parameters and boundary conditions are for both mathematical models the same. The convective terms $u_i c_{,i}$ will be neglected, because, to first order, currents in the hypolimnion are small. The turbulent diffusivities are the same in the entire lake and assume the values: horizontally 1'000 cm^2/s, vertically 0.1 cm^2/s. The flux from the sediment is 360 m^{-2}d^{-1}. At the lake surface the con-centration will be kept constant at the value 100. The reaction rate (for Rn identi-cal with the decay rate) is 0.1812 d^{-1}.

The finite difference model

The discretization was made with a mesh size of 100/250 m in the horizontal direction and 3 m in the vertical direction. In this way a total of 22 x 17 x 18 meshes resulted. The distribution can be inferred from figure 2, for a cross profile from figure 4. Typical for the finite difference method are the step

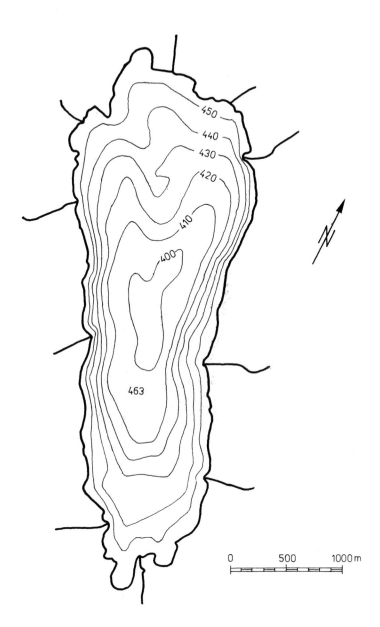

Fig. 1. Baldeggersee. Topography and level lines.

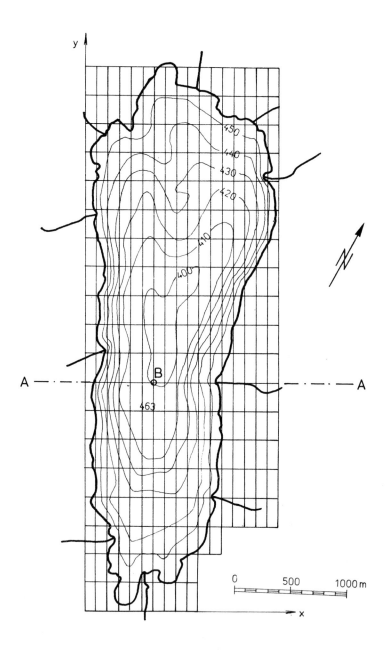

Fig. 2. Baldeggersee. Finite difference mesh (Imboden, 1977).
$\Delta x = 100$ m, $\Delta y = 250$ m, $\Delta z = 3$ m

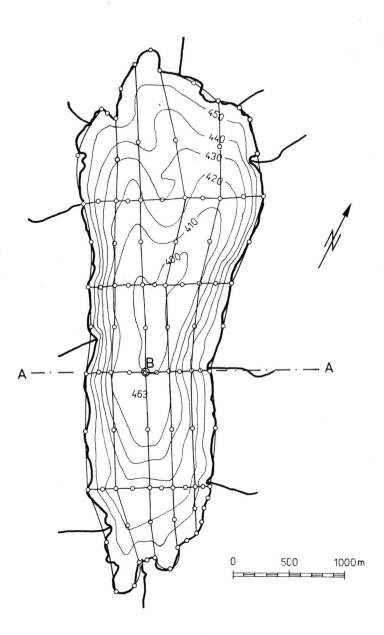

Fig. 3. Baldeggersee. Discretization with finite elements.
Element number = 150, number of nodes = 888.

94

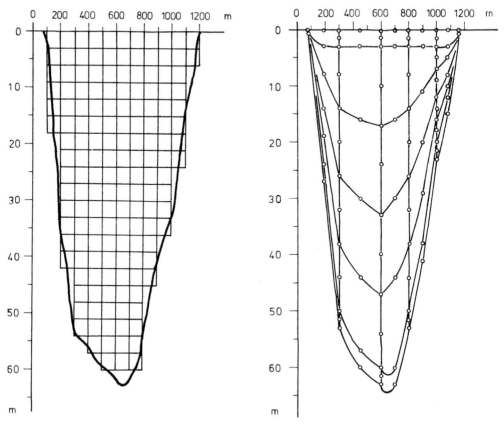

Fig. 4. Cross profile A - A with finite
difference mesh

Fig. 5. Cross profile A - A with partition into isoparametric finite elements

features, which may lead to difficulties, in particular when the lake bottom is
discretized.

Problems are encountered when the flux from the sediments is taken into account.
If this flux is introduced exclusively at the horizontal bottom surface, too high
and too low values of the concentration are obtained at the vertical, over several
mesh sizes extending, side wall, respectively, dependent upon whether one is close
or far from the bottom. If the flux is uniformly distributed among all these boundary cells, the calculated concentrations are somewhat better, obviously because
a certain sidewise flux is simulated thereby.

The finite element model

We choose isoparametric elements with quadratic shape functions. The lake is divided into 150 cubic elements with 888 nodal points. In the neighborhood of the lake bottom and the lake surface the vertical distribution is 1.5 - 3 m and up to 20 m in the interior. The horizontal discretization follows primarily from the topography of the lake. In the average, the nodal points are twice as far apart as in the finite difference model. The discretization is illustrated in the figures 3 and 5, respectively.

There was no difficulty in simulating the flux from the sediments, because the lake bottom could be accurately approximated owing to the flexibility in element choice.

Comparison of the models

The coincidence of the distributions in concentration of the two methods is surprisingly good. In figure 6 the concentration of the profile at the deepest point of the lake is shown. In the neighborhood of the sediment and toward the epilimnion a clear exponential growth of the concentration can be observed. In the interior the decay rate dominates the processes; the concentration is substantially smaller there, and the distribution is uniform. Close to the sediments larger discrepancies between the two models can be observed. At the deepest point the concentration is 330 for the finite difference method and 614 for the finite element method. The cause for this difference is to be sought primarily in the better approximation of the lake bottom by the finite element method, but can also be traced back to the different handling of the flux from the sediment.

To judge the models, computer times and work consumption must be considered, not mentioning the quality of the results.

To calculate a single time step requires in a typical problem approximately seven times more executing time in the finite element method than in the finite difference method. The reason for this are larger matrices. Yet, because the finite element method is implicit, the time steps can be chosen arbitrarily large, without encountering instabilities, quite contrary to the finite difference techniques, in which time steps are limited by the Courant criterion. As a result, for simulations of long duration both methods may lead to comparable executing times.

The discretization and setting up of the input data requires a larger time

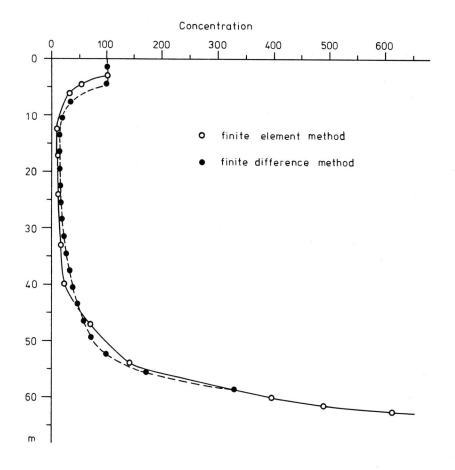

Fig. 6. Distribution of concentration in profile B. Comparison of the methods of finite differences and finite elements

investment in the finite element method. To compete with the finite difference method the finite-element-input facilities should be well developed, otherwise the finite difference method must be favored.

CONCLUSIONS

The comparison of the two methods indicates that the finite difference method bears clear advantages as far as computer time, data preparation and exploitation of the results is concerned. Finite elements are, however, more adjustable and reliable if the lake topography is to be discretized.

Which of the two methods should be applied in a concrete case does not so much depend upon the costs - for such projects computer costs are only a fraction of the total costs - but all the more upon the adaptivity of the mathematical model and on personal preferences.

ACKNOWLEDGEMENT

This comparison was only possible, because Dr. D. Imboden and B. Eid, EAWAG, Dübendorf, made available to us the data of the finite difference model. The translation of this article into the English language was performed by Dr. K. Hutter. The help of these people is gratefully acknowledged.

REFERENCES

Imboden, D.M. and B. Eid, 1977. "Trans 3" User's Manual, (not published).
Imboden, D.M. and S. Emerson, 1978. Natural Radon as limnologic tracer: Horizontal and vertical eddy diffusion in Greifensee. Limnol. Ozeanogr., 23:77-90.

DENSITY INDUCED TRANSPORT PROCESSES IN LAKES AND RESERVOIRS

M. Markofsky

Research Engineer, Institut für Hydromechanik, Universität Karlsruhe

ABSTRACT

The role of density differences in the flow patterns in thermally stratified lakes and reservoirs is discussed. This includes the determination of the inflow level elevation, outlet velocity patterns, and a description of the overturn process. Based on laboratory experiments and the results of a mathematical model for the prediction of thermal stratification and water quality in impoundments, the influence of density currents on the overall water quality of a reservoir is illustrated.

INTRODUCTION

The water quality of reservoirs and lakes is governed both by the biological and bio-chemical reactions taking place within the water body and the hydrodynamical advective and convective transport of the reacting material. The hydrodynamical transport is, in turn, influenced by thermal stratification through which convective transport between the warmer upper layers (epiliminion) and the cooler, lower layers (hypolimnion) is restricted. This can lead to poor water quality in the hypolimnion.

This paper presents the first results of ongoing research at the University of Karlsruhe in the area of lake and reservoir water quality modelling. The goal of the project is the development of a mathematical model which adequately describes the interaction between reservoir hydrodynamics and water quality. This hopefully will be an improvement over such models which neglect or radically simplify the description of hydrodynamical (advective and convective) transport and consequently rely on highly emperical dispersion coefficients to "transport" a pollutant within the reservoir in accordance with observed data.

A dissolved oxygen prediction model for lakes and reservoirs is used to indicate the affect which a variation in the description of the reservoir hydrodynamics can have on water quality predictions.

A QUALITATIVE DESCRIPTION OF THE THERMAL STRATIFICATION PHENOMENA

The thermal stratification process in deep reservoirs is described with the aid of Figure 1.

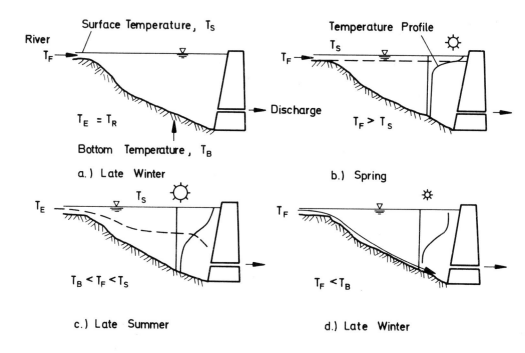

Fig. 1. Schematic Representation of the Thermal Stratification Phenomena

A reservoir with one inflow and one outflow is schematically shown. In the spring the reservoir is fully mixed of constant temperature (isothermal). Since a stream warms faster than a large body of water, the stream temperature in the spring and summer is warmer than the main body of the reservoir and the incoming water enteres at the reservoir surface. In addition the reservoir temperature increases due to warming through the reservoir surface. In the fall and winter the opposite occurs. The stream cools faster than the reservoir and, as the incoming temperature is lower than that of the reservoir surface the stream enters the reservoir at some intermediate depth corresponding to its temperature (density). Cooling of the water surface, associated with decreasing air temperature , solar radiation etc. in the fall and winter, additionally results in density instabilities which lead to the mixing of the reservoir. Throughout the year the temperature structure in the vicinity of the outlet may result in selective withdrawal causing water to be withdrawn from a layer of restricted depth.

The thermal stratification, through the density variation, has a predominant influence on the flow patterns and circulation within the reservoir. Vertical motions are inhibited. Since oxygen transfer occurs at the water surface, transport of oxygen into the lower layers of the reservoir is restricted often leading to high oxygen deficits, or even anaerobic conditions in this region.

Due to the changing temperature field, any pollutant or water quality parameter contained in the inflowing water will enter the reservoir at different elevations throughout the year, depending on the temperature of the inflowing water and the thermal structure of the reservoir at that time. The elevation at which the flow enters, coupled with the changing thermal structure within the reservoir, will determine the detention time of that water in the reservoir. The longer the detention time, the greater the probability that poor water quality will result.

MATHEMATICAL DESCRIPTION

Thermal Stratification and Density Induced Velocity Field

The proposed mathematical model is based on the MIT Deep Reservoir model developed over the last 15 years by Dake (1966), Huber (1968), Markofsky (1971), Ryan (1971) and Hurley (1977) under the Supervision of Dr. D.R.F. Harleman (coauthor of all of the above cited reports). The model can be used to predict the instationary thermal stratification process in a one dimensional horizontally stratified reservoir, as a function of time varying inflow and outflow rates (including selective withdrawal) variable inflow temperature and heat exchange at the reservoir boundaries and at the water surface under time varying meteorological conditions. An explicit, finite difference scheme is used to solve the Equation

$$\frac{\partial T}{\partial t} + v \frac{\partial T}{\partial y} = \frac{1}{A} \frac{\partial}{\partial y} [A E \frac{\partial T}{\partial y}] + q_i [\frac{T_i - T}{A}] - \frac{p \phi_m}{\rho c_p A}$$

$$+ \frac{1}{\rho c_p A} (1-\beta) \phi_o e^{-\eta(y_s - y)} (-\eta A + \frac{\partial A}{\partial y}) \qquad (1)$$

where

T = T(y, t) = Temperature (^{o}C); t = time (day);

$v = v(y,t)$ = vertical velocity (m/day); y = vertical coordinate (m);

$A = A(y)$ = Area in horizontal plane (m^2); E = Dispersion coefficient (m^2/day);

$q_i = q_i(t)$ = inflow rate/width (m^3/m·day); $T_i = T_i(t)$ = inflow temperature (^{o}C);

$p = p(y)$ = reservoir perimeter (m); ϕ_m = heat flux through reservoir wall (cal/m^2·day);

$\rho = \rho(T)$ = water density (mg/m^3); c_p = specific heat of water (cal/gm·^{o}C);

β = fraction of solar radiation absorbed at the water surface;

$\phi_o = \phi_o(t)$ = solar radiation heat flux (cal/m^2· day);

η = radiation absorption extinction coefficient (m^{-1}); $y_s = y_s(t)$ = surface elevation (m).

Since the time dependent vertical thermal structure of the reservoir is predicted, this model is capable of accounting for hydrodynamic transport resulting from the following four phenomena:

1. The density (temperature) of the inflowing water and the coincident thermal structure of the reservoir determine the elevation of the inflow, i.e. the inflowing water "seeks" its density level within the reservoir.

2. Selective withdrawal at the reservoir outlet varies with time in accordance with the temperature gradient at the outlet.

3. The first two phenomena generate a vertical velocity field $v(y, t)$ which, in addition to the dispersion term (the first term on the right hand side of Equation 1), transports heat vertically within the reservoir ($v \, \partial T/\partial y$).

4. Convective mixing of the reservoir during the breakdown of the thermal stratification due to surface cooling further transports heat vertically within the reservoir.

Details of the solution can be found in Markofsky and Harleman (1971), Ryan and Harleman (1971) and Markofsky and Harleman (1973).

In the latest version of the model (Hurley and Harleman, 1977) both multiple outlets at different depths and wind mixing of the surface layers can be treated. The model has been verified through comparison with both laboratory and field data. Typical comparisons for Fontana Reservoir in the TVA system (USA) (mean flow through time = 1.3 years) for the time dependent outflow temperature and temperature profile in the reservoir are shown in Figures 2 and 3. These results were obtained using only molecular diffusion indicating that the velocity field and the resulting vertical transport was adequately described.

Water Quality Model

The first attempt to couple the MIT temperature model with a water quality model is reported in Markofsky and Harleman (1971). The temperature prediction model (Equation 1)

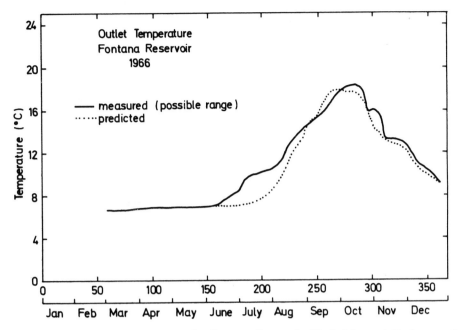

Fig. 2. Outlet Temperature for Fontana Reservoir (Markofsky and Harleman, 1971)

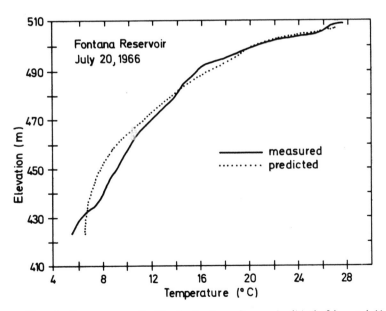

Fig. 3. Temperature Profile in Fontana Reservoir (Markofsky and Harleman, 1971)

was combined with two transport equations for the prediction of dissolved oxygen (DO) and BOD, concentrations:

$$\frac{\partial c}{\partial t} + v \frac{\partial c}{\partial y} = \frac{1}{A} \frac{\partial}{\partial y} [A E \frac{\partial c}{\partial y}] + q_i [\frac{c_i - c}{A}] - K l \qquad (2)$$

and

$$\frac{\partial l}{\partial t} + v \frac{\partial l}{\partial y} = \frac{1}{A} \frac{\partial}{\partial y} [A E \frac{\partial l}{\partial y}] + q_i [\frac{l_i - l}{A}] - K l \qquad (3)$$

in which c = DO concentration (mg/l), l = BOD concentration (mg/l); c_i, l_i = inflow DO and BOD concentrations respectively (mg/l); K = BOD reaction rate (day^{-1}).

It should be noted here that the dispersion term had originally been neglected based on the results in the temperature model. This model was tested against laboratory experiments of a pulse injection of fluorescent tracer in a stratified laboratory model. Although sufficient input data was lacking, a sensitivity analysis indicated that the water quality model reproduced the trends in the dissolved oxygen measured in the outlet of Fontana Reservoir (Markofsky and Harleman, 1973). Thus this water quality model is potentially capable of predicting DO and BOD in reservoirs. At present the model still remains to be field verified.

SENSITIVITY OF DISSOLVED OXYGEN PREDICTIONS TO HYDRODYNAMIC ASSUMPTIONS

Before proceeding with the development of a phosphorus model (to be coupled with Equation 1), it was of interest to test to what degree the predictions of a given water quality parameter could be affected by changing the description of the reservoir hydro-dynamics. Two extreme assumptions are that (1) the water always enters at the water surface or (2) the water enters at the reservoir bottom. This is analogue to either the water always entering the epilimnion (Knoblauch, 1977) or into the hypolimnion (Imboden and Gächter, 1978).

Since the dissolved oxygen model was available, it was used to test sensitivity to the hydrodynamic assumption. The water was made to flow in at the water surface through the assumption that the inflow water temperature was 0.01 °C warmer than the surface water. Similarly bottom inflow was generated through the assumption that the inflow water temperature was 0.01 °C cooler than the reservoir bottom water. These two cases were compared with the dissolved oxygen predictions using the detailed velocity field and varying inflow level and selective withdrawal thickness associated with Equation 1.

Predicted dissolved oxygen profiles in Fontana Reservoir for April, July, September and November 1966 are presented in Figures 4 - 7 and the outlet time dependent dissolved oxygen concentration in Figure 8. Figures 4 and 5 illustrated that during the warming period, little change in the predicted dissolved oxygen profiles occures if one assumes that the water seeks its own density level (curve P–13c) or that it enters at the water surface (curve P–19c). This is because the water, due to its density is typically entering near the water surface anyway. The assumption that the water enters at the reservoir bottom (curve P–20c), however brings the nutrients (BOD) present in the inflowing water into the bottom water and a rapid decrease in dissolved oxygen concentration in the hypolimnion is found. Since cooling has already begun by September large differences between dissolved oxygen concentrations resulting from surface inflow and "density seeking" inflow are seen (Figures 6 and 7). Since no nutrients are directly input to the surface waters if it is assumed that the water enters at the reservoir bottom, the surface DO concentrations under this assumption (curve P–20c) remain high throughout the year. By November the surface dissolved oxygen concentrations are lowest for the case of surface inflow assumption. A consequence of inflow related nutrient input. The predicted outflow dissolved oxygen concentrations (Figure 8) reflect the differences in the predicted profiles and indicate that the assumption of how the water flows through the reservoir affects the predicted concentrations.

Of course some of the differences noted in Figures 4 - 8 can be attributed to the different temperature structures resulting from the assumptions about the inflow water temperature. As illustrated by Figure 2, the results of the thermal stratification prediction model present a realistic description of the temperature field given that the time dependent inflow water temperature is correctly simulated. It should also be noted that although oxygen transfer at the water surface is temperature dependent (in that the saturation value is temperature dependent) care was taken to produce identical surface oxygen transfer in each of the three cases tested. Thus the differences noted in Figures 4 - 8 are primarily attributable to hydrodynamic differences and not to temperature related surface transfer effects.

CONCLUSIONS

The prediction of water quality in stratified reservoirs is sensitive to a description of the reservoir hydrodynamics. The coupling of water quality models with a thermal stratification prediction model has promise in that the hydrodynamic transport can be described

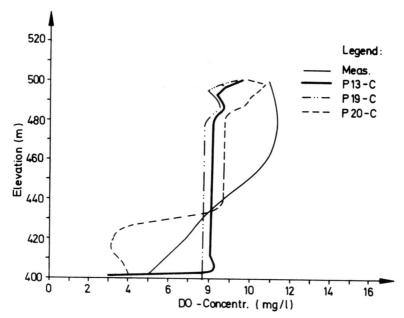

Fig. 4. Fontana Reservoir, April 21, 1966 – Measured and Predicted
D.O. Conc. Profiles. Variables: P13–C: Inflow in Layer of
Same Density; P19–C: Inflow in Surface; P20–C: in Bottom
Layer

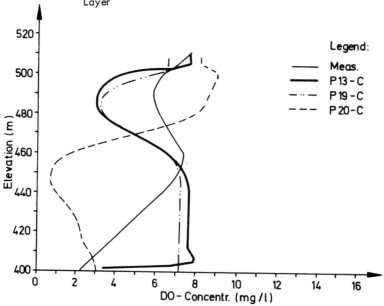

Fig. 5. Fontana Reservoir, July 20, 1966 – Measured and Predicted
D.O. Conc. Profiles. Variables: P13–C: Inflow in Layer of
Same Density; P19–C: Inflow in Surface; P20–C: in Bottom
Layer

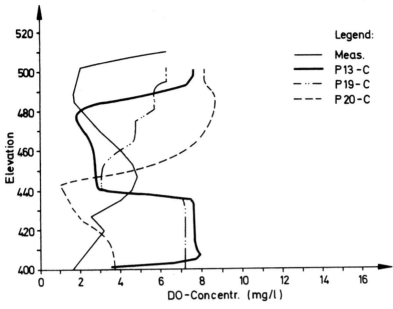

Fig. 6. Fontana Reservoir, Sept. 8, 1966 – Measured and Predicted
D.O. Conc. Profiles. Variables: P13-C: Inflow in Layer of
Same Density; P19-C: Inflow in Surface; P20-C: in Bottom
Layer

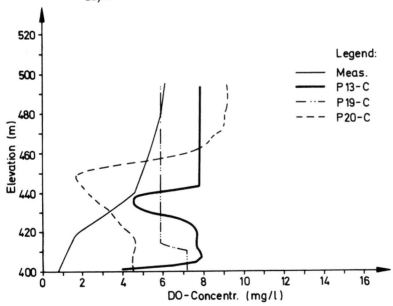

Fig. 7. Fontana Reservoir, Nov. 7, 1966 – Measured and Predicted
D.O. Conc. Profiles. Variables: P13-C: Inflow in Layer of
Same Density; P19-C: Inflow in Surface; P20-C: in Bottom
Layer

108

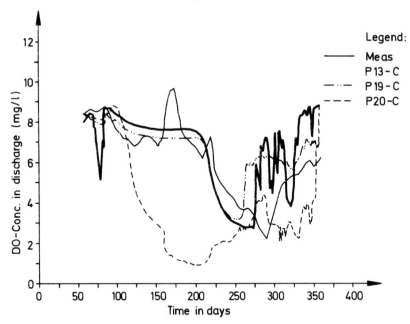

Fig. 8. Fontana Reservoir, 1966 – Measured and Predicted D.O.
Conc. in Outlet. Variables: P13-C: Inflow in Layer of
Same Density; P19-C: Inflow in Surface; P20-C: in Bottom
Layer

in relatively good detail. Further field verification is needed, however, before qualitative
statements related to the accuracy of a coupled thermal stratification–water quality model
can be made. At present research in this area related to a combined thermal stratification–
phosphorus prediction model is underway at the University of Karlsruhe as a joint project
between the Institut für Wasserbau III (Director Prof. E. Plate) – hydrodynamical aspects
and the Institut für Siedlungswasserwirtschaft (Director Prof. H.H. Hahn) – biochemical
aspects. The project is to be supported by the Deutsche Forschungsgemeinschaft (DFG).

ACKNOWLEDGEMENT

The author would like to thank Mr. E. Vock for his highly qualified assistance in the
computer programming and the Deutsche Forschungsgemeinschaft for financing this project.

REFERENCES

Dake, J.M.K. and Harleman, D.R.F., September, 1966. An Analytical and Experimental Investigation of Thermal Stratification in Lakes and Ponds. M.I.T. Hydrodynamics Laboratory, Technical Report No. 99.

Huber, W.C. and Harleman, D.R.F., October, 1968. Laboratory and Analytical Studies of Thermal Stratification in Reservoirs. M.I.T. Hydrodynamics Laboratory, Technical Report No. 112.

Hurley, K.A. and Harleman, D.R.F., June, 1977. Vertical Heat Transport Mechanisms in Lakes and Reservoirs. M.I.T. Hydrodynamics Laboratory, Technical Report No. 112.

Imboden, D.M. and Gächter, R., 1978. A Dynamic Lake Model for Trophic State Prediction. Ecological Modelling 4.

Knoblauch, A., 1978. Mathematische Simulation des Phosphorkreislaufs in einem gestauten Gewässer. (Dissertation TU Karlsruhe) R. Oldenbourg Verlag Munich, Vienna.

Markofsky, M. and Harleman, D.R.F., January, 1971. A Predictive Model for Thermal Stratification and Water Quality in Reservoirs. M.I.T. R.M. Parsons Laboratory for Hydrodynamics and Water Resources, Technical Report No. 134 (also available in Environmental Protection Agency (U.S.A.) Water Pollution Control Research Series No. 16130 DIH 01/71. Water Quality Office, Washington D.C., 1971).

Markofsky, M. and Harleman, D.R.F., May, 1973. Prediction of Water Quality in Stratified Reservoirs. J. Hyd. Dir., ASCE Hy 99.

Ryan, P.J. and Harleman, D.R.F., April, 1971. Prediction of the Annual Cycle of Temperature Changes in a Stratified Lake or Reservoir: Mathematical Model and User's Manual. M.I.T. R.M. Parsons Laboratory for Water Resources and Hydrodynamics, Technical Report No. 137.

Volenweider, R.A., 1971. Scientific Fundaments of the Entrophication of Lakes and Flowing Waters with Particular Reference to Nitrogen and Phosphorus as Factors in Entrophication. OECD Report, Paris.

ON SINK FLOW IN A ROTATING BASIN

C. KRANENBURG

Laboratory of Fluid Mechanics, Department of Civil Engineering,

Delft University of Technology, Delft (The Netherlands)

ABSTRACT

Kranenburg, C., 1979. On sink flow in a rotating basin. In: W.H. Graf and C.H.
    Mortimer (Editors), Hydrodynamics of Lakes. Elsevier, Amsterdam.

    The flow of a homogeneous, viscous liquid towards a sink in the interior of a
rotating basin with a free surface, a horizontal bottom and a vertical side-wall is
considered. The conditions assumed are such that an Ekman layer occurs at the bottom
beyond a small distance from the sink.
    It is shown theoretically and experimentally that eccentric withdrawal from a
circular basin causes a vortex at the sink and a counterrotating gyre attached to the
far wall.

INTRODUCTION

The research under discussion was done to make clear a certain aspect of the flow

caused by the injection of compressed air at the bottom of a thermally stratified lake

or reservoir. Air injection is sometimes used to increase the mixing between

epilimnion and hypolimnion, thus destratifying the lake (Goossens and Van Pagee, 1977;

Kranenburg, 1978, 1979a). Local air injection induces a nearly horizontal sink flow in

epilimnion and hypolimnion which is directed towards the injection point. The water

transported through these layers enters a 'near field' surrounding the injection

point, is mixed due to the turbulence caused by the air injection, and flows outwards

horizontally as an interlayer of intermediate temperature and density. It has been

found from destratification experiments in nature that the Coriolis force causes

azimuthal velocities in epilimnion and hypolimnion which sometimes are larger by an

order of magnitude than the radial components. A mathematical model of the destrati-

fication process in which viscous effects are ignored has been developed (Kranenburg,

1978, 1979a).

To obtain an understanding of the combined effects of viscosity and rotation, a

simpler but related problem is examined in this paper, namely the local withdrawal

from a single, homogeneous layer of viscous liquid in a rotating, shallow basin with a

free surface, a horizontal bottom and a vertical side-wall. The sink through which the liquid is withdrawn is remote from the side-wall. It may be thought of as a vertical line sink extending from the free surface to the bottom, or a point sink at a certain depth. The influence of the actual shape or depth of the sink is likely to be confined to a relatively small region enclosing the sink. The analytical development is based on the Ekman model of rotating flow.

A discussion of existing literature and a more detailed analysis of the problem under consideration is given in Kranenburg, 1979b.

EKMAN MODEL

Equations

It is well known that, if some conditions to be specified later are satisfied, an Ekman boundary layer will develop at the bottom of a rotating basin (e.g. Greenspan, 1968). Assuming a constant viscosity ν or, in the case of turbulent flow, a constant eddy viscosity, the vertical velocity distribution in the Ekman layer is given by ($z = 0$ at the horizontal bottom)

$$u(x,y,z,t) = u_o(x,y,t)(1 - e^{-kz}\cos kz) - v_o(x,y,t)\, e^{-kz}\sin kz \tag{1}$$

$$v(x,y,z,t) = u_o(x,y,t)e^{-kz}\sin kz + v_o(x,y,t)(1 - e^{-kz}\cos kz) \tag{2}$$

in which x,y = horizontal co-ordinates, z = vertical co-ordinate, u,v = horizontal velocity components, t = time, and

$$k = \sqrt{\frac{f}{2\nu}} \tag{3}$$

where f is the Coriolis parameter (= $2\Omega \sin \phi$, Ω is the angular velocity of the earth and ϕ the latitude). The velocity components u_o and v_o representing the flow in the region outside the Ekman layer (the interior flow region), do not depend on the vertical co-ordinate z. An estimate of the thickness δ of the Ekman layer is

$$\delta \sim \sqrt{\frac{\nu}{f}} \tag{4}$$

Equations (1) and (2) imply a transport of mass in the Ekman layer normal to the velocity vector in the interior flow region (Ekman transport).

In terms of a horizontal length scale L, a velocity scale U and a time scale T the conditions for an Ekman layer to occur are

$$\frac{1}{fT} \ll 1, \qquad Ro = \frac{U}{fL} \ll 1, \qquad E = \frac{\nu}{fL^2} \ll 1 \tag{5}$$

in which Ro is a Rossby number, and E an Ekman number. The first two conditions represent the requirement that the inertial terms in the equations of motion should be relatively small, the third condition is related to negligible shear stresses in lateral planes. Appropriate expressions for the scales will be given later.

The equation for the vorticity $\omega_o = \partial v_o/\partial x - \partial u_o/\partial y$ in the interior flow region is

$$\frac{\partial \omega_o}{\partial t} + u_o \frac{\partial \omega_o}{\partial x} + v_o \frac{\partial \omega_o}{\partial y} + (f + \omega_o)(\frac{\partial u_o}{\partial x} + \frac{\partial v_o}{\partial y}) = 0 \tag{6}$$

Because of (5), the vorticity is small when compared with the Coriolis parameter, since

$$\frac{\omega_o}{f} \sim \frac{U}{fL} = Ro \tag{7}$$

Eq. 6 may therefore be approximated in the first instance by

$$\frac{\partial \omega_o}{\partial t} + u_o \frac{\partial \omega_o}{\partial x} + v_o \frac{\partial \omega_o}{\partial y} + f(\frac{\partial u_o}{\partial x} + \frac{\partial v_o}{\partial y}) \simeq 0 \tag{8}$$

The continuity equation for a fluid element extending from the bottom to the free surface (z = h) may be written

$$\frac{\partial h}{\partial t} + \frac{\partial}{\partial x} \int_0^h u\,dz + \frac{\partial}{\partial y} \int_0^h v\,dz = 0 \tag{9}$$

Substituting from (1) and (2), and introducing a 'rigid-lid' approximation ($\partial h/\partial x \simeq \partial h/\partial y \simeq 0$, $\partial h/\partial t \neq 0$), (9) becomes

$$-\frac{Q(t)}{A} + h(\frac{\partial u_o}{\partial x} + \frac{\partial v_o}{\partial y}) \simeq \frac{\omega_o}{2k} \tag{10}$$

in which Q represents the discharge withdrawn, and A the surface area of the reservoir. The RHS of (10) represents the so-called Ekman suction (or injection), a vertical transport of mass from the interior flow into the Ekman layer (or conversely). Eliminating the divergence $\partial u_o/\partial x + \partial v_o/\partial y$ of the interior flow field from (8) and (10) yields as an equation for the vorticity

$$\frac{D\omega_o}{Dt} + \frac{f}{h}(\frac{Q}{A} + \frac{\omega_o}{2k}) = 0 \tag{11}$$

in which $D/Dt = \partial/\partial t + u_o\,\partial/\partial x + v_o\,\partial/\partial y$ is the material derivative. The water depth, h, follows from

$$\frac{dh}{dt} + \frac{Q}{A} = 0, \quad h(0) = H \tag{12}$$

in which H is the initial water depth (Q is assumed to be zero when $t \leq 0$).

Integrating (12) and (11) yields the vorticity of a particular fluid element in the interior flow region as a function of time. However, (11) holds for all fluid elements in the interior flow region. Consequently, these elements all attain the same vorticity at a certain instant, and the vorticity does not change in horizontal directions ($\partial \omega_o/\partial x = \partial \omega_o/\partial y = 0$). Therefore (11) is not only valid for a single element but also for the interior flow region as a whole. Since the fluid is at rest at t = 0, the initial condition for the vorticity equation (11) is $\omega_o(0) = 0$.

The different behaviour of fluid entering the interior flow region as a consequence of upwelling at the side-wall is discussed later.

The solution of (11) in the case of a constant discharge Q (t > 0) is (Fig. 1)

$$\omega_o = - \frac{Q}{A} \sqrt{\frac{2f}{\nu}} \left[1 - (\frac{h}{H})^{1/\alpha} \right] \tag{13}$$

in which

$$\alpha = \frac{Q}{A} \sqrt{\frac{2}{f\nu}} \tag{14}$$

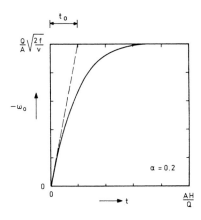

Fig. 1. Time evolution of vorticity, $\alpha = 0.2$.

Since $\omega_o \sim U/L$, and the 'spin-up time' $t_o \sim H/\sqrt{\nu f}$ (Fig. 1), an obvious choice for the scale quantities involved is

$$\frac{U}{L} = \frac{Q}{A} \sqrt{\frac{f}{\nu}} \qquad \text{and} \qquad T = \frac{H}{\sqrt{\nu f}}$$

The length scale L is associated with the size of the reservoir. Therefore $L = \sqrt{A}$ is assumed. The conditions (5) then become, respectively,

$$\frac{\delta}{H} \ll 1, \qquad \alpha \ll 1 \qquad \frac{\delta^2}{A} \ll 1 \tag{15}$$

The first condition indicates that the Ekman layer thickness should be small when compared with the water depth; the second that the time ($\sim H/\sqrt{\nu f}$) to reach the maximum vorticity should be less than the time (= AH/Q) needed to empty the reservoir. The third condition is less restrictive than the first, since in general $A > H^2$.

Boundary conditions at the side-wall

Since boundary layers at the side-wall are of secondary importance for the problem

under consideration, the only boundary condition at the side-wall to be considered
is a zero net flux normal to it, that is

$$\int_0^h \underline{u} \cdot \underline{n} \; dz = 0 \qquad (16)$$

in which $\underline{u}$ is the (horizontal) velocity vector ($\underline{u} = (u,v)$), and $\underline{n}$ is the unit vector
normal to the side-wall. Substituting from (1) and (2), (16) gives

$$\underline{u}_o \cdot \underline{n} \simeq \frac{1}{2kh} \; \underline{u}_o \cdot \underline{s} \qquad (17)$$

in which $\underline{u}_o$ is the (horizontal) velocity vector of the interior flow, and $\underline{s}$ is the
unit vector tangential to the side-wall. $\underline{u}_o \cdot \underline{n}$ and $\underline{u}_o \cdot \underline{s}$ are the normal and
tangential components of the interior flow at the wall. The physical interpretation
of (17) is that the Ekman transport at the side-wall is compensated by an interior
flow normal to the wall and downwelling (Ekman transport inwards, Fig. 2a) or
upwelling (Ekman transport outwards, Fig. 2b) at the side-wall. It follows from (15)
and (17) that $\left| \underline{u}_o \cdot \underline{n} \right| \ll \left| \underline{u}_o \cdot \underline{s} \right|$.

Fig. 2. Flow at side-wall, a downwelling, b upwelling.

Eq. 17, together with the equations of motion, can be utilized to show that the
circulation, $\oint \underline{u}_o \cdot d\underline{s}$, along the side-wall vanishes (Kranenburg, 1979b),

$$\oint \underline{u}_o \cdot d\underline{s} = 0 \qquad (18)$$

This equation indicates that, if $\underline{u}_o$ does not vanish everywhere at the wall, there
must be at least two stagnation points at the wall. It will be seen later that these
two stagnation points are related to the occurrence of a vortex near the sink and a
counterrotating gyre attached to the far wall.

Interior flow field

The definition of the vorticity and the continuity equation (10) yield the
equations for the interior flow,

$$\frac{\partial v_o}{\partial x} - \frac{\partial u_o}{\partial y} = \omega_o \qquad (19)$$

$$\frac{\partial u_o}{\partial x} + \frac{\partial v_o}{\partial y} = \frac{1}{h} \left(\frac{\omega_o}{2k} + \frac{Q}{A} \right) \tag{20}$$

The vorticity of the interior flow follows from (11). It depends on time, but not on the horizontal co-ordinates. The vorticity of the fluid entering the interior flow region at the side-wall (upwelling of fluid transported outwards in the Ekman layer) is different. It can be shown, however, that there is only a relatively thin layer at the wall where the vorticity differs from that in the remaining part of the interior.

Neglecting this effect, the right-hand sides of (19) and (20) are functions of time only. A stream function Ψ and potential functions Φ_1 and Φ_2 not depending on time may then be introduced according to

$$u_o = - \omega_o A \frac{\partial \Psi}{\partial y} + \frac{1}{h} \left(\frac{\omega_o}{2k} A + Q \right) \frac{\partial \Phi_1}{\partial x} + \frac{\omega_o}{2kh} A \frac{\partial \Phi_2}{\partial x} \tag{21}$$

$$v_o = \omega_o A \frac{\partial \Psi}{\partial x} + \frac{1}{h} \left(\frac{\omega_o}{2k} A + Q \right) \frac{\partial \Phi_1}{\partial y} + \frac{\omega_o}{2kh} A \frac{\partial \Phi_2}{\partial y} \tag{22}$$

On substitution of (21) and (22) into (19) and (20), Ψ, Φ_1 and Φ_2 are found to satisfy the equations

$$\frac{\partial^2 \Psi}{\partial x^2} + \frac{\partial^2 \Psi}{\partial y^2} = \frac{1}{A} , \qquad \frac{\partial^2 \Phi_1}{\partial x^2} + \frac{\partial^2 \Phi_1}{\partial y^2} = \frac{1}{A} \quad \text{and} \quad \frac{\partial^2 \Phi_2}{\partial x^2} + \frac{\partial^2 \Phi_2}{\partial y^2} = 0 \tag{23a,b,c}$$

The boundary conditions follow from (17). Since the coefficient $1/2kh$ in this equation is muss less than unity, it suffices to take into account on the RHS of (17) only the leading term of (21) and (22). In order that stream function and potential functions do not depend on time, the following boundary conditions must be satisfied

$$\frac{\partial \Psi}{\partial s} = 0, \qquad \frac{\partial \Phi_1}{\partial n} = 0 \quad \text{and} \quad \frac{\partial \Phi_2}{\partial n} = \frac{\partial \Psi}{\partial n} \tag{24a,b,c}$$

The above equations reveal the physical significance of Ψ, Φ_1 and Φ_2. Initially ($t \ll T$) the vorticity ω_o is still small, and the velocities follow from the potential function Φ_1. The flow is then almost identical to that in a non-rotating reservoir, the transport of fluid towards the sink taking place over the whole depth (Fig. 3a). When time elapses, the vorticity increases, so that the factors multiplying derivatives of Ψ and Φ_2 in (21) and (22) increase. When ω_o has reached its final value $-2kQ/A$ (see (13)), the influence of the potential function Φ_1 vanishes. The RHS of the continuity equation (10) shows that as ω_o increases, the Ekman layer suction increases. The (vertical) suction velocity $\omega_o/2k$ tends to the vertical velocity of the free surface $(-Q/A)$ as ω_o tends to its final value. Consequently, the transport of fluid towards the sink then takes place completely within the Ekman layer, whereas the streamlines of the interior flow are closed (Fig. 3b). This result for (quasi-)steady flow is well known (Greenspan, 1968; Kuo and Veronis, 1971).

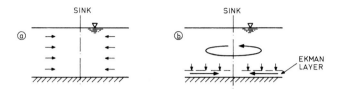

Fig. 3. Principles of flow field, a initial phase, b final phase.

The functions Φ_1 and Ψ turn out to be singular at the sink. Introcuding polar co-ordinates (r, ϕ) with the origin at the sink and velocities (u_r, u_ϕ), the continuity equation when applied to the interior flow region yields for $r \to 0$

$$2\pi r h u_r = - (Q + \frac{\omega_o}{2k} A) \qquad (25)$$

The last term in (25) represents the transport through the Ekman layer. It follows from (25) that

$$\Phi_1 \to - \frac{1}{2\pi} \ln \frac{r}{r_o} \qquad \text{if} \quad r \to 0 \qquad (26)$$

in which r_o is an arbitrary constant. The singularity in the stream function Ψ can be found by applying Stokes' theorem to the region enclosed by the contour shown in Fig. 4. This gives

$$\oint \underline{u} \cdot d\underline{s} - (2\pi r u_\phi)_{r \to 0} = \omega_o A$$

Using (18) it is found that

$$u_\phi \to -\omega_o A/2\pi r \qquad \text{and} \qquad \Psi \to - \frac{1}{2\pi} \ln \frac{r}{r_o} \qquad \text{if} \qquad r \to 0 \qquad (27)$$

The singularity in Ψ will not occur, if the sink is situated at the side-wall. This case is treated by Kuo and Veronis (1971).

Equations (25) and (27) show that the azimuthal velocity u_ϕ in the final phase is an order of magnitude (namely by a factor $h/2k$) larger than the radial velocity u_r in the initial phase.

THEORETICAL AND EXPERIMENTAL RESULTS FOR A CIRCULAR RESERVOIR

The interior flow pattern is determined by the functions Ψ, Φ_1 and Φ_2. Attention is devoted here to the stream function Ψ only, since this function represents the influence of the rotation on the interior flow. It also determines to a large extent the flow in the final quasi-steady phase in the case where Q is constant. The potential function Φ_1 represents the flow pattern in the absence of rotation, and is

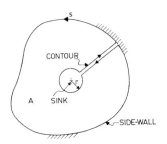

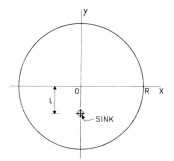

Fig. 4. Application of Stokes' theorem. Fig. 5. Definition sketch of circular reservoir.

of less interest here. The contribution of the potential function Φ_2 is of secondary importance, because of the small factor 1/2kh in (21) and (22).

The solution of (23a) for a circular reservoir (Fig. 5), which satisfies the boundary condition (24a) and has the correct singular behaviour at the sink accordin to (27), is

$$\Psi = \frac{1}{4\pi} \ln \left[\frac{l^2}{R^2} \frac{x^2 + (y + \frac{R^2}{l})^2}{x^2 + (y + l)^2} \right] + \frac{1}{4\pi} \frac{x^2 + y^2}{R^2} \tag{28}$$

in which R is the radius of the reservoir. The co-ordinates of the sink are x = 0, y = - 1.

In the case of centric withdrawal the final velocities for constant discharge Q are (1 = 0, $r = \sqrt{x^2 + y^2}$)

$$u_r = 0, \qquad u_\phi = \sqrt{\frac{2f}{\nu}} \frac{Q}{2\pi r} (1 - \frac{r^2}{R^2}) \tag{29}$$

This result may be derived more simply directly. As an example, Fig. 6 shows the azimuthal velocity u_ϕ at a fixed radius as a function of time. It is seen that initially the viscous and inviscid solutions coincide, but that the viscous solution branches off to a constant final value. Fig. 7 shows the distribution of the final azimuthal velocity in radial direction.

Experiments were done in a circular tank, diameter 1.50 m and maximum water depth 0.20 m, placed on a turntable rotating in clockwise direction. The angular velocitie of the turntable (0.04-0.14 rad/s) were so low that the deformation of the free surface owing to the centrifugal force was negligibly small. In the experiments with centric withdrawal water was withdrawn through a small pipe at some distance above t bottom. The Ekman layer was visualized with potassium permanganate crystals sprinkle on the bottom. Except very close to the sink, the angle between streaklines and azimuthal direction was nearly 45 degrees, which is in agreement with the theory of

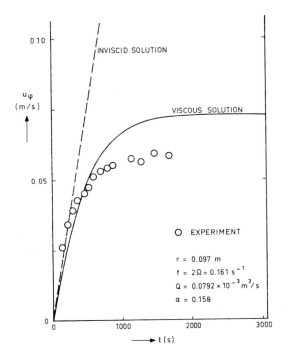

Fig. 6. Time evolution of azimuthal velocity.

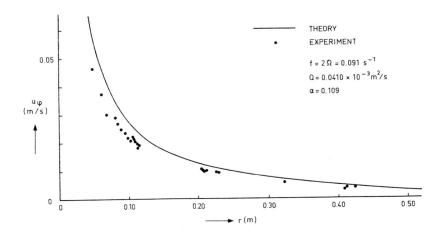

Fig. 7. Radial distribution of final azimuthal velocity.

the Ekman layer. Figs. 6 and 7 show that the theory predicts the velocity distribution correctly. The theoretical values of the final azimuthal velocities are somewhat too large, however. This discrepancy is caused by the neglect in the Ekman layer theory of the inertial terms in the equations of motion.

Fig. 8 shows theoretical and experimental streamlines for l/R = 0.467. It is seen that a vortex with its centre at the sink develops, much as in the case of centric

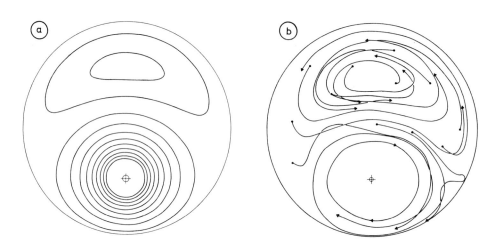

Fig. 8. Streamlines of interior flow, l/R = 0.467, a theory, b experiment.

withdrawal, and that a counter-rotating gyre is generated at the far wall. The stagnation points at the side-wall separate regions with upwelling and downwelling (cf. (24c)), upwelling occurring at the far wall. In the experiments with eccentric withdrawal water was withdrawn through a hole in the bottom of the tank. Fig. 8b shows experimental paths of floats travelled during fifteen rotations of the tank. The agreement between theory and experiments as regards the interior flow pattern is satisfactory.

DISCUSSION

The deformation of the free surface was ignored in the analysis, although a drop in the water level does occur close to the sink. It can be shown that the radius r_1 at which this drop in water level becomes larger than about two per cent of the total depth, is given by

$$r_1 \approx Q \sqrt{\frac{f}{\nu gh}} \tag{30}$$

in which g is the gravitational constant. Eq. (30) in many cases yields fairly small radii r_1. In the case of withdrawal from a constant-density layer in a stratified reservoir, however, the deformation of the interface may be much larger. The gravitational constant in (30) has then to be replaced by εg, where ε is the fractional density difference between the layers. In the case of thermal stratification ε is a small number, and the radius r_1 can become considerable.

Close to the sink, the boundary layer at the bottom is dominated by the inertial terms in the equations of motion, the Coriolis force being negligible. As a consequence, the flow in the boundary layer appeared to become radially directed. This experimental finding is in agreement with the theoretical predictions of Burggraf et al., 1971.

The research reported here is being continued with experiments on selective withdrawal from a two-layer system, and destratification experiments in which air is locally injected at the bottom of a two-layer system. The major interest in these experiments is in the properties of the interface, such as its stability and frictional behaviour.

REFERENCES

Burggraf, O.R., Stewartson, K. and Belcher, R.J., 1971. Boundary layer induced by a potential vortex., Phys. Fluids, 14: 1821-1833.

Goossens, L.H.J. and Van Pagee, J.A., 1977. Modelling of the near field due to air injection in big reservoirs. In: Proc. 17th Congress IAHR, Baden-Baden, 1: 587-594.

Greenspan, H.P., 1968. The theory of rotating fluids. Cambridge University Press, London.

Kranenburg, C., 1978. On the destratification of lakes and reservoirs using bubble columns. Communications on Hydraulics, Report No. 78-1, Dept. of Civil Engineering, Delft University of Technology.

Kranenburg, C., 1979a. Destratification of lakes using bubble columns. J. Hydr. Div., Proc. ASCE. To be published.

Kranenburg, C., 1979b. Sink flow in a rotating basin. J. Fluid Mech. To be published.

Kuo, H.-H. and Veronis, G., 1971. The source-sink flow in a rotating system and its oceanic analogy. J. Fluid Mech., 45: 441-464.

MEASURING ON LAKE GENEVA* (LE LEMAN)

W.H. GRAF, C. PERRINJAQUET, S.W. BAUER, J.P. PROST and H. GIROD

Laboratoire d'Hydraulique (LHYDREP), Ecole Polytechnique Fédérale, Lausanne, Switzerland

ABSTRACT

This article gives a description of a measuring programme on Lake Geneva (Leman). General information on the Basin of the Leman is presented first. Under the heading of Technical work, the measuring installation, the measuring instruments and subsequently the adopted launching procedure of the installation are discussed. Finally, under the heading of Results, the data acquisition system and the data visualization system are presented; a display of all data observed thusfar is included.

INTRODUCTION

Ever since its foundation in 1928 (1932) the Hydraulics Laboratory (LHYDREP) of the EPF-L had had a certain interest in coastal and lake problems. However, it is only in the last few years that problems of the hydrodynamics of lakes receive major attention in our research programme. Presently we are engaged in an extensive field programme, in simulations of lake-circulation, in atmospheric boundary layer research and in wave prediction. The present article deals with our measuring campaign on the Leman. This is an updating of a previous publication by LHYDREP - see Prost et al. (1977); furthermore, we have produced a film showing our procedures (this film is available on loan). In order to obtain both the circulation pattern of the lake's waters and the boundary layer of the atmosphere, it would be desirable to measure synoptically at many points in the lake. This is presently not possible for us, therefore we have started by developing a single measuring unit, giving information on vertical velocity and temperature distributions in water and in air. This measuring unit we deploy for certain time periods at "interesting" locations in the Leman.

---

* While it is a pleonasm there exists also the name "Lac Léman". During the past various names have been used such as lacus Lemannus (by the Romans), lac de Genève or de Lausanne (during the Renaissance), Léman (XIX century) etc. The French language knows presently the name: Léman or Lac Léman; other languages have as "translations": Lake of Geneva, Genfersee and Lago di Ginevra.

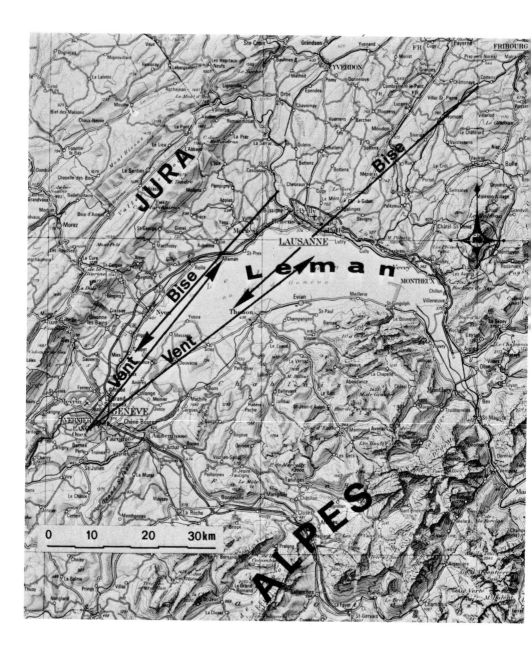

Fig. 1. The Basin of the Leman; and the important winds

THE BASIN OF THE LEMAN

Le Léman

On Fig. 1 we see the basin of the lake surrounded by the Jura mountains in the NW and the northerly parts of the central Alps in the S and SE. The basin of the lake itself is part of the Swiss plateau which is made up of the tertiary of the Alpine foreland, characterized by thick alternating marine and non-marine clastics of orogenic derivation, known to European geologists as molasse (Krumbein et al., 1963). The origin of the Leman - much debated - is said to be due to fluvial erosion, perturbed by tectonic deformation and glacial remodeling (Amberger et al., 1976). Furthermore, one likes to distinguish 3 sub-basins: (i) the alpine Leman - formed by the erosion of the glacier of the Rhône; (ii) the prealpine Leman - formed mainly by an ancient fluviatile basin and (iii) the jurassic Leman - produced by tectonic activity and by deposition of the glacier.

Important general data on the Leman are summarized in Table 1. The bathymetry of the lake is roughly indicated in Fig. 2. It must also be mentioned that, in a certain sense, the Leman is an artificial lake since it is regulated hydraulically in Geneva at its "downstream" end. By an agreement of 1892 the level at Geneva should not exceed 372,30 m at ist maximum and the minimal normal is set at 371,70 m.

Thermodynamic aspects of the Leman are well schematized in Fig. 3. It is a lake with a direct stratification; solar heating combined with wind action is responsible for stratification in summer, and wind action and autumnal cooling produce uniform conditions in winter. At the end of summer, the epilimnion reaches its maximum thickness of about 25 m; the surface temperature can be as high as 25°C or slightly more. The thermocline is in general very steep. During the entire year, the hypolimnion has a quasi-winter temperature profile; at the lake bottom, temperatures of ca. 5°C are recorded. At the end of winter the lake is more or less homogeneous. During the entire year the lake's surface temperature is generally higher than the temperature of the ambient air.

Some meteorological information

Due to its geomorphologic situation the basin of the Leman feels the influence of the following climatic zones: The Atlantic ocean, the Russian plains and the Mediterranean Sea. In addition, the above influences are modified by the Alps, and to a lesser degree, by the Jura. The winds which result from combinations of this situation must be considered as important agents of the circulation

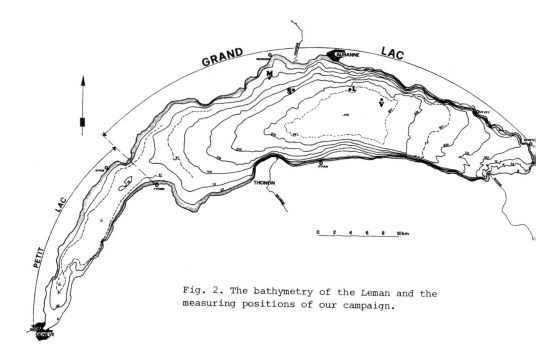

Fig. 2. The bathymetry of the Leman and the measuring positions of our campaign.

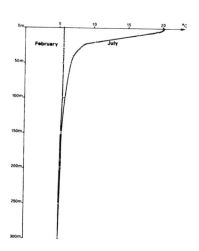

Fig. 3. Stratifications of the Leman for 1974 (Monod et al., 1974).

TABLE I

General information on the Leman

Geographic position (mean)	$46^{\circ}27'$ lat. N $6^{\circ}32'$ long. E. of Greenwich
Waterlevel (mean) of lake	372 m
Max. depth	309,7 m
Mean depth	152,7 m
Area	582 km^2
Great Lake (86 %)	503 km^2
Small Lake (14 %)	79 km^2
Length along its axis	72,3 km
Length of coastline	167 km
Max. width (Morges-Amphion)	13,8 km
Volume	$\sim$ 89 milliards of m^3 = 89 km^3
Great Lake	85,7 " " "
Small Lake (1/28 of lake)	3,2 " " "
Drainage basin (without the Leman itself)	6380 km^2
Inflow all tributaries	8 milliards of m^3 per year
Rhône: Q_{mean}	181 m^3/s
Q_{max}	500 m^3/s
Dranse: Q_{mean}	19 m^3/s
Venoge: Q_{mean}	3 m^3/s
Outflow (the only one is the Rhône at Geneva; it is regulated)	240 m^3/s

in the Leman. There are various winds known in the Leman basin (Primault, 1972). However, if one considers a typical wind-rose - see Fig. 4 - one is immediately persuaded that only two (2) winds should be of major importance. From the NE comes a wind known as "Bise"; it is dry, cold and at times violent and can last for days. From the SW comes a wind known as "Vent"; it is humid, warm and sometimes violent. Other meteorological generalities are given in Table 2.

Measuring positions

The measuring positions of our campaign are indicated in Table 3. Given are the coordinates X and Y as utilized in the "cartes nationales" of the Swiss Topographic Service. (It should be noted that the origin of the system is the old observatory of Bern (X = 200 km, Y = 600 km) given at $46^{\circ}57'07''$ N and $7^{\circ}26'22''$ E).

TABLE 2

Meteorological information of the basin

	Genève	Lausanne	Montreux
Air temperature (mean)	10,6°	9,6° [1]	10,3°
Number of frosty days per year (temperature below 0°C)	63	66	68
Number of rainy days per year (light showers included)	128	146	143
Precipitations (mm of water per year)	889 mm	1064 mm	1151 mm
Numbers of sunshine hours per year	2036	1971	1673 [2]

[1] The observatory of Lausanne is at a higher altitude than the other two.
[2] The observatory of Montreux is not well situated for insolation.

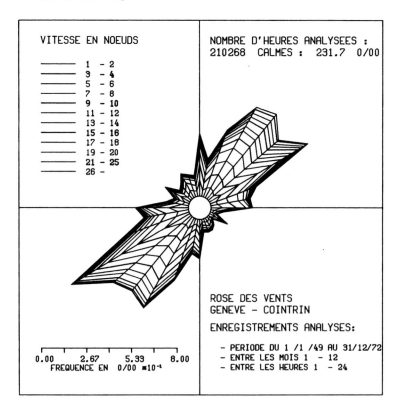

Fig. 4. A typical wind rose (1949-1972).

TABLE 3

Measuring positions

Site	Position	Duration
Morges **m**	X = 149,18 km Y = 528,28 km Z = 75 m (depth)	February 2, 1977 - March 1, 1977
St Sulpice **s**	X = 148,07 km Y = 531,24 km Z = 199 m	March 2, 1977 - April 25, 1977
Lausanne **l**	X = 148,68 km Y = 538,39 km Z = 293 m	June 17, 1977 - August 24, 1977
Villette **v**	X = 147,48 km Y = 542,02 km Z = 299 m	September 1, 1977 - April 22, 1978

The geographic locations of our 4 positions - indicated with M, S, L and V -
are found in Fig. 1. The time of exploration is indicated in the table.

TECHNICAL DATA

The measuring installation

   As shown in Fig. 5, our present measuring installation is made up of the following 3 units: a chain of current meters, an anemometric station and a signal
buoy.

(a) The chain of current meters consists of up to 6 current meters (1)* which
    can be installed at different levels with a variable length steel cable (2)
    of 5 mm diameter. This measuring chain is dynamically independent of the
    other units. Tension of the cable is assured by means of floats (3).

(b) The anemometric station (two variants built at LHYDREP), is shown in Fig. 6.
    The first variant was made of a helicoidal cylinder of PVC (4), having a
    length of 2,50 m and a diameter of 0,75 m; the interior was filled with plastic
    foam. A 50 mm aluminum "pipe" of 5 m length transversed the cylinder, serving
    simultaneously as support for a dead-weight of lead. An identical "pipe" was
    rigidly fixed on the upper part of the cylinder; this pipe served as a mast
    (5), where the anemometers (6), the wind direction sensor (8), a magnetic
    compass (7) and a large wind vane (9) were attached. On top of the mast was

*The numbers in parentheses are indicated in Fig. 2

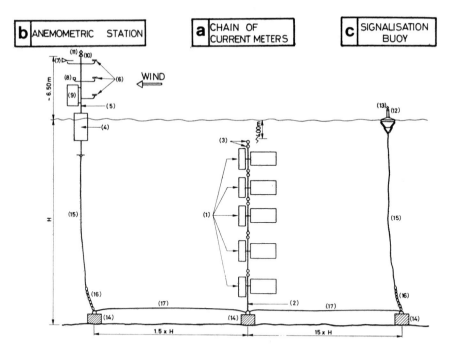

Fig. 5. Scheme of the measuring installation

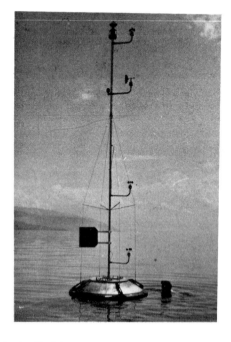

Fig. 6. Anemometric stations: first variant (left); second variant (right)

mounted a signal light (10) and a radar reflector (11). Measured from the water surface the height of the anemometric station was about 6,50 m and its total weight was approximately 600 kg.

The <u>second</u> variant had the form of a double cone with a diameter of 1,75 m and a height of 0,8 m; it was fabricated of aluminum and filled with plastic foam. As counterweight served a 1 m long and 0,2 m wide cylinder containing lead. The mast was made of stainless steel tubing with dimensions identical to those of the first variant; however, it was not rigidly fixed and 4 steel cables kept it in place.

(c) <u>The signal buoy</u> fabricated of aluminum, was constructed as a double cone, 0,70 m high and 1,15 m in diameter. On top was installed a cylinder. At an elevation of 1 m from the water-surface the signal light (12) and the radar reflector (13) were fixed. The only use of this buoy was to help locating our installation and to serve as a warning buoy to lake traffic. At times it also facilitated emergency recovering of our chain of current meters.

Concrete blocks and/or chains of lead were used as dead weight (14); and were linked with our units by steel cables of 9 mm (15) and "large" chains of 12 mm (16). For reasons of security a link between the dead-weights and the measuring chain was provided by a cable of 9 mm (17).

The measuring instruments

After a careful investigation LHYDREP decided to purchase all electronic measuring instruments from AANDERAA Instruments, Bergen, Norway. The principal instruments were the current meters and the anemometric instruments.

(a) The current meters - see Fig. 7 - are commercially known as "Recording Current Meters (RCM), Model 4" and are extensively described in AANDERAA's (1978) operating manual. Measured are the following quantities: (i) the current speed is "sensed by a rotor located at the top of the recording unit. The revolutions of this rotor are transferred magnetically to the inside of the unit, where an electronic counter counts the number of revolutions. This gives the current speed as an average speed over the sampling interval"; (ii) the current direction is "measured by the orientation of the instrument. The direction sensor consists of a magnetic compass located at the bottom of the recording unit. The direction measurement is a momentary measurement taken at the moment the instrument is switched on"; (iii) the pressure is measured "by a pressure sensor consisting of a potentiometer driven by a bourdon tube" and (iv) "the temperature is measured by a thermistor fitted into a stud extending into the water". The instrument records the data on 1/4" magnetic tape, while a quartz clock triggers the measuring cycle at regular and preset

132

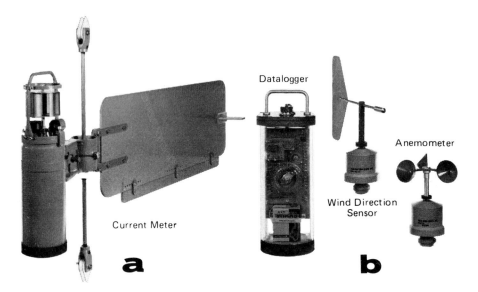

Datalogger

Anemometer

Wind Direction
Sensor

Current Meter

a

b

Fig. 7. Measuring instruments   a) for current
b) for wind

intervals; a battery powers the complete unit. An assembled current meter consists of 3 parts, namely the recording unit, the vane assembly and the spindle
rod (to be shackled into the mooring line). Aanderaa (1978) gives the following range specification: (i) for the current speed a range of 2,5 to 250 cm/s,
(ii) for the current direction a precision of about $\pm 5^{\circ}$, (iii) for the pressure
from 0 to 500 PSI and for (iv) the temperature from $-2,46^{\circ}$ to 21,48 $^{\circ}$C.

(b) The following anemometric instruments are deployed: (i) An <u>anemometer</u> or wind
speed sensor (Aanderaa WSS 2219) - see Fig. 7 - consisting of a 3-cup rotor
on top of a plastic housing. The speed is measured in integrated form; an
electronic counter records the number of rotor revolutions. A more recent
version of anemometer (used since December 1977) gives both the average and
the maximum speed. According to the manufacturer the instrument has a threshold
speed of 25 to 30 cm/s with an accuracy of ± 2 %. (ii) A <u>wind direction sensor</u>
(WDS 2053) consisting of a light wind vane fixed to a vertical pivot and
mounted on top of a plastic housing. A built-in compass, magnetically coupled
to this vane, is clamped by applying current to a clamping coil inside the
compass; the wind direction is given as a potentiometer rading. Quick vane movements are damped with a silicone fluid, which will permit also to line up the
wind vane even at very light winds. Indicated are threshold speeds of less
than 30 cm/s and an accuracy of $\pm 5^{\circ}$. This system of the wind direction sensor
is in our case coupled with an (iii) independent <u>magnetic compass.</u> In this way

TABLE 4.1

Data for Site **m**

Measured parameter	Position of instrument	Duration	Commentaries
Water velocity, direction and temperature	55.0 m 35.0 m 20.0 m 10.0 m 5.6 m	Feb. 2, 1977 to March 1, 1977	no data: for velocities at 35 m for entire period
Air velocity direction	1.8 m 4.1 m 6.5 m ∿ 5.0 m		no data: for velocities and direction for Feb. 12 to March 1. (The lashing chain broke and put the anemometric station our of order.)

TABLE 4.2

Data for Site **s**

Measured parameter	Position of instrument	Duration	Commentaries
Water velocity, direction and temperature	148.9 m 84.4 m 20.2 m 10.2 m 5.8 m	March 2, 1977 to April 25, 1977	no data: for velocities at 84.4 m for entire period
Air velocity direction	1.8 m 4.1 m 6.5 m ∿ 5.0 m		no data: for velocities and direction for March 9 to April 25 (The base-plate of the anemometric station broke and put it out of order.)

the real wind direction with respect to magnetic north is obtained. (iv) A temperature sensor (Aanderaa TS 1289) consists of a 500 Ω platinum resistance, and it is equipped with a radiation screen. The last instrument was only used since December 1977.

The electronic signals (i.e. measurements) produced by above described instruments are transmitted to the datalogger (Aanderaa DL-1); see Fig. 7. Being compact and watertight and powered by a battery, the datalogger allows for measurements in situ. Both battery and datalogger are housed in the main body of the anemometric

TABLE 4.3

Data for Site ▌

Measured parameter	Position of instrument	Duration	Commentaries
Water velocity, direction and temperature	255.5 m 132.4 m 19.1 m 9.8 m 4.9 m	June 17, 1977 to August 24, 1977	no data: for velocities at 132.4 m for entire period
Air velocity	1.1 m 1.7 m 6.6 m		Installation of second variant of anemometric station. incomplete data: for certain time periods and at various elevations the velocities are not recorded. (It seems (?) that temporarily an electric-static field destroys the recording circuit.)
direction	5.0 m		no data: for direction for entire period. (The magnetic compass does not function.)

station. Similar to the recording current meters, the datalogger records the data
on 1/4" magnetic tape and a quartz clock triggers a preset measuring cycle. Depending on the model, the measuring interval may be selected between 30 seconds
and 4 hours.

Launching of the installation

Due to the complexity of the installation (number of delicate instruments, dimensions and weight of the anemometric station, cables and chains and the deadweights, etc.). a launching of the entire installation is a relatively involved
procedure, especially if it is to be performed during a single day and within the
daylight period. For this operation a pusher-pontoon assembly is hired. The pusher
has a motor of 340 HP and is equipped with radar. The pontoon has a size of
18 m x 9 m and is fitted with a crane whose maximum height is 14 m, as well as
with various winches. The crew of the pusher-pontoon assembly consists of 3 marine technicians; the LHYDREP staff working on bord included 2 researchers and
3 technicians. Furthermore, this operation necessitates that, on the day before
launching, all mechanical and electronic equipment be carefully checked and pos-

TABLE 4.4

Data for Site

Measured parameter	Position of instrument	Duration	Commentaries
Water Velocity, direction and temperature	196.7 m 73.9 m 20.6 m 3.3 m	September 1, 1977 to November 8, 1977	
Air velocity direction	1.1 m 1.7 m 6.6 m ∿ 5.0 m		incomplete data: see remark in Table 4.3
Water velocity, direction and temperature temperature	195.6 m 92.7 m 18.5 m 8.6 m 3.9 m 1.0 m	December 9, 1977 to February 15, 1978	
Air velocity (mean and maximum) direction temperature	0.8 m 2.2 m 6.1 m ∿ 5.0 m 5.0 m		no data: for velocities, direction and temperature for January 4 to January 23. (The entire mast is broken.)
Water velocity, direction and temperature temperature	283.3 m 191.8 m 92.3 m 20.3 m 4.3 m 1.0 m	February 16, 1978 to April 22, 1978	no data: for velocity, di- rection and temperature at 4.3 m, 10.3 m, 92.3 m and 191.8 m for entire period. (False montage of the magnetic tape.)
Air velocity direction temperature	0.8 m 2.2 m 6.1 m ∿ 5.0 m 5.0 m		no data: for velocity, di- rection and temperature, for February 16 to March 7 and March 15 to April 22. (For this period either the datalogger did not work, or/and the magnetic tape was of bad quality or/and the mast was in the water.)

sibly even loaded onto the pontoon. A detailed description of the launching was
given by Prost et al. (1977); here it should suffice to mention that 3 consecutive
stages were adopted for the launch, namely (i) the installation of the anemometric

station, then (ii) the launch of the chain of current meters and finally (iii) the installation of the signal buoy.

Important information on our campaign

In form of tables - Table 4.1 to 4.4 - we give here the important information on the campaign. The measuring positions are indicated on Fig. 1 and their geographic locations given in Table 3. Information found in the subsequent tables will be helpful when regarding the graphical display of the data in Figs. 10-15.

THE RESULTS

Data acquisition system

As has been previously mentioned, each Aanderaa instrument stores the recorded data on 1/4" magnetic tapes, and each instrument produces one such tape. However, the code for storing the data is not standard and the 1/4" tapes are not compatible with standard computational installations. Keeping in mind these problems and the fact that the data should be stored in an easily and safely accessible form, a suite of procedures and programs was established at LHYDREP.

In Fig. 8, the principal operations which are performed at LHYDREP are schematized. Since, as shown in Fig. 8, the 1/4" magnetic tapes on which the measuring instruments record their data are nonstandard, the contents of these tapes has to be transferred onto standard tapes. Therefore, each 1/4" magnetic tape is first read by an Aanderaa tape reader (type 2103) and punched onto standard paper tapes by means of a Facit punch. This results in the same number of paper tapes as 1/4" magnetic tapes. Now, these standard paper tapes can be read by an Eclipse computer (Data-General). At this stage, each paper tape still contains the non-standard code, which, with the aid of the Eclipse, can be translated into decimal code and stored in the form of individual sequential files which in term are stored on one standard 1/2" magnetic tape. This standard magnetic tape now contains the same number of files, in decimal form, as the number of the original nonstandard 1/4" tapes. Each file also contains all information in chronological order and furthermore, each file may have a different starting and ending date. Since generally it is required to retrieve data that have been recorded at the same time simultaneously, the contents of the above mentioned files has to be further manipulated in order to create a data bank which is easily accessible. For that purpose, the above files are read sequentially by the CDC computer of the EPF-L, stored, and then rewritten simultaneously onto still another file containing all

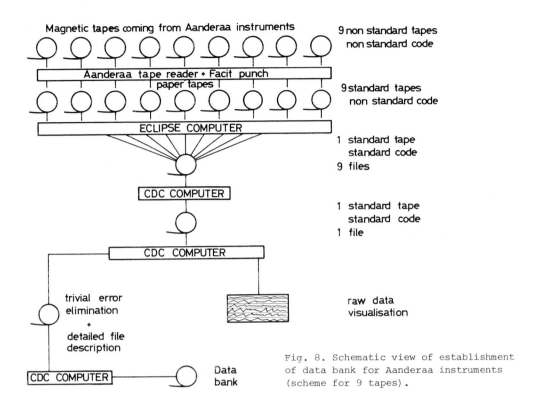

Magnetic tapes coming from Aanderaa instruments — 9 non standard tapes non standard code

Aanderaa tape reader + Facit punch
paper tapes — 9 standard tapes non standard code

ECLIPSE COMPUTER — 1 standard tape standard code 9 files

CDC COMPUTER — 1 standard tape standard code 1 file

CDC COMPUTER

trivial error elimination
+
detailed file description — raw data visualisation

CDC COMPUTER — Data bank

Fig. 8. Schematic view of establishment of data bank for Aanderaa instruments (scheme for 9 tapes).

information recorded in one measuring period. At this stage all data recorded at one point in time are already stored in one line each. With the aid of graphical displays, this file is now checked for trivial errors, and if errors are found, they are manually corrected. To assure absolutely unique identification of this file, a file description containing all necessary information to allow proper interpretation of the file content is added at its beginning. Fig. 9 shows the file description and the beginning of the recorded measurements of the measuring period February 1977. In the established data bank each data period is, for safety reasons, stored 3 times on 3 separate tapes respectively. A more detailed description of the procedures employed is given by Bauer and Perrinjaquet (1979).

Data visualization

As can be seen from Fig. 9, the data bank consists of an enourmous amount of digital information which is practically useless, if not interpreted in some way. Thus, at the very outset of the establishment of the data bank, programs were developed which allow visualization of the recorded data. Also the programs were de-

LEMAN . POSITION Y= 528,28 KM X=149,18 KM MORGES . DU 1 FEV 77 AU 1 MARS 77 .

CONTENU DU FICHIER :   1ER ENREGISTREMENT COMMENTAIRES
                         2ME ENREGISTREMENT DONNEES

        CONTENU DU 2ME ENREGISTREMENT

PERIODE DE MESURES : 1 FEVRIER 77 A 16HEURES 0 MINUTE
                     1 MARS 77 A 9H00 MINUTES

POSITION GEOGRAPHIQUE DE LA STATION DE MESURE :
        Y= 528,28 KM   X= 149,18 KM   AU LARGE DE MORGES

IL Y A UN DATALOGER(VENT) ET 5 COURANTOMETRES
LE FORMAT EST LE SUIVANT :(5I2,24I5)
5I2 : ANNEE,MOIS,JOUR,HEURE,MINUTE. 2 CHIFFRES POUR CHACUN
24I5 : (3VITESSES,1 DIRECTION) VENT
      5 X (TEMPERATURE,PROFONDEUR,DIRECTION,VITESSE) EAU
POUR LA SUITE DES COMMENTAIRES ON SE REFERERA A 24 COLONNES
NUMEROTEES DE GAUCHE A DROITE:SANS TENIR COMPTE DE LA DATE(5I2)

VENT :   VITESSES EN DM/S
         DIRECTION EN DEGRE PAR RAPPORT AU NORD (CLOCKWISE)
EAU :   TEMPERATURE EN 1/100 DEGRE CELSIUS
         PROFONDEUR EN DM
         DIRECTION EN DEGRE PAR RAPPORT AU NORD (CLOCKWISE)
         VITESSE EN MM/S

CONTENU DES COLONNES
COL.1 ANEMOMETRE 1 HAUTEUR PAR RAPPORT A L'EAU :   6,47M
COL.2   "   2   "   "   : 4,12M
COL.3   "   3   "   "   : 1,77M
COL.4 DIRECTION DU VENT
COL.5-8 COURANTOMETRE(RCM2300),TEMPERATURE,PROFONDEUR,DIRECTION,VITESSE
COL.9-12 COURANTOMETRE(RCM2301)
COL.13-16 COURANTOMETRE(RCM2302)
COL.17-20 COURANTOMETRE(RCM2303)
COL.21-24 COURANTOMETRE(RCM2304)

REMARQUES :

- UNE VALEUR DE (-999) INDIQUE QUE LA MESURE EN QUESTION N'EST
  PAS VALABLE.

- IL SEMBLE QUE LES PROFONDEURS INDIQUEES PAR LES APPAREILS NE
  SOIENT PAS JUSTES: CES PROFONDEURS SERAIENT :
                 RCM2300 : 5,6M
                 RCM2301 : 10 M
                 RCM2302 : 20 M
                 RCM2303 : 35 M
                 RCM2304 : 55 M

- LES MESURES CONCERNANT LE VENT NE SONT VALABLES QUE JUSQU'AU
  11 FEVRIER A 13 HEURES 20 MINUTES

- LES MESURES DE VITESSE DU COURANTOMETRES RCM 2303(COL.20) SONT FAUSSES

-LE NOMBRE DE LIGNES DE L'ENREGITREMENT SUIVANT EST DE 3991

DATE	VV	VV	VV	DV	T	P	DE	VE	T	P	DE	VE	T	P	DE	VE	T	P	DE	VE	T	P	DE	VE
77 2 116 0	17	17	16	131	576	74	46	71	576	112	44	58	580	218	46	68	580	358	54	-999	571	557	47	34
77 2 11610	17	17	17	150	578	74	50	68	578	112	49	68	580	218	46	65	580	358	53	-999	571	557	47	37
77 2 11620	19	19	18	146	583	74	43	71	578	112	49	68	580	218	47	68	580	358	54	-999	571	557	45	34
77 2 11630	21	21	21	129	576	74	47	68	576	112	47	68	580	218	45	65	580	358	50	-999	574	557	43	37
77 2 11640	21	21	21	135	576	74	46	68	576	112	46	68	580	218	46	65	580	358	54	-999	571	557	44	37
77 2 11650	22	22	21	134	576	74	47	68	578	112	45	68	580	218	42	65	580	358	52	-999	571	557	43	37
77 2 117 0	17	17	17	141	576	74	48	68	576	112	48	68	580	218	46	68	580	358	55	-999	571	557	38	37
77 2 11710	14	14	14	126	576	74	48	68	576	112	49	68	580	218	46	68	580	358	50	-999	571	557	28	40
77 2 11720	15	15	14	128	576	74	50	68	576	112	47	68	580	218	48	65	578	358	55	-999	571	557	36	37
77 2 11730	11	10	10	140	576	74	51	68	576	112	47	68	580	218	48	68	578	358	58	-999	571	557	36	37
77 2 11740	10	9	9	155	576	74	49	68	576	112	49	68	580	218	49	65	578	358	53	-999	571	557	33	37
77 2 11750	7	6	5	193	576	74	52	68	576	112	47	68	580	218	48	65	580	358	53	-999	571	557	29	40
77 2 118 0	5	5	5	219	576	74	50	68	576	112	49	68	580	218	49	65	580	358	43	-999	574	557	35	40
77 2 11810	5	5	4	162	576	74	49	71	576	112	46	68	580	218	48	65	580	362	54	-999	571	557	39	40
77 2 11820	6	6	5	207	576	74	49	71	576	112	48	68	580	218	44	62	580	362	52	-999	571	557	36	43
77 2 11830	3	3	3	196	576	74	46	71	576	112	47	68	580	218	46	65	580	358	52	-999	571	557	37	43
77 2 11840	5	5	5	183	576	74	51	71	576	112	48	68	580	218	46	65	580	362	54	-999	574	557	39	40
77 2 11850	8	8	7	152	576	74	49	71	576	112	49	68	580	218	46	65	580	358	53	-999	574	557	41	40
77 2 119 0	9	10	9	166	576	74	53	71	576	112	52	68	580	218	49	65	580	358	53	-999	574	557	35	40
77 2 11910	10	10	10	153	576	74	51	68	576	112	49	68	580	218	47	65	580	358	43	-999	571	557	39	40
77 2 11920	11	11	11	152	576	74	53	71	576	112	50	68	580	218	45	62	580	362	50	-999	571	557	29	40
77 2 11930	13	13	12	160	576	74	52	71	576	112	49	68	580	218	46	65	580	362	55	-999	571	557	29	40
77 2 11940	12	12	11	145	576	74	49	68	576	112	48	58	580	218	45	65	580	362	54	-999	571	557	31	40
77 2 11950	14	13	12	168	576	74	49	68	576	112	48	65	580	218	45	65	580	362	51	-999	571	557	28	40
77 2 120 0	13	13	12	170	576	74	55	71	576	112	52	68	580	218	48	62	580	362	53	-999	571	557	28	40
77 2 12010	10	10	10	314	576	74	51	71	576	112	52	68	580	218	46	62	580	362	51	-999	574	557	32	40
77 2 12020	15	15	16	306	576	74	53	71	576	112	51	68	580	218	49	62	580	362	51	-999	574	557	22	40
77 2 12030	16	17	17	293	576	74	53	68	576	112	52	68	580	218	49	62	580	362	51	-999	574	557	33	43
77 2 12040	18	18	17	280	574	74	53	68	576	112	52	68	580	218	50	65	580	362	53	-999	574	557	25	43
77 2 12050	14	14	14	289	574	74	52	71	576	112	51	68	580	218	48	65	580	362	54	-999	574	560	27	43
77 2 121 0	15	15	15	289	574	74	50	68	576	112	50	68	580	218	49	65	580	362	52	-999	574	560	29	45
77 2 12110	12	12	12	283	574	74	52	71	576	112	51	71	580	218	47	65	580	362	54	-999	574	560	32	45
77 2 12120	11	11	11	287	576	74	51	71	576	112	49	68	580	218	47	65	580	362	54	-999	571	560	31	43
77 2 12130	12	12	12	303	574	74	52	73	576	112	50	71	580	218	46	65	580	362	54	-999	571	560	31	47
77 2 12140	14	14	14	328	574	74	53	79	576	112	48	71	580	218	46	65	580	362	54	-999	574	560	29	45
77 2 12150	12	12	12	7	574	74	53	76	576	112	51	68	580	218	46	65	580	362	53	-999	574	560	32	45
77 2 122 0	10	10	9	303	574	74	63	82	576	112	54	73	580	218	46	65	580	362	52	-999	571	560	28	45
77 2 12210	12	12	12	228	571	74	58	76	574	112	54	71	580	218	47	65	580	362	51	-999	574	560	20	43
77 2 12220	54	54	50	242	576	74	56	76	576	112	47	73	580	218	49	65	580	362	51	-999	574	560	24	48
77 2 12230	43	42	41	252	574	74	55	79	574	112	55	73	578	218	49	65	580	362	51	-999	574	560	25	48
77 2 12240	27	26	26	282	571	74	54	79	574	112	52	79	578	218	47	65	580	362	51	-999	574	560	28	48

Fig. 9. Example of datafile description and beginning of datafile (February 1977).

signed to be completely general; i.e., any data file with the same principal
structure as the one shown in Fig. 9, but having for example a different number
of columns should be treatable. Furthermore, the order of horizontal traces
should be independent of the sequence existing in the data file. Finally, the
program should be written for standard computer tracing equipment (e.g. Calcomp
plotter), which allows tracing of only one line at a time. Also, because of the
large amount of data to be handled, the program should be efficient. Keeping in
mind the above requirements, a principal program TRACE has been written, the
output of which will be presented below. A more detailed description of program
TRACE and of some variants of TRACE allowing drawing of vector stick diagrams and
of hodographs is given by Bauer and Perrinjaquet (1979).

Data display

In this paragraph, an analog representation of all data collected thus far
by LHYDREP in the campaigns summarized in Tables 3 and 4 is given in Figs. 10-15.
The same basic principles were employed throughout: The time axis is horizontal,
whereby every 24 hours a vertical line, showing the date in years, months, days,
hours and minutes indicates the start of a new day. The time base used is always
"astronomical" central European time, i.e. without any modifications such as
daylight saving time. The data represented in the topmost band are temperatures.
Proceeding downwards the next band shows the wind velocities followed by the
velocity observations* of the current meters in the order of their positions in
the lake. The subsequent bands show directions, the first being the direction
of the wind* followed by the directions of the current meters, again in the same
order as for the velocity bands. With the exception of the temperature bands, the
vertical scales of all bands in Figs. 10-15 and the horizontal scales in Figs.
10-15 are all the same. The vertical scales - shown every five days - have been
selected such that the wind speed bands extend over a range of 0-10 m/s, the
water velocity bands over 0-10 cm/s and the wind and water direction bands over
$0-360^{\circ}$. The wind direction is given as the direction from which the wind comes
and the current direction is given as the direction in which the current flows.
The temperature bands extend over a range of $5-10^{\circ}$C in Figs. 10, 11, 14 and 15.
In Figs. 12 and 13 the temperature band has a range of $5-21^{\circ}$C. In case these ranges
are exceeded by the data to be plotted, the trace of one band continues over
neighbouring bands but keeps its original scale. As can be seen in Figs. 10-15,
the records are by no means complete, since numerous problems occurred. A rough

---

* In Fig. 12, the wind direction band and the water velocity band at 132,4 m have
  been suppressed in order to gain space, since no records were available.

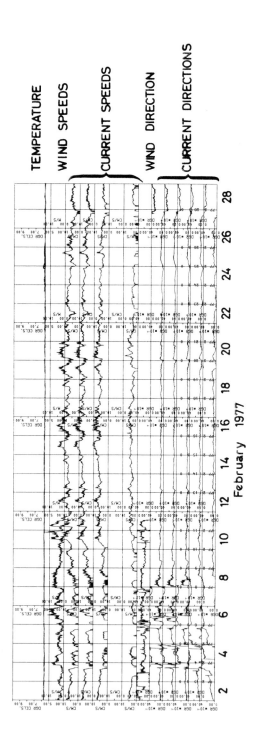

Fig. 10. Morges.

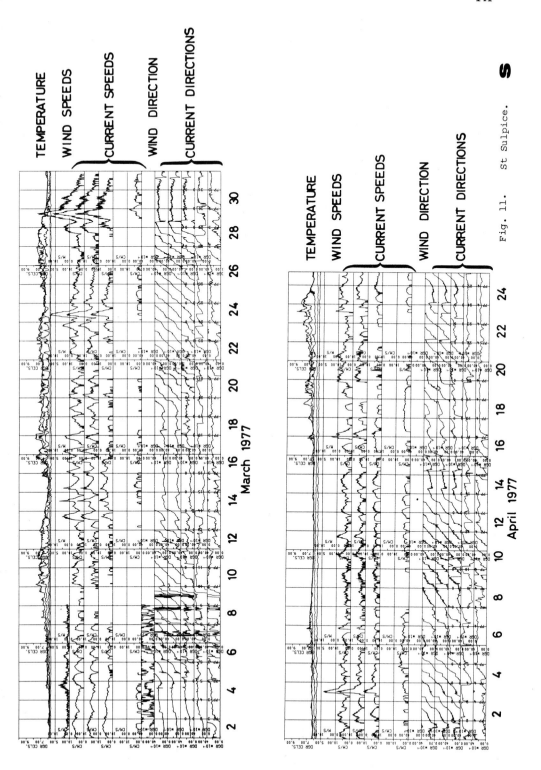

Fig. 11. St Sulpice.

142

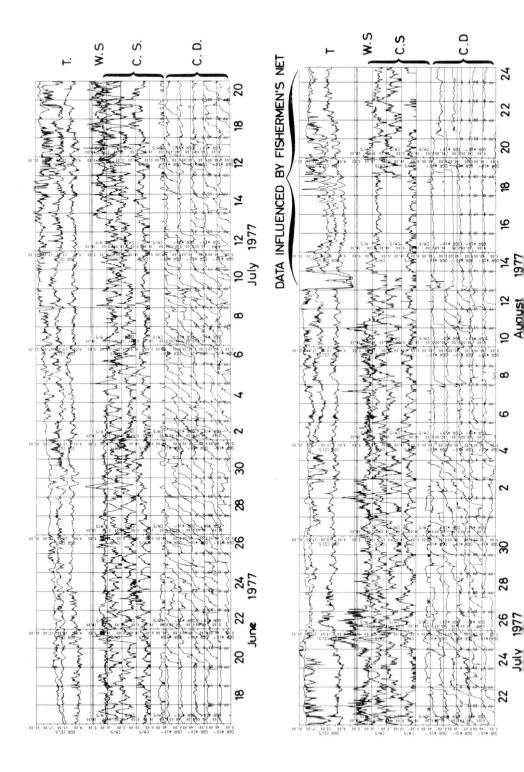

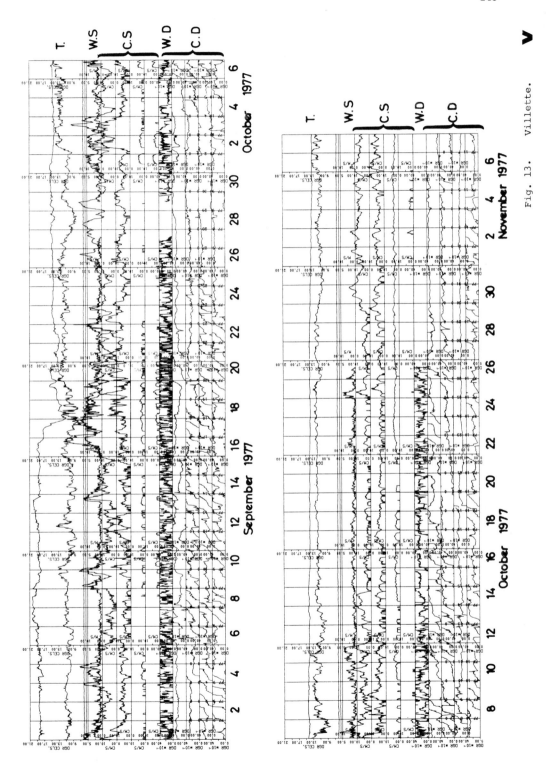

Fig. 13. Villette.

144

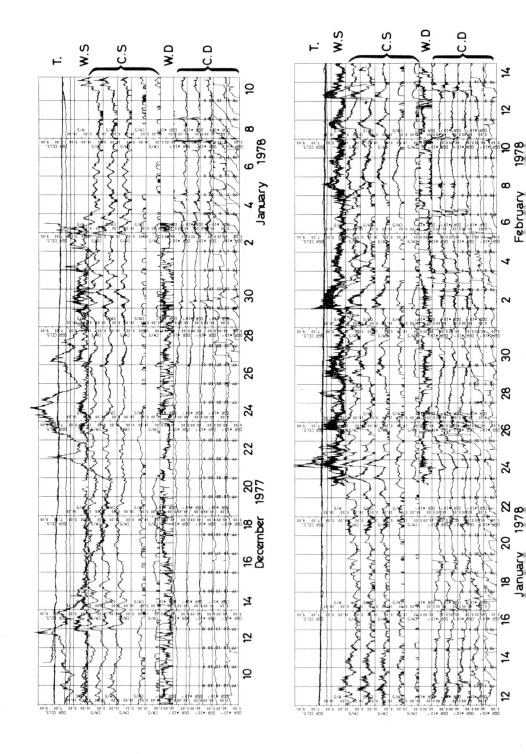

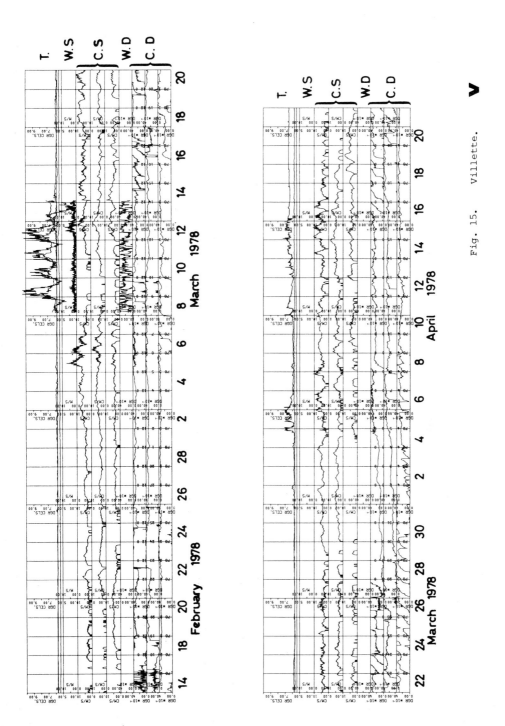

Fig. 15. Villette.

summary of the problems encountered is given in Tables 4.1-4.4. In the followin

some additional observations are given.

Comparing the wind direction bands of Figs. 10 and 11 with those of Figs. 13-15, one notes that the directions of Figs. 10 and 11 appear to be less varying than those of Figs. 13-15. This is most likely a reflection of the change to the second variant of our buoy which took place on June 17, 1977. Apparently, the first variant of the buoy was more stable than the second variant. On January 23, 1978, the standard anemometers were replaced by anemometers recording not only mean velocity but also the maximum velocity observed within one measuring interval. This can be seen in Fig. 14. Also, starting with Fig. 14, air temperature can be readily distinguished from water temperature. The measuring interval used at all times was 10 minutes.

The effects of the entanglement of the measuring instruments with a fisherman's net on the measurements are evident in Fig. 12, where it can be seen, that on August 13, 1977, the temperature recordings drop suddenly and substantially. Investigating the pressure measurements (not shown), it was found that this drop in temperature coincides with an increase of water pressure at all instruments respectively. From this, it can be concluded that the instruments were caught by a drag net. At the end of that day, the pull of this net appears to have decreased thus allowing the chain of instruments to rise again to its standard position. However, after August 13, 1977, the recordings appear to be influenced by remains of the net that were eventually found in the chain (see in particular all the temperature- and direction recordings and the velocity recordings of the two topmost current meters between 15 and 17 August inclusive, and also the velocity recordings of the third current meter between 21 and 24 August inclusive).

In conclusion, it is interesting to note that, with the measuring interval of 10 minutes used throughout, the total number of recorded data is approximately one million, of which about 800,000 have been traced in Figs. 10-15.

ACKNOWLEDGMENT

This work was partially sponsored by the Swiss National Science Foundation (FNSRS) under its special program "Fundamental problems of the water cycle in Switzerland".

REFERENCES

Aanderaa, 1978. Operating Manual for Recording Current Meter, Model 4. Aanderaa
    Instruments, Bergen, Norway.
Amberger et al., 1976. Le Léman, un lac à découvrir. Office du Livre S.A., Fribourg.

Bauer, S.W. and Perrinjaquet, C., 1979. Data bank and -visualization for sequential
    data with special reference to Lake Geneva. In: Hydrodynamics of Lakes, ed.
    W.H. Graf and C.H. Mortimer, Elsevier Scientific Publishing Company, Amsterdam.
Krumbein, W.D. and Sloss, L.L., 1951. Stratigraphy and Sedimentation. Freeman Co.,
    San Francisco.
Monod, R. et al., 1974. Rapports sur les études et recherches entreprises dans le
    Bassin Lémanique, Campagne 1974. Commission international pour la protection
    des eaux du Lac Léman contre la pollution.
Primault, B., 1972.. Etude meso-climatique du Canton du Vaud. Cahiers de l'aménage-
    ment régional 14, Office cantonal vaudois de l'urbanisme, Lausanne 1972.
Prost, J.-P., Bauer, S.W., Graf, W.H. and Girod, H., 1977. Campagne de mesure des
    courants dans le Léman. Bull. Techn. Suisse Romande No 19, septembre 1977.

"LAKE OF ZUERICH 1978" - A PHYSICAL LIMNOLOGICAL EXPERIMENT

WILFRIED HORN

Versuchsanstalt für Wasserbau, Hydrologie und Glaziologie an der Eidgenössischen Technischen Hochschule Zürich

ABSTRACT

Horn, W. 1979. "Lake of Zürich 1978" - a physical-limnological experiment. Proceedings of the Symposium on Hydrodynamics of Lakes, Lausanne.

After a one-month test experiment in March/April the Lake of Zürich was investigated during August and September 1978 to study especially the variations of water circulation and mixing mechanisms in space and time and their relation to the prevailing meteorological conditions. More than 50 current and temperature recorders were moored at 12 positions (Fig. 1); three of these subsurface moorings were completed with meteorological buoys covering the suitable instruments in three levels. The chosen sampling rate for the parameters will permit the spectral analysis of eventual processes within a time scale between 2 minutes and 28 days; the spatial distribution of the sensors yields a length scale between 1 meter and 28 kilometers. The mean stratification of the lake was measured along several sections (Fig. 2, 4, 5, 6). To obtain an insight into the short term variation of the horizontal and vertical distribution of temperature, conductivity, oxygen and pH, two "4-ship" synoptic surveys were carried out for a period of 60 hours each. For this purpose each ship was assigned an area of 1 km^2 in which it manoeuvered in a figure-8 (Fig. 3). In the same area dye diffusion experiments in the thermocline should enable turbulence to be described in terms of Lagrangian variables.
Some results of the spring-time test experiment, which was mainly restricted to the northern part of the Lake of Zürich proved the lake to be a higly fluctuative hydrodynamic system. The lake's response to external forces seems to be demonstrated in segments of time series and some representative spectra (Fig. 7, 8, 9). In spite of the topographic dimensions of the lake the influence of the Coriolis force on the moving water masses is probably not negligible.

INTRODUCTION

The subject of transport and mixing mechanisms in Swiss lakes has received increasing attention in the physical and engineering sciences since 1972, when the Lake Constance was systematically investigated with regard to hydrodynamic processes (Hollan, 1974). In 1978 a joint research programme was started to study especially the response of the physical and chemical system of the Lake of Zürich to atmospheric forces. The participating institutions were the Eidgenössische Anstalt für Wasserversorgung, Abwasserreinigung und Gewässerschutz (EAWAG), the Wasserversorgung Zürich (WVZ), the Geographisches Institut der Universität Bern and the Versuchsanstalt für Wasserbau, Hydrologie und Glaziologie Zürich (VAW). The Lake of Zürich was chosen as a test area for physical-limnological experiments because of the proximity of the neighbouring institutes and also because descriptive knowledge about wind-induced circulation was already available (Nydegger, 1957), as were a systematic analysis on long-term thermal stratification (Kutschke, 1966), qualitative observations of internal wave motions (Thomas, 1949) and modern research work on long term variations of physical, chemical and biological parameters at several fixed positions (Zimmermann and Suter-Weider, 1976). Geologists made the first measurements with moored instruments, recording currents near the bottom for periods up to 6 days. These data contain features (Horn and Lambert, 1979) which gave rise to further detailed investigations. In the following a short report is presented on the activities during the summer experiment, which took place from August 3rd to September 29th, 1978. A selection of results of the test-experiment (March 15th to April 14th) contributes to the knowledge on the hydrodynamics of a small area of the Lake of Zürich.

THE LAKE TOPOGRAPHY

The investigations during 1978 in the Lake of Zürich were restricted to the area of the so-called Untersee which is separated to a great extent from the much smaller Obersee by a moraine. Towards the north this moraine continues below the present mean water level of 406 meters (above sea-level). This rather shallow region and three canals provide for more or less seasonal inflow. The river Limmat beginning at the northernmost region of the lake is fed by the outflow, which is controlled in such a way as to avoid water level changes. The Untersee has a length of 28 km, a mean width of 2.4 km and a mean depth of 54 m. By bottom topography (northwest – southeast direction) the lake is divided into a basin (maximum depth 136 m), a transient zone with a mean slope of about 3% and a shallow region with a mean depth of 22 meters (comp. Fig. 1, 3 and 4). The surface area amounts to 67 km^2, the volume to 3.32 km^3.

THE OBSERVATIONS

In the beginning of the summer-experiment an array of twelve moorings of the

"classical" U-type was set (see Fig. 1) with a total of 42 instruments recording
current, temperature and pressure data. The water depths at the 12 locations varied
from 18 meters (position 12) to 136 meters (pos. 6); the instruments-depths ranged
from 3 meters below the surface to the bottom. The marker-buoys of moorings 4, 6
and 11 were replaced by meteorological buoys measuring wind speed and direction,
air temperature and pressure as well as radiation in three levels up to 5.8 meters
above the lake surface. For a period of 8 weeks four different types of instruments
sampled data as follows:

1.   3 Aanderaa (Bergen) data loggers for the meteorological data
     (sampling rate: 10 minutes);

2.   11 Aanderaa current meters with temperature sensors, two of them with
     pressure sensors, (10 minutes);

3.   10 Aanderaa thermistor cables of lengths between 10 and 20 meters,
     (20 minutes);

4.   1 Aanderaa water level recorder, (60 minutes);

5.   21 Current meters constructed at the VAW, (20 minutes).

After having recovered most of the instruments about the end of the experiment, at
position 9 an additional mooring was launched with 9 current meters and 2 thermistor
cables, completed as usual with a meteorological buoy. All the recorded parameters
were sampled with a time interval of one minute for a period of 3 days. During the
test-experiment in March/April only 3 moorings were set at positions 2, 3 and 4,
yielding 34 temperature records and only one current record worth processing. Repeated cross-sections and sections along the lake axis (Fig. 2) show the hydrographic situations during the test- and summer-experiment. The measuring devices
were a temperature-conductivity-depth recorder (accuracy of temperature approx.
$\pm$ 0.05 $^{\circ}$C, of conductivity approx. $\pm$ 1 μmho, of depth $\pm$ 0.2 meters), a temperature-
depth recorder (accuracy of temperature $\pm$ 0.003 $^{\circ}$C) and modern Nansen-bottles with
reversing thermometers. To get further detailed information of the variability of
temperature, conductivity, oxygen and pH of the stratified lake the transient zone
between the southern part of the lake and the deep basin was chosen for two "4-ship"
synoptic surveys (comp. Fig. 3). Each ship was assigned a square of 1 km^2 in which
it manoeuvered in a figure-8. The surveys took 60 hours each and consisted of 5
laps. This caused altogether 520 stations, which were carried out in the course
of considerably altering weather conditions. In the same area dye diffusion experiments took place by means of in situ measurements of the Rhodamine-concentration
within the thermocline to describe turbulence in terms of Lagrangian variables.

152

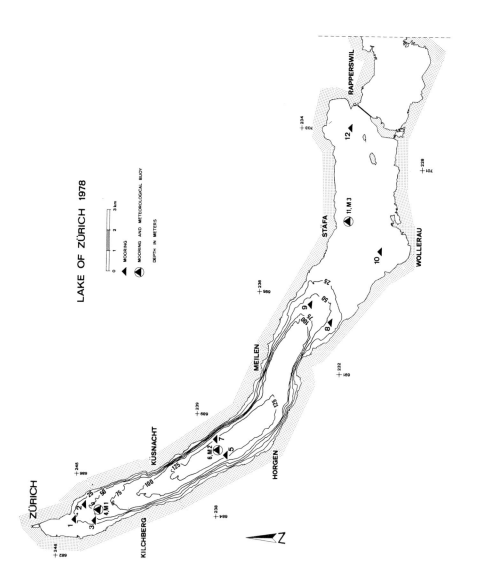

Fig. 1. Station chart (positions of moorings and meteorological buoys)

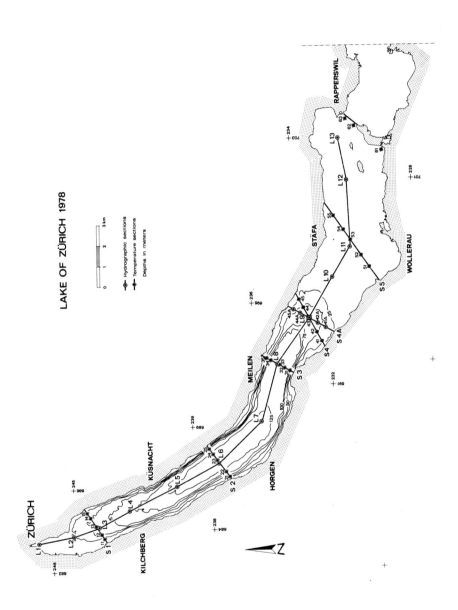

Fig. 2.   Station chart (positions of hydrographic sections)

154

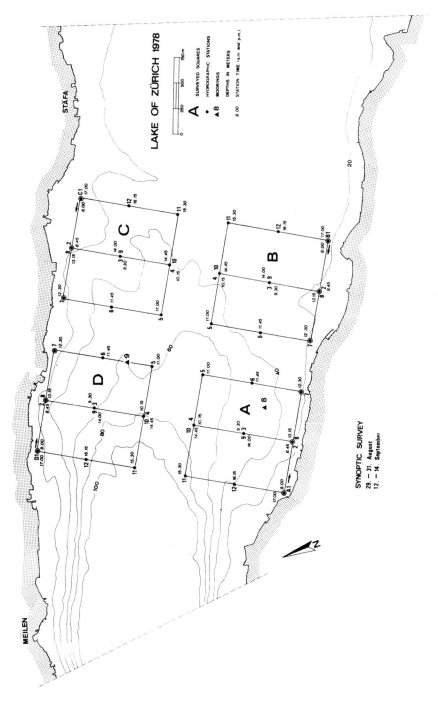

Fig. 3. Area of Synoptic Surveys with track and station chart.

THE HYDROGRAPHIC CONDITIONS DURING THE TEST - EXPERIMENT

According to the character of a test-experiment only a small amount of data is available, which only permit a description of some phenomena occuring during the survey. As an example the temperature section along the lake axis (Fig. 4; comp. Fig. 2) shows essentially the beginning of a stratification which is typical for the period of observation (compare Kutschke, 1966).

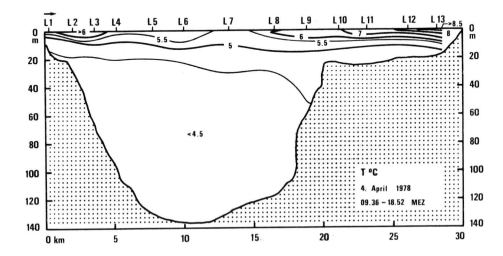

Fig. 4. Temperature section along the lake axis (St. No L1 - L13)

Whereas the temperatures of the upper layer of the basin region range from 4.5 ° to 6.5 °C and show a weak vertical gradient, the southern part of the lake is covered by a large patch of warmer water with temperatures of more than 8.5 °C and stronger vertical gradients. Both the inflow of usually warmer water from the Ober- see and the greater rate of heating in a shallow region as present produce a north- ward spreading water mass. The change of the temperature field within 25 days is shown in the pattern of the repeated cross sections S1 (Fig. 5, 6; compare Fig. 2), which run through the area of the 3 moored systems. The situation of March 16th, represents rather small horizontal and vertical temperature gradients; the measu- rements of April 10th, indicate the beginning of the seasonal heating which has already built up a weak thermocline. Taking into account the shortcomings of de- terminating the density of lake water from temperature and conductivity alone it turns out, that the accuracy of the CTD-instrument used is not sufficient

156

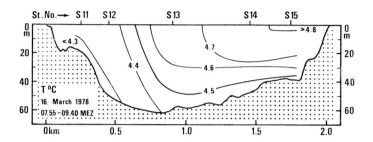

Fig. 5. Temperature section S1 at the beginning of the test-experiment.

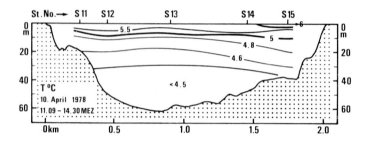

Fig. 6. Temperature section S1 at the end of the test-experiment.

to reproduce a relevant non-uniform density field. Even one month later the vertical density gradients are so small - for the given example $O(10^{-8})$ cgs for the upper 10 meters - that barotropic motions are expected to be predominant.

THE CURRENT AND TEMPERATURE FLUCTUATIONS MEASURED BY THE MOORED INSTRUMENTS

As mentioned above only 1 current record is available, namely from position 3 at 11 meters depth. Due to the threshold of about 2.5 cm sec^{-1} the record contains numerous spikes and gaps, i.e. periods in which the current velocity was less than the value given above. It is obvious that a sensible statistical treatment, e.g. a spectral analysis is impossible. Apart from two events, when the speed increases up to 5 cm sec^{-1} for periods of about 2 days (certainly caused by "föhn"), the variation of current direction alone still enables some qualitative statements about the time scale of the fluctuations to be made. The mean flow is directed to the north, long term deflections of about $\pm$ 40 $^{\circ}$ from the mean over a period of about 3 days seem to be significant. Other periodicities are within the range from 12 to 48 hours; here the changes of direction indicate not only east-west oscilla-tions but also circular motions. Although the test-experiment was carried out

during a phase of a quasi-homogeneous lake all the 34 temperature records show
distinct variations in space and time. Throughout the whole record length (approx.
24 days) longterm oscillations are obvious. These are superposed by motions of
higher frequencies especially at that time when the weak stratification was built
up. A typical example of temperature variations in space and time is presented in
Figure 7, namely in segments of the temperature series (hourly means) in 15 meters
depth at positions 2, 3 and 4 (the corresponding record numbers are 780221, 780321,
780421).

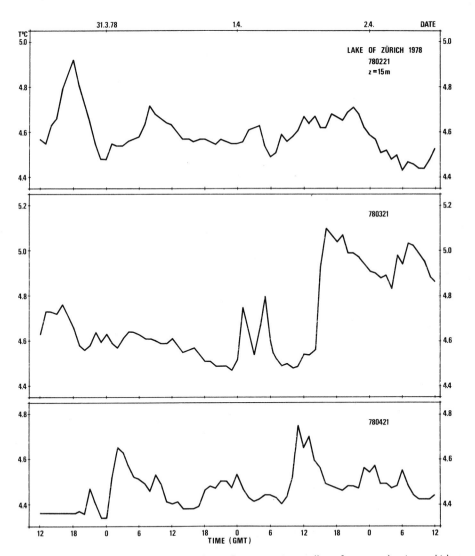

Fig. 7. Segments of the time series of temperature (hourly means) at position
2, 3 and 4 (780221, 780321, 780421).

158

This period of observation was characterised by rapid changes of meteorological conditions in the southern region of the lake, just as 10 days later, when temperature oscillations with increasing amplitudes are somehow generated (Fig. 8).

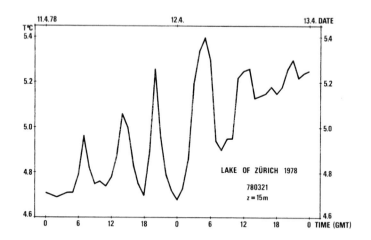

Fig. 8. Segment of the time serie of temperature (hourly means) at position 3 during a föhn-period.

From spectral analysis of the time series the following results are apparent (compare Fig. 9, where a selection of 5 spectra is plotted - all the other spectra look quite similar): The low frequency part of the amplitude spectrum, i.e. where the frequencies are smaller than the local inertial frequency f (for the Lake of Zürich f = 6.13 · 10^{-2} cph, which corresponds to a period of 16.3 hours), is characterised by a peak at 9 · 10^{-3} cph, which also occurs when analysing the meteorological data of the weather-station at Zürich. The second significant amplitude maximum is concentrated around the inertial frequency and the previously described circular motion of the current at position 3 has the same frequency range. The time lag between the temperature maxima appearing with this same frequency at positions 2, 3 and 4 (comp. Fig. 7) give rise to the assumption that either inertial or Kelvin- or Poincaré-type waves (clockwise rotation) occur in a relatively small and narrow lake like the Lake of Zürich. The third significant peak at 0.12 cph should possibly be assigned to a higher mode of the above mentioned wave-types, towards the higher frequencies the spectral amplitudes decrease following the ω^{-1} law.

These interesting problems will have to be further investigated with the data of the summer-experiment in order to explain properly the phenomena described above.

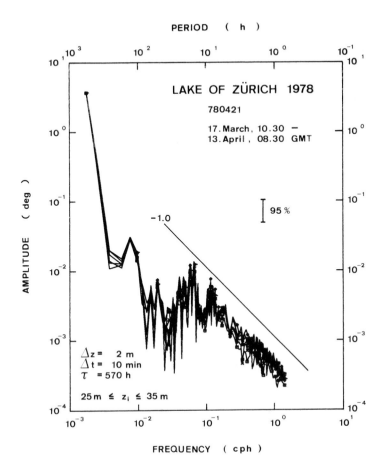

Fig. 9. Amplitude spectra of temperature records at position 4.

ACKNOWLEDGEMENTS

The efforts of all the collegues of the Versuchsanstalt für Wasserbau preparing and carrying out the experiment are gratefully acknowledged. Thanks are due to Prof. D. Vischer for generously supporting the project. Further acknowledgement must go to E. Hollan, Landesamt für Umweltschutz Baden-Württemberg (Germany), D. Imboden, Eidgenössische Anstalt für Wasserversorgung, Abwasserreinigung und Gewässerschutz, K.P. Koltermann, Deutsches Hydrographisches Institut, U. Zimmermann, Wasserversorgung Zürich, P. Hirsig and B. Werthemann, Geographisches Institut der Universität Bern, the lake police authorities and the Eidgenössische Amt für Wasserwirtschaft, Bern for cooperation and finally to the Schweizerische Nationalfonds for financial support.

REFERENCES

Hollan, E., 1974. Strömungsmessungen im Bodensee. Arbeitsgemeinschaft Wasserwerke
    Bodensee-Rhein, 6. Bericht, 111-187
Horn, W. and A. Lambert, 1979. Near bottom current measurements in Swiss lakes (in
    preparation)
Kutschke, I., 1966. Die thermischen Verhältnisse im Zürichsee zwischen 1937 und
    1963 und ihre Beeinflussung durch meteorologische Faktoren. Vierteljahresschrift
    der Naturforschenden Gesellschaft Zürich, 111, Heft 1, 47-124
Nydegger, P., 1957. Vergleichende Untersuchungen an sieben Schweizer Seen. Beiträge
    zur Geologie der Schweiz - Hydrologie, Nr. 9.
Thomas, E.A., 1949. Sprungschichtneigung im Zürichsee durch Sturm. Schweiz. Zeit-
    schrift für Hydrologie, 11, 527-545.
Zimmermann, U. and P. Suter-Weider, 1976. Beiträge zur Limnologie des Walen-, Zürich-
    Ober- und Zürichsees. Schweiz. Zeitschrift für Hydrologie. 38,2, 71-96.

WATER CIRCULATION IN LAKES. RESEARCH IN SITU, USING REVOLVING LAKE-MODELS (AS
SHOWN IN THE FILM) AND COMPARISONS WITH THE LATEST LIMNOSEDIMENTOLOGICAL RESULTS

P. NYDEGGER

University of Bern, Department of Hydrology-Limnology, Bern (Switzerland)

ABSTRACT

Up to now the role of the inflow of tributaries was, in our opinion, underrated
in favour of the importance of the wind. This is particularly true for the lakes of
our alpine regions with their vigorous through currents and is probably due to the
fact that ocean flow research where the wind effects are extremely dominant was
splendidly carried on and because exceptional results from Scottish lakes under
strong wind exposure are available (MORTIMER et al). Therefore, this communication
will deal primarily with the influence of the tributaries and the Coriolis effects
on the flow pattern.

It is shown how the inflow, after stratification at the depth corresponding to
its density, will form a clockwise vortex induced by the Coriolis force, and how
water masses shed from the vortex are pushed on by the following ones. Therewith they
press, owing to the Coriolis effect, to the right and must, by virtue of the "con-
straint force" resulting from the shore boundary, rotate in the lake in a counterclockwise direction. Thereby a counterclockwise rotation takes place at the strati-
fying depth of the inflow (clockwise rotation in the southern hemisphere) which
gradually draws along the entirety of over- and underlying layers.

INTRODUCTION

In the following article, the most important results of observations and measurements carried out on the lakes of Brienz, Murten and Biel as well as on their models are summarized. They were done in close cooperation with my assistant E. Münger.
We selected those lakes because each one represents a different type. On the other
hand, they have in common their intensive through currents. This is very important,
because we concentrate mainly on currents caused by the inflow of rivers. It is our
impression that, until now, these were neglected, whereas many researchers, as for
instance MORTIMER, have presented excellent results related to induced water movements. We are aware of the fact that our results are related to lakes with large
catchment areas, as is true of the piedmont lakes. Whereas in the lakes with weak
through currents and big surfaces, the inflowing streams are more or less "over-
lapped" by wind-caused movements.

THE EXAMINED LAKES (Fig. 1)

Common characteristics

     As already mentioned, the three lakes have strong through currents. The relation
between the lake's surface and the catchment area is, for the lake of Brienz, 1 : 38,
for the lake of Murten 1 : 30, and for the lake of Biel 1 : 143 (without the contributing area of the lake of Neuenburg). Accordingly all three lakes show defined
turbid horizons in the depths of the stratified inflows (Fig. 4).

     The lakes also have comparable climatic conditions because they are located at
almost the same latitude between 46 ° 43 ' (lake of Brienz) and 47 ° 05 ' (lake of
Biel), and between 564 m (lake of Brienz) and 429 m (lakes of Murten and Biel above
the sea level). All three water bodies are oriented from SW to NE.

     The time for water renewal is for the lake of Murten 1,7 years, for the lake of
Brienz 2,7 years, and for the lake of Biel 0,2 years.

Differences

     The important differences are doubtlessly in depth and volume.* The lake of
Brienz is a deep piedmont lake with steep shores and a big hypolimnion. The other
two lakes are rather flat and not very deep.

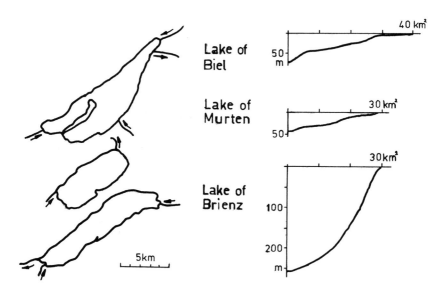

Fig. 1 Surface form and volume of the examined lakes

Furthermore the following facts must be considered:

- The lake of Murten has an inflow which enters on the left side at the upper end of the lake. It thus finds enough space to produce a clockwise vortex.

- Inflows are at the top (the Aare) and the end (the Lütschine) of the lake of Brienz. One (the Aare) finds space to form a clockwise vortex, whereas the other (the Lütschine) flows along the northeastern shore. As such this lake is very simply formed.

- The lake of Biel consists of three basins. It also has three definite inflows. The most important one being the Aare, flows into the lake in "unnatural" lateral manner.

Finally it has to be mentioned that, from all three lakes, limnosedimentological results are available which allow interesting comparisons with our investigations.

EXAMINATION METHODS

Drift measurements

Plastic folios are stretched on iron frames. They are placed at certain depths and hang on a float. Through theodolite measurements, the movements of the floats can be measured according to the streams in the depth.

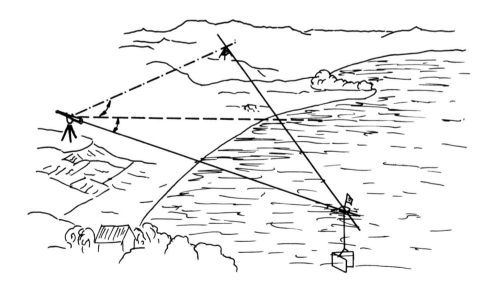

Fig. 2   Determination of the stream trajectories with floats

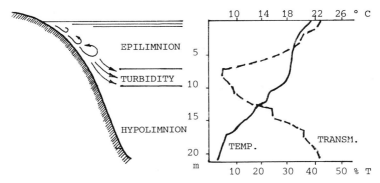

Fig. 3   Stratification of the inflow and the forming of the turbid horizon (scheme
and measurement in lake of Murten from 21.9.1966)

Fig. 4   Construction of
research model

Research model

In order to simulate the rotation of the earth and the effect of the force of
coriolis, a round wooden plate with a diameter of 140 cm, was erected so that it
could rotate on its verticale axis; the lake therefore turned on one axis, which itself drew a circle (Fig. 4). The three mentioned lakes were formed out of Polyester,
and coloured water flowed in and out through built-in-pipes. A camera, which was
put on the wooden plate, filmed the streams of water in the model.

GENERAL FACTS ABOUT THE LAKE STREAMS AND THE IMPORTANCE OF THE FORCE OF CORIOLIS

Fig. 3 shows, schematically the measurements of transmission from 21.9.1966 in the lake of Murten, how the inflow of water at that depth of the lake is stratified in which occurs the according density. This is caused by the temperature, salt content and turbid substance.

Our system has the coordinates x, y and z, and in the x-, y-, z-direction the acceleration of the force of coriolis work f_x, f_y, f_z.

The horizontal component is important $f_x = 2\omega v \sin\varphi$, whereas according to PRANDTL, the other two could be neglected.

ω = angular velocity of earth rotation = 7,29 $10^{-5} s^{-1}$

v = speed of stratification

φ = geographical latitude

As the acceleration is vertical to the direction of the flow, a mowing mass, free from friction, will draw a circle. The radius of the "circle of inertia" can be calculated with the formular:

$$r = \frac{v}{2 \omega \sin\varphi}$$

The whirlpool in Fig. 5 has a diameter of about 1500 m. It is important to consider the following:

1. As new waters constantly push their way in, parts of the whirlpool break off the main whirlpool and are pushed further on.

2. These parts of the water are diverted towards the right, and therefore pushed towards the shore.

3. Due to the forced streams along the shore, a left rotation of the main water arises in the depth of stratification of the inflows. This exerts a force which has a vertical effect on the direction of motion. The water masses below and above are, as a result of viscosity, "dragged along" with decreasing speed upwards and downwards.

Fig. 5   Mouth of the Aare near Hagneck, airphoto by NYDEGGER 1967

OBSERVATIONS AND EXPERIMENTS LAKE OF MURTEN

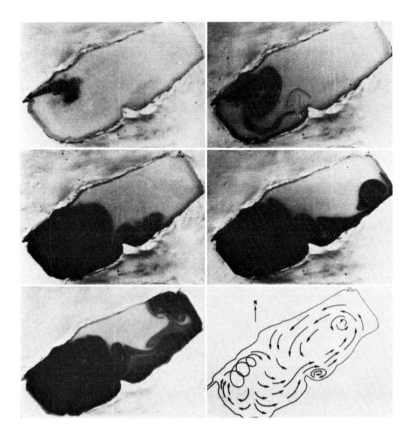

Fig. 6   Photos of an experiment in the lake of Murten and scheme of the streams

OBSERVATIONS AND EXPERIMENTS LAKE OF BRIENZ

Fig. 7   shows photos of the movement of the inflow water from the Aare and Lütschine
         in the model.
         In the pictures 1-4, the clockwise rotations (northern hemisphere) are there,
         whereas picture 5 the expected stream by counter clockwise rotation, sou-
         thern hemisphere, is demonstrated.

Fig. 8   STURM and MATTER found the carbonate distribution in the surface sediments,
         which is shown in Fig. 8. This result clearly confirms our research ex-
         periences.

Fig. 9   shows two cross-sections of transmission in the lake of Brienz. Cross-
         section a is at the height of Ebligen (Aare is dominating) and cross-
         section b is the height of Niederried (Lütschine dominating). It is clear
         to see that the Lütschine stratifies at about 10 m deeper than the Aare
         (more turbid substances). The numbers of the legend show the transparency
         in %/m-level in the green sphere.

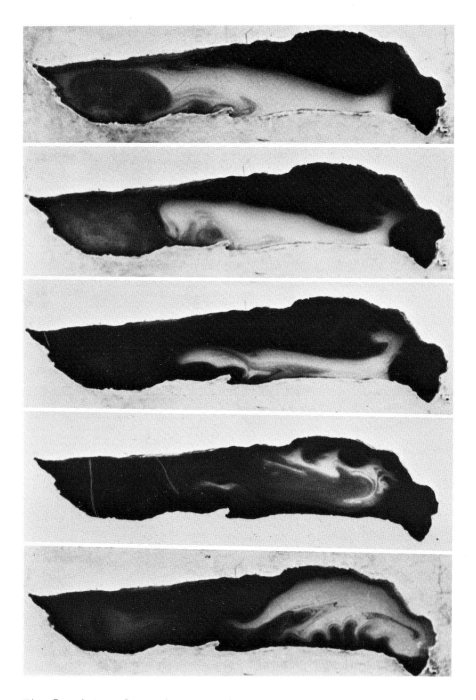

Fig. 7   Photos of experiments on the lake of Brienz

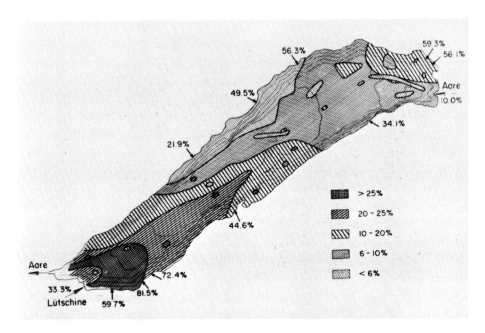

Fig. 8

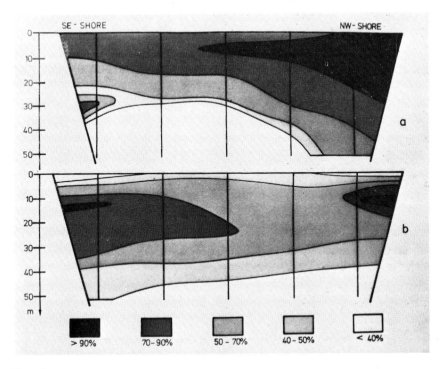

Fig. 9

OBSERVATIONS AND EXPERIMENTS LAKE OF BIEL

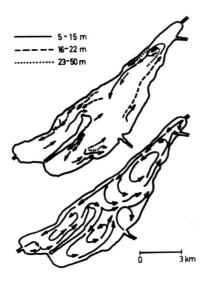

Fig. 10 Lake of Biel. a. Streams observed during the summer month 1971/72
                        b. Scheme of streams

REFERENCES

NYDEGGER, P., 1967. Untersuchungen über Feinstofftransport in Flüssen und Seen,
    über Entstehung von Trübungshorizonten und zuflussbedingten Strömungen im Brien-
    zersee und einigen Vergleichsseen. Beiträge zur Geol. der Schweiz, Hydrologie Nr.
    16.
NYDEGGER, P., 1976. Strömungen in Seen. Untersuchungen in situ and an nachgebildeten
    Modellseen. Beiträge zur Geol. der Schweiz, kleinere Mitteilungen Nr. 66.
    Kommissionsverlag Kümmerly + Frey, Bern.
STURM, M., 1976. Die Oberflächensedimente des Brienzersees. Geologisches Institut
    der Universität Bern. Publikation in "Eclogae geol. Helv.".
STURM, M., MATTER, A., 1976. Geologisch sedimentologische Untersuchungen im Thuner-
    und Brienzersee. Separatdruck aus "Jahrbuch Thuner- und Brienzersee", Thun.

EXPERIENCES FROM A COMPUTERIZED WATER QUALITY IN SITU INSTRUMENT

L.T. LINDELL

National Swedish Environment Protection Board, Limnological Survey, University of Uppsala, Uppsala (Sweden)

ABSTRACT

Lindell, L.T., 1979. Experiences from a computerized water quality in situ instrument.

To analyse the distribution of water parameters in the large lakes of Sweden, a system has been developed for collection and instantaneous processing of field data by means of a minicomputer system.
The instrumentation consists of a sensor unit (pressure, specific conductance, temperature, transmission, oxygen and pH), a cable for vertical sampling and a minicomputer for control of sampling and data processing. The computer system also controls the surface sampling which is routinely done while underway.
The minicomputer collects and processes information from the sensor unit and also controls the electronics within the sensor unit. Immediately after the processing, the data are presented on a screen (CRT).
This minicomputer system is a development of a sampling system without a computer. The old system was in use 1970 through 1975 and has operated almost troublefree acquiring 95 % valid data.

INTRODUCTION

The National Swedish Environment Protection Board has a research group (Limnological Survey) at the University of Uppsala, Sweden, which deals with applied limnological studies in the large lakes of Sweden - Lakes Vänern, Vättern and Mälaren. In 1969 a group within the Survey was established to handle the physical limnology. The first work for this group was to construct an efficient in situ instrument to measure physical variables, because conventional techniques of collecting water samples and wet analyses in the laboratory were quickly found to be too inexact and time-consuming.

An automatic in situ instrument (ATOS I) was constructed for use on small boats. It was used in 1970 for the first time (Wikström and

Håkanson, 1970). This instrument measured and recorded depth, temperature, specific conductance and light transmission. The signals from
the sensors were digitized and stored on paper tape. The system was
gradually modified (ATOS II) and has been used continuously on Lakes
Mälaren and Vänern, Sweden (Lemming et al., 1973).

This system has been further developed and now a minicomputer has
been added for the measurement control, and evaluation of water quality information (ATOS III). The advantages of the new system are:
a better control over the collecting phase and a possibility to modify a sampling program in response to the information collected,
since the processing of data is instantaneous. The system is used
both for the control and collection of data of surface water while
underway and for vertical sampling at different stations. The physical dimensions of the system as well as the power consumption are
kept low to permit use on board small cruisers.

The design of the system

The design of the system can be seen in Fig. 1. It consists of

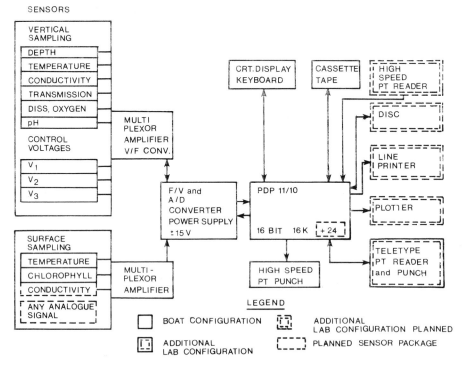

Fig. 1. The computerized water quality recording system.

a number of sensors for vertical sampling in situ and a number of
sensors on board the boat for the analysis of surface water. The submersible unit as well as the unit on board have each been provided
with a multiplexor and amplifier. An A/D converter is placed on board
the boat. The signal is transmitted through the cable by frequency
multiplexing technique. The central unit consists of a PDP 11/10 (Digital Equipment) which is a 16-bit computer provided with 16 k memory. For communication with this unit there is a CRT-key board (VT 05,
Digital Equipment). Programs and data are stored on cassette tape
(TU 11, Digital Equipment) and final storage is on paper tape (Facit).

The submersible unit at present consists of sensors for depth,
temperature, specific conductance, transmission, oxygen and pH.

On board the boat there is a temperature sensor and a fluorometer
(chlorophyll a) for continuous surface monitoring. An autoanalyzer
may be added to the system and a sensor for conductivity is anticipated. The system for continuous surface sampling is also used when
pumping water at a station.

The complete instrumentation weights only about 100 kg and the
power consumption is below 1 kW.

The sensor unit

The submersible sensors are adapted to a stainless steel cylinder
containing among other things all sensors with electronics, a multiplexor and amplifiers (Fig. 2-3).

The depth sensor is a diaphragm stress membrane (Transducers Limited) with an accuracy of 0.1 m in the interval 0 - 70 m. It can be
used below this range to 140 m but with slightly less accuracy.

The temperature sensor is our own construction consisting of a
thermistor with an amplifier. The absolute accuracy is $\pm 0.1^{\circ}$ C. The
sensor has been calibrated many times without showing any tendency
for longterm drift. An extra temperature sensor is always connected
for checking purposes and in the case of a breakdown.

The conductivity cell is constructed according to the 4-electrode
principle (Kemotron AS) and modified for our system so that the time
constant is in parity with the other sensors.

The transmissometer is a completely new construction of ours, because of the fact that the commercial units and our earlier modifications have not been sufficiently stable and handy in the field. Our
new meter has only 15 cm (2 · 7.5 cm) path length. It is insensitive
to surrounding light. All electronics are placed together and a prism

Fig. 2. The top of the sensor unit with the pressure sensor (arrow).

(tripple mirror) has been used to move and reflect the transmitted lightbeam back. The prism reflects the light parallel to the incoming light independent of the adjustment of the prism. The use of the prism has also further reduced the physical size of the instrument and increased the ruggedness. The source of light is a special red (635 nm) light diode. This keeps the power consumption and heat emission low and the wave length approximately constant and narrow ($\Delta\lambda$ 40 nm). The absolute accuracy is determined by how well cleaned and calibrated the instrument can be. The accuracy is better than 0.15 % for the interval 75 - 100 % transmission and better than 2 % in the rest of the interval. The relative accuracy is better than 0.05 %. The temperature drift is less than 0.1 %/$^{\circ}$ C. The time drift is less than 0.01 % per month. The instrument is using ±15 V. The power consumption is about 50 mA. The transmissometer sensor is not yet commercially available.

The oxygen sensor is a slightly improved commercial unit (Yellow Springs).

The pH-sensor is a commercial unit (Beckman and Lazaran) sofar not useful in our system due to very long internal time constant.

The sensor unit for the surface sampling consists of our self-constructed temperature sensor (thermistor, amplifier) and a fluorometer (Turner) which can be used for measuring chlorophyll a (Lorenzen, 1966). Alternatively the fluorometer is used for lignin measurements according to our own method (Wilander et al., 1974). The autoanalyzer that we have been testing is a modified version similar to most commercial units (Technicon).

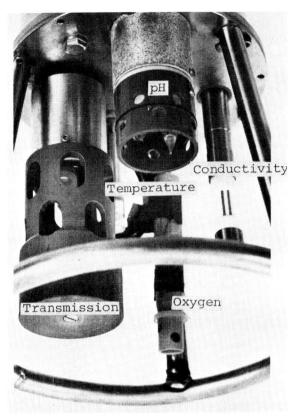

Fig. 3. The lower part of the probe with the different sensors.

We are using a cable containing 16 conductors for the transmission of the signals from the submersible unit to the boat.

The interfacing unit is designed in the following manner: beside the signals from the sensors there are a few control voltages transferred which are connected to a 16 channel analogue multiplexor and programmable amplifier. Transfer of the recorded signals is frequency multiplexed; other signals to and from the sensor unit are transferred parallel in the form of 5 V levels.

For the surface sampling 16 analogue inputs are available. These inputs are connected to an analogue multiplexor, a programmable amplifier and an A/D converter is in common for both modules and thus the frequency multiplexed signals have to be converted.

Both modules also contain control logics etc. The multiplexing units and A/D converters are based on commercial modules (Analogic), but with our own interfaces.

Operating procedure

System ATOS III is collecting the following information (Fig. 4):
1. Surface distribution records from temperature and chlorophyll a (lignin);
2. Vertical profiles obtained by in situ sensors of temperature, specific conductance, light transmission, dissolved oxygen and pH. A depth sensor determines the precise depths of the samples.

At the different sampling stations water may also be pumped and analysed for other constituents.

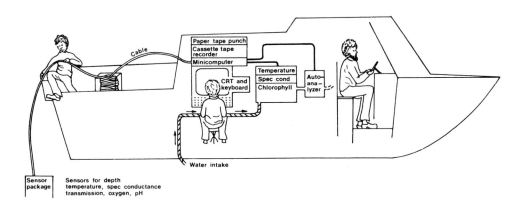

Fig. 4. The function of the ATOS III system.

Surface sampling is performed through a water intake in the bottom of the boat and water is continuously supplied to the sensors by the pitot principle. The sampling can be controlled in two different ways
a) sampling at distinct time intervals (software control by an internal clock);
b) sampling at distinct distance intervals by using the log of the boat (manual control at present).

Vertical sampling is normally carried out by stopping the boat at a station and lowering the sensor unit manually to the bottom with a brief stop (a few seconds) at two meter intervals (or more frequent) for sampling.

By manually lowering the sensor unit it is much easier to avoid undue tension on the cable than by using a winch arrangement since the wave action on board a small boat is sometimes severe. Sampling can be conducted quickly; for example, at a normal sampling station on Lake Vänern, a complete profile (60 m) sampling takes about 7 minutes including stopping and starting of the boat, as long as no pumping is performed.

Pumping at a station is presently performed by a separate hose and a pumping system (a 12 V DC pump), not connected to the vertical sampling unit. A new combined system is, however, anticipated in which the hose and the cable will be fastened together.

The unit for vertical sampling is never towed for surface mapping purposes.

The minicomputer is used for both surface and vertical sampling. It controls the voltages, collects information, and makes necessary computations.

All information is handled in real-time mode and is immediately presented on the CRT (Fig. 5). By a command from the consol the information is stored on cassette tape and paper tape for more involved calculations on a larger landbased computer.

DEPTH	TEMP	COND	TRANS	EXT	OXYG	%	DENSITY
.5	18.46	86.7	95.6	.234	11.2	87	.1234
2.0	18.20	86.7	95.1	.237	11.0	86	.1333
4.1	18.11	85.9	96.0	.212	10.8	87	.1334
6.0	18.03	85.7	96.1	.211	10.7	87	.1335
8.2	17.44	_					

DATE 17/4 1974
TIME 0915
VERTICAL 97/83

5 .95

SENSOR 5 SEEMS TO GIVE WRONG VALUES

Fig. 5. A fictive layout of the CRT. The parameter values are listed for the different depths. To the right the numbers 5 and .95 appear, indicating that something is wrong with sensor five. The last line is used for input and output of information.

A vertical sampling sequence could also be performed automatically (without consol command) so that the probe could be lowered continuously or even dropped. The sampling frequency and the appropriate sensor is chosen by the computer (software), the highest possible frequency being 300 Hz. The most suitable sampling frequency has been found to be 80. The mean value of 10 consecutive recordings for a certain parameter will be the actual measured value. This principle can thus be looked upon as "software filtering".

It should be stressed that the vertical sampling technique with ATOS III is identical to that with the older system, i.e. the sensor unit halts for sampling at two meter intervals. This differs

from the ordinary way of using the STD-(CTD)-probe in the ocean environment and thus most of the technique of filtering for this purpose (Roden and Irish, 1975) is not applicable.

The programming is performed in Basic with a few assembly routines
and the program package is modularly built to create the greatest
flexibility. To change between the two different program units for
vertical or surface sampling, a call is made from the consol.

Experiences

The older systems (ATOS I-II), which were used 1970 - 1975, collected about half a million values from the three largest lakes
in Sweden. The main task for that instrument was to make synoptical
measurements all over the lakes, but lately there has been an increasing need for local investigations in embayments close to waste
water inflows. Therefore ATOS III will be used also for this purpose.

The effectiveness of the ATOS system compared to conventional
water sampling and laboratory analyses can be illustrated with work
from Lake Ekoln (Mälaren). The synoptic network on this lake consists
of 42 stations which covers the entire lake surface (21.5 km^2). With
conventional methods it took about 2 days to collect water samples
in the field and after that about the same time to complete laboratory analyses. The evaluation of data, including drawings and plots
took about 4 - 6 weeks. With the ATOS system the same work requires
about 2 hours in the field and about 1 - 2 minutes (+10 to 15 minutes
for plotting) computation time. Although the time saved is notable,
the big advantage with the system is the accuracy of the measurements
As an example, a detailed distribution picture of several parameters
(Fig. 6) is shown. The type of patterns that can be seen in Fig. 6
has never been observed by conventional methods (Kvarnäs and Lindell,
1970), especially not the small but clear differences in the physical
character of the southern part of the lake. The figure shows how heav
ly polluted water is supplied to the lake via the River Fyris, whose
high specific conductance values can be used as a natural tracer. It
can be seen that the polluted water is supplied to the depth in the
lake that approximates its density, in this case the upper part of
the thermocline. Note the very limited vertical and lateral dispersion of the polluted water. The Coriolis force is also quite clearly
detectable in spite of the limited size of the lake. At the outlet
of the lake all parameters show the same distributional pattern, thus
indicating the process of the outflow.

179

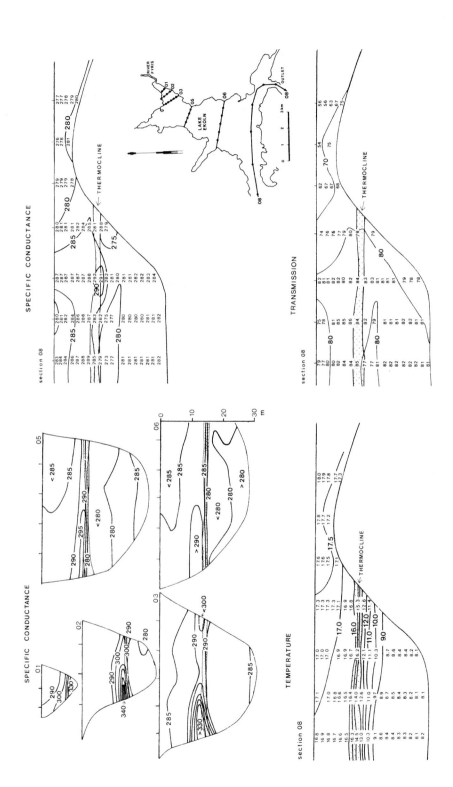

Fig. 6. The variations of different parameters in Lake Ekoln, August 31 1970, as recorded by ATOS II.

In Lake Vänern, ATOS II has mainly been used for synoptic studies and from these, computations of the geostrophic stream pattern (Kvarnäs, 1975 and 1978) were made.

Special studies have also been carried out in limited regions of Lake Vänern and showing the very valuable physical information from ATOS II necessary for the adequate interpretation of the distribution of chemical and biological parameters (Welch, 1974; Lindell, 1975a, b).

These recordings described are examples from investigations that would have been almost impossible to perform without the aid of an automatic in situ device or at least would have been very time-consuming and less accurate.

During the last two years the ATOS II instrument functioned extraordinary well. From all measurements, including those made under very rough conditions with snow and temperatures below 0° C, almost all data have been correct, according to frequent calibrations and comparisons with simultaneously collected data.

The disadvantage with the old system was, however, that it was difficult to be completely certain of the validity of the data while sampling, since only relative values in the form of millivolts were presented. The addition of the minicomputer has provided the capacity of immediately processing and presenting the information in understandable form and furthermore to control the function of the whole system and make rough checks of the computed values. This will help the manual control of the sampling procedure. The instant display of the values also provides the possibility of modifying the measuring program while it is still in progress based on the collected data and it will be a great aid in optimizing future more extensive sampling program involving many time-consuming analyses of chemical and biological variables.

The most positive experience with ATOS III is the reliability of the system. We had expected a number of hardware and software problems but so far (2 years) there has been less malfunctions than with the older system. Also it has been possible to use unskilled people to handle the instrument due to the simplified commanding procedures.

However, the system would be most beneficial to the experienced limnologist who can use the real-time information for judgement of the data during a continuing survey e.g. when tracing plumes etc. Then ATOS III offers a flexibility for you to choose appropriate sampling positions and sampling depths.

The change of transmissometer in ATOS III has been very successful. The sensor has been extremely stable and accurate compared to
our ten years of experiences with commercial and improved commercial
units.

REFERENCES

Kvarnäs, H., 1975. Den geostrofiska strömningen i Värmlandssjön
    (Vänern). SNV PM 561/Naturvårdsverkets limnologiska undersökning
    79, Uppsala, 14 pp.
-    1978. Dynamiska studier i Vänern och Ekoln. SNV PM 1030/Naturvårds-
    verkets limnologiska undersökning, Uppsala, 84 pp.
Kvarnäs, H. and Lindell, T., 1970. Hydrologiska studier i Ekoln.
    Uppsala Naturgeografiska Institution Report 3, Uppsala, 39 pp.
Lemming, J., Lindell, T. and Kvarnäs, H., 1973. Mobilt instrument
    för vattenkvalitémätning in situ. Naturvårdsverkets limnologiska
    undersökning Report 61, Uppsala, 7 pp.
Lindell, T., 1975a. Vänern. In: Vänern, Vättern, Mälaren och Hjälmaren
    - en översikt. SNV Publications 1976:1, Stockholm, pp. 21-35.
-    1975b. Water movements and exchange of water within nearshore
    areas of Lake Vänern. SNV PM 672/Naturvårdsverkets limnologiska
    undersökning 85, Uppsala, 84 pp.
Lorenzen, C.I., 1966. A method for the continuous measurement of in
    vivo chlorophyll concentration. Deep Sea Research 13, Oxford,
    pp. 223-227.
Roden, G.I. and Irish, J.D., 1975. Electronic digitization and sen-
    sor response effects on salinity computation from CTD field
    measurements. J. Phys. Oc. Vol. 5:1, pp. 195-199.
Wikström, A. and Håkanson, L., 1970. Nytt automatiskt instrument
    för vattenundersökningar. Vatten Årg. 26, No. 2. Lund, pp. 120-125.
Welch, E., 1974. The water quality of nearshore areas in Lake Vänern
    - causes and prospects. SNV PM 509/Naturvårdsverkets limnologiska
    undersökning 77, Uppsala, 31 pp.
Wilander, A., Kvarnäs, H. and Lindell, T., 1974. A modified fluoro-
    metric method for measurement of lignin sulfonates and its in situ
    application in natural waters. Water Research Vol. 8, 1037-1045 pp.

STRATEGIES FOR COUPLING DATA COLLECTION AND ANALYSIS WITH DYNAMIC MODELLING OF
LAKE MOTIONS[*]

C. H. MORTIMER

Center for Great Lakes Studies, University of Wisconsin-Milwaukee, Milwaukee, WI, USA

ABSTRACT

Mortimer, C. H., 1979. Strategies for coupling data collection and analysis with
    dynamic modelling of lake motions.

    The lecturer selects lake-seiche motion to illustrate interactive coupling
between experiment and theory in physical limnology, which has taken the form of
an evolving *pas de deux* between (i) in-lake data-gathering and (ii) conceptual or
mathematical modelling. For example, F. A. Forel's classic seiche investigations
on Léman led directly to E. M. Wedderburn's pioneering studies of internal seiches
in Scottish lakes and, in turn, to theoretical and experimental advances elsewhere,
including the Great Lakes of North America. Because of its anticipated importance
for the physical and biological economy of Léman, the internal seiche in that lake
is here examined in some detail, and a new adaptation of Defant's procedure for
seiche calculation is appended. The influence of Earth's rotation is demonstrated;
and the non-linear character of internal seiche waves in Léman is inferred from
examples from other lakes.
    The role of seiche-induced currents--and other types of flow which introduce
current shear into stratified lakes--is illustrated by recent theoretical and
experimental advances made by S. A. Thorpe and co-workers.
    In the light of this review and of experience elsewhere, promising strategies
are suggested for future research.

INTRODUCTION

    The above long-winded title, proposed before this lecture was composed, was

deliberately chosen to allow me to discourse rather freely on some philosophical

concepts of limnological research, to ride a hobbyhorse or two, and to emphasize

above all that notable advances have been and will be dependent upon intimate

coupling, step by step, between experiment and theory. In doing so, I make no

distinction between physical limnology and other branches of geophysical fluid

dynamics; because advances in one branch--oceanography for example--often directly

---

[*]Contribution No. 177 from the Center for Great Lakes Studies, University of
    Wisconsin-Milwaukee, Milwaukee, Wisconsin 53201, USA.

influence advances in another. At school I was taught chemistry by the historical method; and, although we had to toil through what seemed like centuries of the phlogiston theory before arriving at the enlightenment of Lavoisier and Priestley, that dawn was all the brighter because of it. Therefore, here, I attempt to deliver my message with the help of examples from a much briefer limnological history, where possible choosing those examples from researches on Léman or from other research findings likely to have special significance for lakes of that size class.

Those fortunate enough to take part in this meeting, and others who hear of it, will surely exclaim: "What more fitting *venue* could there be for a symposium on the hydrodynamics of lakes than Léman?" F. A. Forel's three volumes ("Le Léman" 1892-1904) launched and christened limnology as a sub-discipline of general oceanography and geophysical fluid dynamics. Entitling his volumes "Monographie Limnologique," Forel explains:

> *"Je dois expliquer ce néologisme, et m'en excuser si cela est nécessaire. J'ai voulu faire une généralisation résumant dans une vue d'ensemble les faits détaillés, appuyant chaque étude spéciale sur les données fournies par les autres études. Le thème de ma description étant une partie de la terre....j'aurais donc dû lui donner le titre d'océanographie d'eau douce. Mais un lac, quelque grand qu'il soit, n'est pas un océan; son espace limité lui donne un caractère propre, bien différent de l'espace illimité de la vaste mer. J'ai donc dû chercher un mot plus modeste....le mot limnologie. La limnologie est donc l'océanographie des lacs."*

In those volumes we see the first attempt to build diverse results into a unifying theme, clearly recognizing the indivisible unity of limnology and oceanography. Incidentally Volume 2 also secured a place for Léman vernacular--"seiche"--in the hydrodynamicist's vocabulary.

Léman was also the scene of other "firsts": Saussure (1799) with thermally-lagged thermometers discovered that the bottom temperature in Léman and other deep Swiss lakes in summer was near that of maximum density; and an English geologist with the un-English name of de la Bèche (1819) made a series of temperature soundings with a minimum thermometer. Although his estimates of deep-water temperature were a degree or so too high--probably because of the effect of hydrostatic pressure on his instrument--he discovered the shape of the autumn thermocline (open circles in later Fig. 3).

Driven by scientific curiosity to probe beneath the surface, those earlier investigators aspired to understand the responses of a lake to the forces acting

upon it, i.e. responses to the seasonal cycle of heat flux, to the wind, and to
other interactions with the atmosphere and inflows. That remains the general
objective of modern-day limnologists, now armed with improved tools, including
a prospect of predictive modelling capability. But since Forel's time a more
immediate, related objective has assumed growing importance, i.e. improvement in
understanding and prediction to a point at which useful advances can be made in
the parallel understanding of chemical and biological events and processes, leading to enlightened ecosystem management. In this lecture I attempt to focus on
some of the physical questions, selecting for examination those which appear to
have a bearing on lake ecosystem dynamics.

THE *PAS DE DEUX* BETWEEN EXPERIMENT AND THEORY

In physical limnology the coupling between theory and experiment--the mainspring
of advance in any science--has taken the form of interaction between in-lake
measurements and mathematical models, analytical or numerical. History shows
that such coupling can be tight or loose, immediate or delayed. In some cases
a theoretical result has prompted field observations, sometimes the reverse;
and often it has taken a long time for essential connections between available
theory and existing experimental results to be perceived. There has been a
parallel evolution, not always in step, of (i) measuring techniques, (ii) methods
of data-analysis, and (iii) concepts or models, leading to further experiment.
That evolution is well illustrated by a Léman example, Forel's beautiful set of
seiche data.

Surface seiches

Although Forel recognized the features of a standing wave and applied Merian's
equation as a simple model, contemporary theory (for example du Boy's modification
of Merian) was inadequate to accurately predict the period, elevation and current
structure of the seiche modes in basins of even moderately irregular shape. Chrystal
(1905), a mathematician, took the next step. His was an analytical approach, in
which the morphometry of the real basin was transformed into an equivalent "normal
curve," to which could be fitted known analytical expressions for basins of
mathematically treatable shape (parabolic, quartic, for example). This mathematically innovative method yielded accurate estimates of seiche period, when used

---

* In an obscure military report (1872) a U.S. Army Engineer surveyor, C. B.
Comstock, interpreted a conspicuous transverse seiche in Lake Michigan as a
standing wave, thereby antedating Forel's first report (1873) by one year
(see Mortimer, 1965).

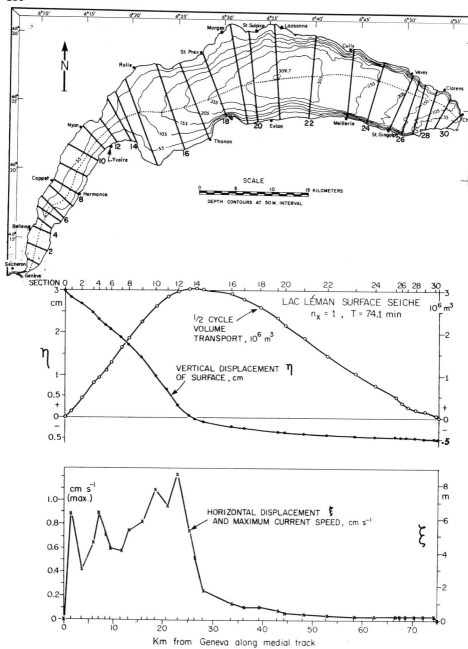

Fig. 1. Defant analysis (see appendix) of the first (uninodal) surface seiche mode in Léman (period T = 74.1 min). The 31 sections were drawn on 1:50000 "Carte des sondages du Lac Léman 1891" from positions given by Doodson, Carey, and Baldwin (1920); and a medial track (dotted) was superimposed. Illustrated are distributions, along the medial track, of: ½-cycle transport through each section; vertical displacement (η, relative to 3 cm amplitude at Geneva); and corresponding horizontal displacement (ξ, ¼ cycle) and maximum speed, i.e. mean speed ($4\xi/T$) multiplied by $\pi/2$.

on not-too-irregular ·basins (Chrystal and Wedderburn 1905, Chrystal 1908); but-- as often happens--numerical methods proved more convenient to use and, in the example (Defant 1918, 1960) examined below, provided additional information on the distribution of vertical and horizontal displacements attributable to each free seiche mode. Later, analytical and numerical methods of solving the seiche problem in irregular basins proliferated. Some are reviewed in Servais (1957) and in Defant (1960). They provide many examples of mathematical skill poorly matched by observations. For example, there are none to test Servais' elaborate computations for Lake Tanganyika. In fact most of the lake seiche theories shed little light on processes <u>within</u> the basins.

Because Forel's excellent data set provided a good test, some of those methods have been applied to Léman, notably Defant's method (Servais, 1957) and Proudman's method (Doodson, Carey, and Baldwin, 1920). Both of those treatments sought to reproduce the observed seiche periods and the positions of nodes; and in this they succeeded quite well (see Table 1). My interest here, in using Defant's method and the same 31 Sections which Doodson et al. employed, is (i) to explore the contribution of surface seiches to water motions in Léman, (ii) to adapt the method for use as a simple but useful model of the much more significant internal seiche motions in that lake, and (iii) to test both models against observations.

The results of a Defant calculation for the first Léman surface seiche mode are presented in Figure 1. The computed period is 74.1 min. The greatest amplitudes occur in the Petit Lac with a node at the mouth, exactly where Forel's

TABLE 1

Comparison of the periods (in minutes) of longitudinal surface seiches observed in Léman by Forel (1895) and Bircher (1954) with those calculated by two different methods.

Author and Method	Mode Number				
	1	2	3	4	5
Observed					
Forel (1895) multi-series average, p. 122;	73.5	35.5		20(rare)	
single series, March-April 1891	74.0				
Bircher (1954) observed 1949-50	73.5-74.2				
Computed					
Doodson et al. (1920) Proudman's method	74.45	35.1			
Servais (1954), Defant method[*]	71.45	34.92			
Mortimer (this paper) Defant method[+]	74.1	35.5	29.1	21	18

[*]25 cross-sections equally spaced along a medial track of length 73.9 km.
[+]31 cross-sections (positions and areas tabulated in Doodson et al., 1920)
   unequally spaced (to accomodate changes in basin sections, see Fig. 1) along
   a medial track 74.9 km long.

observations placed it (his Fig. 74, Vol. 2, p. 127). From Forel's long and thorough studies and from more recent surveys (for example Bircher, 1954), the periods of the first two Léman surface (longitudinal) modes are known with considerable precision. Less precise are estimates of mean and maximum amplitude and the distribution of amplitude around the shores. Forel's measurements (1895, Vol. 2, pp. 120-122) of many series of uninodal seiches at several stations yield a mean period of 73.5 min with a standard deviation of the order of half a minute. It is noteworthy that the longest most regular series, which Forel illustrates for March-April 1891, was obtained when the lake level was 0.3 m below the mean and yielded a period of 74 minutes. Bircher (1954), in an analysis of 14 months of continuous recording at 17 stations, illustrates a dependence (in the expected sense) of period on lake level over a level range of about 1.4 m and a seiche period range of 73.5 to 74.2 min. Forel's 74 min estimate falls on Bircher's line. For the binodal seiche, Forel examined six series ranging in period from 35.3 to 35.7 minutes, average 35.5. The comparisons with the computed periods (Table 1) shows remarkable agreement, even more remarkable when one considers that motions transverse to the medial track are excluded in the Proudman and Defant procedures. Because errors might therefore be expected to arise at the abrupt section change between the Petit Lac and the main basin, Doodson et al. spaced their cross-sections more closely there than elsewhere.

Concerning amplitude distribution, Forel and others have noted that large amplitudes occur in the Petit Lac and that the uninodal seiche is the one most commonly excited. Forel estimated daily averages of seiche amplitude at Sécheron for the whole of 1891 and computed an annual mean range of ± 2.25 cm. For a 14-month interval (1949-1950) at Bellevue, Bircher (1954) counted 9 days when the seiche "amplitude," which I take to mean range, was > 10 cm, 50 days > 5 cm, and 129 > 3 cm. Therefore a uninodal seiche amplitude of ± 3 cm at Sécheron (Geneva) is commonplace; and that was the scale adopted in Figure 1, and which determines the along-basin distribution of vertical and horizontal displacements at each cross-section and the corresponding volumes transported across each section during half of the seiche cycle. Horizontal displacement can also be scaled in velocity, in this case the maximum velocity attained, taken as $\pi/2$ times the mean velocity, assuming simple harmonic motion. As observed, Figure 1 shows the greatest amplitudes in the Petit Lac. The maximum horizontal displacement ± 8 m from equilibrium occurs at the narrow cross-section 12, just inside the mouth of the Petit Lac. The corresponding maximum current speed, attained every 37 min, is 1.2 cm s^{-1}. Larger seiches will, of course, produce larger motions. All scales in Fig. 1 change in proportion to change in seiche amplitude.

Internal seiches

In the preceding paragraphs I have given more space to surface seiches than they perhaps merit in this symposium, not only because of the Léman connection, but to demonstrate precision, which Defant's one-dimensional model can achieve if sufficient cross-sections are taken, and to also illustrate (with a two-layered Defant adaptation) the iterative progress from an initial data set,

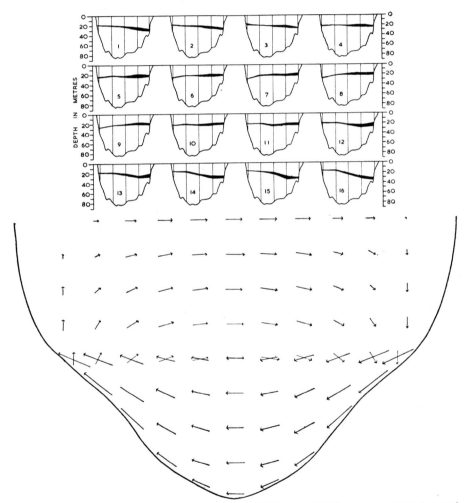

Fig. 2. Upper portion: hourly positions (0100 to 1600 hours, 9 August 1911) of the thermocline (black area bounded by the 9° and 11°C isotherms) on a longitudinal section of Loch Earn, redrawn from Wedderburn (1912). The vertical lines are the station positions. Lower portion: Wedderburn and Williams' (1911) model of Loch Earn as a two-layered lake, the "interfacial normal curve" of which is a parabola. Motion of water particles is shown above and below the interface which oscillates about a central uninode.

leading to primitive theory, followed by further experiment to test the theory, and so on.

In themselves, surface seiches play a minor role in the physical and biological economy of a lake, but interest in them led directly to the study of a more important class of oscillatory motion, the internal seiche. The story now turns to Scotland where Wedderburn and collaborators, in the course of testing Chrystal's surface seiche equations, discovered internal (thermocline) oscillations often of large amplitude in Loch Ness. The standing-wave character of this oscillation was recognized by giving it the name: "temperature seiche" (Watson, 1904; Wedderburn, 1907) therby confirming Thoulet's (1894) conjectured *sorte de seiche intérieure*. The model evolutionist may note that Wedderburn and William's (1911) model of an internal seiche (Fig. 2) was a two-layered adaptation of Chrystal's surface seiche model and subject to the same limitations when applied to real, irregular basins. That model was tested by very detailed data-sets from the Madüsee, Pomerania, and from Loch Earn, Scotland, where Wedderburn and Young's (1915) team made 20 reversing-thermometer measurements by hand-winch every hour for five days in one of the Loch Earn examples. That 1915 publication--Wedderburn's last before embarking on a very successful career in law--marks, not only the monumental labor just noted, but also introduced spectral techniques and complex demodulation to limnological analysis and also the earliest recognition of the non-linear nature of the internal seiche (see later discussion). Surprisingly, Wedderburn's findings lay relatively neglected or even disputed by limnologists (Birge, 1910) until I demonstrated their universality (Mortimer, 1953).

But the two-layered Chrystal model proved to be a *cul de sac*; and for internal (as for surface) seiches it appears that Defant's numerical procedure can yield more useful results. I have here adapted it (details in appendix) to calculate internal seiches in a two-layered model adjusted to the dimensions and density distribution in Léman. The same assumptions--absence of friction, absence of rotation, and no transverse motion--apply; but in this case the seiche is an internal one, occurring at the interface between an upper homogeneous layer of density ρ_1 and a lower homogeneous layer of density ρ_2. Figure 3 serves to specify $(\rho_2 - \rho_1)$ at about 1.4×10^{-3} and the equilibrium depth of the interface at 15 m. In the figure I have also included four August 1890 profiles obtained by T. Turrentini at a 30 m station in the Petit Lac, 2.4 km from the jetty at Geneva. Forel, who presented Turrentini's results for the whole summer (Vol. 2, p. 367), noted the great variability and the dependence of the temperature profile on wind. For example, the 28 August profile was taken after several days of strong wind. We should therefore expect large wind-induced changes in temperature structure and correspondingly large internal seiches in the Petit Lac, an expectation confirmed by summer temperatures at the Geneva waterworks

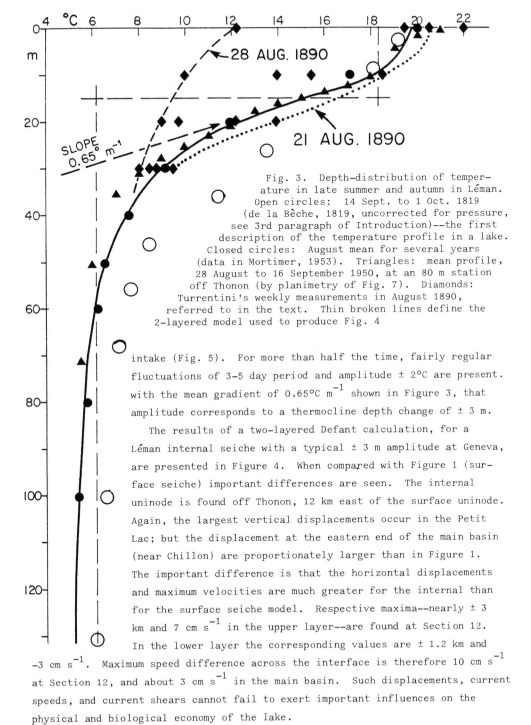

Fig. 3. Depth-distribution of temperature in late summer and autumn in Léman.
Open circles: 14 Sept. to 1 Oct. 1819
(de la Bèche, 1819, uncorrected for pressure,
see 3rd paragraph of Introduction)--the first
description of the temperature profile in a lake.
Closed circles: August mean for several years
(data in Mortimer, 1953). Triangles: mean profile,
28 August to 16 September 1950, at an 80 m station
off Thonon (by planimetry of Fig. 7). Diamonds:
Turrentini's weekly measurements in August 1890,
referred to in the text. Thin broken lines define the
2-layered model used to produce Fig. 4

intake (Fig. 5). For more than half the time, fairly regular
fluctuations of 3-5 day period and amplitude ± 2°C are present.
with the mean gradient of 0.65°C m^{-1} shown in Figure 3, that
amplitude corresponds to a thermocline depth change of ± 3 m.

The results of a two-layered Defant calculation, for a
Léman internal seiche with a typical ± 3 m amplitude at Geneva,
are presented in Figure 4. When compared with Figure 1 (surface seiche) important differences are seen. The internal
uninode is found off Thonon, 12 km east of the surface uninode.
Again, the largest vertical displacements occur in the Petit
Lac; but the displacement at the eastern end of the main basin
(near Chillon) are proportionately larger than in Figure 1.
The important difference is that the horizontal displacements
and maximum velocities are much greater for the internal than
for the surface seiche model. Respective maxima--nearly ± 3
km and 7 cm s^{-1} in the upper layer--are found at Section 12.
In the lower layer the corresponding values are ± 1.2 km and
-3 cm s^{-1}. Maximum speed difference across the interface is therefore 10 cm s^{-1}
at Section 12, and about 3 cm s^{-1} in the main basin. Such displacements, current
speeds, and current shears cannot fail to exert important influences on the
physical and biological economy of the lake.

Although the two-layer Defant model is primitive and ignores several important

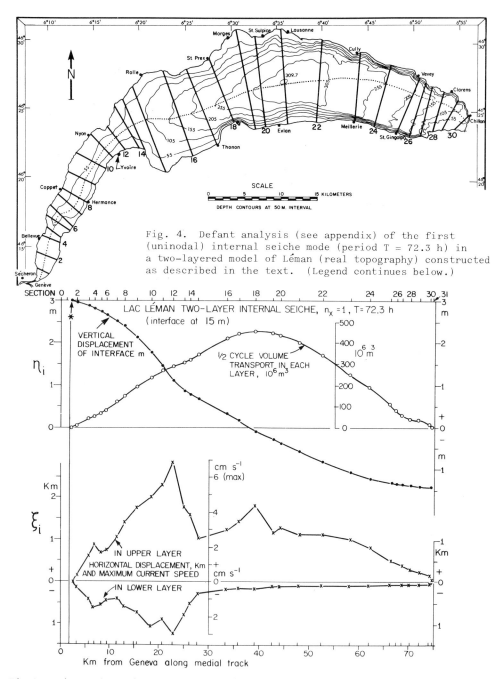

Fig. 4. Defant analysis (see appendix) of the first (uninodal) internal seiche mode (period T = 72.3 h) in a two-layered model of Léman (real topography) constructed as described in the text. (Legend continues below.)

Fig. 4. (Legend continued from above.) The first sentence of the Fig. 1 legend applies; the layer density difference $(\rho_2 - \rho_1)$ is assumed to be 1.41×10^{-3}; the interface depth is taken as 15 m; and the basin (interface) ends are placed at the asterisk (between Section 1 and 2) and at Section 31. Illustrated are: ½-cycle volume transport in each layer; vertical displacement of the interface (η_i, relative to 3 m amplitude at Geneva); and the corresponding horizontal displacements (ξ_i, ¼-cycle) and maximum speeds in each layer. Mean speeds are ($4\xi_i/T$); maximum speeds are $\pi/2$ times greater, assuming simple harmonic motion.

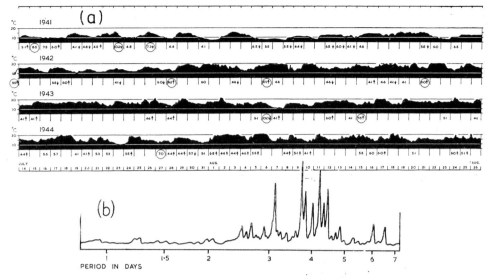

Fig. 5: (a) Temperature at the lake intake pipe (3.5 km from shore, 15 ı deep) at Geneva waterworks, 14 July-21 August, 1941-1944; (b) periodgram derived from the silhouettes in (a) using the "wave analyzer" of Barber et al. (1946) and Tucker (1956)--reproduced from Mortimer (1953). Daily mean wind velocities in km h^{-1} at Geneva Observatory are entered in (a) whenever the mean exceeded 4 km h^{-1}. Entries above 7 km h^{-1} are circled. Rising and falling arrows indicate N-NE and S-SW direction, respectively. Absence of an arrow indicates variable direction.

factors, the results reveal avenues for further exploration. For example, the Defant model (Fig. 4) predicts a free (first mode) internal seiche period of 3.0 days, corresponding perhaps to the isolated energy peak near that period in Fig. 5(b). But most of the energy is contained in a broader period band, 3.8 to 4.4 days, which (it turns out) coincides with the observed average range of intervals between the passage of wind impulses. Apparently therefore, the strong and persistent responses of the lake over that period range during each summer (Fig. 5a) represent meteorologically forced oscillations in near-resonance with the first free internal mode.

The influence of Earth's rotation

Because lake motions take place on the rotating Earth, complete theory must take the influence of rotation into account. For surface seiches in Léman that influence can be neglected, not so in larger basins. In this field also, there has been an interplay between observations and theory and between analytical and numerical modelling. Analytical treatment has been confined to basins of simple geometric shape (rectangular, Rao, 1966, 1977; elliptical

194

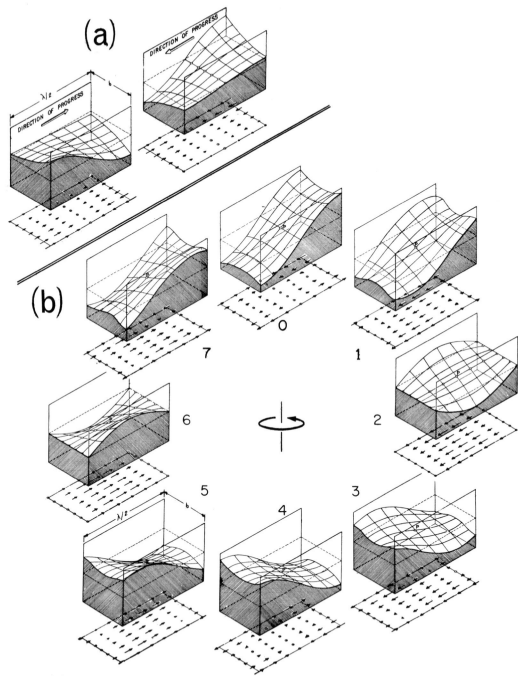

Fig. 6. (a) two oppositely propagating but otherwise identical Kelvin waves of cross-channel amplitude ratio 100/17; (b) combination of the two waves in (a) to produce an amphidromic "double Kelvin" wave, shown at 1/8 cycle intervals in a straight, rotating channel of rectangular cross-section, with the amphidromic point at P. (Assembled from figs. in Mortimer, 1975).

paraboloid, Ball, 1965), while numerical procedures have been devised for
prediction of the seiche frequencies and structures in basins of more complex
shape (Platzman, 1972; Rao and Schwab, 1976). The numerical methods have
performed satisfactorily when tested against adequate data sets. In Lake
Superior and Lake Michigan, for example (Mortimer and Fee, 1976), the numerical
and experimental results both show seiche structures in which nodal lines (without
rotation) have been replaced by nodal points of amphidromic systems, from which
the co-phase lines radiate, and around which "high water" completes one cyclonic
rotation every seiche period.

An approximate model of such an amphidromic system is provided by a pair of
identical Kelvin waves travelling in opposing directions along a straight rotating
channel of unchanging rectangular cross-section (Fig. 6). (For the purposes of
illustration, the elevation and current amplitudes illustrated under (b) in
Figure 6, are not always the sum of the contributions from the two progressive
waves under (a). Half-wavelength portions are shown, and the wave topography
can be viewed either as that of the water surface, or as that of a "thermocline"
interface in a two-layered model, in which case horizontal components of the wave
currents in the lower layer are projected onto the plane below the channel.) Wave
amplitude (and corresponding current amplitude) is at a maximum along the channel
side lying to the right (in N. Hemisphere) of the direction of wave progress.
The amplitude decreases exponentially in an offshore (x) direction, being proportional to $\exp(-fx/c)$, in which f is the Coriolis parameter ($f = 1.056 \times 10^{-4}$ at
Lat. 46°24' for Léman), x is distance along a perpendicular to the channel side,
and c is the wave phase speed or celerity. If g is the acceleration of gravity
and h is the channel depth, the celerity of a surface Kelvin wave, C_o, is given
by $\sqrt{gh}$. The celerity, C_i, of an internal Kelvin wave in a two-layered channel
is given by $C_i^2 = g(\rho_2 - \rho_1)h_1 h_2/\rho_2(h_1 + h_2)$ in which h_1 and h_2 are the thicknesses
and ρ_1 and ρ_2 the densities of the upper and lower layer, respectively. For a
Léman-equivalent channel (8 km wide, 170 m deep, $f = 1.056 \times 10^{-4}$, and with the
two-layer parameters as used to construct Fig. 4 the surface and internal Kelvin
wave speeds are: C_o 40 m s^{-1}; and C_i 43 cm s^{-1} respectively. Important to note
is that the amplitude of the surface Kelvin wave in mid-channel is only 1% less
than the maximum amplitude at the channel side, whereas it is 63% less for the
internal Kelvin wave. Therefore Figure 6, with a cross-channel amplitude ratio
of 100/17, is an approximate representation of the Léman internal seiche; but it
is only an approximation, and Figure 6 is not a true standing wave, because the
currents (at the ends of the half-wavelength sections shown) fall to low values
but are not always zero (except at the center-channel point). Therefore Figure
6 cannot satisfy the solid boundary conditions of any cross-channel barrier. The
complete closed basin solution (i.e. solving the problem of Kelvin wave reflection)
was given by Taylor (1920) and more directly in Rao's (1966, 1977) treatment of

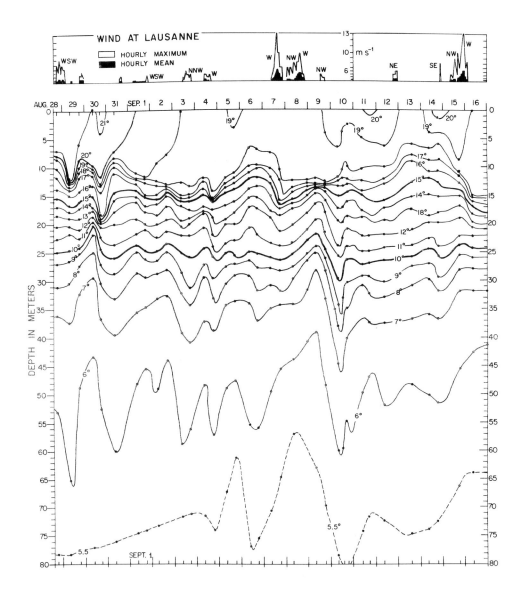

Fig. 7. Léman 1950: fluctuations in isotherm depth at a station 1.2 km off
Thonon (Haute Savoie), water depth 80 m, 28 Aug.–16 Sept.; wind at Lausanne
Cité. The survey (profiles approximately twice-daily) was carried out in
collaboration with Dr. B. H. Dussart and colleagues, Station de Biologie
Lacustre. (Published with other information in Mortimer 1963, in which wind
speeds were erroneously scaled in km h^{-1}.)

the rectangular rotating basin case. In those solutions, as in Figure 6, the unimodal interface wave progresses cyclonically in a counterclockwise direction around the basin (see later Fig. 10).

Does the real internal seiche show cyclonic progression in Léman? As I pointed out in 1963 and 1974, a fortunate set of circumstances permitted that question to be answered. Thermocline seiche waves are accompanied by very small surface waves of the same period but opposite in phase. The surface/internal amplitude ratio is roughly $(\rho_2 - \rho_1)/\rho_2$; and so small a signature can only be detected if the much larger surface seiches and short-period fluctuations are filtered out. That was possible for Léman--but not yet for any other lake to my knowledge-- because, in a 1949-50 leveling survey (Bircher, 1954), French and Swiss engineers obtained nearly continuous records from seventeen recorders around the lake, and were kind enough to provide me with copies. By chance also in the same year, Dr. B. H. Dussart and I measured temperature profiles at an 80-m deep station off Thonon at roughly twice-daily intervals from 28 August to 16 September (Fig. 7).

Consider now the comparisons in Figure 8. The "surface deviations" of Thonon and Sécheron (Geneva), St. Sulpice, and Chillon were obtained by low-pass filtration of the records from each station (6-hourly means centered at 3 h intervals) followed by subtraction of the ensemble mean level for all eight stations used in the preparation of later Figure 9. The mean thermocline depth at Thonon was determined by planimetry of whole-degree isotherms, 13° to 18°, in Figure 7. The average density of the 0-80 m water column on each sampling occasion was obtained by conversion of the temperature profile, using density tables for pure water uncorrected for pressure. The deviation of the column average from the mean for all profiles is plotted over the range ±0.1 σ_t, i.e. in units of $10^3 (1 - \rho)$. The correlations are remarkably close and of correct sign. For example, temperature rise (falling thermocline) at the Geneva intake is corre- lated with a rising water surface at nearby Sécheron; and surface rise at Thonon accompanies an increase in thermocline depth and a decrease in mean column-density there. It appears that surface deviation may be used with confidence to follow local movements of the thermocline at other stations, for example at St. Sulpice and at Chillon in Figure 8.

The interval covered by Figure 8 includes two storm episodes: a short WSW impulse on 28 August which set the internal seiche in motion; and a westerly storm of longer duration on 7-8 September. The first response to both storms was not--as might have been expected--a thermocline descent (positive surface deviation) at Chillon coupled with a thermocline ascent (negative deviation) at Geneva, but was a marked thermocline descent (strongly positive deviation) at Thonon, i.e. on the shore lying to the right of the wind direction. That thermo- cline descent was caused by the deflecting (Coriolis) force of Earth's rotation acting upon the storm-generated upper-layer current, turning it to the right.

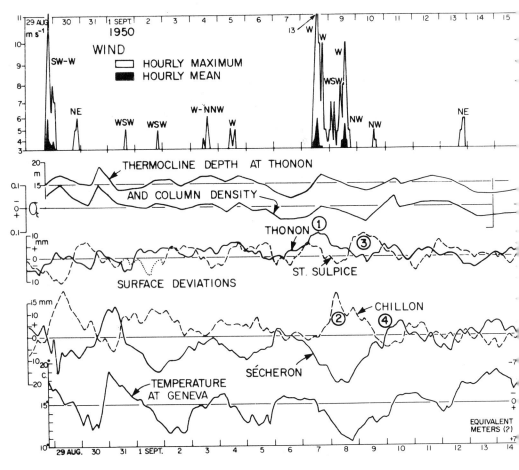

Fig. 8. Léman, 28 Aug. to 14 Sept. 1950: deviations, from the whole-lake mean (defined in the text), of water level at Thonon, St. Sulpice, Chillon, and Sécheron, compared with wind at Lausanne Cité. Surface deviation at Thonon is compared with inverted thermocline depth (mean of 13° to 17° isotherms, Fig. 7) and deviation of water column density (0-80 m, $\sigma_t = 10^3 (1 - \rho)$) from the mean for the whole interval (Fig. 7). Surface deviation at Sécheron is also compared with temperature at the Geneva city water intake (depth 15 m)--the "equivalent m" conversion is based on a gradient of 0.65° m^{-1} (Fig. 3).

Both storm perturbations set a train of internal seiche waves in motion marked by counterclockwise progress of surface deviation maxima, illustrated for example by the number sequence 1 to 4 in Figure 8 and more fully in Figure 9. At an internal Kelvin wave speed of 43 cm s^{-1}, computed and defined earlier, the wave would require 4 days to travel 150 km around the basin. That period is longer than the "observed" period in Figure 9, i.e. approximately 3.5 days during the episode following the 28 August storm. The period given by the Defant's calculation (Fig. 4) is even shorter, 3.0 days. A further step in

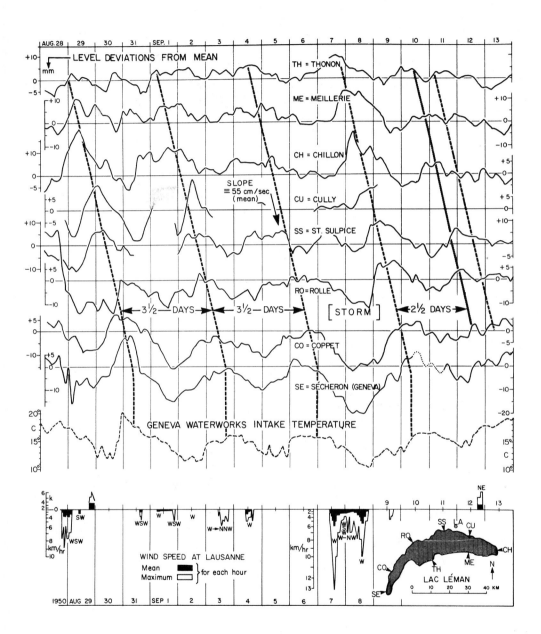

Fig. 9. Léman, 28 Aug. to 13 Sept. 1950: deviations (defined in the text) of water levels at eight shore stations from the whole-lake mean, compared with wind at Lausanne Cité and with temperature at Geneva city water intake (15 m depth). (From Mortimer 1974)

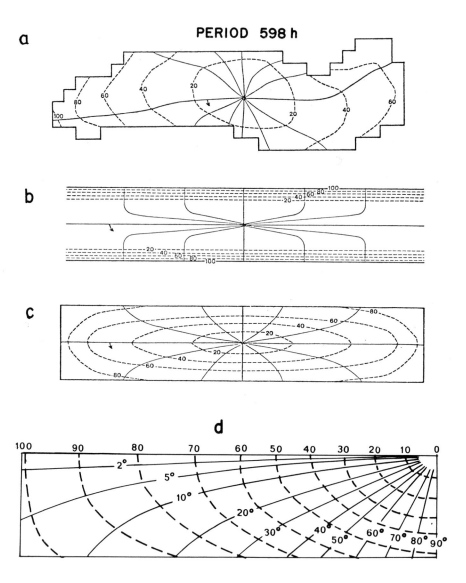

Fig. 10. Models of internal Kelvin-like waves on the interface between two layers: (a) amplitude (% of maximum, shown as broken lines) and phase (in increments of 30°, 0° marked by arrow indicating direction of propagation) associated with lowest Kelvin-type mode calculated for Lake Ontario (Schwab, 1977); (b) comparable calculation for two oppositely-propagating internal Kelvin waves in a channel (Schwab, 1977); (c) comparable calculation for a rectangular basin (Schwab, unpublished); (d) amplitude distribution and phase progression of an interfacial wave in a physical model, a 2-layered rotating basin (redrawn from Suberville, 1976, rotation period 50.4 s, wave period 36.6 s, ¼ of basin illustrated, cf. also Chabert-d'Hières and Suberville, 1974).

model evolution is clearly needed, comparable to the step taken for surface seiches in going from Defant's one-dimensional numerical procedure to the two-dimensional calculation of the period and structure of free surface modes in irregular basins, taking rotation into account (Rao and Schwab, 1976).

That step has, in fact, recently been taken by Schwab (1977) with an application of Rao and Schwab's single-layer technique to a two-layered model fitted to Lake Ontario's outline. Although the method does not permit depth variation—i.e. the "equivalent depth" $(h_1 h_2)/(h_1 + h_2)$ must be kept constant—the results are encouragingly realistic, reproducing the structure of Kelvin-like modes with periods much greater than intertial and Poincaré-like modes with periods close to but slightly less than inertial. (The correspondence of the predicted structures with those observed in Lake Ontario and other very large lakes goes beyond the scope of this paper. Internal Poincaré waves are the subject of research in progress, Mortimer, 1977.) For qualitative[*] comparisons with the Léman internal seiche, Figure 10 illustrates the amplitude distribution and phase progression of the first Kelvin-like mode in Schwab's Lake Ontario model and the comparable structures he computed for a rotating rectangular basin and channel. Of interest also is the experimental result of Chabert-d'Hières and Suberville, 1974 (see also Suberville, 1976) in a two-layered rectangular basin on the rotating table at the University of Grenoble. An experiment, on that table, with a two-layered model of Léman, with appropriate ratios of seiche mode periods to rotation periods, would yield interesting results.

Before committing a great deal of effort to large numerical models of the two-layered type (for example, Kizlauskas and Katz, 1974, Lake Michigan) or the multilayered type (for example, Simons, 1973, 1974, 1975) I believe an application of Schwab's model to Léman would reproduce the principal features of the real internal amphidromic seiche. Another short cut is possible, which appears justified in the light of the good performance of the Defant procedure in predicting the surface seiche periods of Léman (Table 1) when enough well-placed cross-sections are used. That short cut was taken by F. Defant (1953) in a study of the effect of Earth's rotation on surface seiches of Lake Michigan. He used his father's method to compute the distribution of current speed (as in Fig. 1) and then made the assumption—not unreasonable as it turned out (Fig. 11)—that the along-basin currents were everywhere in geostrophic equilibrium, i.e. that the Coriolis force was balanced by a pressure gradient created by a cross-basin slope of the water surface. The pattern created by Defant's combination of the seiche contribution and the geostrophic contribution is an amphidromic one, with counterclockwise progression of high water.

---

[*] Not quantitative because the ratios of rotation period to seiche period are very different.

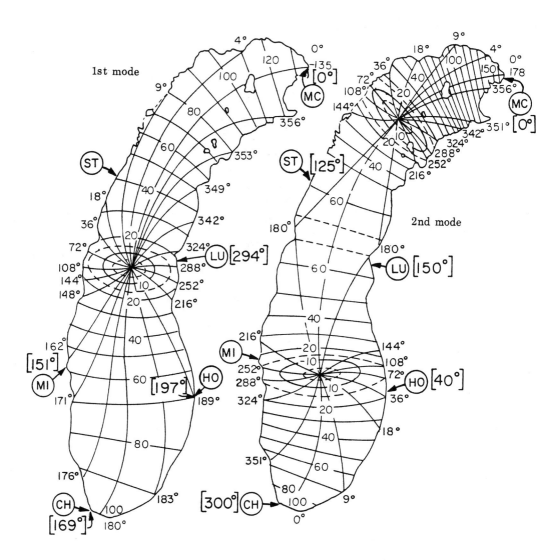

Fig. 11. Defant's (1953) model of the phase progressions (co-tidal lines with phase angles relative to 0° at MC) and elevation distributions (co-range lines relative to 100 at CH) of the first and second free longitudinal surface modes of oscillation of Lake Michigan. Compared with the model are <u>observed</u> station phase angles [in square brackets] also relative to 0° at MC, <u>determined</u> (Mortimer and Fee, 1976) by cross-spectral analysis of water level records at pairs of stations, yielding interstation coherence and phase information.

Adapting F. Defant's scheme to the two-layered Léman case, the velocity
differences between the upper and lower layers (taken from Figure 4 at each
section and at appropriate intervals throughout the seiche cycle) may be used
to calculate the transverse slopes (angle α) of the interface at each section
from Margules equation: $\tan \alpha = f(u_1 - u_2)\rho_2/g(\rho_2 - \rho_1)$, in which f is the
Coriolis parameter (1.56×10^{-4} at Lat. 46°25'), g is the acceleration of gravity,
and $u_1 u_2$ and $\rho_1 \rho_2$ are the respective current speeds and densities of the upper
and lower layers. For example, at the point in the internal seiche cycle illustrated in Figure 4 at Section 12 (interface width 3.3 km) $(u_1 - u_2)$ is 10 cm s^{-1};
and the geostrophic cross-channel interface slope at that section is 76 cm km^{-1},
yielding a 2.5 m difference in interface level between the two ends of the
section. At Section 18 (speed difference 4.6 cm s^{-1}, interface width 8.9 km)
near the internal uninode, the corresponding slopes and level differences are
35 cm km^{-1} and 3.1 m. The full calculation has yet to be done. Kanari (1975)
has compared the results of a similar calculation with a two-layered numerical
model used to interpret the observed, apparently amphidromic internal seiche in
Lake Biwa, Japan.

The emphasis placed in this lecture on whole-basin internal responses to
wind impulses must not be taken to suggest that other responses are unimportant
in Léman. Shorter internal waves with periods of minutes (Brunt-Väsälä waves)
and near-inertial waves in the central region of the lake with periods of 16 h
and less are to be expected. As I have reviewed these in some detail elsewhere
(1971, 1974, 1977) further discussion here is *de trop*. All these components
and various internal and surface seiche modes will contribute intermittently
to the complexity of current patterns and will appear as perturbations, sometimes
weak sometimes strong, on the steadier wind- and gradient-driven circulations
of the kind which Bauer et al. (1977) have begun to model (initially during the
unstratified season) and which Prost et al. (1977) are proceeding to verify by
in-lake measurement.

The non-linear character of internal seiches

Each of the models which I have so far described or suggested are based on
linear shallow-water theory. While the simplicity of that theory assists the
interpretation of surface seiches and small-amplitude internal waves, the large
amplitudes of real internal seiches, relative to layer thicknesses, introduce
non-linear effects more complex to simulate and with important consequences for
exchanges of energy and materials within a lake. For example, the simple two-
layered seiche model in Figure 4 is clearly inadequate near the end of the Petit
Lac with an interface swing of ±3 m and average upper layer thickness of only 15
m. Simple harmonic motion can no longer be assumed, and the wave-form will

204

change. Wedderburn and Young (1915) were the first to demonstrate this phenomenon (Fig. 12) and to attempt to model it with a two-layer adaptation of Chrystal's
surface seiche equation:

> "Since this equation is not linear a simple harmonic type of oscillation
> is not possible, and as the oscillation progresses there will be a change
> of type. In the deeper parts of the loch the ratio between amplitude
> and depth is smaller, and a change of type will be the more easily
> averted by a slight adjustment of the velocities of the water particles.
> Towards the ends of the loch, however, when the amplitude is large,
> considerable distortion of the wave surface may be expected. The
> suddenness of the fall of the isotherms which has been noted is also
> probably largely due to the change in type of the wave in shallow
> water. Where the amplitude of the oscillations is large, it is
> probable that the isotherms will move very rapidly indeed, and possibly
> the wave may break, just as travelling surface waves break on a shelving
> beach. If there is such breaking of the density wave strong currents
> will probably occur. . . ."

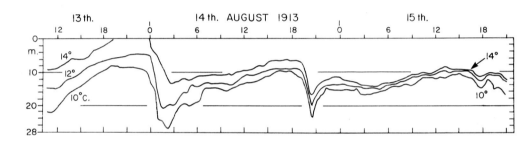

Fig. 12. Variation in isotherm depth at a station about 250 m from the W end
of Loch Earn, Scotland, in 30 m of water (Wedderburn and Young, 1915).

To explore the internal seiche in Loch Ness I moored (1955) three thermistor
chains (at stations FA, FE, and FW in later Figure 14) and connected them to
recorders ashore. Records from FA, near the SW end of the loch, showed large
oscillations of thermocline depth associated with wind forcing or with the free
internal seiche oscillation. Isotherm descent (downwelling) was much more
rapid than ascent, as in Loch Earn. An example is shown, with a primitive
graphical analysis, in Figure 13. When the harmonic components of the seiche
(in the form of damped sinusoids) are removed, an internal surge remains, which
travels to-and-fro along the basin with decreasing amplitude. It can be seen
passing the mid-loch stations (FE, FW) and returning again after reflection at
the end. As the 9° FE and FW isotherms show (at the bottom of Figure 13), the
surge amplitude is noticably greater on the basin side lying to the right of
the direction of surge progress--a consequence of Earth's rotation. Internal
Kelvin-type waves were also seen in temperature records from waterworks intakes
from Lake Michigan (Mortimer, 1963). They also exhibit non-linear features,

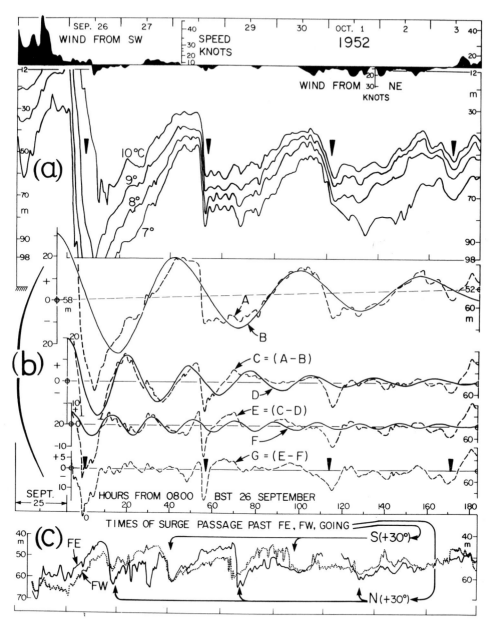

Fig. 13. Loch Ness 1952, internal seiche and surge response following a storm: (a) Hourly mean depths of thermocline isotherms, 24 Sept.-3 Oct., at FA near SW end of basin (Fig. 14i) interpolated from temperature at 9 depths, 12 to 98 m (bottom at 112 m); wind speed (10 knots = 5.15 m s^{-1}) on land near FA; (b) graphical analysis of the 9°C isotherm oscillation (arrowheads indicate fundamental period 57 h) using damped cosine "harmonics" (amplitudes in m, time t in h, r = t/57) as follows: A = 9° isotherm; B = 32 cos 2πr.exp(-0.55r); C = (A - B); D = 20 cos 4πr.exp(-0.48r); E = (C - D); F = 6 cos 6πr.exp(-0.21r); (c) 30-min mean depths of 9° isotherm at stations FE and FW (see Fig. 14i).

206

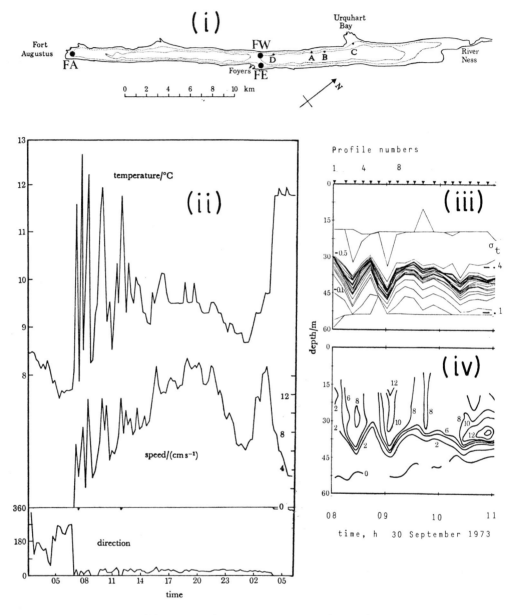

Fig. 14. Loch Ness: (i) map showing depth contours (dotted) at 91 and 183 m; positions of moorings (A, B, D) and thermistor chain (C) referred to by Thorpe (1977); and positions (FA, FE, FW) of thermistor chains (Mortimer, 1955) referred to in connection with Fig. 13; (ii) temperature, speed and direction of the current measured every 15 min at 35 m depth and about 50 m NE of mooring A from 0200, 30 September, to 0600 1 October 1973, showing the passage of the internal surge at about 0700, 30 September, and its return at about 0400 on 1 October (all times are G.M.T.); (iii) contours of density (σ_t) and (iv) contours of current (cm s^{-1}, 036° component) on 30 September. Profiles 1–8 are reproduced in Fig. 17. (These figure and part-figures are assembled from Thorpe, 1977.)

modelled by Bennett (1973).

In a series of field and laboratory experiments, which will surely serve as a paradigm for future research, Thorpe and collaborators (Thorpe, Hall and Crofts, 1972; Thorpe, 1971, 1974, 1977) have demonstrated that the Loch Ness internal surge has the character of an internal undular bore, analogous to a tidal bore, propagating at a speed of about 35 cm s^{-1} with a steep leading front followed by a train of internal undulations. The example illustrated in Figure 14(ii) is typical. Generated at the SW end of the loch by a large wind-induced depression of the isotherms (a mechanism was proposed by Thorpe, 1974) the surge moved northeastward past station A at about 0700 on 30 September, producing a rapid rise in temperature (fall of the thermocline) followed by a series of internal waves of about 40 min period and 1 km wavelength, illustrated in more detail in Figure 14(iii) and (iv). After reflection at the NE end of the basin (also seen in Fig. 13) the surge returned to A at about 0400 on 1 October. The steep surge front was retained, but the undulations had disappeared. A similar undulatory internal bore was observed by Hunkins and Fliegel (1972) in Seneca Lake; and it appears likely that a similar phenomenon will probably be seen in Léman, particularly in the Petit Lac, when large internal seiches are in progress. Note the surge-like responses of the thermocline at Thonon after each wind impulse in Figure 7.

Seiche-linked internal surges were also observed during high-resolution, cross-basin temperature surveys (Boyce and Mortimer, 1978) in Lake Ontario; but in that case the surges propagated not along, but across the basin, away from a region of strong downwelling (isotherm descent) along the southern shore, i.e. the shore lying to the right of the wind direction during the storm, which produced the downwelling and initially set the internal seiche and surges in motion. In other words, the small-lake (Loch Ness) picture is turned through a right-angle in the large lake (Ontario); and this is a consequence of Earth's rotation. Earlier we examined one class of internal seiche model (the Kelvin model) generated in basins large enough to show substantial influence of rotation. Another class, to which I drew attention in 1963, is the internal Poincaré wave model, which describes some features of observed cross-basin seiches in very large lakes, i.e. clockwise rotation of seiche-currents and wave periods little less than the local inertial period. These "near-inertial" waves are not considered in this lecture; but, in their case also, it appears that large-amplitude Poincaré waves and their precursors--downwelling events--generate surges similar to those seen in smaller lakes.

The Ontario internal surge, with rotating currents, has recently been analyzed and modelled by Simons (1978); and because his numerical simulations of this particular episode showed satisfactory agreement with the observations, he concludes:

"that the basic dynamics of the downwelling front are explained by the nonlinear wave principles considered here. The recurrence of the front after an inertial period and the proper phase relationship between thermocline deflections and inertial currents, confirm that the observed downwelling fronts are intimately connected with the oscillatory action of the inertial motion in deep water. Thus, while less detailed observations of similar temperature distributions could easily be interpreted as manifestations of baroclinic jets, the fronts are to be visualized as part of the oscillatory rather than the quasi-geostrophic response of the Lake to wind. Although disturbances from the opposite upwelling shore may eventually combine with those from the downwelling shore to create standing Poincaré waves (Mortimer, 1977), the scale of the frontal zone is sufficiently small that it can be treated independently of this effect. Thus, similar phenomena can be expected to occur in any near-shore region for suitable stratification conditions."

GENERATION OF TURBULENCE AND MIXING

While internal seiches, including those in Léman, remain fascinating objects of study--with much still to be learnt about their generation by wind action-- their principal interest for limnologists and lake managers lies in their contribution to the generation of turbulence and consequent mixing. Seiche currents represent only one class of flow contributing to generation of turbulence-- wind-driven currents are another important class--but internal seiche currents and internal wave currents generally are characterized by development of internal shears in stratified layers, for example across the thermocline interface between an upper and a lower layer, moving in opposing directions. It has long been recognized (since Richardson, 1920) that the growth or suppression of turbulence in a vertically stratified fluid, subject also to vertical shear, depends on the balance between mechanical energy supplied by the shear and the loss of energy in opposing the buoyancy force associated with the vertical density gradient. On which side that balance falls--turbulence suppression or growth--is determined by the well-known dimensionless ratio, the Richardson Number, Ri. If Ri is greater than ¼, the shearing flow remains stable; if Ri is less than ¼, instability can develope as illustrated in Figure 15. Initially small perturbations of the flow grow into steepening internal waves, which curl up as rolling vortices, intensifying turbulence and mixing. That type of unstable flow is often termed Kelvin-Helmholtz (K-H) instability. Thorpe and Hall (1974) named the rolling vortices "K-H billows." The K-H instability is a most important mixing agent in lakes; but it occurs very episodically, is usually generated during and just after storms, and is localized in regions of temporarily high shear. The products of the mixing are later transported to other regions by advection (Mortimer, 1961).

The controlling influence of instrument development on progress in limnology is clearly but painfully illustrated by the paradox that Ri, recognized as perhaps the most important parameter in physical limnology, has rarely been determined in the field. The reason is simple. Whereas it has long been easy

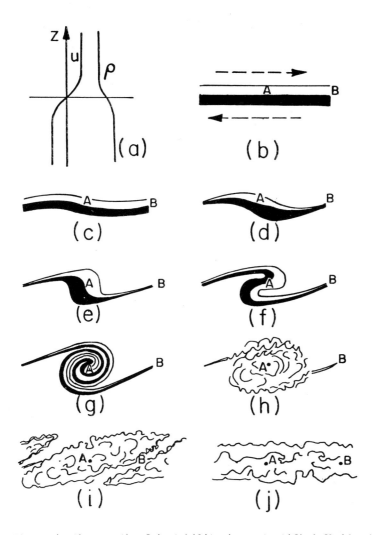

Fig. 15. Stages in the growth of instability in a stratified fluid subject to shear and with a Richardon Number below the critical level: (a) initial vertical distributions of current speed (u) and density (ρ); (b) the initial configuration with A and B as fixed points; (c) to (f) growth of unstable internal waves; (g) vortex ("billow") formation; (h) to (j) convectional collapse of the vortices and spread of the mixed product (redrawn from Thorpe, 1969).

to measure vertical density profiles with precision, it has only recently become possible to obtain sufficiently detailed profiles of vertical shear using novel instruments, for example the cyclesonde (Van Leer et al., 1974) and Thorpe's profiling current meter (P.C.M.) illustrated in Figure 16(i). In Loch Ness (Thorpe, 1977) the P.C.M. was tethered to a sheave on the bottom at a point (A in Fig. 14) 250 m from shore and 174 m deep. A cable, connecting the P.C.M. to a shore recorder, was also used with a winch onshore to raise and lower the

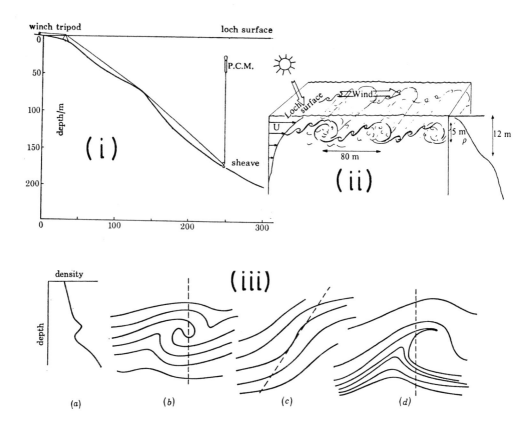

Fig. 16. (i) Arrangement for mooring and operating the Profiling Current Meter P.C.M. in Loch Ness; (ii) schematic diagram and estimated dimensions of billows in the upper layer of a lake, driven by the wind and heated by the sun and with mean vertical gradients of horizontal current and density, as shown; (iii) sketch of a density profile containing an apparent inversion, which would be recorded if the P.C.M. passed along the dotted-line track through either of the isotherm structures illustrated in (b), (c), or (d). Portions (i) and (iii) are from Thorpe (1977); portion (ii) is from Thorpe and Hall (1977).

instrument. I mention these details because this is a technique which could be used on steep shores of Léman.

Operated in this way, the P.C.M. provides a detailed picture of the vertical variation of density and of horizontal current (examples in Fig. 14 iii and iv). Interpretation of the profiles is not without difficulty, when the P.C.M. traverses the complexity of a K-H billow (Fig. 16 ii and iii); but Thorpe's painstaking and ingenious investigations--in Loch Ness where the study of internal waves in lakes began--represent a major step forward in our understanding of the turbulence-generating mechanisms in the thermocline and the upper wind-driven layers (Thorpe and Hall, 1977; Thorpe et al., 1977). The nature of the insight

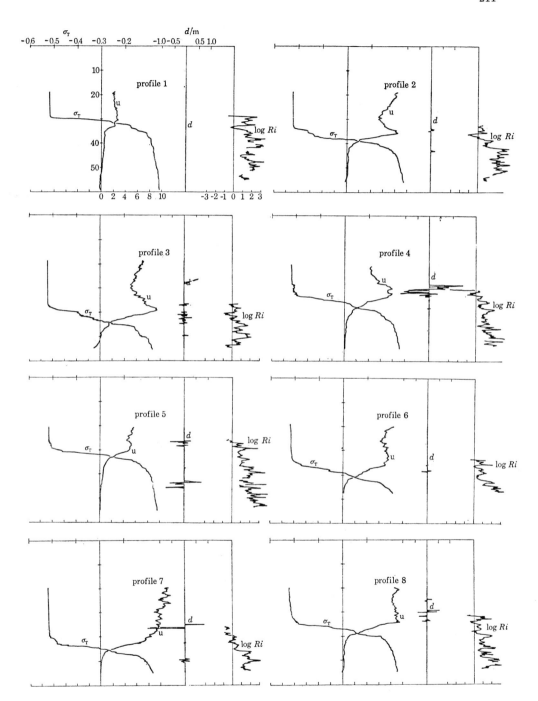

Fig. 17. Loch Ness, 30 Sept. 1973: profiles obtained with the P.C.M. (Thorpe, 1977): density (σ_t); current (u, 036° component, cm s⁻¹); displacements (d, defined in the text) and log Richardson number (Ri, computed for 1.06 m vertical interval)--the first eight profiles marked in Fig. 14(iii).

is disclosed by a fuller examination of the internal surge passage illustrated
in Figure 14.

The righthand portion of Figure 14 presents the density and along—basin
current—speed contours, determined from P.C.M. profiles made at the 10 min
intervals shown by arrows along the top of the figure. The profiling started
with the second undulation after arrival of the surge. Those undulations
measured 5 m from trough to crest. The wave currents, in phase with the troughs,
produced a 2 cm s^{-1} modulation on an 8 cm s^{-1} mean northeasterly flow in the
upper layer. Results from the first eight profiles (those numbered in Fig. 14)
are assembled in Figure 17. Displayed are the measured profiles of density,
$\sigma_t = 10^3(1 - \rho)$, and the NE component of horizontal current. From those profiles
are computed the Richardson Number (Ri over an interval of 1.06 m and plotted on
a log scale) and "displacement." The latter quantity is calculated when and
where temperature inversions (presumed instabilities) appear in the profile. To
do this, the observed profile is "rearranged" with minimum vertical movement of
its parts to achieve a stable profile, while conserving heat and mass. Those
minimal movements, computed for each profile increment corresponding to each
0.5 s time interval during ascent of the P.C.M., are the displacements. They
mark the depths at which instabilities are found and they provide a scale of
the vertical motions which those instabilities are expected to generate.

It is evident that the information content in Figure 17 is high. To indicate
its nature, I can do no better than quote Thorpe (1977, p. 161):

"The first profile, immediately preceding the second wave, is entirely
stable with no inversions which exceed the noise level of the P.C.M.,
but with small Richardson numbers developing in the thermocline at the
trough of the second wave, instability is observed (profile 3) with
inversions first occurring in the main gradient region of the thermocline and later at the edges, a pattern following that of Kelvin-
Helmholtz instability in laboratory experiments (Thorpe, 1973). It
is not evident from the profiles that the whole thermocline has become
involved in violent instability. What is likely, judging by the
Richardson numbers involved, is that very weak billows of small amplitude are produced (see Thorpe, 1973, figure 2e, f). Their wavelength
may be inferred from the density or velocity structure to be approximately 10-20 m, much less than the length of waves. The amplitude
of the displacements is at first about 25 cm (profile 3) but assumes
a larger scale at the edges of the main thermocline (profiles 4, 5).
The profiles of Richardson number are very irregular as expected in
internal wave trains....Profiles 2-4 show an interesting jet-like
feature near the regions of largest density gradient. In the third
wave (profiles 6-8) the Richardson number at the main thermocline
does not fall below 0.3 and the displacements which indicate the
presence of gravitational instability are neither so numerous or as
large as those which followed the passage of the second wave."

CONCLUDING REMARKS AND SUGGESTED RESEARCH STRATEGIES

The picture presented in this lecture has been deliberately selective, in order to focus on the evolutionary interplay of experiment and theory. Concentrating on whole-basin oscillatory motions and on smaller-scale instabilities in stratified shearing flow, I have no space left for discussion of other important classes of motion: (i) wind-driven currents; (ii) gradient-driven currents arising, for example, from non-uniformity in horizontal density distribution; (iii) whole-basin circulations which may be regarded as aperiodic on the time scale we have been considering (see Csanady, 1977, for discussion of mean cyclonic circulation in large lakes); (iv) inertial and near-inertial motions (my present interest); and (v) the whole spectrum of less organized horizontal and vertical turbulence. Turbulence greatly complicates the picture by superimposing eddy-like motions of varying intensity and scale on the mean circulations, on wind- and gradient-driven mean flows and on internal wave currents. Furthermore, as a consequence of basin geometry, eddy scales in the horizontal are very much greater than those in the vertical. Much theoretical and experimental effort has been devoted to studies of turbulent diffusion in natural waters; but predictive modelling of the turbulent transport and dispersal of materials--a matter of great practical concern--remains an uncertain art. This remains so, not only because of the chaotic and indeterminate nature of turbulence itself--which has engaged the best brains in geophysical fluid dynamics, since L. F. Richardson, Wilhelm Schmidt, and G. I. Taylor entered the field sixty years ago--but also because of the complexity of the mean flows upon which the turbulent fluctuations are superimposed. That complexity arises from the variety of origins and from the highly episodic and intermittent nature of force application (storm impulses). The underwater "weather" is no less complex than the above-water weather which drives it.

Forel knew this well. Although he only commanded one reversing thermometer and one small boat--no thermistor chains or current meters, no meteorological buoys or research vessels--he nevertheless observed and correctly interpreted responses of Léman to wind, including a number of coastal upwelling events and movements into and out of the Petit Lac, inferred from Turrentini's weekly temperature profiles mentioned earlier. As a shore-bound observer, *faute de mieux*, he noted evidence of occasionally strong sub-surface currents, often running against the wind, as disclosed by displacement of fishermen's drift nets (later systematically studied by Mercanton, 1932).

"Ces exemples montrent la grande irrégularité des courants. Peut-être si j'avais pu poursuivre plus longtemps l'observation, serais-je arrivé a y demeler des lois....Je recommande cette étude aux personnes en position de la faire utilement." (Le Léman, Vol. 2, p. 288)

Eighty years later, although much is known, much remains to be explored.

In conclusion therefore, and to justify my title, I give my "top ten" selection of strategies for meeting Forel's challenge, placing greater weight on signals from the lake itself, as clues to better physical understanding and as the only tests for realism in models.

1. Develop new tools (or improve old ones) to provide data-sets adequate to answer the questions posed, thereby exploiting the below-mentioned strategies to the fullest extent. Instrument development I have here put in a separate category, because repeated experience has shown that new tools have opened new doors to knowledge (for example Thorpe's profiling current meter) but that research-funding agencies have been generally reluctant to provide adequate development funds. The tools I have in mind are: profilers (tethered and free-floating) to repeatedly measure physical and chemical structure; depth-undulating instrument packages, towed by moving vessels (Boyce and Mortimer, 1978); drifting instruments which transmit their position and environmental information from various depths in the water column to shore-based recorders. Data resolution must be adequate to answer critical questions and to remove aliasing errors where spectral and cross-spectral analyses are to be performed. At the same time some preliminary analysis can be carried out, for example by microprocessors built into the instruments, in order to lighten the enormous data-processing load, as is done in vector-averaging current meters, for example. And, as instruments increase in sensitivity and cost, more attention must be paid to methods of mounting and recovering them.

2. Provide better coverage, in space and time, of meteorological forces acting on the water surface. Wind stress and its horizontal distribution over the whole water surface is a critical variable, but it is usually the least well defined.

3. Explore whole-basin circulations and horizontal dispersal and diffusion patterns. To study the complete anatomy of dispersal and diffusion in a coherent, near-synoptic manner is a difficult task, not fully attempted as yet. A combination of Eulerian (fixed instrument) and Lagrangian (drifting instrument) measurements are needed to characterize motions over a wide spectrum of length-scales, to elucidate the linkages and energy fluxes between them, and to provide an integrated description of a lake's response to meteorological forcing. To perform this task adequately requires expensive multi-station networks of instruments. These should be shared on a national and international basis, re-deployed where needed in other lakes or oceans.

4. Explore episodic and localized instabilities in stratified flows and subsequent advection. Because it is the local value of the Richardson

Number which determines whether or not turbulence decays or grows in a
stratified fluid subject to shearing flow, the instabilities are as episodic
as the storms which generate them; and they are often very localized, at
the nodes of internal waves for example, or at the downwind end of a wind-
blown lake basin. After the instability subsides, the products of mixing
(see Fig. 15) then spread by advection; the newly mixed layers seek their
appropriate density levels.

5. Explore the vertical microstructure of density and current distribution
   using repeatedly profiling instruments, attended and unattended. Examination of profiles in detail can, as thorpe has shown, provide clues to the
   mechanisms generating or suppressing the instabilities discussed in
   paragraph 4.

6. Design programs of in-lake measurements to provide, not only long data
   series from fixed stations or frequent visits by research vessels, but
   also repeated scans of the whole basin cross-sectional distributions of
   significant variables, using depth-undulating instruments towed from ferries
   or research vessels. Where possible the fixed-station recorders should be
   deployed along the vessel tracks. This strategy has demonstrated its value
   in the International Field Year Program on Lake Ontario (examples in
   Mortimer, 1977; Boyce and Mortimer, 1978).

7. Collect data-series and clues to lake behavior from all available recording
   points, for example municipal or industrial lake-water intake pipes, level
   recording stations, meteorological services, and other routine sampling
   agencies. Water temperature and chemical data from intakes can be a valuable
   source of information on intermittent events as well as long-term changes.

8. Use naturally occurring and introduced isotopes to study water-mass exchanges
   and water mass aging on time scales which cannot be approached by other
   methods. (No examples of this strategy are given here; they were the
   subject of another workshop and another lecture, Mortimer, 1978).

9. Exploit simple analytical and numerical models for the physical insight they
   provide, and as stepping-stones to further model evolution and verification.
   The use of more elaborate numerical models as research tools for exploration
   of particular mechanisms in detail (air-water interaction or unstable stratified flow, for example) will then lead to a fuller understanding and
   provide the best foundation for building universality and predictive
   capability into lake circulation models and for designing new field
   experiments to test them.

10. And finally--although more of a distant objective than a strategy--
    develope improved couplings between hydrodynamic and ecosystem models.
    The development of limnology as an integrated science and the design of
    enlightened public management of lakes both require such couplings to be

soundly established. That, in my view, is the main challenge facing limnology today and one which we should constantly have in mind while concentrating, as we do in this symposium, on lake hydrodynamics.

REFERENCES

Ball, F.K. 1965. The effect of rotation on the simpler modes of motion of a liquid in an elliptic paraboloid. J. Fluid Mech. 22: 529-545.

Barber, N.F., F. Ursell, and M.J. Tucker. 1946. A frequency analyser used in the study of ocean waves. Nature, London, 158: 329-332.

Bauer, S.W., W.H. Graf, and E. Tischer. 1977. Les courants dans le Léman: Les courants dans le Léman en saison froide une simulation mathematique. École polytech. féd., Lausanne, Switzerland, Publ. 164: 1-7.

Bèche, H-T de la. 1819. Sur la profondeur et la température du Lac de Genève. Bibl. Univ. Sci. et Arts, Genève.

Bennett, J.R. 1973. A theory of large amplitude Kelvin waves. J. Phys. Oceanogr., 3: 57-60.

Bircher, H. 1954. Les dénivellations du Lac Léman. Comm. Serv. féd. Eaux, 40: 103 pp., 18 graphs, tables. Dept. féd. postes, chemins de fer, Berne, Switzerland.

Birge, E.A. 1910. On the evidence for temperature seiches. Trans. Wisconsin Acad. Sci. Arts. Lett., 16: 1005-1016.

Boyce, F.M.* and C.H. Mortimer.* 1978. IFYGL Temperature Transects: temperature distributions across three sections of Lake Ontario continuously traversed over four-day intervals in July, August, and October 1972. Technical Bull. No. 100, Inland Waters Directorate, Environment Canada, 315 pp. (*principal investigators with collaboration of: D.N. Baumgartner, J.A. Bull, D.L. Cutchin and W.J. Moody.)

Chabert-d'Hières, G. and J.L. Suberville. 1974. Ondes internes à l'interface de deux fluides de densités voisines contenus dans un bassin rectangulaire tournant. La Houille Blanche, 1974: No. 7/8, 623-630.

Chrystal, J. 1905. On the hydrodynamical theory of seiches. Trans. Roy. Soc. Edinburgh, 41: 599-649.

_____. 1906 and 1908. An investigation of the seiches of Loch Earn by the Scottish Lake Survey. Parts I and II, Trans. Roy. Soc. Edinburgh, 45 (1906): 361-396. Parts III-V, 46 (1908): 455-516.

Chrystal, J. and E.M. Wedderburn. 1905. Calculation of the periods and nodes of Lochs Earn and Treig from the bathymetric data of the Scottish Lake Survey. Trans. Roy. Soc. Edinburgh, 41: 823-850.

Comstock, C.B. 1872. Tides at Milwaukee, Wisconsin. Ann. Rep. Survey of the Northern and Northwestern Lakes, Appendix A, p. 9-14, Pl. I-V.: Irregular oscillations in surface of Lake Michigan at Milwaukee. Appendix B, p. 14-15.

Csanady, G.T. 1977. On the cyclonic mean circulation of large lakes. Proc. Nat. Acad. Sci., U.S.A., 74: 2204-2208.

Defant, A. 1918. Neue Methode zur Ermittlung der Eigenschwingungen (Seiches) von abgeschlossenen Wassermassen (Seen, Buchten, usw.).--Ann. Hydrogr. Berlin 46: 78-85.

_____. 1960. Physical oceanography--Pergamon, London, Vol. II, 598 pp.

Defant, F. 1953. Theorie der Seiches des Michigansees und ihre Abwandlung durch Wirkung der Corioliskraft. Arch. Met. Geophys. Bioklimatol. Wien. A 6, 218–241.

Doodson, A.T., R.M. Carey, and R. Baldwin. 1920. Theoretical determination of the longitudinal seiches of Lake Geneva. Trans. Roy. Soc. Edinburgh, 52: 629–642.

Forel, F.A. 1873. Première étude sur les seiches. Bull. Soc. Vaudoise des Sci. Natur., 12: 213.

_____. 1892, 1895, 1904. Le Léman: Monographie limnologique. Vol. 1 (1892), 539 pp., Vol. 2 (1895), 651 pp., Vol. 3 (1904), 715 pp. F. Rouge, Lausanne.

Hunkins, K. and M. Fliegel. 1972. Internal undular surges in Seneca Lake: a natural occurrence of solitons. J. Geophys. Res., 78: 539–548.

Kanari, S. 1975. The long-period internal waves in Lake Biwa. Limnol. Oceanogr., 20: 544–553.

Kizlauskas, A.G. and P.L. Katz. 1976. A numerical model for summer flows in Lake Michigan. Arch. Met. Geoph. Biokl., Vienna, Ser. A, 23: 181–197.

Mercanton, P-L. 1932. Étude de la circulation des eaux de Lac Léman. Mem. Soc. Vaudoise Sci. Nat., 4: 225–271, 5 pl.

Mortimer, C.H. 1953. The resonant response of stratified lakes to wind. Schweiz. Z. Hydrol., 15: 94–151.

_____. 1955. Some effects of the earth's rotation on water movements in stratified lakes. Verh. Int. Ver. Limnol., 12: 66–77.

_____. 1961. Motion in Thermoclines. Verh. Int. Ver. Limnol., 14: 79–82.

_____. 1963. Frontiers in physical limnology with particular reference to long waves in rotating basins. Proc. 6th Conf. Great Lakes Res., Univ. Michigan, Great Lakes Res. Div., Publ. No. 10: 9–42.

_____. 1965. Spectra of long surface waves and tides in Lake Michigan and at Green Bay, Wisconsin. Proc. 8th Conf. Great Lakes Res., Great Lakes Res. Div., Univ. Michigan, Publ. No. 13, 304–325.

_____. 1971. Large-scale oscillatory motions and seasonal temperature changes in Lake Michigan and Lake Ontario. Center for Great Lakes Studies, Univ. Wisconsin-Milwaukee, Spec. Rept. No. 12: Part I text, 111 pp.; Part II illustrations, 106 pp.

_____. 1974. Lake Hydrodynamics. Mitt. int. Ver. Limnol., 20: 124–197.

_____. 1975. Substantive corrections to SIL Communications (IVL Mitteilungen) Numbers 6 and 20. Verhandl. int. Verh. Limnol., 19: 60–72.

_____. 1977. Internal waves observed in Lake Ontario during the International Field Year for the Great Lakes (IFYGL) 1972: Descriptive survey and preliminary interpretations of near-inertial oscillations in terms of linear channel-wave models. Center for Great Lakes Studies Spec. Rept. No. 32, Univ. Wisconsin--Milwaukee, 122 pp.

_____. 1978. Some central questions of lake dynamics. Introductory lecture in report by Advisory Group on "Applications of nuclear techniques to the study of lake dynamics", International Atomic Energy Agency, Vienna, 29 August–2 September, 1977.

_____ and E.J. Fee. 1976. Free surface oscillations and tides of Lakes Michigan and Superior. Phil. Trans. Roy. Soc., London, A, 281: 1–61.

Platzman, G.W. 1972. Two-dimensional free oscillations in natural basins. J. Phys. Oceanogr. 2, 117–138.

Prost, J-P., S.W. Bauer, W.H. Graf, and H. Girod. 1977. Les courants dans le Léman: Campagne de mesure des courants dans le Léman., École polytech. féd. Lausanne, Switzerland, Publ. 164: 5, 8–11.

Rao, D.B. 1966. Free gravitational oscillations in rotating rectangular basins. J. Fluid Mech., 25: 523–555.

_____. 1977. Free internal oscillations in a narrow, rotating rectangular basin. Mar. Sci. Directorate, Dept. Fish. Environ., Ottawa, Ms. Rept. Ser. No. 43, 391–398.

_____, and D.J. Schwab. 1976. Two-dimensional normal modes in arbitrary enclosed basins on a rotating earth: Application to Lakes Ontario and Superior. Phil. Trans. Roy. Soc., London, A, 281, 63–96.

Richardson, L.F. 1920. The supply of energy from and to atmospheric eddies. Proc. Roy. Soc., A, 97: 354–373.

Saussure, H-B de. 1799. Voyages dans les Alpes.,Neuchâtel.

Schwab, D.J. 1977. Internal free oscillations in Lake Ontario. Limnol. Oceanogr. 22, 700–708.

Servais, F. 1957. Étude théorique des oscillations libres (Seiches) du Lac Tanganika, "Exploration hydrobiologique du Lac Tanganika (1946-1947)", Resultats Scientifiques: Vol. II, Fasc. 3, 311 pp. Inst. Roy. Sci. Nat. de Belgique, Brussels.

Simons, T.J. 1973. Development of three-dimensional numerical models of the Great Lakes. Sci. Ser. No. 12, Canada Ctr. for Inland Waters, Burlington, Ont., Canada, 26 pp.

_____. 1974. Verification of numerical models of Lake Ontario: Part I. Circulation in spring and early summer. J. Phys. Oceanogr. 4: 507–532.

_____. 1975. Verification of numerical models of Lake Ontario: Part II. Stratified circulations and temperature changes. J. Phys. Oceanogr. 5: 98–110.

_____. 1978. Generation and propagation of downwelling fronts. J. Phys. Oceanogr. 8: 571–581.

Suberville, J-L. 1974. Ondes internes en fluide tournant: contribution théorique et expérimentale. Dr.-ing. thesis, Univ. Grenoble, 291 pp.

Taylor, G.I. 1920. Tidal oscillations in gulfs and rectangular basins. Proc. Lond. Math. Soc., 2nd Ser. 20: 148–181.

Thorpe, S.A. 1969. Experiments on the stability of stratified shear flows. Radio Sci. (Amer. Geophys. Un.), 4: 1327–1331.

_____. 1971. Assymetry of the internal seiche in Loch Ness. Nature, London, 231: 306–308.

_____. 1973. Turbulence in stably stratified fluids: a review of laboratory experiments. Boundary-Layer Meteorol. 5: 95–119.

_____. 1973. Experiments on instability and turbulence in a stratified shear flow. J. Fluid Mech. 61: 731–751.

_____. 1974. Near resonant forcing in a shallow two-layer fluid: a model for the internal surge in Loch Ness? J. Fluid Mech. 63: 509–527.

_____. 1977. Turbulence and mixing in a Scottish loch. Phil. Trans. Roy. Soc. London, A., 286: 125–181.

Thorpe, S.A., and A.J. Hall. 1974. Evidence of Kelvin-Helmholtz billows in Loch Ness. Limnology and Oceanography 19: 973–976.

_____, and A.J. Hall. 1977. Mixing in upper layer of a lake during heating cycle. Nature, Lond. 265: 719–722.

_____, A.J. Hall and I. Crofts. 1972. The internal surge in Loch Ness. Nature, Lond. 237: 96–98.

_____, A.J. Hall, C. Taylor, and T. Allen. 1977. Billows in Loch Ness. Deep–Sea Res., 24: 371–379.

Thoulet, J. 1894. Contribution a l'étude des lacs des Vosges. Geogr. Bull. Soc. Geogr., Paris, 15:

Tucker, M.J. 1956. The N.I.O. wave analyzer. Proc. 1st Conf. Coastal Engineering Instrumentation, Berkeley, Cal., Coll. Repr. Nat. Inst. Oceanogr., Wormley, Surrey, England, 5: 129–133.

van Leer, J., W. Düing, R. Erath, E. Kennelly, and A. Speidel. 1974. The cyclesonde: an unattended vertical profiler for scalar and vector quantities in the upper ocean. Deep–Sea Res., 21: 385–400.

Watson, E.R. 1904. Movements of the waters of Loch Ness as indicated by temperature observations. Geog. J. 24: 430–437.

Wedderburn, E.M. 1907. The temperature of the fresh water lochs of Scotland, with special reference to Loch Ness. Trans. R. Soc. Edinb. 45: 407–489.

_____. 1912. Temperature observations in Loch Earn; with a further contribution to the hydrodynamical theory of the temperature seiche. Trans. Roy. Soc. Edinburgh, 48: 629–695, 6 pt.

_____, and A.M. Williams. 1911. The temperature seiche, Pt. II, Hydrodynamical theory of temperature oscillations. Trans. Roy. Soc. Edinburgh, 47: 628–634.

_____, and A.W. Young. 1915. Temperature observations in Loch Earn, Part II, Trans. Roy. Soc. Edinburgh, 50: 741–767.

APPENDIX: ADAPTATION OF DEFANT'S (1918) PROCEDURE FOR SURFACE SEICHE ANALYSIS TO THE CALCULATION OF INTERNAL SEICHES IN TWO–LAYERED LAKES OF IRREGULAR SHAPE

I. Summary of the procedure for surface seiche analysis

Defant (1918, summarized 1960) applied a method of stepwise integration of the one–dimensional equations of continuity and motion, in finite–difference form, to a simulation of seiche motion in irregular basins. His procedure satisfied the solid boundary conditions at the ends of the basin and determined, not only the periods and node positions of the seiche modes, but also provided estimates of the relative vertical and horizontal displacements at given points along the basin. In this last respect, Defant's method is more useful than the variety of others developed to predict period and nodal position only. The tedium of the calculation is no longer a deterrent (see Fee's 1968 computer programs). Before discussing the adaptation to internal (two–layer) seiche analysis, the surface seiche procedure must be briefly outlined (for more detail, consult Defant 1960, Fee 1968, Fee and Bachmann 1968).

In application to a given lake, the first subjective step is to draw a smooth "medial track," as the x axis on the bathymetric chart, which follows more or less the "valley bottom" (Talweg) of the basin, and which is assumed to be the axis along which the linear one-dimensional equations of continuity and motion apply. Normal to the x axis, a number of sections (cross-sections) are drawn, usually more than 20, and in any case sufficient to ensure that cross-sectional area does not change too abruptly from one section to the next (Fee and Bachmann, 1968). The sections need not be equally spaced; in fact it is advantageous (as was done in Figure 1 of the main lecture) to space them closer together where there are large changes in basin shape.

The following information is then tabulated (using Defant's notation):

Δx, distance along the Talweg between adjacent sections $(x - 1)$ and x;

ℓ, total length of the Talweg;

S_x and b_x, area and width (at the lake surface) of the section at x;

v_x, area of lake surface between sections $(x - 1)$ and x

The following quantities are derived in the course of the calculation:

η_x and ξ_x, vertical and horizontal displacement of water particles at section x;

q_x, volume of water passing through the section at x.

Defant's difference equations were respectively derived from the following one-dimensional differential equations of continuity and motion:

$$\frac{\partial(S\xi)}{\partial x} = -\eta b \tag{1}$$

$$\frac{\partial^2 \xi}{\partial t^2} = -g\frac{\partial \eta}{\partial x} \tag{2}$$

Equation (2) states that acceleration of a water particle is proportional to the slope of the free surface above it, g being the acceleration due to gravity. Assuming simple harmonic motion, the elevation at point x and time t is given by $\xi_x = \xi_{max} \cos 2\pi(t/T)$, in which T is the seiche period. Double differentiation yields $\partial^2\xi/\partial t^2 = -(4\pi^2/T^2)\xi$. Using equation (2) and introducing finite differences, Defant obtained $\eta_x = \eta_{x-1} + \alpha\xi$, in which $\alpha = \Delta x(4\pi^2/gT^2)$. Assumption of linearity in ξ yields:

$$\eta_x = \eta_{x-1} + (\xi_{x-1} + \xi_x)(\alpha/2) \tag{3}$$

in which subscripts x and $(x - 1)$ refer to successive sections. Bearing in mind that the volume increment, Δq, in the slice of the lake bounded by the two sections is approximately $[v_x(\eta_{x-1} + \eta_x)/2]$ the total volume passing through section is:

$$q_x = q_{x-1} + \Delta q \tag{4}$$

Manipulation of equations (1), (3), and (4) yield an analogous and more convenient relation for displacement:

$$\xi_x = \frac{-1}{\left(S_x + \dfrac{\alpha v_x}{4}\right)} \left[q_{x-1} + v_x \left(\eta_{x-1} + \frac{\alpha \xi_{x-1}}{4} \right) \right] \tag{5}$$

Equations (3), (4), and (5) are those which Defant used in his iterative procedure, designed to determine a set of periods which yield distributions of ξ which satisfy the boundary condition that q_x is zero at the ends of the basin. To start the calculation, a trial value of T is taken (usually from Merian's formula, $T = 2\ell/\sqrt{(gh)}$, in which h is the mean depth of the basin and the other terms have been defined), η_o is set at 100 and q_o and ξ_o are set to zero at one end of the basin (Section 0). Equation (5) is then used to compute ξ_1 for Section 1; the result is then used in equation (3) to compute η_1. With knowledge of η_1, equation (4) yields q_1. Those three quantities are then used to compute the corresponding three parameters for section 2, and so on. In the unlikely event that the trial value of T was correctly chosen, q and ξ fall to zero at the last section, i.e. the other end of the basin. If this is not the case, the residual value of q is noted, the calculation is run a second time with a different value of T, yielding a different residual q. Interpolation between the two residuals usually yields a value of T very close to the one sought, which can then be used in a final calculation to provide the information displayed in the Figure 1 example in the main lecture.

II. Two-layered internal seiche analysis

For the lake under investigation, the observed density profile is fitted to a two-layered model with real basin topography but containing two homogeneous layers: an upper layer (subscript 1) of depth h_1 and density ρ_1; and a lower layer (subscript 2) of density ρ_2 and occupying the portion of the basin which lies below the interface. The mean depth of the lower layer is h_2. A Talweg is drawn from one end of the interface to the other, and sections erected normal to it, dividing the basin into a series of slices. Sections are more closely spaced where the basin shape changes rapidly. Compared with the whole basin considered in the surface seiche calculation, the two-layered model basin is truncated at the ends of the interface; and section width, b_i, and area of interface between sections, v_i, are measured on the interface as indicated by subscript i. Section areas are determined not only for the whole section, S_w, but also for the sub-section, S_2, below the interface. Sub-section area, S_1, above the interface is then given by $(S_w - S_2)$.

As John Crease (Institute of Oceanographic Sciences, Wormley, Surrey, England) kindly communicated to me over 20 years ago, the two-layered form of the equation of continuity (1) becomes:

$$\frac{\partial (S_2 \xi_2)}{\partial x} = -\eta_i b_i \tag{6}$$

In which ξ_2 is the horizontal displacement through the sub-section S_2 and η_i is the vertical displacement of the interface. The two-layered form of the equation of motion (2) becomes:

$$\frac{\partial^2 \xi_2}{\partial t^2} = -g(\rho_2 - \rho_1) \left(\frac{S_1}{S_w \rho_2} \frac{\partial \eta_i}{\partial x} \right) \tag{7}$$

In a manner analogous to that described above for surface seiche analysis, equations (6) and (7) are transformed into two-layer equivalents of equations (3), (4), and (5) simply by replacing g by $g(\rho_2 - \rho_1)S_1/\rho_2 S_w$ and α by $\Delta x(4\pi^2 S_w)\rho_2/T^2 g(\rho_2 - \rho_1)S_1$. Using those three modified equations, the calculation then proceeds--exactly as in the surface seiche case--to search for values of T which satisfy the boundary conditions, q_i and ξ_i zero, at both ends of the interface and to provide estimates of η_i (relative to an arbitrary value chosen for section 0) and ξ_2 for each section. The procedure is amenable to machine operation (modification of Fee's 1968 programs, for example). Merian's equation may be used, in two-layered form, to estimate T for an initial trial, i.e. $T^2 = 4\ell^2(h_1 + h_2)\rho_2/h_1 h_2 g(\rho_2 - \rho_1)$ with terms already defined.

The calculation yields estimates of lower-layer displacement and transport, ξ_2 and q_2, for each section. Assuming (reasonably) that the lake surface level does not change, the upper-layer transport, q_1, must equal $-q_2$; and the upper-layer displacement is therefore given by: $\xi_i = -\xi_2 S_2/S_1$.

The mean upper-layer and lower-layer current speeds during ¼ seiche cycle are obtained by dividing ξ_1 and ξ_2 by T/4; and it follows from the assumption of simple harmonic motion that the maximum speeds are $\pi/2$ greater than the means. That is how the values presented in Figure 4 of the main lecture were obtained.

III. References for Appendix

Defant, A., 1918. Neue Methode zur Ermittlung der Eigenschwingungen (Seiches) von abgeschlossenen Wassermassen (Seen, Buchten, usw.).--Ann. Hydrogr. Berlin 46: 78-85.

_____, 1960. Physical oceanography--Pergamon, London, Vol. II, 598 pp.

Fee, E. J. 1968. Digital computer programs for the Defant method of seiche analysis. Center for Great Lakes Studies, Univ. Wisconsin-Milwaukee, Spec. Rept. No. 4: 27 pp.

Fee, E. J. and R. W. Bachmann, 1968. An empirical study of the Defant method of seiche analysis. Limnol. Oceanogr., 13: 665-669.

OBSERVATIONS OF INTERNAL WAVES IN LAKE VÄNERN, SWEDEN

J. SVENSSON

The Swedish Meteorological and Hydrological Institute, Norrköping (Sweden)

ABSTRACT

Svensson, J.,1979. Observations of internal waves in Lake Vänern,Sweden.

The linear internal wave model of Mortimer (1974, 1977) has been applied to the two basins of Lake Vänern. Both basins have an irregular, not very channel-like shape. Nevertheless long records of current and thermocline oscilliations with periods close to computed Poincaré wave periods are found in field measurements. Examples of uninodal, binodal and manynodal waves are given and compared with theory. The same Poincaré wave cell can in some of the records be traced on six current meters and three thermistor chains simultaneously.

INTRODUCTION

Lake Vänern is the largest lake in Sweden, with a volume of 150 km^3. The lake is devided into two basins which are connected by a shallow sound. The maximum depth ($\approx$ 100 m) is situated in the eastern basin. The western basin has a maximum depth of about 70 m. The two basins have a rather irregular shape and near the coast skerries and shoal areas points towards rather bad reflexion possibilities for internal waves. It was therefore quite a surprice when in many registrations of temperature and current from the lake we found long and clear records of internal oscillations. The period was a little less than the local inertial period. The records were taken during part of 1971, 1972 and 1973 to study the circulation and temperature structure of the lake.

Figure 1 show the lake and the stations occupied by moored current meters and temperature chains.

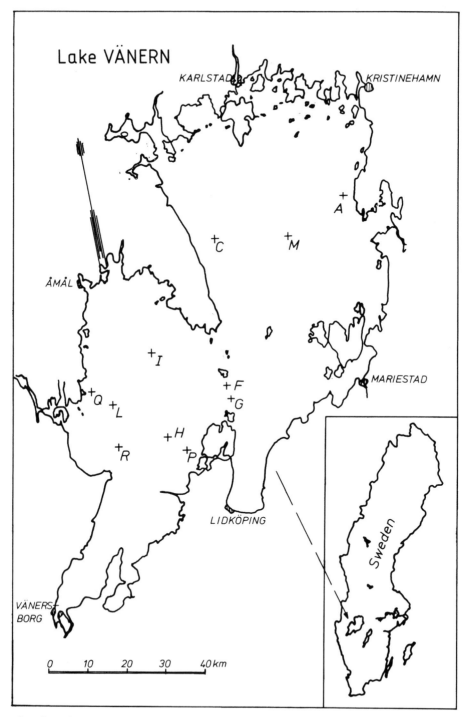

Fig. 1. Lake Vänern.

Mortimer explains the theory of standing Poincaré waves and compares it with measurements in several articles (Mortimer 1974, Mortimer 1975, Mortimer 1977).

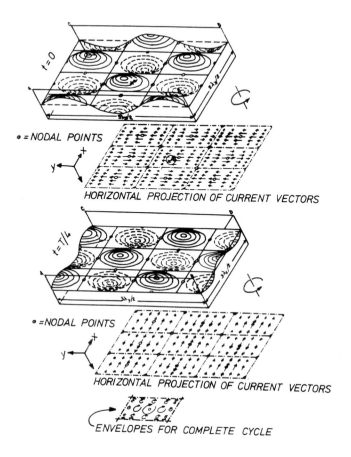

Fig. 2. A standing Poincaré wave, of cross-channel nodality three, in a wide rotating channel of rectangular cross-section (from Mortimer 1974).

The fact that velocities along the cell-end walls do not fall to zero should be pointed out.Two oppositely progressive Poincaré waves alone can therefore not meet a solid-wall boundary condition at the cell-end walls. This does not affect Poincaré waves in an elongated basin (channel) very much but may disturb a comparison between theory and observation in Lake Vänern.

The present study, however, shows a good agreement between linear wave theory and observation, despite the fact that only one or few "Poincaré cells" are studied. The same conclusion is drawn in Schwab (1977) where results from a Lake Ontario model of irregular plan but uniform depth are presented.

226

Mortimer gives the wave spead of the Poincaré wave:

$$C_p{}^2 = C_0{}^2 \, (1 + R^2) + (2b \, / \, n_x P_i)^2$$

C_0 = wave spead without rotation
R = the cross channel to along-channel wavelength
b = channel width
n_x = cross channel nodality
P_i = local inertial period

If the wavelength along and across the channel is about the same ($R = 1$) the second term becomes dominant when the channel width increases. For Lake Vänern the first term is in some cases important and can not be neglected.

The relationship between cross basin wavelength and Poincaré wave period for the two basins is shown in fig. 3.

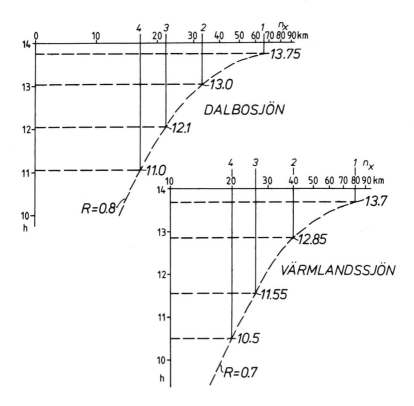

Fig. 3. Explanation see the text.

An example of a measured Poincaré wave in the western basin is given in fig. 4. The period taken e.g. from the current record of station H agrees well with the period of a uninodal Poincaré wave.

The oscillation is present at all 6 current meter stations in Dalbosjön. The instantaneous direction of the current is the same at all stations which shows that the wave is uninodal in both across and along basin direction. The information from thermistor chains and temperature sensors on current meters is not evident. However stations H and P show a crest when station Q shows a trough which also indicates a uninodal wave.

During the days before the wave the wind was blowing from NE and E, 3 to 5 m/s. This caused a deep-laying thermocline at station Q. The Poincaré wave was started by a sudden SW-wind (8 m/s) which was blowing a few hours around noon on the second of July. After that there was half a day of calm weather followed by light SW-winds.

Mortimer has in Lake Ontario found waves with 1, 3 and 5 nodes but not 2, 4 etc.. This seems natural if the waves are produced by uppwelling at one coast and down-welling at the other. In the eastern basin of Lake Vänern, Värmlandssjön, the temperature record from the middle of the lake shows clear oscillations. The period of these waves is most of the time close to a computed period for a binodal wave and once during the observational period coincides with the theoretical period for a four-nodal wave. One example of a binodal wave is shown in fig. 5. Both the period of the wave and the comparison between observations at stations M and C indicates a binodal wave. E. g. a deep laying pycnocline in the center of the lake is accompanied by a south going current at the western side.

A very clear and about 6 periods long series of oscillations was recorded on the thermistor chain at station M in late July. The period is close to the one calculated for a 4 node Poincaré wave. The records from temperature sensors and current meters from other stations do not show clear oscillations. However they can fit the theory for a 4 node wave (fig. 6).

Other remarks on the records are:
a) Current fluctuations often have a period slightly longer than temperature oscillations.
b) The waves with 1 or 2 nodes have big amplitude in the current record. The waves with 4 nodes can only be seen at thermistor records.
c) The period of both current and pycnocline fluctuations seems to grow shorter as the fluctuation goes on.

228

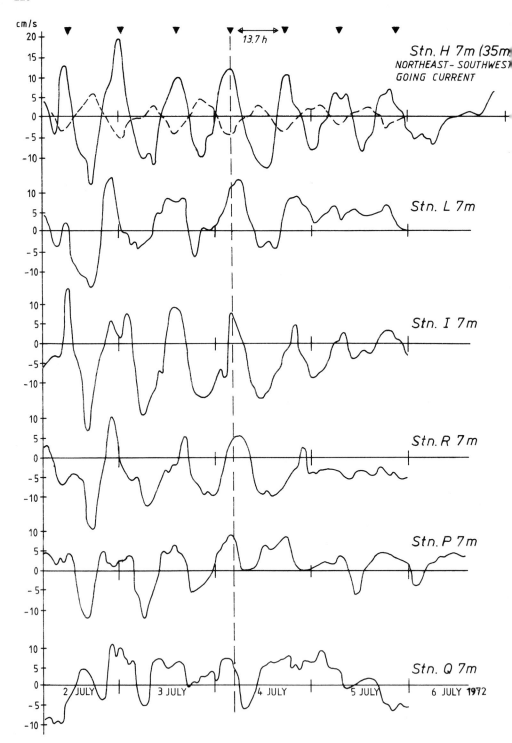

Fig. 4. Example of a measured uninodal Poincaré wave (current).

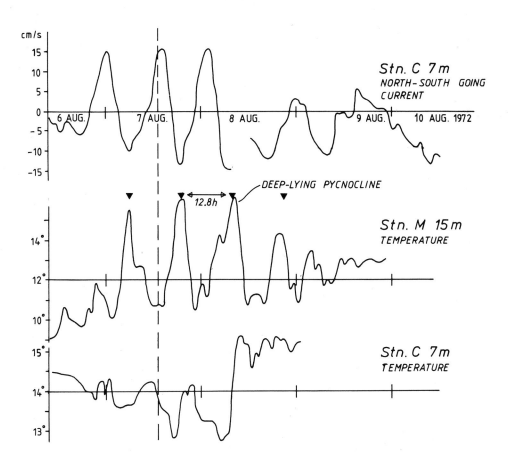

Fig. 5. Example of a measured binodal Poincaré wave.

230

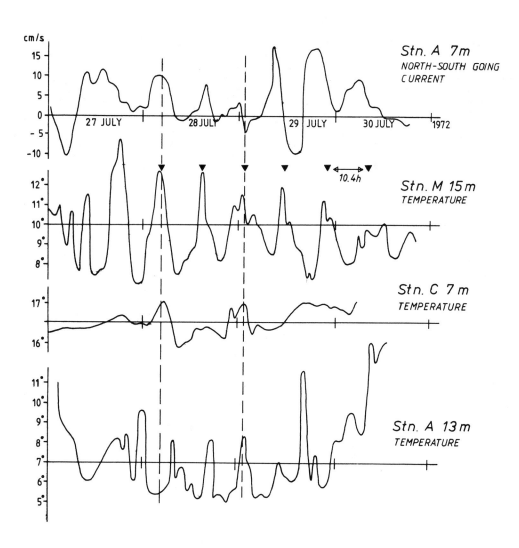

Fig. 6. Example of a measured four-nodal Poincaré wave.

REFERENCES

Mortimer, C.H., 1971. Large-scale oscillatory motions and seasonal temperature changes in Lake Michigan and Lake Ontario. Spec. Rept. No. 12, Ctr. for Great Lakes Stds., Univ. Wisconsin--Milwaukee.

Mortimer, C.H., 1974. Lake Hydrodynamics. Mitt. Internat. Verein. Limnol. 20: 124-197 (50th Jubilee Symp., Int. Assoc. Limnol., Kiel 1972).

Mortimer, C.H., 1975. Substantive corrections to SIL Communications (IVL Mitteilungen) Numbers 6 and 20. Verh. Internat. Verein. Limnol., 19: 60-72.

Mortimer, C.H., 1977. Internal Waves Observed in Lake Ontario During the International Field Year for the Great Lakes (IFYGL) 1972. Spec. Rept. No. 32, Ctr. for Great Lakes Stds., Univ. Wisconsin--Milwaukee.

Schwab, D.J., 1977. Internal free oscillations in Lake Ontario. Limnol. Oceanogr. V. 22(4).

EXPERIMENTAL SET UP OF AN INTERNAL WAVE, GENERATED BY THE WIND, AND OF SHORTER
PERIOD THAN THE CORIOLIS PERIOD

G. CHABERT d'HIERES and D. RENOUARD

Institut de Mécanique de Grenoble, Grenoble (France)

ABSTRACT

In order to study, under laboratory conditions, the generation of internal waves
by a suddenly applied wind, taking account of the Coriolis effect, the authors
have built on the rotating platform of Grenoble University a large flume
(8.0 x 2.0 x 0.6 m) at present equipped with a wind tunnel, but capable of recei-
ving at some future date, a mechanism for simulation of the driving effect of the
wind. They first describe the experimental installation and the measuring instruments it supports. Then they submit a theoretical interpretation of the phenomena
observed. As a rotating tank is involved, the following are observed : 1) variation in the mean level of the interface ; 2) the organization of a Poincare-
Kelvin amphidromy ; 3) an internal inertial wave, with a shorter period than the
inertial period and related to the impulsive character of the wind. Comparison
between the experimental results and the theorical forecast reveals the limits of
a theory which, at present, does not take account of particularities due to the
limited nature of the channel.

INTRODUCTION

In nature, for instance in summer, at the laboratory buoy BORHA II in the Mediter-

ranean sea, one can observe internal waves the period of which is shorter than

the local Coriolis period, and of large amplitude (Crepon et al., 1972). It can be

seen that they occurred after a sharp variation of the wind (wind impulsional with

time). Numerous theories have been proposed to explain this phenomenon, and we

have chosen and particularly studied Crépon's theory (Crépon, 1969) according to

which these perturbations first appear at the coast, a zone of spatial disconti-

nuity, and propagate from the coast to the open sea, with a pseudo-period slightly.

shorter than the local Coriolis period. In fact, the observations in nature never

clearly show the progressive character of these waves, and in addition, the high

cost and hazardous character of such measurements has to be considered. Consequently,

on the large rotating platform of Grenoble University we built a flume fitted with

a wind tunnel in which, over the last few years, we have studied the generation

of internal waves by the wind, while keeping the main parameters constant : densi-

ty and thickness of the salt and fresh water layers, wind speed, period of rotation

of the platform. We present here the first conclusions of this experimental work.

LABORATORY FACILITIES

To approximate, as closely as possible, the theoretical model of wind-induced internal waves, and thus be in possession of an instrument of quality capable of being used for other studies, such were our objectives when we built our laboratory facility.

In order to achieve these objectives, the flume had to be sufficiently long and wide to enable level rises engendered near a wall to be analysed, taking into account the Coriolis force, before their superimposition with level rises generated from other boundaries of the liquid domain. Since we will be dealing with internal waves, it is essential to provide excellent flow observations facilities. As we are in a revolving medium, and owing to the fact that the flume has to be large in order to be able to study the effect of the Coriolis force alone, the effect of the centrifugal force has to be eliminated. For this reason, therefore, the flume floor must be capable of adapting to equipotential surfaces in a resolving medium, i.e., paraboloïds of revolution. Finally, since the flume is fitted to the revolving platform of the "Institut de Mécanique de Grenoble", which still carries the scale model of the English Channel, its characteristics must be consistent with this installation, and it must not therefore create a load in excess of 1 tonne/m^2 which is the maximum acceptable load of the supporting concrete slab, nor must possible platform deformations be transmitted to the basin. The basin must therefore be both light and rigid.

The internal waves that we are studying are generated by the sudden application of a tangential stress identical in intensity at all points of the free surface and constant with time. The flume must thus be equipped with a wind-tunnel fulfilling these conditions. Since it is clearly apparent that it will be difficult to meet these conditions, we must study the possibility of simulating the driving effect of the wind on the free surface by other means.

We have therefore designed a parallelepipedic flume 8 m long, 2.0 m wide and 0.60 m deep ; the vertical sides being made of glass in order to have good visualisation, the main structure of the flume being made of steel.
The flume is equipped with the following :

<u>a</u>. a wind-tunnel consisting, from upstream to downstream, of a tapering inlet of the flume fan connection circuit and ensuring equal flow distribution in the air stream and, finally, a fan and flow control valve ;

<u>b</u>. a recirculation circuit, with possible head-loss compensation by means of valves and a system of adjustable discharge injectors ; this circuit can be controlled by means of flow meters ;

<u>c</u>. a "false-bottom" of variable shape, mainly to compensate for centrifugal force effects ;

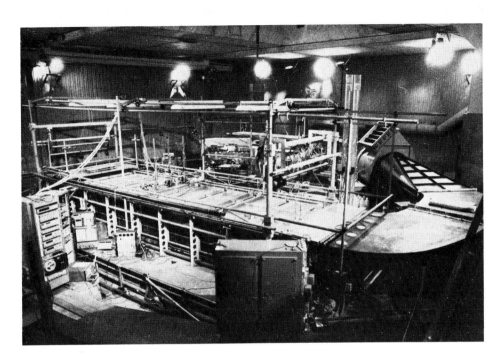

Fig. 1. Photograph of the flume equipped with the wind tunnel, on the rotating platform of Grenoble University.

<u>d</u>. a carriage allowing the experimental worker easy access to any point of the flume and to move, adjust or monitor the instrumentation without difficulty, this instrumentation being installed on an another carriage.

To complete this installation, two tanks are situated off the rotating platform and are used for preparing the large quantities of salt water needed for each experiment.

THE INSTRUMENTATION

For the filling operations we use a fixed-point water level gauge to measure water height.

The wind field created by the previously adjuste a wind-tunnel is explored by means of Prandtl tubes connected to a high precision pressure gauge. In the future, we will measure the turbulence in the air flow section by using hot-wire anemometers.

The water velocities are very small, of the order of 1 cm/s, so they cannot be measured with micro-current meters. We will thus use hot-film current-meters and, if we wish to measure the two velocity components and their fluctuations, it is possible that we will have to use a laser current-meter. As far as the velocity of the surface layer is concerned, the only significant method is chronophotography of small, suitably ballasted floats.

The level differences of the interface are known thanks to interface followers. The characteristics of these conductivity meters, in which a probe is slaved to follow a layer of liquid of selected conductivity, i.e., of selected density, are described elsewhere (Chabert d'Hières and Suberville, 1974). The signal obtained is converted either into immediately exploitable analogue recordings or into digital recordings in which case the serialisation of the data and its transfer on to punched tape is carried out by a data acquisition unit and the data is then processed on a computer. We now have five interface followers.

At the beginning of each experiment, we measure the density of each layer and, during the experiment, we can follow the temperature of each layer with great accuracy.

THE AIR VELOCITY FIELD

In order to be as near as possible to the theoretical hypothesis, in each point of the free surface we have to have a wind-stress impulsional with time, then constant in intensity and direction, and uniform, with as small a pressure gradient as possible.

We first verified that, when the pneumatic valve is closed, the time elapsing before steady flow conditions are set up is shorten than 1.5 s in all points of the flume. This time is shorter than all characteristic periods of the flume, particularly, the barotropic longitudinal period which is equal to 7.2 s in our normal experimental conditions. In addition, this wind is constant with time at every point, to an accuracy of 1 % in velocity and a few degrees in direction.

Looking at the cross-sectional profiles of the horizontal velocity component, it can be seen that they are symmetrical with respect to the centre-line of the flume, to within 1 or 2 % , the difference can be attributed to the effects of rotation of the platform. In the first sections of the flume there is a small velocity deficit due to insufficient guiding of the air stream at the wind-tunnel inlet.

However, a relative difference between the mean velocities upstream and downstream can be observed. As there is no possibility of air-entrance in the air- section, we assume that this difference is linked to a variation in the wind-stress on on the free-surface. This hypothesis seems possible because of the difference in amplitude of the small waves at the free surface between upstream, where they are

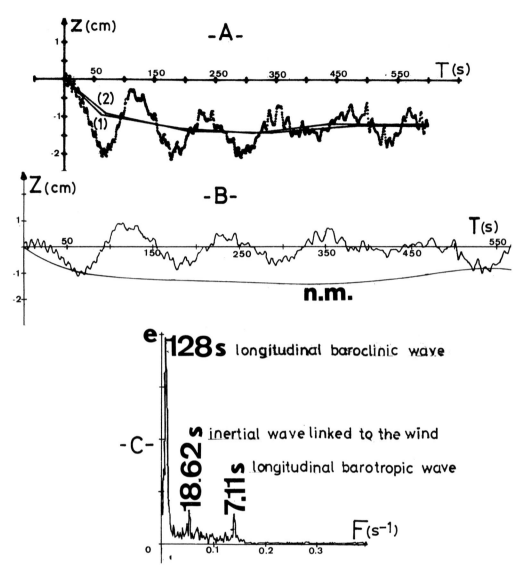

Fig.2.a. – Analogical reproduction of interface height variation with time in
the middle of the Channel, 25 cm from the rifht-hand side; the movements start from rest, the platform is in rotation (T_{rot} = 40.0 s).

This reproduction includes two tests for determining the mean curve,
with blocks of (1) 250 and (2) 275 points respectively.

2.b.(1) – curve showing the variation in the mean level of the interface.
(2) – residual signal resulting from the subtraction, of the mean level
height – cf.b(1) – from the true experimental height-cf.a-for each
point.

2.c. – Frequency spectrum of the residual signal, obtained by the Fast Fourier
transformation on 1024 points. Peaks corresponding to the longitudinal
baroclinic wave, to the inertial wave due to the suddenly applied wind,
and to the longitudinal barotropic wave are clearly apparent.

a few millimeters high and downstream, where they are up to 3 or 4 centimeters high.

If we consider the vertical profiles of the horizontal velocity components, it can be seen that they are regular but that the velocity is slightly greater near the "ceiling" of the wind-section. This is probably due to the difference of roughness between the horizontal "ceiling" and the free-surface.

From this rapid revue of the wind field we can conclude that, along the flume, there is a small variation in the wind-stress at the free-surface, but we cannot say what is its exact law of variation. So, in our experiments, the theoretical hypotheses are not totally satisfied.

SPECTRAL ANALYSIS OF THE VARIATION IN HEIGHT OF THE INTERFACE

At a given point, for instance in the central section of the flume, 25 cm from the right-hand side, the interface height variation, starting from rest, is the superposition of a variation in the mean level of the interface due to the currents generated by the wind, longitudinal baroclinic and barotropic oscillations, and the inertial wave we are looking for, the latter being characterised by its shorter period than the Coriolis period. To make the spectral analysis of such a signal it is necessary to eliminate the mean-level variation.

Therefore, we developed an automatic treatment of the data obtained. From the digital recording we calculate mean values in blocks - generally with between 250 and 300 values while the whole tape contains 1200 values, one every 0.5 s - and, by a broken line we visualise the mean curve obtained (cf. fig.2a). since the system of calculus allows a large number of fits, we choose the one which gives the best mean curve. We then make the hypothesis that the variation of the mean level of the interface passes through these points and may be approximated by a Lagrangian poly-nominal calculated from these points. Then, for each point, we calculate the difference between the experimental data and this approximation of the mean level. We then have a residual signal, and we make sure that it is really periodic with time and has no mean level variation (cf. fig. 2b). It is on such a signal that we make the spectral analysis.

On all the spectras obtained, corresponding to a platform rotation period between 35 an 150 seconds, we first observe barotropic and baroclinic period of the basin. In general, as with the transversal barotropic or baroclinic waves, the harmonics of these periods do not appear. However, relatively high turbulence is apparent on every recording.

But, and here is the new point illustrated by these experiments, the spectral analysis clearly shows an energy peak for a slightly shorter period than the iner-tial period, and this for every experiment in which the wind is impulsional with

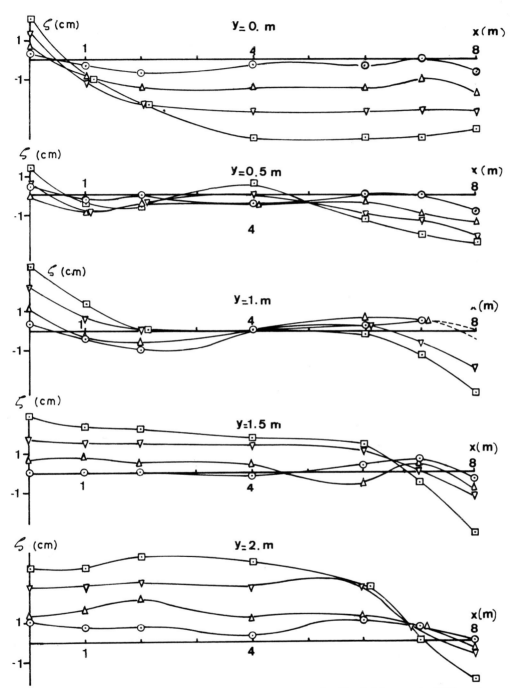

Fig.3.- Interface height variation, along five longitudinal lines, at different times after the beginning of application of the wind. In this experiment $h_1=h_2=26$ cm, $\mathcal{C}_1=0.9987$, $\mathcal{C}_2=1.0168$, $w=4.68$ m/s, $f=0.24933$ s^{-1} $(T_{rot}=50.4s)$, the internal radius of deformation $R_D=0.60$m.

time. The period found is between the Coriolis period and the period given by an approximated theory of the phenomenon (G. Chabert d'Hières and D. Renouard, 1977). We have verified that this difference between the experimentally found period and the Coriolis period is linked to the impulsive character of the wind.

EXPERIMENTAL RESULTS

If we examine the interface, along five longitudinal lines, at different times after the beginning of application of the wind, it is found that, during the first seconds, the height variations along three-quarters of the longitudinal sides are identical. This confirm that the inertial wave first appears along the sides and propagates from the sides through the centre of the Channel. Also of note is the progression, along these sides, of the perturbations which first appear at the side ends (cf. fig.3).

We obtain identical results if we have a smaller depth or if with the same rota-tion velocity of the platform, depth and wind, we change the thicknesses of the salt and fresh water layers.

In order to define the organisation of the pseudo-Poincaré Kelvin amphydromy which appears in the flume, we put, in function of the abscissa, the amplitude of the two first extrema of the same sign, along the longitudinal sides. We find that they make two parallel curves, and they enable us to determine the line of mean level of the interface, along the axis of the basin. The slope of this line depends on the wind speed and, for the same wind, the total depth (cf. fig.4).

We also see that the amplitude of these extrema is proportional to the square of the wind velocity. However, for the same wind, we do not find any relationship between this amplitude and the internal radius of deformation. The last two results are already classical ones. Finally, in a given point, the amplitude of the free oscillations, after the end of the wind, depends on the duration of this wind : it is greatest when this duration is equal to an odd number of half baro-clinic periods of the basin.

If we now consider a transverse section, for instance the central one (cf. fig.5) we observe that, near the sides, there is response time of the order of 7 s, between the beginning of application of the wind and the time for which the rise in height of the interface exceeds 1 mm. This time is independent of the section studied, and probably corresponds to the response time of the upper layer to the excitation of the wind. Especially we notice in particular that, for the rise in height there is a propagation time from the sides towards the centre of the Channel

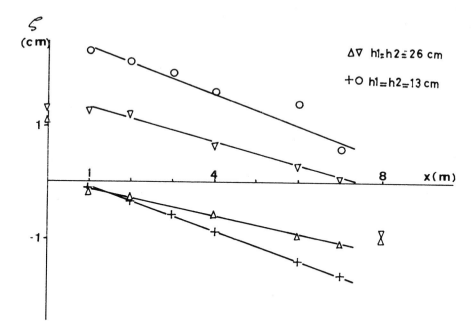

<u>Fig.4</u> - *Loci of the first extremum after the beginning of application of the wind, along the two longitudinal sides (+$\triangle$ right-hand side ; O $\triangledown$ left-hand side), when (1) ($\triangle\triangledown$) h_1=h_2 = 26 cm, $\mathcal{C}_1$ = 0.9987 , $\mathcal{C}_2$ = 1.0168 , v = 4.68 m/s and (2) (+ 0) h_1 = h_2 = 13 cm , $\mathcal{C}_1$ = 0.9985 , $\mathcal{C}_2$ = 1.0111, v = 4.47 m/s (f = 0.24933 s^{-1}).*

This time corresponds to a propagation velocity of about 10 cm/s, which is of order of the propagation velocity of the baroclinic wave, and of the inertial wave.

CONCLUSIONS

If the existence of a wave, related to the impulsional character of the wind, and of shorter period than the inertial period, appearing first at the sides and then propagating towards the centre seems to be demonstrated, we do not at present possess an analytical solution to describe it correctly, nor experimental methods to specify its shape and phase.

Nevertheless, this experimental evidence of such a wave seems both new and interesting.

242

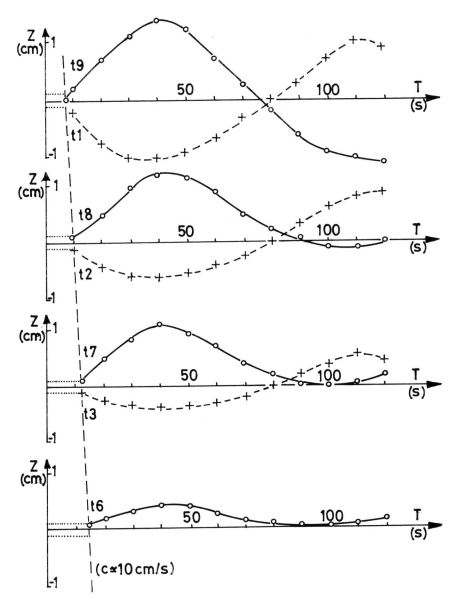

Fig.5.- *Interface height variation, with time, for different points of the*
transverse section, in the middle of the Channel, from top to bottom,
near the sides (t1, y=0, t9, y=2m) and at 25 cm (t2, y=0.25m, t8,
y=1.75 m), 50cm (t3, y=0.50cm ; t7, y=1.50m) and 75 cm (t6, y=1.25m)
from the sides. Dashed lines indicate heights ± 0.1 cm.

REFERENCES

Chabert d'Hières G. and Renouard D., 1976. Canal équipé d'une soufflerie et d'un moyen mécanique de simulation, sur la plaque tournante de Grenoble. Houille Blanche, 1:45-51.

Chabert d'Hières G. and Renouard D., 1977. Ondes internes engendrées par le vent dans un canal parallélépipèdique en milieu tournant. Ann. Hydrogr. 5e serie, 5:127-134.

Chabert d'Hières G. and Suberville J.L., 1974. Ondes internes à l'interface de deux fluides de densité voisines contenus dans un bassin rectangulaire tournant, Houille Blanche, 7-8:623-630.

Crépon M., 1969. Hydrodynamique Marine en régime impulsionnel. Cah. Océanogr. 21:863-877.

Crépon M., Gonella J., Lacombe H. and Stanislas G., 1972. Participation Française à l'opération Cofrasou I, rept. CNEXO, 04-1972:91-106.

WIND-WAVES IN THE BAY OF GENEVA

J. BRUSCHIN and L. SCHNEITER

Laboratoire d'Hydraulique (LHYDREP), Ecole Polytechnique Fédérale, Lausanne,
Switzerland

ABSTRACT

Hydraulic works in lakes are increasing steadily in number and size. As a result a strong demand for wave-data for the large Swiss lakes, practically non-existent only 10 years ago, is developing very fast.

This paper completes a previous one where some results of wind-waves measurements performed since 1974 on the Petit Lac (south-western part of the Lake of Geneva) are reported. Specific comments on refraction effects, on the analysis of wind and wave-data, on aerial photographs and the corresponding image analysis are offered, together with some new results on period statistics and energy spectra.

Some as yet unexplained facts are also reported. A wind-wave model is proposed for the bay of Geneva. A few remarks on specific meteorological conditions like the generation and influence of breezes are also included.

INTRODUCTION

The number of fairly large hydraulic lake structures built or designed during the last 10 years surpasses 50 if all Swiss lakes ar considered. The Lake of Geneva has over 15 such structures. Typical works are new small harbors, extensions and improvements of existing ones, shore protections, underwater pipelines, outlets and intakes. If investments are considerable - hundreds of millions of Swiss Francs look like a reasonable estimate - the design relies essentially on tradition, know-how, personal judgment of local conditions, etc. The only well-known, published measurements on the Lake of Geneva belong to the 19th century and are a wave-period at Morges on February 20, 1879 in the late evening, of 4.7 sec, and a maximum wave-height of 1.5 m observed in deep water under unspecified circumstances (Forel, 1969).

Fresher outlooks, a couple of expensive breakdowns, a need for floating breakwaters and -piers, generated a stringent demand for more extensive and accurate information.

That is how we were able to start measuring wind and wave characteristics in the bay of Geneva in December 1974. These measurements are still going on to some extent but records up to May 1978 were analyzed and some results published (Bru-

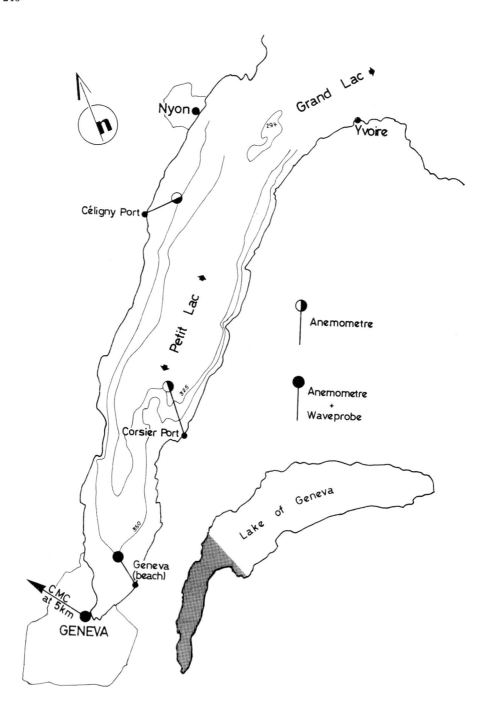

Fig. 1. Petit Lac with wind and wave-stations.

schin and Schneiter, 1978). Further analyses and results are presented here.

SITE AND MEASUREMENT EQUIPMENT

This is already described by Bruschin and Schneiter (1978). We will summarize and offer further comments here.

Site

Starting wind-wave measurements with rather small means and without any previous experience makes one cautious - fortunately. We were therefore looking for places where siting, measurements, direct observation of the equipment and its maintenance, survey of the lake and even more than anything else interpretation of results would be as simple and straightforward was possible.

From the main winds likely to generate strong waves on our lakes only the "bise" (NNE) blows under a clear (cloudless) sky, making direct or aerial surveys possible. Lakes with a long enough fetch for the "bise" are those of Geneva and Neuchâtel. In their SW parts the "bise" is also the only wave-generating wind. After some pondering over geometrical and bathymetrical features, facility of access, availability of meteorological information and help of all types, we decided on the bay of Geneva and a location next to the beach (GP - Genève Plage).

Equipment

The equipment is already described extensively by Bruschin and Schneiter (1978) and the locations are given in Fig. 1. Here we will only offer some comments which we consider useful for further understanding.

Our wave-probe was located in shallow water. Moreover, despite poor knowledge of bottom topography (the bathymetric maps also belonged to the end of the last century and are rather inconsistent with some more recent measurements) it appeared that deep-water conditions (for estimated wavelengths L_o = 40 m) were available at more than 700 m off-shore. Since refraction calculations under these circumstances were scarcely reliable and bottom topography measurements at this scale could not even be considered, we had to rely on estimations of refraction effects. With wave directions in deep water varying from N10E to N40E and a bottom slope supposed uniform and directed at some angle between N and N45W, the error with respect to deep-water amplitudes H_o after shoaling up to our probe is:

> 5 % for L_o > 13 to 17 m

> 10 % for L_o > 17 to 36 m corresponding respectively to incidence angles

$$10^O < \alpha_o < 60^O \quad (L_o > \text{when } \alpha_o <)$$

However, since the general form of the Petit Lac - see Fig. 1 - is that of a submarine valley, more energy is transferred laterally than evaluated precedingly so that the expected error, in the limits of our measurements, when writing

$$H_{measured} = H_o$$

should be smaller than the standard deviation of H_o resulting from the combination of the 5 min. records, that is 10 % or less (Bruschin and Schneiter, 1978). Further confirmation of this statement comes from aerial photography for waves of $L_o \simeq 24$ m and wave statistics which will be discussed later.

DATA ANALYSIS

First results have already been published. More interest will be attached here to some of the problems encountered while collecting, analyzing and explaining the results.

Wind measurements had to be made with two types of anemometres with outputs in 3 different formats: 5 min. averages on punched paper-tape, continuous graphical recording (CMC[1]), hourly averages in km/h and 3 significant figures for velocities, rounded to the nearest 10° above for directions and 4 of the 6 anemometres. Results are obviously not fully comparable. That is why we believe that the observed differences in wind velocities $U_{GP,10} < U_{CMC}$ while corresponding to those predicted by Bruschin and Falvey (1976) are not really significant. Moreover, these differences decrease with wind velocity. Since for significant waves $H_s > 1.0$ m, $U_{GP,10} > 12$ ms^{-1}, we will admit $U_{GP} = U_{CMC}$ for all practical purposes of wave hind- or forecasting.

Not so however for wind directions. The stations next to the lake, on the shoreline, describe the "bise" as blowing on the Petit Lac with an average N3OE $\pm$ 10° direction, while the stations on land (Cointrin, Payerne) give directions around N6OE $\pm$ 10°! Note that the "bise" is generally depicted as a NNE-NE wind. If we were prepared for some differences bearing in mind geographical features (funneling) as well as some channeling due to roughness and thermal effects, we were startled by their size. The problem is still open.

With respect to waves, at least two features should be mentioned here. During the strongest recorded storm - March 29, 1977, records were analyzed from 10:50 am to 8:50 pm. While wind direction and velocity (17 ms^{-1}) remained practically un-

---

[1]   Centre Météorologique Cointrin

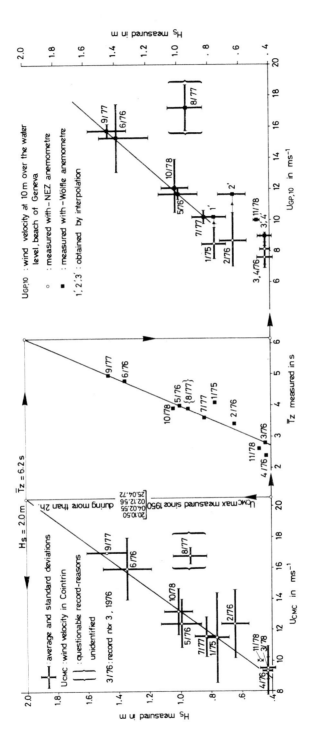

Fig. 2. Wind-wave-periods relationships for the bay of Geneva.

changed for the duration of the record, a jump in wave characteristics was obvious within the hour from 5:50 to 6:50 pm: H_s increased from .93 m to 1.45 m,
$\bar{T}_z$, the zero-crossing wave-period, from 3.9 to 5.0 seconds. Other changes will be
apparent in wave statistics as will be shown later.

Another troubling fact was revealed by aerial photographs and image analysis.
During the storm of May 10, 1978, the whole Petit Lac was photographed from 1200 m
and 5000 m altitude between 10:59 and 11:45 am. In the higher altitude pictures
a crossed-wave pattern could be seen in deep water south of a line Yvoire-Pro-
menthoux over the full length of the Petit Lac (20 km). The first group of waves
comes from the Grand Lac maintaining its direction N30 to 35E, which is also the
measured direction of the wind, the second is directed some 45° eastwards (N60
to 70E). Wave length appears to be of the same order of magnitude but the second
group has longer crests and looks better defined. No satisfactory explanation is
available as yet for this rather unexpected feature.

DISCUSSION OF RESULTS

A first control was made with respect to the intrinsic consistency of the
$H_s(\bar{H}_{1/3}) - U_{GP,10}$ and $U_{CMC} - \bar{T}_z$ relationship. As shown by the SMB charts (Corps
of Engineers, 1975), the H-U part of it is quasi-linear for the limited field of
our measurements and an estimated fetch of 20 km which was computed by the Wiegel-
Saville method for width-limited fetches (Corps of Engineers, 1975; Wiegel, 1954).
On the other hand

$$\frac{H_s}{\bar{T}_z} = \frac{2}{\pi} \sqrt{m_2} \tag{1}$$

where m_2 is the second moment of the energy spectrum. From our ten records we get

$$H_s = .23 \, \bar{T}_z \tag{2}$$

with an estimated standard deviation s = .04; i.e. less than 17 %. Despite some
dispersion this relation also appears as quasi-linear.

Fig. 2 shows these results and points to the very particular case of the storm
8-9/77: for its first part 8/77, H_s is consistent with its $\bar{T}_z$ but inconsistent
with the other H_s values; for its second part 9/77, overall consistency is achieved.

Another control was made by extending wave-statistics analysis to the stronger
storms: 6/76, 8 and 9/77. Experimental and theoretical distributions of standardized
wave-heights and periods were compared as shown in Figs. 3, 4 and 5.

$$p(\xi) = 2\xi \, \exp(-\xi^2) \qquad \xi = H/H_{rms} \tag{3}$$
$$p(\eta) = \tfrac{1}{2}(1 + \eta^2)^{-3/2} \tag{4}$$

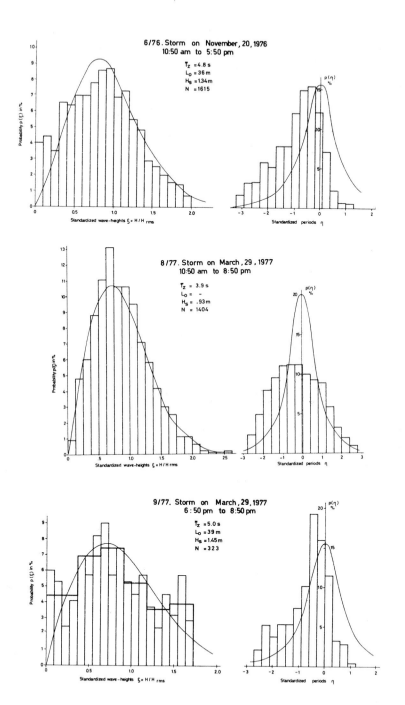

Figs. 3, 4, 5. Standardized wave-heights and -periods statistics for 3 records.

with $\eta = \dfrac{2(T_z - \bar{T}_z)}{\varepsilon \bar{T}_z}$ and $\varepsilon^2 = 1 - (\dfrac{\bar{T}}{\bar{T}_z})^2$

$\bar{T}$ is the average period of all waves ($\bar{T} < \bar{T}_z$) and ε is the spectral width.

Just as for the record 10/78 shown by Bruschin and Schneiter (1978), the distribution of wave heights is well explained by theory. Since H_{rms} (see Bruschin and Schneiter, 1978) is practically unaffected by shoaling, it is interesting to see that not only does refraction not affect the higher waves but also that they are not overestimated by the Rayleigh distribution as ocean waves apparently are (Corps of Engineers, 1975; Forristall, 1978). Wave periods however demonstrate an obvious bias to the higher frequencies with respect to theory (only record 8/77 is clearly different and of a rather symmetrical aspect). This happens because the average spectral periods are larger than the average zero-crossing periods as can be seen from the spectra (Bruschin and Schneiter, 1978), an unusual fact for ocean waves (Subrata et al., 1977).

In the process of computing the wave statics some interesting data on wave periods and spectral width were also obtained - see table 1.

TABLE I

Record nbr	Number of waves	$\bar{T}_{z,1/3}$ seconds	$\bar{T}_{z,1/10}$ seconds	ε
6/76	1616	4.9	5.8	.68
8/77	1404	4.3	5.2	.63
9/77	323	5.4	6.2	.66
10/78	1458	–	–	.61

Silvester (1974) mentions $.6 < \varepsilon < .8$ for ocean waves, while Subrata (1977) calculates $\varepsilon \simeq .75$ for 2 Atlantic storms. Our results are nearer to the lower limit as confirmed by the spectra showing that 90 % of the energy is contained in a 1 to less than 4 times, 80 % in a 1 to less than 2 times frequency band.

WAVE HINDCASTING

With the few reservations already mentioned, the "bise"-waves in the bay of Geneva appear as fully predictable from the SMB charts. The wind velocities can be taken from the CMC records for $U > 12$ ms^{-1}. The effective fetch F_e as obtained by numerical and graphical optimization methods from the data is 18 km, very near to the computed 20 km mentioned before, far however from the 45 km of the longest straight distance.

These results put us, at least for the present time, in a happy position as compared to published results on the Great Lakes (Resio and Hüpakka, 1976). 9 storms (11 records) is certainly not a large enough sample. It proved however to be consistent and well explained by a simple, widely accepted wind-wave model. We believe that engineers may use it confidently.

FINAL REMARKS

What we learned in these four years is perhaps more important than the wave model produced, even if it is so much more difficult to quantify. After all, waves are only one result of the wind-water coupling and the design-storms for hydraulic structures are rare events in the life of a lake.

We learned that rather strong winds on the lake are not always general winds. That even then they may be strongly influenced by breezes (thermal winds) to the point of changing directions and velocities along the fetch. This is particularly true for the "bise", or what is perceived to be one on the Petit Lac, except under stable winter-conditions and velocities exceeding 8 to 10 ms^{-1}. That is one good reason explaining the dispersion of results in Fig. 2 for lower velocities.

The Lake of Geneva is big enough to work like a thermal machine for local atmospheric conditions. Breezes are produced radially as if somewhere on the Grand Lac between Lausanne and Evian there would be alternately a source or a sink. A "bise" can be deviated and weakened on the Grand Lac, strengthened and redirected to the NNE on the Petit Lac; or vice-versa. Moreover, clouds, geographical features, positions of the sun and the synoptic gradient also come into the picture (Ganter, 1978). For these reasons and various others, large parts of the lake may be simply off-wind while rather strong winds are measured elsewhere. Also densimetric flows of 5-6 ms^{-1}, without any synoptic pressure gradient are frequent in the cold season.

That is why we firmly believe that forecasting or real-time general models for waves and/or currents cannot be achieved both for technical but even more for economical reasons.

ACKNOWLEDGEMENT

We express our gratitude to Dr. M. Bouët and Mr. B. Dunand, meteorologists, for their help and good advice.

REFERENCES

Bruschin, J. and Falvey, H.T., 1975 and 1976. Vagues de vent sur un plan d'eau
    confiné. Bull. Techn. Suisse Romande, nos 14 and 2.
Bruschin, J. and Schneiter, L., 1978. Caractéristiques des vagues dans les lacs
    profonds. Bull. Techn. Suisse Romande, no 19.
Corps of Engineers, 1975. Shore Protection Manual. Coastal Eng. Research Center,
    Va., USA.
Forel, F.A., 1969. Le Léman. Slatkine Reprints, Genève.
Forristall, G.Z., 1978. On the Statistical Distribution of Wave Heights in a
    Storm. Journ. Geophys. Res., Vol. 83, No C5.
Ganter, Y., 1978. Contribution à l'étude des brises du Léman". Rapports de travail
    de l'Institut Suisse de Météorologie, Novembre.
Liu, P.C., 1976. Application of Empirical Fetch-Limited Spectral Formulas to
    Great Lake Waves. Proceedings of the 15th Coastal Eng. Conference.
McClenan, C.M. and Harris, D.L., 1975. Wave Characteristics as Revealed by Aerial
    Photography. Offshore Technology Conference, Dallas.
Resio, D.T. and Hŭpakka, L.W., 1976. Great Lakes Wave Information. Proceedings
    of the 15th Coastal Eng. Conference
Silvester, R., 1974. Coastal Engineering, Vol. I. Elsevier.
Subrata, K. et al., 1977. Ocean Wave Statistics for 1961 North Atlantic Storm.
    Journ. Waterways, Harbors and Coast. Eng. Div., ASCE, WW4
Wiegel, R.L., 1954. Oceanographical Engineering. Prentice-Hall, N.J.

STATIC AND DYNAMIC RESPONSE OF A MOORING SYSTEM

G. RAGGIO and K. HUTTER

Laboratory of Hydraulics, Hydrology and Glaciology annexed to the Federal Institute of Technology Zürich

ABSTRACT

Raggio, G. and Hutter, K., 1979. Static and Dynamic Response of a Mooring System. Proceedings of the Symposium on Hydrodynamics of Lakes, Lausanne.

Static and dynamic response of moorings under plane motions is analysed. First, the single chain is treated. It is shown that its response depends on two parameters, a buoyancy and a friction parameter. Using the method of transfer matrices mooring systems consisting of chain segments measuring units and spherical floats are then analysed. Their response is compared with that of a single chain. It does not appear that an approximate method for the prediction of the eigenfrequency can be suggested.

INTRODUCTION

Because lake currents are not steady but continuously shift direction and change speed, a mooring cannot remain in static equilibrium; it must move according to the current imposed on it. Such mooring motions are undesired but unavoidable; they lead to uncertaintities in the position of the buoy system and, furthermore, falsify the velocity measurements if the latter is recorded classically with a rotor measuring device. Ideally, the true motion should be determinable from measured flows past the mooring, so that in principle this flow could be corrected for the motion. A computational method achieving these adjustments would be of value. For relatively soft moorings it appears that they must be large and thus more important than for stiffer ones.

Rather than developing a numerical technique with the aid of which the measured velocities are corrected for, we aim at deriving rational design criteria, which would allow a selection of float-units, chain segments and measuring units such that these elaborous corrections are avoided as far as possible. These design criteria would have to give information on the size of the buoys and perhaps on their distribution within a mooring system.

Lake currents are largely influenced by atmospheric conditions. They, in turn, initiate the motion of the moorings, mainly through viscous friction set up by the motion around the floats, chain segments and apparatus-units. The restoring force counterbalancing these viscous effects is buoyancy, and it is intuitively obvious that a mooring system becomes stiffer the larger the floats. Dependent upon buoyancy and friction a mooring possesses a certain frequency spectrum, which should lie outside the dominant frequency range of the currents, because otherwise currents could produce resonance and would falsify the data set.

There are several questions that should be answered in connection with such measuring systems: Among these we mention:

(i) What are the important physical parameters that govern the motion of a single chain? How does the chain react to these parameters? How does the frequency spectrum depend on them?

(ii) Is a single chain a reliable model to treat mooring systems consisting of chains, instruments and floats? If not,

(iii) Is there an efficient mathematical method by which such systems could be relatively easily analysed?

(iv) Are there, perhaps, lakes for which amplification of mooring deflections cannot occur?

The aim of this paper is to provide answers to these questions. In so doing we shall restrict ourselves to plane motions. In certain aspects our approach is more rigorous than that of Fofonoff (1965, 1966) in previous articles, because we treat the chain as a continuous flexible string with uniformly distributed weight and hydrodynamic drag, whereas he did not. We are less general than he was insofar as he, in his second paper, treated non-planar motions, whereas we do not systematically. Methodologically, we use the method of transfer matrices. This method, inspite of its numerical drawbacks, bears the advantage that arbitrary mooring systems can be straightforwardly analysed. Indeed, the approach used here and proved useful can, if needed, be generalized to more complicated motions and chain systems.

Since the method of transfer matrices is well known and since we are only interested in the physical significance of the mooring motion, all mathematical details will be left aside. Interested readers may consult the authors.

BEHAVIOR OF A SINGLE CHAIN

Consider a flexible chain or string under planar motion. The plane of this motion will be assumed to be fixed in space and thus can be described by a Cartesian coordi-

nate system with the x-axis pointing horizontally and the z-axis pointing upwards.
The origin O of this system will not coincide with any point of the chain, in general, but for the purpose of this section we may identify O with the lower endpoint
of the chain. The chain is assumed to be held close to a vertical position by buoyancy forces transferred to the chain through its upper endpoint. The interest in
this section is the planar motion of this chain, its frequency behavior and its
response to external forces.

In figure 1 the geometry is depicted. $U(z, t)$ denotes a given velocity profile
of the fluid which the chain is exposed to. The lower and the upper endpoints will
be denoted by S and E , respectively. The arc length along the cord measured from
S is denoted by s and the entire length of the chain is L , and it is assumed
that the latter is constant. The chain is thus inextensible. We also assume that any
bending rigidity is negligible.

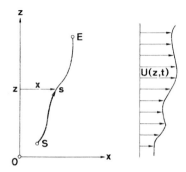

Fig. 1. Geometry of a single chain and definition of coordinate system

Consider a chain held fixed at S and subject to a buoyancy force B at E .
Its motion depends on the following list of parameters:

B   buoyancy force induced at E

g   gravity constant

μ   (constant) mass of chain per unit length

ρ_w density of water

A   cross sectional area of chain

$g^* := (\mu - \rho_w A)g/\mu$, reduced gravity constant

c, ℓ hydrodynamic friction parameters of a linear and quadratic friction law,
        respectively.

$U(x, t)$ Velocity profile the chain is exposed to.

In this list the friction parameter neads further explanation. To this end, let W be the friction force per unit length exerted on the chain by the fluid. It can be defined as

$$W = c(\dot{x} - U) = \frac{\rho}{2} \mathcal{C} (\dot{x} - U)|\dot{x} - U| ,$$

where $(\dot{x} - U)$ is the velocity of the chain relative to the fluid; c is the phenomenological coefficient of a linear friction law, $\mathcal{C}$ that of a quadratic law. For small relative velocities a linear representation is more appropriate.

Dependent on the type of problem the above list of parameters can be reduced in number; this will now be done.

a) <u>static response</u>

If $U = U(x)$, the long time response of the chain will be steady state. It can be shown to depend on a buoyancy and on a friction parameter

$$B^* := \frac{B}{\mu g^* L} > 1 , \quad F^*_{St} = \begin{cases} F^*_{\mathcal{Q}} = \dfrac{\frac{1}{2} \rho_w \mathcal{C} U^2_{Ref} L}{\mu g^* L} & \text{quadratic law} \\[4mm] F^*_{L} = \dfrac{c U^2_{Ref} L}{\mu g^* L} & \text{linear law} \end{cases}$$

and on the distribution $u^*(x)$ of the current along the chain, $U(x) = U_{Ref} u^*(x)$. Of particular interest is the deflection x/L at the upper end E . As an example this is shown in figure 2 for the case that $u^* = 1$. It is seen that, as expected, the deflection of the upper endpoint decreases with increasing buoyancy parameter. For $B^* > 2$ this deflection stays very small, so that from this point of view B^* should not be increased very much beyond $B^* = 2$. Knowing the horizontal deflection we can give an estimate for the maximal vertical displacement Δh as follows

$$\Delta h \cong L \left(\frac{x}{L}\right)^2$$

At the thermocline these displacements give rise to errors in the temperature well in the range of the accuracy of common thermistors. This should be born in mind.

b) Eigenfrequencies

The eigenfrequencies of a single cord depend on B^* and on the dimensionless frictional parameter

$$F^* = \frac{c \sqrt{g^* L} \; L}{\mu g^* L}$$

Intorducing $\omega_o := \sqrt{g^*/L}$ the frequency relation can be expressed in the dimensionless form

$$\omega^* = \frac{\omega}{\omega_o} = \omega^*(B^*, F^*)$$

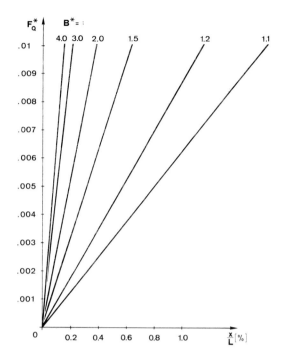

Fig. 2. Horizontal deflection of upper endpoint for a single cord as a function
of F* and B*.

Its numerical value follows from an exploitation of the governing equations. For
a chain held fixed at S and subject to a buoyancy force B at E we have in
figure 3 plotted ω* as a function of F* and B*. There is an infinite number of solutions but figure 3 contains the first and second modes only. It is seen that for a given buoyancy parameter there is an upper bound of the friction parameter beyond which
lowest order eigenmodes are not possible. In this case, however, higher order
modes may very well exist, because the response point of the system in figure 3
may then jump from the lowest order mode to the next higher one. Numerical calculations have also indicated that the amplitude of the upper end point, normalized
such that the inclination of the chain at the lower endpoint is fixed, depends
only on B* (and not on F*).

c) Forced vibration of a single chain

Time dependent response of single chains is caused by unsteady currents U(x, t).
If the frequencies of such currents are close to the resonance frequency of the
chain, large amplifications of the deflection will occur. They cause corresponding
errors in the velocity recordings. The width of the frequency band in which such

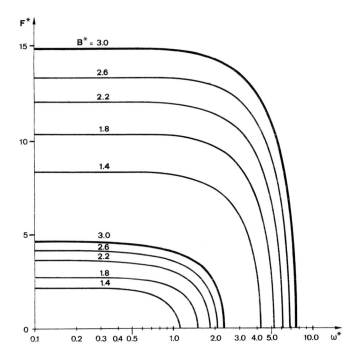

Fig. 3. First and second dimensionless eigenfrequency as a function of the buoyancy parameter B* and the friction parameter F*.

amplifications arise is of practical interest. Of course, hydrodynamic friction will diminish the amplitudes in size and with time. But with F* = 0 upper bounds will generally be obtained.

Let σ be the forcing frequency of a spatially uniform current motion. Denote by A the dimensionless amplitude at the upper endpoint E . Neglecting hydrodynamic friction we then have A = A(σ*, B*), where σ* = σ/√g*L . In figure 4 this function is plotted for two distinct values of B* and in the neighborhood of the first eigenmode. It is seen that the frequency band, in which amplification of the deflection occurs, decreases with increasing B*. The figure also indicates that chains become stiffer the larger B* . At the higher modes the general behavior of the curves is not altered, but the frequency band where amplification occurs becomes very narrow. Consequently, care must be observed when designing single chains so that forcing frequencies lie far from the lowest order eigenfrequency. If this cannot be achieved a high value for B* will both narrow down the frequency band and move the resonance frequency to higher values.

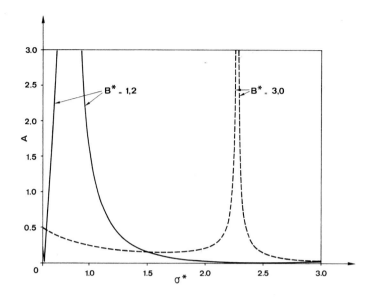

Fig. 4. Dimensionless amplitude as a function of the driving frequency σ for
B* = 1.2 and B* = 3 .

DYNAMIC BEHAVIOR OF MOORING SYSTEMS

In this Section we shall be concerned with the eigenvalue problem of mooring
systems. The restrictions will be the same as in Section 2, namely, planar motion,
neglect of vertical acceleration and small inclinations. We shall further use a
linear law for the viscous forces and shall assume motions around steady state which
are periodic in time. The forces acting on these mooring systems are gravity, horizontal viscous friction, buoyancy and retaining forces.

Mooring systems consist of chain segments, buoys and measuring units. Their
steady state and time dependent response cannot be described in an as simple way
as was the case for a single chain; but chain segments may be treated as flexible
strings, floats and measuring units as rigid bodies. Their mass, moment of inertia
with respect to the center of mass and their hydrodynamic frictional behavior govern
their motion. We have developed a mathematical model describing the motion of the
entire systems. It consists of using the method of transfer matrices. Our interest
was, in particular, in the determination of the system eigenfrequency. Figure 5
contains the necessary information about two mooring systems used in lake Zürich in
a campain in spring 1978. In tables 1 and 2 we give the numerical results for the
first few eigenfrequencies. In the first columns the results are listed when friction
is neglected. In columns 2 the complex frequencies are listed when friction is

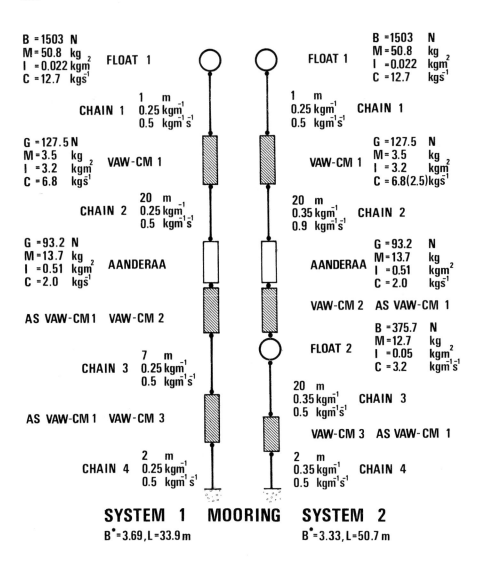

B =1503 N
M=50.8 kg
I =0.022 kgm^2 FLOAT 1
C =12.7 kgs^{-1}

FLOAT 1 B =1503 N
M=50.8 kg
I =0.022 kgm^2
C =12.7 kgs^{-1}

CHAIN 1 1 m
0.25 kgm^{-1}
0.5 kgm^{-1}s^{-1}

1 m
0.25 kgm^{-1} CHAIN 1
0.5 kgm^{-1}s^{-1}

G =127.5 N
M=3.5 kg
I =3.2 kgm^2 VAW-CM 1
C =6.8 kgs^{-1}

VAW-CM 1 G =127.5 N
M=3.5 kg
I =3.2 kgm^2
C =6.8(2.5)kgs^{-1}

CHAIN 2 20 m
0.25 kgm^{-1}
0.5 kgm^{-1}s^{-1}

20 m
0.35 kgm^{-1} CHAIN 2
0.9 kgm^{-1}s^{-1}

G =93.2 N
M=13.7 kg
I =0.51 kgm^2 AANDERAA
C =2.0 kgs^{-1}

AANDERAA G =93.2 N
M=13.7 kg
I =0.51 kgm^2
C =2.0 kgs^{-1}

AS VAW-CM 1 VAW-CM 2

VAW-CM 2 AS VAW-CM 1

B =375.7 N
M=12.7 kg
FLOAT 2 I =0.05 kgm^2
C =3.2 kgm^{-1}s^{-1}

CHAIN 3 7 m
0.25 kgm^{-1}
0.5 kgm^{-1}s^{-1}

20 m
0.35 kgm^{-1} CHAIN 3
0.5 kgm^{-1}s^{-1}

AS VAW-CM 1 VAW-CM 3

VAW-CM 3 AS VAW-CM 1

CHAIN 4 2 m
0.25 kgm^{-1}
0.5 kgm^{-1}s^{-1}

2 m
0.35 kgm^{-1} CHAIN 4
0.5 kgm^{-1}s^{-1}

SYSTEM 1 MOORING SYSTEM 2
B*=3.69, L=33.9 m   B*=3.33, L=50.7 m

Fig. 5. Two mooring systems as used in Lake Zürich in Spring 1978. The various numbers indicate: for the floats: B = buoyancy force, M = mass, I = moment of inertia, C = coefficient of hydrodynamic friction, for the instruments: G = weight under water, M = mass, I = moment of inertia relative to the center of gravity, C = coefficient of hydrodynamic friction, for the chains: length (m), mass per unit length 0.25 kg m^{-1}, hydrodynamic friction 0.5 kg m^{-1}s^{-1}.

TABLE I

First 3 eigenfrequencies of mooring Nr. 1. ω_S calculated neglecting friction, ω with friction, ω_E is an estimation according to formula (*).

$\omega_S \left[s^{-1}\right]$ without Friction	$\omega_S \left[s^{-1}\right]$ with Friction	$\omega_E \left[s^{-1}\right]$ Estimation
2.988	(2.871, 1.81	1.0
6.189	(5.935, 1.77	8.5
12.099	(11.921, 1.81)	13.0

TABLE II

First 6 eigenfrequencies of mooring Nr. 2, ω_S is calculated neglecting friction, ω with friction. ω_E is an estimate according to (*)

without Friction $\omega_S \left[s^{-1}\right]$	with Friction $\omega \left[s^{-1}\right]$	with reduced Friction of the VAW - CM (c_τ=2.5 kg/s)	Estimation $\omega_E \left[s^{-1}\right]$
1.505	(1.46, 0.65)	(1.48, 0.50)	1.9
4.285	(4.23, 1.78)	(4.28, 1.42)	5.8
5.988	(5.79, 1.57)	(5.83, 1.35)	9.2
8.491	(8.46, 0.98)	(8.46, 0.97)	16.4
10.560	(10.51, 1.15)	(10.51, 1.14)	19.2
11.630	(11.59, 0.96)	(11.59, 0.96)	

taken into account. The first number gives the real part and represents the frequency. The second number is the attenuation. To estimate the influence of the hydrodynamic friction we have listed in column 3 of table II the results for reduced friction coefficients of the VAW-current meters. It is seen that the influence of the size of the friction coefficient is relatively unsignificant. In the last column of tables I and II we have also listed an estimate ω_E for ω. This estimate was determined on the basis of the results for a single chain as follows:

$$\omega_E = \omega^* \sqrt{g^*_{virt}/L} \qquad (*)$$

In this formula ω^* is the dimensionless frequency for a single chain whose buoyancy parameter

$$B^* = \frac{\text{total buoyancy forces of the mooring}}{\text{total reduced weight of the mooring}}$$

is the same as that for the mooring under consideration and for which $F^* = 0$. g^*_{virt} is the reduced gravity constant evaluated such that

$$\mu_{chain}\, g^*_{virt} = \left\{ \begin{array}{l} \text{total reduced weight} \\ \text{of the mooring} \end{array} \right\}$$

This method of simplified determination of the eigenfrequency is obviously very
bad for the present moorings, but has been found to be rather accurate (see next
section) for very long chains which carry only a few measuring units and a few buoys.
Better approximate schemes were not found. Consequently, a simplified determination
of the motion of a mooring, although reasonable in certain instances, is not possible
in general. In the next section we shall also give corroboration for the importance
of the deformation and motion of the chain.

FURTHER REMARKS; CONCLUSIONS

In this article the static and dynamic behavior of mooring systems has been analysed using the method of transfer matrices. The single chain was investigated, and
it was found that its dynamic response depends on two dimensionless parameters, a
buoyancy and a friction parameter. Both parameters have a sizeable effect on the
eigenfrequency of the chain, but the forced vibration response and the near resonance behavior depend chiefly on the buoyancy parameter. With increasing buoyancy
the chain does not only become stiffer, but the frequency band in which amplification of the vibration occurs becomes simultaneously more narrow.

The response of actual mooring systems consisting of chain segments, measuring
units and floats is more complicated than that of chains and no direct connection
with single chains exists. The latter is nevertheless a useful tool, because under
certain circumstances it may serve as a first approximation in the design of mooring
systems. This is the case if moorings carry only very few instruments and buoys.
To corroborate this and in order to compare our technique with that of Fofonoff we
determined the first few eigenfrequencies of his "Bermuda mooring". This mooring
is 2'100 m long, carries a 50 kg current meter at a depth of 150 m and a buoy of
mass 565 kg and buoyancy 4710 N. Fofonoff calculated the eigenfrequency on the basis
that the chain is massless and weigthless and that current meter and buoy are idealized mass points. He obtained for the eigenfrequencies $\omega_1 = 0.063$, $\omega_2 = 0.856$
$[s^{-1}]$. There are no others in a two-degrees of freedom system. Not knowing the mass
of the cables and the moment of inertia of the Bermuda-mooring, we could only guess
these. We chose $\mu = 0.25$ kg/m, $I_{current\ meter} = 6$ kg/m^2 and $I_{buoy} = 8$ kg/m^2.
With these we obtained the results of table III. Very roughly they indicate that
Fofonoff only obtained the first and sixth order eigenfrequencies. All others are
missing. This is a serious drawback of his method and implies that the mass of the
chain and its continuous distribution must not be neglected. This impression is
even more intensified if normalized amplitudes are looked at. For $\omega_3 \div \omega_6$ the
largest amplitudes occur at the current meter! Hence large errors of the velocity

TABLE III

First 6 eigenfrequencies of the "Bermuda mooring". ω_C corresponds to a single chain with the same B^* as for the Bermuda mooring. ω_E gives an estimate calculated according to $\omega_E = \omega_C\sqrt{g^*_{virt}/L}$. ω_B is the actual frequency of the mooring.

	ω_C $[s^{-1}]$	ω_B $[s^{-1}]$	ω_E $[s^{-1}]$
1	0.044	0.022	0.045
2	0.202	0.269	0.207
3	0.484	0.395	0.496
4	0.624	0.516	0.639
5	0.764	0.632	0.782
6	0.903	0.867	0.924

data must be expected in the neighborhood of these frequencies – and these are not even detected by Fofonoff. Data corrections with his approximate method are therefore illusory. We have also determined the eigenfrequency with the approximate single-chain method explained in Section 3. The approximate estimates ω_C and ω_E are resonably close to the frequency evaluated by exact methods. This is no surprise, because the mooring is indeed close to a single chain, but more importantly and unlike Fofonoff, our approximate method gives the correct number of eigenfrequencies at a better accuracy than that of Fofonoff.

It should be noted that from a data exploitation point of view resonance phenomena play only a role if the eigenfrequencies of the mooring lies below, or in the neighborhood of the Nyquist frequency. Common recording intervals are roughly 10 min so that $\omega_{Nyquist} \cong 0.01\ s^{-1}$. Nyquist frequencies are seldom above $0.2\ s^{-1}$. This indicates (see tables I,II) that there is no harm if the frequency analysis is disregarded for the Lake Zürich moorings. Yet they should be taken into account for low buoyancy parameters and for long chains in deep lakes and in the Ocean.

Several other questions can be answered with the use of single chain. As an example: Is it advantageous in a mooring system to replace chains by lighter ones and to reduce the buoyancy correspondingly? In practice this is achieved by changing the cross section and/or the material of chain. We have analysed this question and came to the conclusion that the answer depends on several factors which require a separate analysis for each individual case.

We have in the above dealt only with plane motions and have disregarded any 3-dimensional response. Clearly, this response should also be considered. An estimate on it can be obtained if it is assumed that the chain moves in a plane rotating with constant angular velocity Ω. It is not hard to see that these rotations decreases the system eigenfrequency. The plane case is thus indeed the critical one.

REFERENCES

Fofonoff, N.P., 1965. A technique for analysing buoy system motion. Geo Marine
    Technology, 1:V222-225
Fofonoff, N.P., 1966. Oscillation modes of a deep sea mooring. Geo Marine Techno-
    logy, 2:V327-331

DATA BANK AND -VISUALIZATION FOR SEQUENTIAL DATA WITH SPECIAL REFERENCE TO
LAKE GENEVA

S.W. BAUER and C. PERRINJAQUET

Laboratoire d'Hydraulique (LHYDREP), Ecole Polytechnique Fédérale, Lausanne,
Switzerland

ABSTRACT

A field program of observations on the Lake of Geneva using sophisticated
electronic equipment yields a large amount of digital information. In order to
store these data in form of a data bank a suite of procedures and programs has
been established at LHYDREP. Furthermore, means have been developed to allow
visualization of the data in different forms of graphical representation.

INTRODUCTION

Measuring of hydraulic phenomena of the Lake of Geneva (Le Léman) has been done
for a long time. The first scientifically significant measurements were probably
undertaken by F.A. Forel (1895) who performed continuous, high precision measurements of water level fluctuations of the Leman. These measurements allowed him
to verify his physical explanation of the well known periodic water fluctuations
of the Leman (seiches) and to resolve the classic problem of the alternating,
violent currents in the straights of Euripe (Forel, 1879), which for over 2300
years had remained unsolved. A first systematic study of currents of the Leman
appears to have been undertaken by Kreitmann (1931) and Mercanton (1932) who, in
a small "fishery war" between France and Switzerland, observed the drift of fishermen's nets and submerged floats to investigate allegations by fishermen that
the nets at times traverse the entire lake in only one night. Measurements in
the Leman using current meters (Mertz Strommesser) were performed first by Bétant
and Perrenoud (1932), who undertook measurements in the "Petit Lac" to obtain a
better knowledge of the lake in the vicinity of the Geneva waterworks. In order
to study nonperiodic denivellations of the Leman, the Swiss hydrographical service
set up a series of additional water level recorders for a period of about one
year (Service fédéral des eaux, 1954). This campaign gave some insight into wind
generated changes in water levels and allowed Mortimer (1953, 1963, 1974) to prove

that there exist large <u>internal seiches</u> in the Leman. Studying littoral drift currents at the northern coast of the Leman, Plauchu (1970) used submerged floats and electronic current meters. It appears that the Hydraulics Laboratory (LHYDREP) of the Swiss Federal Institute of Technology in Lausanne (EPFL) was the first to use sophisticated electronic recording current meters, which allow continuous observation over long time periods without interruption.

The procedures to be described in this article were established in conjunction with an extensive measuring program on the Leman, which was started in 1977 by LHYDREP. The instruments used in the LHYDREP field program of observations have all been of the type Aanderaa of Aanderaa Instruments, Bergen, Norway. A detailed description of the measuring program is given by Prost et al. (1977) and Graf et al. (1979). The measuring instruments and their working principles are described by Aanderaa Instruments (1975, 1976, 1977).

ESTABLISHMENT OF DATA BANK

Aanderaa instruments record all data on 1/4" magnetic tapes, one tape for each instrument. Thus, in one measuring period there will be the same number (or even more) of tapes as there are instruments. All tapes are non-standard and contain information in non-standard code. If the establishment of a data bank is required, the contents of the 1/4" magnetic tapes must first be transferred onto standard tapes and the code must be translated into some standard code. In establishing the data bank, special care must be taken to store all data in such a way that they can be easily retrieved. This means that all data which have been observed at the same time, should be located next to each other in the data bank. Finally each file in the data bank must be absolutely uniquely identified and the contents must be appropriately described.

The principle operations for the establishment of a data bank are schematized in Figure 1. As can be seen in Figure 1, the contents of each 1/4", non-standard magnetic tape are fist transferred onto standard paper tape with the aid of the Aanderaa tape reader (type 2103) and a Facit punch. This results in the same number of paper tapes as magnetic tapes. Now these standard paper tapes can be read by an Eclipse computer (Data-General). At this stage, each paper tape still contains the non-standard code. To translate this code, a program TRANS has been written, which translates the original code into decimal code and which also converts the raw data into physically significant values (degrees, m/s etc.) by means of the appropriate calibration curves. For each band a sequential file is created containing in each line the time and all measurements of one measuring cycle. Thus

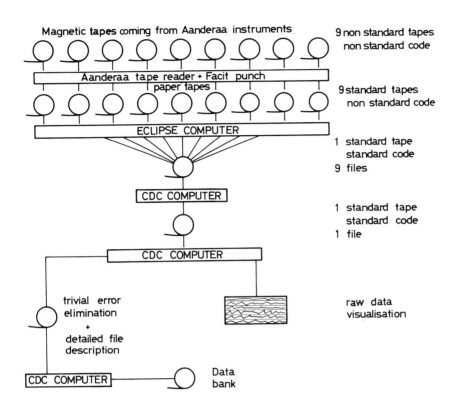

Fig. 1. Schematic view of establishment of data bank for Aanderaa Instruments (scheme for 9 tapes).

one such file will have the same number of lines as there are measuring cycles, all information being in chronological order. Furthermore, each file may have a different starting and ending date. Since generally it is required to retrieve data that have been recorded at the same time, simultaneously, the contents of these files must be amalgamated into one single file by program FUSION. Due to the large storage requirements of this amalgamation procedure, it is performed on the CDC computer of the EPFL. In the same process a preliminary control for errors is included. If faulty information is encountered, it is replaced by the code -999 to indicate that there are no data available. Once this first file has been created, a numerical listing is printed. Also, using program TRACE to be described later, all data are graphically displayed and checked for trivial errors (for example 40°C air temperature in winter, excessive velocities lasting only one measuring cycle, etc.). If such errors are encountered, they are manually replaced by -999. Finally, a detailed file description is added to ensure proper interpretation of the entire file contents.

The data bank resides on magnetic tape and is organized in a multifile set. Each file corresponds to one measuring period and has a label allowing ready access to any specified data period. For safety reasons, each multifile is stored in triplicate on different tapes. An example of a data file is shown in Figure 9 of Graf et al. (1979).

DATA VISUALIZATION

Thus far, about ·one million individual data have been collected in the LHYDREP measuring program. Due to the large number of data it is indispensable to develop some means of analog representation to allow glancing over the collected data and to arrive at some first conclusions. This is also the only way to select periods of special interest which might then be used for further analysis (see for example Bauer and Graf, 1979).

Thus program TRACE was developed to allow tracing of the raw-data in the form in which they are stored in the data bank. Also, two variants of TRACE, programs ARROWS and HODOGR were written to allow drawing of vector stick diagrams and of hodographs. Finally, program ROSE has been developed to perform frequency analyses of the observed data and to draw wind- and current roses.

All programs have been coded in FORTRAN IV and are conceived for standard tracing equipment of computers (e.g. Calcomp plotter), which allow drawing of only one line at a time.

Program TRACE

Program TRACE is completely general. Thus, any data file having the same principal structure as the data file shown in the lower portion of Figure 9 of Graf et al. (1979) can be treated. Figure 2 is an example of output from program TRACE (see also Figures 10-15 of Graf et al., 1979).

Since, as has been stated, standard tracing equipment does not allow the simultaneous tracing of more than one line at a time, it is necessary that program TRACE first reads a given number of lines and stores their contents in its memory. Tracing is then performed in such a way, that one parameter only is drawn for the given period. The next parameter will then be traced once the tracing of the former parameter has been completed. Once the given number of lines has been drawn, a new batch of lines is read replacing the old contents of the memory. Only the last values of each column of the earlier batch have been kept in memory to serve as a starting point when drawing the new batch of data.

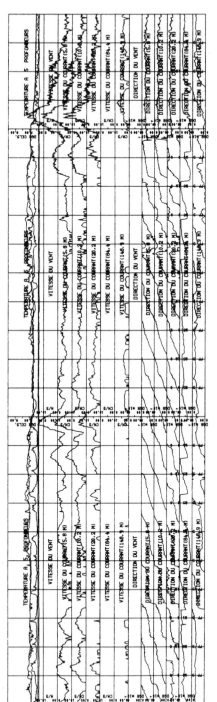

Fig. 2. Trace of data observed between March 19, 1977 and March 31, 1977.

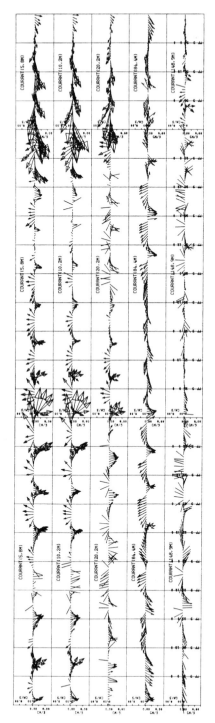

Fig. 3. Vector stick diagram for mean hourly vectors between March 19, 1977 and March 31, 1977.

In Figure 2 it can be seen that the time axis is horizontal and that the data ar
drawn within horizontal bands; furthermore: the sequence of the data traced within
bands is independent from their sequence within the data bank, any number of parameters may be traced within one band, the vertical scale and its starting point
may be different in each band, the width of each band may be different, each band
may or may not be identified by a descriptive text, any number of bands may be
traced. In case the range of a band is exceeded by the data to be plotted, the
trace of these data is continued over neighbouring bands whereby the trace keeps
its original scale. Tracing of data of a time period may be started and terminated
anywhere within the data file. The scale of the horizontal axis corresponding to
the time scale can be freely selected according to the requirements. To allow ready
identification of the data with respect to time, the date may be marked at specified intervals. The only limit of presenting data by program TRACE is the memory
available in the computer and the physical limits of the tracing equipment used.

Program ARROWS

Program ARROWS is a variant of program TRACE to produce vector stick diagrams as
shown in Figure 3. To produce such vector stick diagrams, a certain interpretation
of the data read by program ARROWS is necessary. The vectors shown in Figure 3 are
mean hourly vectors and they correspond to the water velocities and -directions
shown in Figure 2.

There are various output options of program ARROWS. One option is to draw either
every observed vector, or to draw mean vectors for time increments which are mul-
tiples of the observation time increment. Another parameter necessary is an indication showing if the vectors to be drawn are for wind- or for water data. This
is necessary since in meteorology the wind direction is indicated by the direction
from which the wind comes, and in oceanography the current direction is indicated
by the direction in which the current flows. Digital output from the Aanderaa air
and water sensors corresponds to this principle.

A further complication arises due to the fact that a vector is defined by two
quantities of which one may be missing. In case a scalar quantity, such as for
example temperature, is faulty or nonexistent, this value is simply lost. Since
vectors are composed of two components, i.e. magnitude and direction, a vectorial
quantity is lost entirely only if both components are missing. There are thus four
possibilities:
a) both magnitude and direction have been observed,
b) the velocity observation is zero,
c) the velocity observation is faulty (missing) and

d) the directional observation is faulty (missing).

Program ARROWS has been written such that "zero quantity- and faulty information vectors" are either entirely suppressed or drawn as schematized in Figure 4. In Figure 4 it can be seen that "faulty vectors" are distinguishable by their arrow

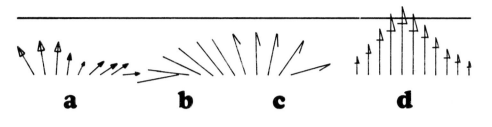

Fig. 4. Schematized vector stick band produced by program ARROWS

tips. If the magnitude is zero or missing, the faulty vectors will be drawn all with a same specified size; if direction is missing, the faulty vectors will be drawn pointing upwards. Thus, if it is desired to suppress the drawing of "faulty or zero" vectors, this size must be specified to be zero. The arrow tips shown in Figure 4 correspond to the four possibilities mentioned above. It may be noted that the above possibilities b and c have actually occurred in Figure 3.

Program HODOGR

Program HODOGR is still another variant of program TRACE to produce vector- and integrated vector diagrams. A vector diagram is the trace of the tip of a vector, which changes its magnitude and direction, but not its origin. Thus a so defined vector diagram corresponds to the observations of an instrument which is fixed in place. An integrated vector diagram consists of a sequence of vectors drawn in such a way that the origin of each vector coincides with the tip of the previous vector. Thus, in an integrated vector diagram the positions of the vectors drawn and the position of the observing instrument no longer coincide.

Figure 5 shows integrated vector diagrams for four current meter observations between March 2, 1977 and April 25, 1977. As can be seen in Figure 5, there is a strong lateral distortion of distances according to the ellipses which have been drawn in broken lines. This distortion can however be eliminated if one chooses an angle of 90° between the x and y axes. The appropriate scales are shown on the edges of the prism surrounding the vertical axis of the measuring station. To allow identification with respect to time, the traces for each instrument are connected by straight lines every given number of times. Also, the date can be marked at

274

specified intervals.

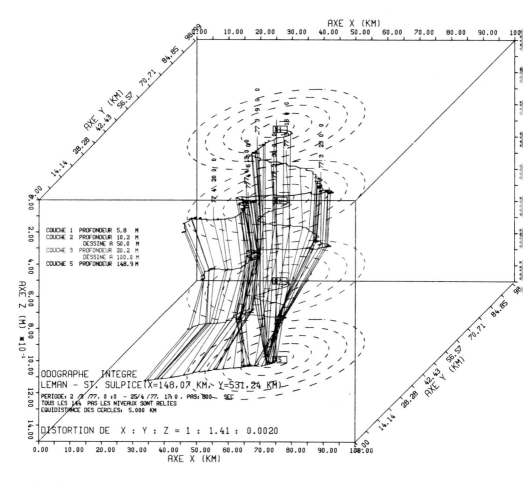

Fig. 5. Integrated vector diagram

Program ROSE

If it is desired to establish tendencies of wind- or current observations, it
is necessary to perform a frequency analysis. Program ROSE has been written to
allow such a frequency analysis and to present the results graphically in form of
wind- and current roses. Figure 6 is an example of wind roses determined for the
airport Cointrin-Genève using 24 years of hourly records. The results of the frequency analysis may also be tabulated by program ROSE in a neat form ready for
publication.

As can be seen in Figure 6, the frequency analysis has been performed for 36

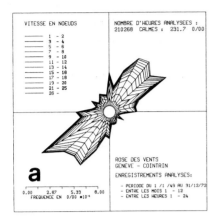

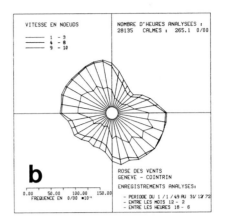

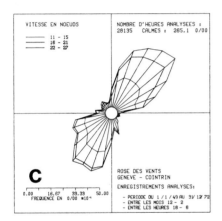

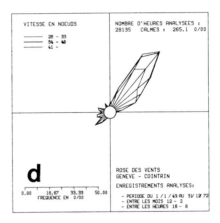

Fig. 6. Wind roses for the airport Cointrin-Genève

directions, i.e., each group for an angle of 10 degrees, whereby the velocities
have been grouped as tabulated in Figure 6. If it is required, program ROSE may
draw frequency roses, using only 12 directions, i.e. each group for an angle of
$30°$. In Figure 6a it can be seen that the frequency diminishes rapidly for strong
winds. Thus program ROSE can draw several roses having different frequency scales
for the same time period, whereby each rose is drawn for a group of velocities.
In Figure 6a the overall sum of all frequencies is 1000 ‰. Since at times it is
required to draw roses with a repartition such that each direction sums up to
1000 ‰ (Aubert, 1963), this option has been included in program ROSE as well.

Finally, program ROSE may perform the frequency analysis only for specified
times. For example, one could determine the frequency distribtuion of winds occur-

ring only in the day-light hours of the summer months. Figures 6b-6d are frequency roses for the same period as that of Figure 6a, but with a partition into three groups of different wind intensities. The analysis shown in Figures 6b-6d has been done only for winter nights, i.e. between December and February inclusive and between 18 and 6 hours. While in Figure 6a the total sum of all frequencies is 1000 %, the sum of the frequencies is 1000 % in each direction in Figures 6b-6d.

ACKNOWLDGMENT

This work was partially sponsored by the Swiss National Science Foundation (FNSRS) under its special program "Fundamental problems of the water cycle in Switzerland".

REFERENCES

Aanderaa Instruments, 1975. Various technical information on Datalogger DL-1. Leaflet No. 102, Bergen.

Aanderaa Instruments, 1976. Various technical information on recording current meter model 4 and 5. Leaflet No. 101, Bergen.

Aanderaa Instruments, 1977. Tape Reader 2103. Technical Description No. 115, Bergen.

Aubert, C., 1963. Climatology of Geneva-Cointrin Airport. Swiss Meteorological Institute, Zurich.

Bauer, S.W., and Graf, W.H., 1979. Wind induced water circulation of Lake Geneva. In: Marine Forecasting, ed. J.C.J. Nihoul, Elsevier Scientific Publishing Company, Amsterdam.

Bétant, A. and Perrenoud, G., 1932. Etude sur la partie occidentale du Lac de Genève. Mém. Soc. phys. et d'hist. nat. de Genève, Vol. 41, Fasc. 2.

Forel, F.A., 1879. Le problème de l'Euripe. Compt. rend. acad. Sciences, Vol. 2.

Forel, F.A., 1895. Le Léman, Monographie Limnologique. Tome second, Slatkine Reprints, Genève, 1969.

Graf, W.H., Perrinjaquet, C., Bauer, S.W., Prost, J.-P. and Girod, H., 1979. Measuring on Lake Geneva (Le Léman). In: Hydrodynamics of Lakes, ed. W.H. Graf and C.H. Mortimer, Elsevier Scientific Publishing Company, Amsterdam.

Kreitmann, L., 1931. Etude des courants du Lac Léman. Les Etudes Rhodaniennes, Vol. 7, No 2.

Mercanton, P.L., 1932. Etude de la circulation des eaux du Lac Léman. Mém. Soc. Vaud. Sc. Nat., Vol. 4, No 27.

Mortimer, C.H., 1953. The resonant response of stratified lakes to wind. Revue Suisse d'Hydrologie, Vol. 15, Fasc. 1.

Mortimer, C.H., 1963. Frontiers in physical limnology with particular reference to long waves in rotating basins. Proc., 6th Conf. Great Lakes Res., Publ. No 10, The University of Michigan.

Mortimer, C.H., 1974. Lake Hydrodynamics. Mitt. Intern. Verein. Limnol., Vol. 20.

Plauchu, J., 1970. Etude des courants du Lac Léman du Rhône à la frontière Vaud-Genève, 1969-1970. Bureau d'Etudes et des Travaux Hydrologiques et d'Océanologie Côtière, Genève.

Prost, J.P., Bauer, S.W., Graf, W.H. and Girod, H., 1977. Campagne de mesure des courants dans le Léman. Bull. Techn. Suisse Romande, Vol. 103, No. 19.

Service fédéral des eaux, 1954. Les dénivellations du Lac Léman. Recherches exécutées de 1949 à 1951. Dép. féd. des postes et des chemins de fer, Berne.

EXCHANGE PROCESSES AT THE WATER SURFACE

E.J. Plate and P. Wengefeld

Institut Wasserbau III, University of Karlsruhe (West Germany)

ABSTRACT

Plate, E.J. and Wengefeld, P., 1979. Exchange Processes at the Water Surface.

A short survey is given of the transport of momentum,heat and mass at the surface of lakes. It is shown in section 1 of this survey that the air flow does work on the water body which results in water drift currents and in wind waves. The unresolved problem is pointed out of how the partitioning of the work is accomplished. When there are no waves, the transferred part of the energy of the wind goes into drift current and water surface set-up, which together with the problem of water surface shear stress is treated in Section 2. Section 3 gives a short survey of the physically different regions of wind-generated waves, with emphasis given to the non-linear saturation region. Finally, in Section 4 heat and mass transfer coefficients are discussed in the light of recent experimental findings.
  Although emphasis is placed on describing the physical processes and regions rather than on quantitative results of analytical or experimental treatments, a set of formulas is given which will enable the user to calculate all the important parameters of the energy transfer process.

1. INTRODUCTION

Of all the lots which human beings can draw one of the closest to perfect bliss must be that of a Swiss limnologist. Like many of his fortunate countrymen he can enjoy at all times the beauty of his country's lakes: their ever changing texture and colour, the coolness and calm of their shores on hot summer evenings, or the spectacle of their agitated surfaces during fall storms. But in addition to the sensual pleasure of seeing and feeling he can enjoy the deep intellectual pleasure of trying to discover and understand the physical and biological reasons behind the phenomena which he observes - a pleasure which is not diminished by the game of hide and seek which nature plays with his mind by the randomness of the causes and the time delays and non-linearitie of the effects.

But the randomness may make it difficult for him to quantify his discoveries in terms of physical principles and formulas. He then should turn to evidence which has been derived from experiments conducted in the laboratory, where some of the variability of the natural processes can be controlled. Such evidence, as it has accumulated over the years, shall be given in this paper for the subject of water surface transport processes. Much of it he will have known already, from observations or from other sources, and all we can do to make it interesting to him is to offer a somewhat personal view, which has developed over many years of doing laboratory tests on wind generated waves and turbulent transport processes.

The background from which we view these phenomena is that of boundary layer theory. We start from the assumption of a steady wind which blows off-shore onto a water surface, as is shown in Fig. 1. The off-shore wind which reflects the properties of the roughness and heat transfer over the land gradually adapts to the water surface properties. The most remarkable differences between this adaptation process and that of a boundary layer flow from one surface to another is the fact that there exists a feed back loop between the air flow and the water flow through the effects of water surface shear and water wave generation.

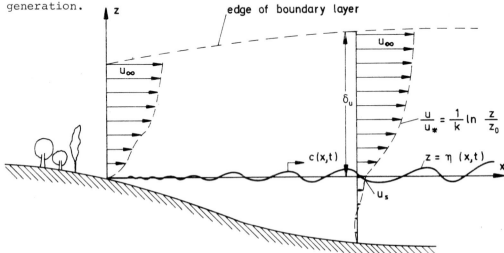

Fig. 1. Wind over water as boundary layer problem

This feed back loop works as follows. If we neglect the effect of pressure gradients of the large scale atmosphere circulation, the driving force for the motion in the water surface is the shear stress which is exerted by the earth on the atmosphere, i.e. the friction which tends to slow down the air currents. In response to this friction, the water surface shows two effects: a drift current is induced, and a wave pattern is generated. Both of these are boundary layer effects: the drift velocity profile develops with space and time, and so does the wave pattern. Both these responses modify the air flow: the drift current imposes a "slip" condition at the lower boundary of the air flow, and the wave pattern changes the roughness. As a consequence, the shear stress is altered. Fortunately, the adjustment time of the air flow to the water surface is very rapid compared to the time that it takes for the wave pattern to change, so that air flow and water surface are locally in equilibrium even during the time of development of a response to a rapid change of air flow conditions - for example during a storm.

The described response of the water body to the wind means that unlike air flow along a solid boundary, air flow along a water surface can do work on the water - work which is partitioned into two parts: one which maintains the wave pattern, and one which produces the energy change of the mean water motion. For each of these parts, the energy balance can be written separately.

The energy balance of the water body is obtained by writing the conservation equation for the energy of the temporal mean velocity field a system of fluid particles:

$$\frac{dE_W}{dt} = \frac{dE_{KW}}{dt} + \frac{dE_{PW}}{dt} - D_W + \frac{dW_W}{dt} = 0 \tag{1}$$

where the index W stands for water, E_K, E_p and E are time mean of the kinetic, potential and total energy, respectively, while W_W is the work done on the water body and D_W is the mean energy dissipation inside the water.

The second part of the work done by the air flow transfers energy to maintain the wave pattern against energy losses caused by wave radiation and dissipation, according to the equation of conservation of the energy E_O of the wave field:

$$\frac{dE_O}{dt} = \frac{dE_{KO}}{dt} + \frac{dE_{PO}}{dt} - D_O + \frac{dW_O}{dt} = 0 \tag{2}$$

where the index O stands for the wave field, the energy terms are
those related to the fluctuating motions of the wave field, and W_O is
that part of the work of the air motion on the water surface which
goes into the water wave field.

It is quite evident that the total work done on the surface is the
sum of W_W and W_O. But it is one of the most intriguing and at present
quite unresolved problems to assign percentages of the total to W_W
or W_O. A solution to this problem requires that it be possible to
partition the shear stress to mean and fluctuating motions of the
surface, which is perhaps identical to the problem of splitting the
total surface stress into form drag of the waves and skin friction
of the surface. This is illustrated in Fig. 2.

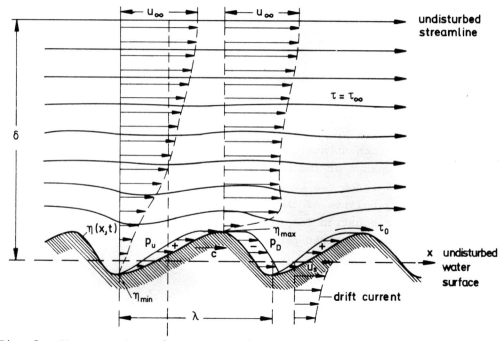

Fig. 2. Momentum transfer over surface waves

For a flow in which the mean does not change with x, the vertical
momentum flux at the height δ is constant and equal to τ_∞. In regions closer to the surface, a part of the momentum flux is transferred downward through shear stress, leading ultimately to a surface
shear stress equal to τ_D. The remainder of τ_∞ is converted through
the variation of the streamline curvatures, into a pressure pattern
which is attached to the waves and which excerts a form drag given
as an average stress $\tilde{\tau}_F$ through the relation

$$\tilde{\tau}_F = \frac{1}{\lambda} \int_{\eta_{min}}^{\eta_{max}} (p_u - p_D) \, dy \qquad (3)$$

The evaluation of the integral (3) represents a very difficult problem. Theory fails to a large extent, because it is very likely that the flow is separated - see Chang et al. (1971). And experimental determinations of pressure distributions are possible only on non-moving wave models which might not be representative.

It may seem a bit academic to dwell on this point. After all, aerodynamists have solved this problem when they encountered the situation of the friction factor for rigid rough boundaries. They have obtained very satisfactory results for all practical purposes by specifying the total shear stress as function of the roughness pattern without bothering about the details of the local pressure field. But there are two important reasons why the situation is different in air sea interaction work.

The first reason lies in the determination of the work integral, because there are different velocities associated with either of the two shear stress components. We obtain

$$\frac{dW}{dt} = \tau_F \cdot c + \tau_O \circ u_s \tag{4}$$

as the work done by the air on the water, and we can only solve this expression if τ_O or τ_F is explicitly known. We only have $\tau_\infty = \tau_F + \tau_O$, and we must admit that we cannot set up a theoretical model that allows to predict wave fields.

The second reason is concerned with mass transport and heat transport. It is well known that the proportionality between heat- and momentum transport, resp. mass- and momentum transport from a flat surface derives from the similarity of the molecular forms of the transport equations at the surface. This similarity breaks down when form drag comes into play, because pressures can transfer momentum, but cannot transport either heat or mass. And so we cannot make a theoretical prediction, based on Reynolds analogy or similar closure assumptions, of the magnitudes of surface fluxes.

As a consequence one must rely on direct experiments and on extrapolation of their results in order to quantify transport processes at the air-water interface. It will be the purpose of the remainder of this paper to present some of the more important laboratory results for these quantities.

2. WIND SHEAR STRESS AND WIND DRIFT

For low wind velocities, the water surface acts like a smooth flat
plate, and its friction factor can approximately be represented by
that of a smooth plate. For higher wind velocities, waves spring up
and add to the roughness of the surface. The roughness which is caused
by the waves will depend both on fetch and on the wind velocity itself
because the wave growth depends on both of these quantities. Only in
the laboratory can one measure the fetch (=x) dependency of the friction coefficient c_{fx}, as was done by Wengefeld (1978). Some of his
data are shown in Fig. 3.

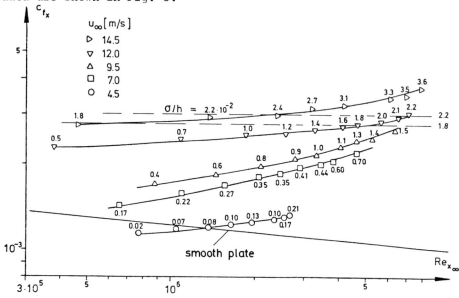

Fig. 3. Friction factor as function of Reynolds number. The data
were taken by Wengefeld (1978), the smooth plate data by suppressing
waves with a net placed on the water surface. σ is the rms-value of
the water surface elevation, h is the depth of flow.

They were calculated by means of the momentum integral equation of
boundary layer theory (Schlichting, 1965). A dependency of c_{fx} on the
distance parameter x (made dimensionless through the introduction of
the Reynolds number $Re_{x\infty} = \frac{u_\infty x}{\nu}$ of the wind velocities) is not large.
Over open water surfaces it can easily be obscured: by the unsteadi-
ness of the air motion, to whose variability the water wave field
reacts only with some time delay, as well as by the fact that the
waves are results of an integration over the history of the wind
field which the waves have encountered in their travel from the

generation area to the point considered.

Also, there is a possibility that the variability of c_f is a secondary effect caused by the increased roughness which comes through the development of the wave field. Such an effect can be inferred by looking at the variability of the roughness parameter σ/h , where h is the depth of the water and σ the rms value of the water surface elevation η . For the largest σ-values of the laboratory data, i.e. values which correspond to high velocities, c_f seems to be constant for constant σ/h values, as is indicated by the curves shown in Fig. 3.

But the question of the dependency of the friction factor on wave parameters is not fully clarified. One often finds the opinion expressed that for a random wave pattern in nature the roughness and the friction factor is solely dependent on the small, high frequency waves which ride on top of the big waves. Consequently, while in a laboratory the roughness-effective waves are the only waves present, in nature they are only a small part of the wave pattern, and thus the rms-value of η would be a very poor representative of its effect on the friction factor. Instead, since the wave part containing small waves remains roughly constant independent of fetch and perhaps of wind speed, the friction factor also becomes independent of these quantities, and there might exist a one to one correspondence between friction factor and wind velocity for all fetches and all wave pattern. This consideration may justify the usual way of presenting surface friction, i.e. through a drag coefficient $C_D = \tau_\omega / \varrho\, u_R^2$ - where u_R is the velocity at a reference height z_R - which is plotted as function of velocity. A diagram of this kind which has recently been published by Hicks (1972) is shown in Fig. 4, which indicates an approximately linear increase of C_D with u_R. However, the diagram Fig. 4 is only a good guess of the true relationship, because the determination of C_D (or u_*) is quite difficult (see Busch, 1976, for a summary of the techniques which can be used for this purpose).

It is only through the momentum integral equation that reliable estimates of the shear stress can be obtained. Two other methods which are considered appropriate for homogeneous terrain do not work so well. The first method which is considered generally to be the most reliable is the measurement of the vertical momentum transport $-\varrho_L \overline{u'w'}$ Over homogeneous terrain this quantity is equal to the shear stress. Over a wave surface, however, part of the transport is through pressures, as was described above, and this part is not known.

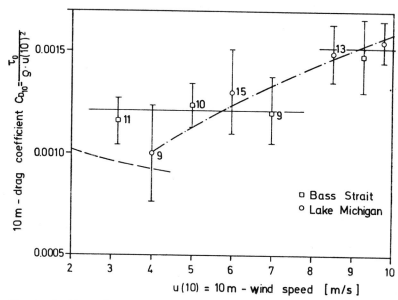

Fig. 4. Neutral 10-m drag coefficients from data obtained over Bass Strait and Lake Michigan. The dashed curve at low wind speeds corresponds to an aerodynamic wavy smooth surface, while the dotted curve is that of Wu (1969). (From Hicks (1972))

The second method is based on the assumption that the velocity profile over the water surface can be represented by a logarithmic law:

$$\frac{u}{u_*} = \frac{1}{k} \ln \frac{z}{z_o} \tag{5}$$

with k, the Karman constant, usually set equal to 0.4. If this equation does indeed represent the velocity profile everywhere, then it is possible to determine the shear velocity u_* and the roughness height z_o from measured velocities at different elevations. This method is often used, sometimes with corrections for the stability of the air flow, but laboratory results indicate that the shear stress calculated from the profiles' $u_* = \sqrt{\tau_\infty / \rho}$ is usually smaller than the value found from the momentum equation.

Knowledge of C_D is sufficient to determine z_o, if validity of Eq. 5 is assumed, because with $u_* = \sqrt{C_D} \cdot u_R$ inserted into Eq. 5 one gets

$$\frac{k}{\sqrt{C_D}} = \ln \frac{z_R}{z_o} \tag{6}$$

in which all quantities are known except z_o. Yet there has been considerable effort to infer z_o directly from the properties of the water surface. Laboratory data show that z_o is proportional to the rms value of the water surface elevation, but apparently this is not valid for very large fetches. Under natural conditions, it seems that the quantity $b = gz_o/u_*^2$ which is termed Charnock's constant lies around the value 0.011 for all wave pattern. However, there is tremendous scatter in the data, as was shown for older data by Roll (1965), and more recent results are not much more definite. A constant Charnock b implies that

$$C_D(z_R) = f\left(\frac{gz_R}{u_*^2}\right) \tag{7}$$

making C_D dependent on a sort of Froude number. It remains to be proved whether this is indeed true. For practical purposes, the relationship of Hicks in Fig. 4 may suffice to calculate the shear stress.

As has been discussed above, if the shear stress is known it must be partitioned into that part which is associated with the drift, and the part belonging to the wave. This is easy for low wind speeds in which case the waves do not take up much of the energy and practically all the shear stress does work to produce drift currents. Plate (1970) has shown that in this case the air flow is unaffected by the drift current, and can be calculated from flat plate relations. As long as the flow stays laminar exact solutions can be obtained for water surface velocity u_s and the drift current profile.

The establishment of the drift current is an unsteady process, much like that of all the generation processes of air sea interaction. According to the energy equation Eq. 1, the work done by a step input of surface stress initially transfers energy into a kinetic energy of a thin drift layer near the surface (for a model see Larnaes, 1976). This energy is converted in part into heat through dissipation, but some of it is converted into a set up, i.e. into potential energy which is manifested in the tilt of the water surface. Eventually, a steady state is reached in which $dE_W/dt=0$ and the work done on the surface is balanced by dissipation, while a steady set up is maintained which provides the driving force for the reverse current required for preserving continuity of the velocity field.

Most of the analyses of water drift currents were based on the assumptions of a steady surface velocity as function of fetch both for laminar flow and for turbulent flow. It was shown that the flow development showed different characteristics in each of the four regions shown in Fig. 5.

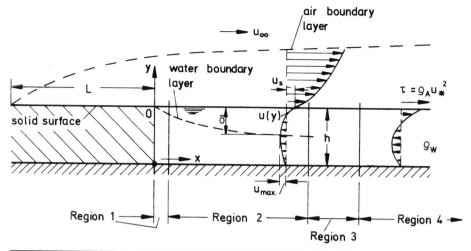

Fig. 5. Regions of water surface drift velocity and results (from Plate (1970))

For each of these Plate derived solutions based on the assumption of an externally imposed shear stress on the surface, a laminar flow in the water or alternatively by a turbulent flow in the water body. For laminar flow, excellent agreement of the theory was found with experimental results of Keulegan (1951). For turbulent flows, an assumption had to be made for the eddy viscosity ε_W in the water, for which the relation:

$$\varepsilon_W = \alpha \cdot u_S \, l_{ch} \tag{8}$$

was chosen. The choice of $l_{ch} = \delta$, the thickness of the boundary layer in region 1, or of $l_{ch} = h$ the depth of flow in region 4 rendered the solution independent of the vertical coordinate, and the solution

$$\frac{u_S}{u_*} = \beta \, \frac{u_{*W} h}{\varepsilon_W} \tag{9}$$

was found, where β is a constant. The quantity u_{*W} is the friction

velocity of the water current, which because of continuity of shear
stress at the water surface is related to the air shear velocity u_*
by $u_{*W} = (\rho_A/\rho_W)^{1/2} u_*$. A comparison with experimental data showed
that the factor α is very likely proportional to the friction factor
c_D. For practical purposes, it appears to be sufficient to put

$$u_S \approx 0.03 \, u_R$$

with u_R measured at 10 m height. Although this relationship is certainly not exact, it is not possible to improve the relationship without more detailed investigations of the interface mechanics. An attempt to include wave dynamics into the consideration of wind induced
water velocity profiles was made by Csanady (1978), who derived a
dependency of ε_W on the ratio of the frictional to the gravitational
forces which is expressed through the Keulegan parameter

$$\Theta = \frac{u_{*W}^3}{g\nu} \tag{10}$$

which plays an important role in the theory of the stability of stratified flows.

Most analyses of the drift current below the surface (for example
that of Csanady, 1978) have started directly from the assumption of
a logarithmic profile, instead of the constant eddy viscosity model
which yields profiles described by error functions or polynomials
(Plate, 1970). A generally valid model is as yet not available.

3. WIND GENERATED WAVES

It is well known that for a given point of the water surface the wind
wave pattern observed there depends on the wind speed, fetch length,
and wind duration. Only when the wind duration is large enough do we
obtain fetch limited waves whose statistical characteristics do not
change with time. These are the maximum possible waves for a given
wind intensity and fetch - in the sense that the individual waves
follow some random distributions for their properties, but that the
parameters of these distributions are stationary. The minimum duration necessary for a fetch limited case to occur after a step change
in wind velocity equals fetch divided by wind velocity - so that at a
fetch of about 50 km even a very strong wind of 40 m/s must have persisted unchanged for at least 20 minutes.

Because of the variability of the natural wind, truly fetch limited
conditions do not often occur on large lakes. But fetch limited waves
are the only ones which can be analysed with some hope of establishing

the dependency of the wave pattern on the wind field: a duration limited wind field can be anywhere in its state between integrated effects of earlier winds and the fetch limited state of the present
wind.

A striking observation for fetch limited data is that for high enough
winds there exist four different regions of flow development which
are schematically shown in Fig. 6.

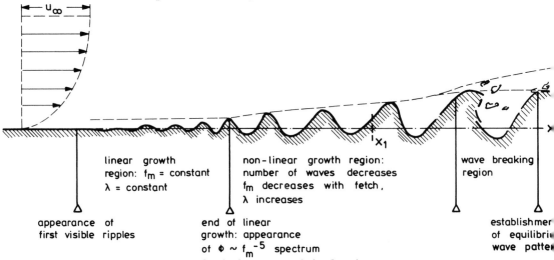

| linear growth region: f_m = constant λ = constant | non-linear growth region: number of waves decreases f_m decreases with fetch, λ increases | wave breaking region |
| appearance of first visible ripples | end of linear growth: appearance of $\phi \sim f_m^{-5}$ spectrum | establishment of equilibrium wave pattern |

Fig. 6. Development of wind waves with fetch

At shortest fetches lies the region of wave generation with clearly
visible, distinctly two dimensional waves established at the end of
the region. Then follows the region of linear instability. The wave
pattern is two dimensional, but not necessarily consisting of long
crested waves. Its most significant characteristic is that the dominant frequency in the spectrum does not change with fetch while the
amplitude of the waves corresponding to this frequency is increasing
exponentially. The next region is the region of saturation growth:
the waves increase in amplitude but at a slower rate, while their
frequency decreases with fetch. It might change into the mixing region in which air and water become mixed. This begins when the waves
start to show white caps, and in its most developed form it has all
the appearances of a layer with continuous transition of an air-water
mixture from clear air to a dense mixture of air, water droplets, and
mist near the water surface - much as in the mixing region of density
stratified fluids with small interfacial Richardson numbers. For air-
water flows this region has not been well observed because wind speeds

and/or fetches have to be very large for it to become fully developed.
It therefore shall not be discussed here. Neither can we discuss the
final state of the surface which must exist at long fetches, when the
work done on the waves is converted into dissipation through the in-
termediary of a steady and homogeneous pattern of waves whose statistical properties remain constant with time and fetch. At low winds,
this state can of course be reached long before wave breaking occurs,
but research on the occurrence of the different stages is not well
developed.

Any of the fetch limited wave pattern is an asymptotic pattern also
for the case of duration limited wave development. After a gradual
change of wind velocity from zero to some large value of u_∞ one observes for example for fetch x_1 of Fig. 6 that the temporal development of the wave pattern goes through all the stages of region 1 to 3
until it becomes stationary.

Fig. 6 shows that it is useful to distinguish two types of stability
limit: a lower one at which the first ripples become visible, and a
higher one at which the waves start breaking. The lower one seems to
correspond to conditions at which wind field and waves become linearly
coupled: waves occasionally seen at shorter fetches than the one corresponding to the lower stability limit have wave heights which decrease
with time, i.e. the waves are damped. The upper limit, on the other
hand, corresponds to a breakdown of the stable waves: it is the stability limit investigated by Jeffreys (see Phillips, 1966).

Although a great deal of effort has been invested in explaining the
occurrence of the first water surface undulations, there exists at
present no theory which really predicts what can be observed. The
state of our theoretical knowledge is presented in Phillips (1966),
the disagreement of theory and experiment has been summarized for the
case of laboratory experiments by Plate (1978). However, for practical
purposes, neither generation region nor region of linear growth are
very important, since most of the time during moderate to strong winds
the water surface will be in a state of non-linear growth. The region
of non-linear growth can at present only be described by taking re-
course to empirical data which are combined with theoretical approaches. Elements of a semi-empirical theory are based on the energy
equation Eq. 2. For the wavefield kinetic and potential energy can be
combined into the term

$$E = E_{KO} + E_{WO} = \gamma \sigma^2 \tag{11}$$

where E is the total wave energy per unit area, and σ^2 the variance of the water surface elevation. Because the wave energy is associated with many different frequencies it is customary to consider the individual wave components, through the frequency spectrum $S(\omega)$ which then is integrated

$$\sigma^2 = \int_0^\infty S(\omega)\,d\omega \qquad (12)$$

to yield the total energy at a point. The energy equation Eq. 2 is then written (for example: Hasselmann et al., 1976) separately for each spectral component:

$$\frac{\partial S}{\partial t} + v\frac{\partial S}{\partial x} = \sum T \qquad (13)$$

where S is the directionally averaged spectrum at angular frequency ω, v an average progression speed of the wave energy at frequency ω and $\sum T$ is the sum of the source terms, which include the work and dissipation terms of Eq. 2 as well as one term representing the non-linear contributions of waves of other angular frequencies (= non-linear interaction terms).

A prediction of the wave energy at a point in space then requires the solution of Eq. 13 from the beginning of a storm (or much earlier, to include swell and distributed sources) to the instant considered. This has been attempted with uncertain success, and quite a bit of research in the field of physical oceanography is directed towards a better understanding of the source terms, and towards solving Eq. 13.

For lakes, it is likely that swell and the effects of directional variability of the wind are of minor importance and one is most concerned with the steady state. In that case, the first term on the left hand side is zero, and the source terms combine to yield a stable and stationary wave pattern which does not change with time, so that its generation history is no longer important. A simple model for the prediction of the wave-field can then be obtained from the assumptions:

1. the probability distribution of the water surface elevation is gaussian,

2. the energy spectrum is narrow banded and can be described by a similarity form proposed by Hidy and Plate (1965): (with $\omega = 2\pi f$ = angular frequency, and the index m denoting the peak in the spectrum)

$$\frac{S(\omega)\omega_m}{\sigma^2} = \phi(\frac{\omega}{\omega_m}) \tag{14}$$

Assumption 1 and the first part of assumption 2 have been used by Longuett-Higgins (1953) to show that the distribution of the wave heights must follow a Rayleigh distribution. A consequence of the Rayleight distribution is that there must exist a relation between the height $H^{1/3}$ which is the average height of the highest one third of all waves, and the mean height H_m

$$H^{1/3} = 1.6 \, H_m \tag{15}$$

Actually, a close inspection shows that the Rayleigh distribution does not really fit the observed data too well. However, the relation Eq. 15 has been observed to fit very well in laboratory as well as in natural conditions (for a summary see Plate, 1978). Also, the variance σ^2 must be related to $H^{1/3}$ by the formula:

$$H^{1/3} = 4\sigma \tag{16}$$

This equation permits to connect the wave height with the spectrum, so that the one is known the other can, through Eqs. 14 and 16, be determined also.

Non-dimensional spectra have been observed by numerous workers, with an exceptionally fine set given by Liu (1971) for lake conditions which is shown in Fig. 7. These curves can be described by the relation:

$$\phi(\tilde{f}) = 4.08 \cdot \tilde{f}^{-5} \, e^{-1.02\tilde{f}^{-4}} \tag{17}$$

given by Liu (1971), where $\tilde{f} = f/f_m$. For the dependency of f_m and σ on fetch the following equations have been given by Mitsuyasu (1978)

$$\frac{g\sigma}{u_*^2} = 1.31 \cdot 10^{-2} \, (\frac{gx}{u_*^2})^{1/2} \tag{18}$$

$$\frac{u_* f_m}{g} = (\frac{gx}{u_*^2})^{-1/3} \tag{19}$$

Together, Eqs. 17 to 18 are sufficient to fully describe the wave spectrum in frequency space. But for a reproduction of individual waves, the spectrum does not suffice. A knowledge of the progression

292

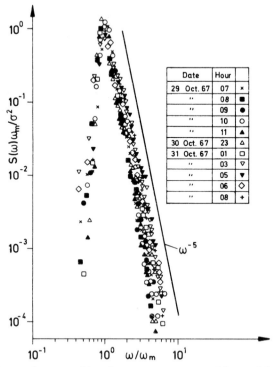

Fig. 7: Examples of normalized wave spectra (from Liu (1971))

speed of the individual waves must be available to translate frequencies into wave length. For the highest waves, experiments have shown
(Mitsuyasu, 1978) that its progression speed is that of an infinitesi-
mal gravity wave with a period equal to $(1.05 \ f_m)^{-1}$.

This discussion did have to be very brief, and could not begin to
do justice to the fascinating theory of wind generated waves. Even
though water waves are one of the most obvious and regular natural
phenomena, their motions are not fully understood, with existing
theories clashing with the experimental evidence. The reader need only
to compare the papers by Hasselmann et al. (1976) and Plate (1978) to
get some impression of this difference.

4. HEAT AND MASS TRANSFER

Heat transfer at a free water surface takes place through the processes of radiation, turbulent convection and evaporation. Only the
latter two effects will be dealt with in this lecture. Both are strongly
influenced by the wind and wave fields already described in Section
2 and 3. Unfortunately the difficulties and uncertainties in the calculation and prediction of these fields are fully reflected in the
heat transport. Therefore empirical methods have been invented which,
for example, have been critically reviewed by Sweers (1976). The resulting empirical formulas give, however, only a very general estimate.
For an improved interpretation it is necessary to fully understand
the aerodynamic problem as a boundary layer problem (see Fig. 8) with
boundary conditions set by the wind and temperature fields, and by
the waves.

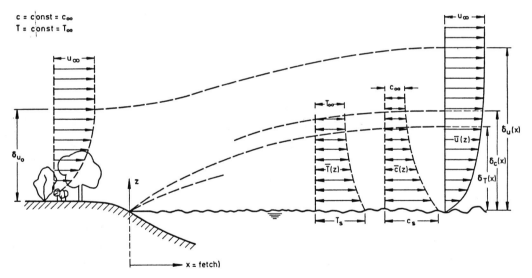

Fig. 8. Definition-sketch for the boundary layer problem of momentum-,
heat- and mass transfer at a water surface

Let us briefly consider the nature of this boundary layer problem.
Under the influence of the wind which blows from the shore onto a
water surface, vertical and horizontal transport of heat and water vapour takes place. In addition to the momentum boundary layer of thickness $\delta_u(x)$ a boundary layer of the humidity of the air with thickness

$\delta_c(x)$ and concentration profile c(x, z) develops. Also, a temperature boundary layer of thickness $\delta_T(x)$ and temperature profile T(x, z) forms. The boundary layer equations which describe these processes cannot be solved exactly. Simplifications are necessary which have to be applied in the light of results of laboratory investigations.

In the theoretical treatment the flow field can be divided into three regions. The characteristic of the first region (very short fetches x) is that the transition from the shore to the water surface has an effect on the heat transfer. For a lake, however, this region is very small. In the second region the local heat transport decreases with increasing fetch due to the development of the profiles. In this region one can apply the relations for the dependence of the heat transport on the fetch x developed from an analysis of the boundary layer equations to the natural boundary layer above a water surface (see Schlichting, 1965). For the evaporation for example, a unique relation between the dimensionless rate of mass transport (the Sherwood number) and the Reynolds number is valid:

$$Sh = f(Re) \tag{20}$$

The Sherwood number is defined as follows:

$$Sh = \frac{E}{D} \frac{L}{\rho_L (c_s - c_R)} \tag{21}$$

with E(gr/m^{2}s) the total evaporation rate, a length scale L(m) which characterizes the size of the lake, the molecular diffusivity of water vapour in air D(m^2/s), the density of air ρ_L(gr/m^3) and the concentration of water vapour c(-) at the water surface and the reference height z = R. The definition of the Reynolds number is:

$$Re = \frac{u_R \ L}{\nu} \tag{22}$$

The difficulty in the application of equation (20) is to find a suitable reference velocity u_R and length scale L. Cermak and Koloseus (1953/54) recommended to use the quantity $\sqrt{A}$ for the length scale L where A is the area of the lake, and the shear velocity u_* as defined by equation (5) for the reference velocity u_R. Meteorologists often use the so-called anemometer height (z = 1.5m) as a reference height. The values of the air humidity and the wind velocity at that reference height and the length scale L (the fetch in the prevailing direction of wind) have to be inserted into Eqs. (21) and (22).

In the third region (very large fetches x) the profiles no longer
change along the flow direction. Consequently the vertical fluxes are
constant and equal to the values at the water surface ($z = 0$, i.e.
the boundary layer equations reduce to:

$$\tau = \tau_0 = \rho_L (\nu \frac{\partial \bar{u}}{\partial z})_{z=0} = \rho_L K_M \frac{\partial \bar{u}}{\partial z} \tag{23}$$

$$-Q = -Q_0 = \rho_L c_p (\lambda \frac{\partial \bar{T}}{\partial z})_{z=0} = \rho_L K_H \frac{\partial \bar{T}}{\partial z} \tag{24}$$

$$-E = -E_0 = \rho_L (D \frac{\partial \bar{c}}{\partial z})_{z=0} = \rho_L K_E \frac{\partial c}{\partial z} \tag{25}$$

where K_M, K_H and K_E are the turbulent exchange coefficients for momentum (the eddy viscosity), heat and water vapour respectively. Their
values are considerably greater than the equivalent molecular coefficients. They express the effect of the turbulence and as such are
not physical constants of the fluid but depend on properties of the
flow field and exhibit a directional dependence. The problem of obtaining solutions to Eqs. (23) to (25) is to find analytical expressions for the exchange coefficients.

A simple solution in the region of constant fluxes is achieved by
assuming that according to the Reynolds analogy the turbulent exchange
coefficients of momentum and water vapour are equal ($K_M = K_E$) and that
the concentration profiles and velocity profiles are similar. By combination of Eqs. (23) and (25) the following expression for the evaporation rate results:

$$E = -\tau_0 \frac{dc/dz}{du/dz} \tag{26}$$

With the definition of $C_D(z)$ - according to which there exists the
following relationship between the shear stress at the ground and
the wind velocity at the height z:

$$\tau_0 = \rho_L \cdot C_D(z) \cdot u^2(z) \tag{27}$$

one finally obtains:

$$E = \rho_L \cdot C_D(z) \cdot u(z) (c_s - c(z)) \tag{28}$$

With a value of $C_D(10)$ of $1.2 \cdot 10^{-3}$ (Fig. 4) (this implies a value
of $C_D(1.5)$ of $1.72 \quad 10^{-3}$ at anemometer height) and several transfor-
mations the following relationship between Sherwood and Reynolds
number results:

$$Sh = 0.0011 \quad Re \tag{29}$$

This formula is practically identical to that given by Coantic (1974).

In the developing region of the profiles (region 2) the exchange rates at the surface become fetch dependent. It is no longer possible to infer the fluxes from one measurement only. A critical survey of the methods available for transport rate calculations has been given by Mangarella et al. (1971), which shows that the best method probably consists in determining profiles and calculating from them the fluxes analogous to the shear stress calculation through the boundary layer momentum equation. This method has also been used by Wengefeld (1978), whose results shall be discussed below.

Results of Wengefeld (1978) for the developing region are shown in Fig. 9, together with experimental results from many sources. The straight line 1 with a slope of 1 holds for long fetches and corresponds to Eq. 29. The straight line 3 was derived by Cermak and Koloseus (1953/54) from different evaporation measurements including field measurements of Lake Hefner and wind tunnel data obtained by them, with Re defined through Eq. 22. Straight line 3 has an exponent of 0.87. Line 2 corresponds to data of Marmottant (1974) and Coantic and Favre (1974) and has a slope of 0.75. While for $10^6 \leqq Re \leqq 10^8$ only small differences exist between the different curves, extrapolation to $Re \sim 10^{10}$ gives results which differ almost by an order of magnitude. One must therefore conclude that the exponent is probably not constant, but approaches 1 asymptotically, which is in agreement with balance calculations.

Since Eq. 29 fits all data fairly well, it is recommended to use it for evaporation at long fetches and high wind velocities, although the true situation is much more complex, as is evident from a closer inspection of the data of Wengefeld (1978). They show that one can distinguish 3 regions; a first region - up to a wind speed of about 4.5 m/s - in which the water surface is smooth along the whole fetch of 10 m, a transition region in which the water surface is partly smooth and partly rough, and a third region with a fully rough surface along the whole measuring section for wind velocities in excess of 9 m/s. In this last region the data of Wengefeld are well represented by the relationship of Coantic and Favre.

The increase in the evaporation rate in the last region is caused by the roughness of the surface. If one takes the data for a wind velocity of 4.5 m/s (closed circles in Fig. 9) the water is smooth along the whole length of the channel (data of Wengefeld). Coantic´s data

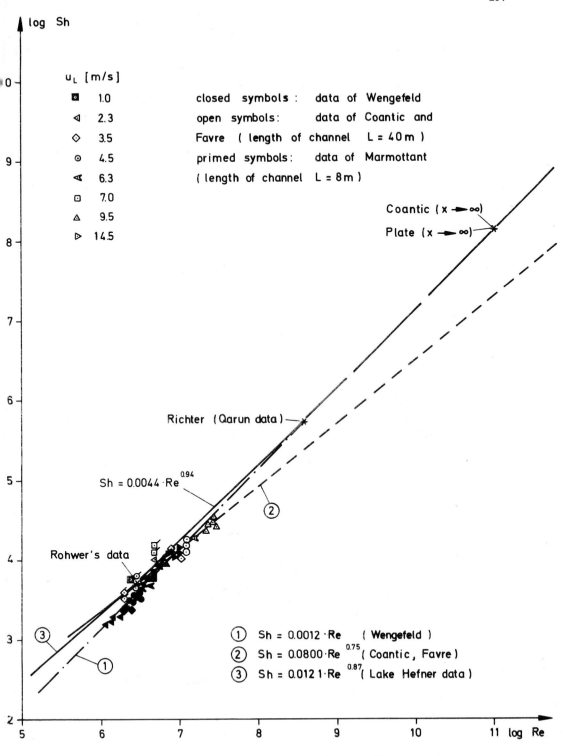

Fig. 9: Comparison of evaporation prediction equations with experimental data of different authors

(open circles) were taken at a channel with a measuring section of
40 m length. Along this fetch even at the low velocity of 4.5 m/s
waves have developed to such a height that the evaporation rate is
enhanced compared to the evaporation from a smooth surface.

The preceding description was limited to the problem of evaporation
since most of the information available concerns this process. However, the sensible heat transport also contributes significantly to
the heat energy balance of a body of water. For atmospheric flow con-
figurations this quantity is difficult to estimate from formulas as
it depends on the temperature gradient between the body of water and
the air and can change its sign. For the computation of transport of
sensible heat one therefore applies the Bowen ratio method, which was
employed for the first time by Bowen (1926). The Bowen ratio BV re-
lates the sensible heat flux Q_H to the latent heat flux Q_E = r · E(r =
heat of vaporization of water). If an equation similar to Eq. 28 is
derived for Q_H, if furthermore the reference height is choosen equal
to the boundary layer thickness δ, where $\varrho_D(z) = \varrho_{D\infty}$ and $T(z) = T_\infty$,
and if equality of the factors $C_D \cdot u_\infty$ is assumed, one obtains:

$$ BV = \frac{Q_H}{Q_E} = 0.493 \frac{T_s - T}{\varrho_{D_s} - \varrho_D} \tag{30} $$

where $\varrho_D (gr/m^3)$ is the density of water vapour in the air. With the
help of this equation one can calculate Q_H if Q_E has been determined
by means of the approximation formula Eq. 28 as described earlier.
Eq. 30, however, has not yet been verified by experiments. Becker
(1964) states that, following field measurements, a factor of
$(1 \pm 0.4) \cdot 0.493$ has to be inserted instead of 0.493. This spread of
40 % leads to considerable uncertainties in the calculation of the
sensible heat transport by Eq. (30). Fig. 10 shows laboratory results
of the Bowen ratio taken by Wengefeld (1978). For a positive temperature difference $T_s - T_\infty$ (for negative values there are no experimental results available) the measured Bowen ratio can be well represented by the following equation:

$$ BV = (1 \pm 0.2) \cdot 0.52 \frac{T_s - T}{\varrho_{D_s} - \varrho_D} \tag{31} $$

By means of these experimental results the scatter can be reduced
from 40 to 20 %. It would be desirable to prove the above relationship for negative temperature differences. An air-conditioned wind

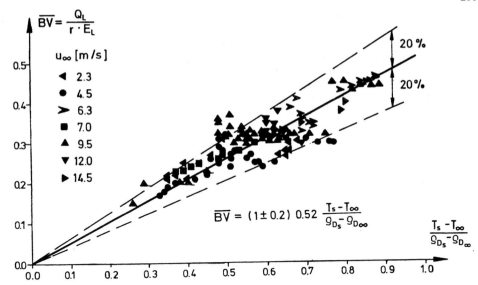

Fig. 10. Bowen-ratio for heat- and mass transfer from a wavy water surface (from Wengefeld (1978))

wave tunnel as used by Coantic and Favre could very much contribute to such an investigation.

It is possible that the assumption, leading to Eq. 30 are not correct because the processes of water vapour and heat transfer differ. For example, an important source of humidity in the air is found in the direct separation of droplets from the surface. A direct indication is seen when the waves show white caps, i.e. for droplet generation the wind speed at large fetches very likely must exceed 6 - 10 m/s. It is interesting to note that white caps and spray formation are usually caused by air entrainment from breaking waves. The breaking wave crest entraps small air bubbles and plunges with them into the water body. Due to their uplift, the bubbles rise to the surface and in penetrating it with a fairly large vertical velocity they carry ring droplets along in their upward motion which then are caught by the horizontal wind and dispersed by the turbulence. Only at large wind speeds does one find droplets which are generated directly by the action of the wind which tears away the tops of wave crests. Wang and Street (1976) have recently summarized previous and their own experimental results which indicate that the number of droplets per unit volume are distributed with height according to a logarithmic profile - which indicates that to a first approximation droplets behave like passive additives to the turbulent motion of the wind - much like the other transported quantities. However, there is no reason to expect that the generation process has any similarity to heat or mass transport from the surface. Quantitative results which make it possible to interpret droplet distributions with humidity or air density are at present not available.

ACKNOWLEDGEMENTS

The researches leading to this work have been sponsored by the German Research Association (DFG) through the Sonderforschungsbereich 80 at the University of Karlsruhe.

REFERENCES

Becker, A., 1964. The thermal capacitance of inland waters. Bes.Mitt. zum gewässerkundlichen Jahrbuch der DDR, Nr. 2.
Bowen, I.S., 1926. The ratio of heat losses by conduction and by evaporation from any water surface. Phys. Review, Vol. 27, p. 779.
Busch, N.E., 1976. Fluxes in the surface boundary layer over the sea. Research Establishment Risø Rep. No. 343, Denmark.
Chang, P., Plate, E.J. and Hidy, G.H., 1971. Turbulent air flow over the dominant component of wind generated waves. Journ. of Fl. Mech., Vol. 47, p. 183.
Coantic, M., 1974. Formules empiriques d´évaporation. Inst. de Méchanique Statistique de la Turbulence, Univ. d'Aix-Marseille.

Coantic, M. and Favre, A., 1974. Activities in and preliminary results of air-sea-interactions. Research at I.M.S.T., Advances in Geophysics, Vol. 18, p. 375.
Cermak, J.E. and Koloseus, H., 1953/54. Lake Hefner model studies of wind structure and evaporation. Final Report, Part I and II, Agric. and Mech. College, Fort Collins, Colorado.
Csanady, G.T., 1978. Turbulent interface layers. Journ. of Geoph. Res., Vol. 83, No. C5, p. 2329.
Hasselmann, K., Ross, D.B., Müller, P. and Sell, W., 1976. A parametric wave prediction model. Journ. of Phys. Ocean., Vol. 6, p. 200.
Hicks, B.B., 1972. Some evaluations of drag and bulk transfer coefficients over water bodies of different sizes. Boundary Layer Met., Vol. 3, p. 201.
Hidy, G.M. and Plate, E.J., 1965. Frequency spectrum of wind generated waves. The Physics of Fluid, Vol. 8, No. 7.
Keulegan, G., 1951. Wind tides in small closed channels. Journ. of Res. of the Nat. Bureau of Standards, Vol. 46, p. 358.
Larnaes, G., 1976. Formation of wind waves. Inst. of Hydrodyn. and Hydr. Eng., Techn. Univers. of Denmark, Series Paper No. 10, Lyngby.
Liu, P.C., 1971. Normalized and equilibrium spectra of wind waves in Lake Michigan. J. Phys. Ocean., Vol. 1, p. 249.
Longuett-Higgins, M., 1952. On the statistical distribution of the heights of sea waves. Journ. Marine Res. 11(3) 245-266.
Mangarella, P.A., Chambers, A.J., Street, R.L. and Hsu, E.Y., 1971. Energy and mass transport through an air water interface. Techn. Rep. No. 134, Dept. of Civ. Engg., Stanford Univ., Stanford, Calif.

Marmottant, M., 1974. Contribution à l' étude de l'évaporation dans une couche limite turbulente d'interface air-eau. Thèse Dr.-Ing., Univ. de Provence, Marseille.

Mitsuyasu, H., 1973. The one-dimensional wave spectra at limited fetch. Rep. Res. Inst. Appl. Mech. Kyushu Univ., No. 30, p. 183.

Mitsuyasu, H., 1978. The growth of duration-limited wind waves. J. of Fluid Mech., Vol. 85, Part 4, p. 705.

Mitsuyasu, H., 1979. Air-sea interactions. Chapt. 8 in the book "Engineering Meteorology". E.J. Plate, Editor, to be published by Elsevier, Publishing Co., The Netherlands.

Phillips, O.M., 1966. The dynamics of the upper ocean. Cambridge Univ. Press.

Plate, E.J., 1970. Water surface velocities induced by wind shear. Proc. ASCE, Vol. 96, J. of the Engg. Mech. Div., p. 295.

Plate, E.J., 1977. Turbulent transport phenomena. Lecture held at Univ. of Karlsruhe, Germany.

Plate, E.J., 1978. Wind generated surface waves: the laboratory evidence. Proc. of a NATO Symp. at Isle de Bandor, 1977, to be published by Plenum Press.

Richter, D., 1969. A contribution to the evaluation of evaporation from free water surface demonstrated with the example of Lake Stechlin. Abhandlungen d. Meteor. Dienstes der DDR, Nr. 88, Band XI, Akademie Verlag, Berlin.

Schlichting, H., 1965. Boundary layer theory. Verlag G. Braun, Karlsruhe, Germany.

Wang, C.S. and Street, R.L., 1978. Measurement of spray of an air-water interface. Dynamics of the Atmosphere and Ocean, Elsevier Publ. Co., The Netherlands, Vol. 2, p. 141.

Wengefeld, P., 1978. Momentum-, heat- and mass transfer at the surface of an open channel flow under the influence of the wind. Dissertation Inst. Wasserbau III, Universität Karlsruhe, Germany

THE AERODYNAMIC DRAG; EXPERIMENTS ON LAKE GENEVA

W.H. GRAF and J.P. PROST

Laboratoire d'Hydraulique (LHYDREP), Ecole Polytechnique Fédérale, Lausanne, Switzerland

ABSTRACT

The presently available data, obtained during a measuring campaign on the Lake Geneva, permitted a preliminary study on the aerodynamic drag coefficient, C_y. The LEMAN data are obtained for 3 different periods at a single station (buoy) on the lake. The presently available data are presented and compared with the literature. It is recommended to use for wind speeds - 5 m/s $\leqslant U_{10} <$ 15 m/s - a Charnock relation with a = 81; for wind speeds - $U_{10} <$ 5 m/s - a dispersive trend is evidenced which apparently depends on a stability criterion.

INTRODUCTION

The sea and the atmosphere are a coupled system; exchanges of momentum, heat and moisture take place at its interface. The fluxes are (Webb, 1965) (for symbols see end of paper):

momentum flux : $\tau = - \overline{\rho u'w'} = \rho K_M \dfrac{\partial u}{\partial y}$ (1)

moisture flux : $E = \overline{\rho q'w'} = -\rho K_E \dfrac{\partial q}{\partial y}$ (2)

heat flux : $H = \rho c_p \overline{\Theta'w'} = -(\rho c_p) K_H \dfrac{\partial \Theta}{\partial y}$ (3)

It is often suggested that these fluxes are nearly constant "in the first tens of meters" (Pond, 1972). In above equations (1) to (3) the fluxes are expressed as turbulent fluxes as well as with the "bulk aerodynamic method" in terms of mean gradients. As a first approximation the transfer coefficients K_M, K_E and K_H are taken equal to unity and yet another convenient way to express these fluxes is (Neumann and Pierson, 1966, p. 413):

$\tau = \rho C_y u_y^2$ (4)

$E = \rho C_y (q_s - q_y) u_y$ (5)

$H = (\rho c_p) C_y (\Theta_s - \Theta_y) u_y$ (6)

These relations represent "for operational, parametric usage ... as good an estimate as can be justified on the basis of routine observations" (Kraus, 1972,

p. 164). The purpose of this paper is to present preliminary information on the C_y-value obtained from measurements over the water surface of the Leman.

THEORETICAL CONSIDERATIONS

Proposed is that the aerodynamic drag or frictional coefficient, C_y, is determined from eq. 4 which with the frictional velocity $u_* = \sqrt{\tau/\rho}$ renders:

$$C_y = (\frac{u_*}{u_y})^2 \tag{4'}$$

The right side of eq. (4') is an indication of the velocity distribution in the air-boundary layer.

The diabatic wind profile shall be given as:

$$\frac{ky}{u_*}\frac{\partial u}{\partial y} = S_M\left(\frac{y}{L}\right) \tag{7}$$

with $S_M\left(\frac{y}{L}\right)$ as an unspecified stability function; L is the so-called Monin-Obukhov length expressed with: $L = -(\rho u_*^3)/(k\ g\ \overline{\rho'w'})$ being a ratio of momentum and heat flux. In this way the $S_M(y/L)$ function is related with the gradient Richardson number, Ri, or:

$$Ri = \frac{\dfrac{g}{T}\dfrac{d\Theta}{dy}}{(\dfrac{du}{dy})^2} = fct\left(\frac{y}{L}\right) \tag{8}$$

and was given in Plate (1971, p. 74). For unstable conditions Ri and $\left(\frac{y}{L}\right)$ are negative, for stable conditions Ri and $\left(\frac{y}{L}\right)$ are positive and for neutral conditions Ri and $\left(\frac{y}{L}\right)$ are zero. The $S_M(y/L)$ term is frequently expressed with a power series or

$$S_M\left(\frac{y}{L}\right) = 1 + \alpha\frac{y}{L}\ ... \tag{9}$$

There exists an extensive literature (Plate, 1971; Kraus, 1972) on the form and the α-values in eq. (9), with average values of $4 < \alpha < 5$. If eq. (9) is substituted into eq. (7) and integration is performed, a log-linear velocity profile is obtained, or:

$$\frac{u_y}{u_*} = \frac{1}{k}[\ln y + \alpha(\frac{y}{L})] + Cte \tag{10}$$

Evaluation of the constant, Cte, is obtained by introducing the so-called roughness-length, y_o, and eq. (10) reads thus:

$$\frac{u_y}{u_*} = \frac{1}{k}[\ln y/y_o + \alpha(y - y_o)/L] \tag{11}$$

For neutral conditions, with $S_M(y/L) = 1$ - "the lowest meter of the atmosphere is approximately neutral, except when the windspeed is low" (Tennekes et al., 1972, p. 100) - eqs. (7) and (11) read respectively:

$$\frac{ky}{u_\star} \frac{\partial u}{\partial y} = 1 \tag{7'}$$

and

$$\frac{u_y}{u_\star} = \frac{1}{k} \ln \frac{y}{y_o} \tag{11'}$$

The roughness length, y_o, for a flat plate with sand of diameter, d, was given (Schlichting, 1968) as $y_o = d/30$ and for vegetation of crop height, h_c, (Plate, 1971, p. 27) as $y_o = 0.15\ h_c$. For wind over a water surface no conclusive information seems to be available. It appears, however, that the y_o value must be dependent on the "sea-state" and that there exists a feedback mechanism between wind velocity, u_y, and the roughness length, y_o.

From the available literature one is lead to conclude that there exist 3 zones, classified according to the types of wind (velocities), namely: breezes, light winds and strong winds.

For strong winds the roughness values, y_o, and thus the drag coefficient are constant or

$$C_{10} = Cte \tag{12}$$

Kraus (1972) - postulating a constant relationship for $u_\star/u \simeq 0.05$ - derives theoretically this constancy and states "that the wind interacts primarily with the high frequency part of the waves spectrum, which is quickly saturated and has the same power over a wide range of wind velocities; ... above a level which is a small function of most wavelength, the wind apparently does not know what the waves are like". However, there exists disagreement as to what this values of constancy is and for what wind-velocity range it is applicable. Kraus (1972) proposed a theoretical value of $C_y = 2 \times 10^{-3}$; reviewing experimental data, this value is given as $C_{10} \simeq 1.3 \times 10^{-3}$. Wu (1969) proposed: $C_{10} = 2.6 \times 10^{-3}$ if $u_{10} > 15$ m/s, while Sethuraman et al. (1975) find constant values, which depend on the roughness categories and all for $u_6 > 3.5$ m/s. Furthermore Kraus (1972, p. 161) indicated that the y_o-values are almost independent upon the stratification (Ri-Number) for $u_{10} \gtrsim 11$ m/s since for the strong winds convection is always forced.

For light (medium) winds there seems to be agreement that the drag coefficient varies "weakly" with wind velocity or

$$C_{10} = f(u^n) \tag{13}$$

Again considerable disagreement is evidenced in the literature as to wind range of application of this dependency and the numerical form of above relation. Much of the data have been compared with the "Charnock" dimensionless roughness scale of:

$$y_o = \frac{u_\star^2}{ga} \tag{14}$$

where a is a constant. Stewart (1974) seems to imply that this constant lies between $28.5 < a < 81$ for a data range of $3 < u_{10} < 13$ m/s. However, Stewart (1974) also demonstrates that the same data have a constant C_{10} value "in the neighbourhood of 1.3×10^{-3} plus or minus some 20 %". It should be mentioned that Wu's (1969) conclusion is in agreement with $a = 64$. Since the variation of C_{10} values with u_{10} is not conclusive, Pond (1972) in a review article suggested: $C_{10} = 1.5 \times 10^{-3} \pm (10\text{-}20 \text{ %})$, apparently valid for a windrange from 2 to 16 m/s.

For breezes (weak winds) there exists neither much nor conclusive literature. It is probably theoretically sound to expect that weak winds act aerodynamically "smooth" and a Reynolds number relationship such as

$$C_{10} = (\frac{yu_*}{\nu})^{-m} \tag{15}$$

is important. With meager experimental evidence Wu (1969) proposed a relationship for eq. (15). Of importance is the experimental work of Mitsuta and Boullery (1977); for a velocity range of $0.1 < u_2 < 4$ m/s, the drag coefficient was $4 \times 10^{-4} < C_2 < 10^{-1}$. The enormous dispersion could be explained with the fact that density stratification plays a most important role at low wind velocities; this is evidenced by Kraus (1972, p. 161). Furthermore, there is a tendency for y_o values to be larger in stable than in unstable stratification; neutral stratification data falling somewhere in between.

In addition to the wind velocity and the density stratification, other parameters have more recently been studied which possibly could explain the scatter in the C_y values. Donelan (1977) investigated the "sea state" as it affects the drag coefficient. The importance of the fetch is shown by Donelan (1974) and Stewart (1974). Boullery (1977) found the drag coefficient to vary with the gustiness of the wind. However, none of above "new" parameters bring sufficient order into the data.

Finally one cannot help but agree with the strong warning by and to many researchers, and so well said by Stewart (1974): "There is always a substantial amount of scatter in published drag coefficient results. Much of this is undoubtedly due to the technical difficulties of making measurements themselves".

DESCRIPTION OF EXPERIMENTS

The measurements

A detailed description of our experimental programme has been given by Graf et al. (1979) and Prost et al. (1977). The instruments used were: (i) 3 wind speed sensors (Aanderaa WSS 2219), (ii) a wind direction sensor (Aanderaa WDS 2053),

(iii) a magnetic compass and (iv) 2 temperature sensors (Aanderaa TS 1289). All the "air" instruments were mounted on the mast of the anemometric station (see Fig. 6 in Graf et al., 1979) and as such were subject to the flow and wave in-duced movement of this station. No effort was made to "clean" the data of this effect.

The data utilised were obtained at the site "V" described by Graf et al. (1979, Figs. 2 and 14) where the measuring campaign lasted from 9.12.1977 to 15.2.1978. All aerodynamic parameters were, for various reasons (see Graf et al., 1979, Table 4.4), recorded for only a limited duration of 23.1.1978 to 15.2.1978. The parameters - measured every 10 minutes - were: the wind velocity (average velo-cities during 10 minute intervals at 6.1 m, 2.2 m and 0.8 m) and its direction (instantaneous at 5.0 m) and the temperature (its instantaneous values in air at 5.0 m and at the water surface, ca. - 1.0 m).

Within the above duration of registration, 3 periods of 24 hours have been se-lected for analysis. This selection aimed at obtaining a maximum spread in in-tensity of winds. Furthermore, for this site only fetches for SW winds can rea-sonably be calculated. The 3 periods are:

Period 1 (29.1.78 at 13.00 to 30.1.78 at 13.00): with medium winds of
$5 < u_{6.1} < 12$ m/s and some weak winds of $u_{6.1} < 5$ m/s, coming from SW; the preceding aerodynamic situation was similar.

Period 2 (2.2.78 at 0.20 to 3.2.78 at 0.20): beginning with a strong wind (gust) from SW (with values up to 15 m/s) after a relatively calm preceding aero-dynamic situation. All winds are > 7.5 m/s.

Period 3 (31.1.78 at 0.00 to 1.2.78 at 0.00): with weak winds of $2 < u_{6.1} < 6$ m/s coming more or less from NWW and SEE.

The data

The 3 periods resulted in $144 \times 3 = 432$ recordings. However, given the precision of the anemometers and their positioning on the mast, one sometimes obtains (i) at all levels the same velocities or (ii) at higher levels lower velocities than at lower levels. Even if the data reflect a "real" phenomenon, they had to be eliminated, since the analysis bases itself upon the "logarithmic distribution". In this way the recordings reduce themselves for period 1: 142 profiles, for pe-riod 2: 139 and for period 3: 90.

With the wind velocities measured at the three levels a regression analysis based on a logarithmic distribution allows the determination of u_{10}, u_5, u_* and y_0; subsequently the "experimental" velocities are corrected for a wind induced surface current, $u_s = 0.55 u_*$.

308

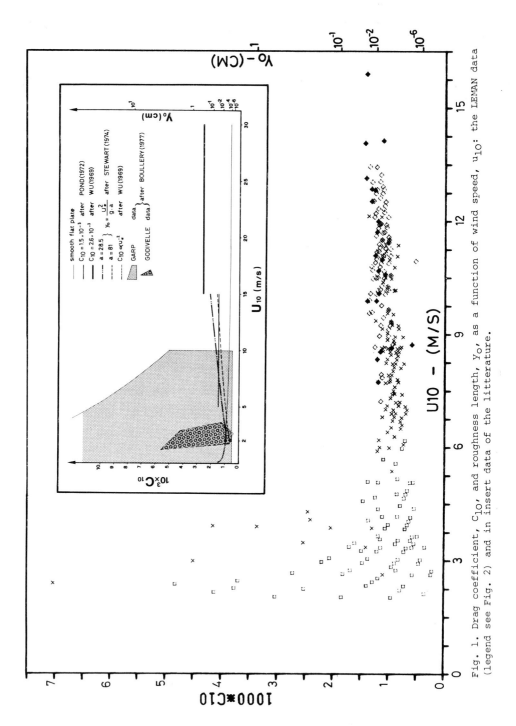

Fig. 1. Drag coefficient, C_{10}, and roughness length, Y_0, as a function of wind speed, u_{10}: the LEMAN data (legend see Fig. 2) and in insert data of the litterature.

Finally we should like to stress that our recordings - the LEMAN data - were used as such and were not "corrected" for supplementary effects caused possibly by the recording instruments and/or the floating anemometric station.

PRESENTATION OF DATA

Drag coefficient and roughness length

A most useful - and indeed often employed - display of the data is obtained by plotting C_{10} and/or y_o versus u_{10}. In the insert of Fig. 1 this is done for relationships as discussed in the previous section; all of these data are obtained for neutral conditions. For the sake of comparison, the smooth flat plate is also indicated; to be noted is that the latter presents a lower limit to above relations. Since relationships for low wind speeds are scarce, we indicated also two sets of data for low wind speeds; these data are for neutral and non-neutral conditions. On Fig. 1 and Fig. 2 the data of our field experiments, the LEMAN data, are represented;

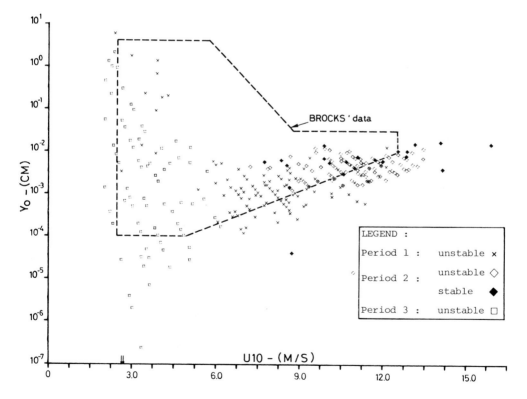

Fig. 2. Roughness length, y_o, as a function of wind speed, u_{10}; the LEMAN data compared with Brocks' data.

310

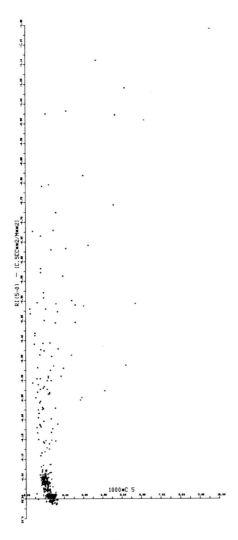

Fig. 3. Drag coefficient, C_5, as a function of a stability criterion, RI(5-0); the LEMAN DATA (legend see Fig. 2).

plotted is the wind speed, u_{10}, against the drag coefficient, C_{10}, and the roughness length, y_o, respectively. Comparing now the LEMAN data with the literature, as displayed in the insert of Fig. 1, one notices: (i) for wind speeds, 5 m/s $\leqslant u_{10} <$ 15 m/s, the LEMAN data (neutral and non neutral) fall slightly underneath the Charnock relation with a = 81; realizing the fact that the LEMAN data are collected with certain experimental difficulties, we are led to conclude that a Charnock relation with a = 81 might be sufficiently appropriate; (ii) for wind speeds, $u_{10} <$ 5 m/sec, the LEMAN data exhibit the dispersive trend similar to the one of Boullery (1977) and Brocks et al. (1970); no specific conclusion can be drawn.

If the LEMAN data are compared with the values supplied by Brocks et al. (1970), above remarks are further evidenced; this is done with Fig. 2. Our conclusion corroborates with Kraus (1972, p. 160): "The influence of the density stratification ... is larger at low wind speeds ... The resulting decrease in the spread of y_o with increasing wind velocity is illustrated ..." The Brocks' data seem to show that for unstable stratification the y_o-values are in general lower than the stable ones. The LEMAN data do not show this pronounced tendency which is also indicated in Fig. 3.

Atmospheric stability

Stability of the atmosphere is described with either the stability function, $S_M(\frac{y}{L})$, or the gradient Richardson-Number, Ri - see eq. (8). In the present study we used a bulk Richardson Number, R_b, indicating the difference between the air layer temperature at 5 m, T_5, and the water surface temperature, T_s, or:

$$R_b = \text{const.} \left[\frac{T_5 - T_s}{u_5^2}\right] = \text{const. } [RI(5-0)] \tag{16}$$

where u_5 is the wind velocity at 5 m. A similar stability relation was used by Donelan et al. (1974) and Boullery (1977). Either of the above criteria becomes zero for neutral conditions; it is numerically positive for stable and negative for unstable conditions.

In Fig. 3, the LEMAN data are plotted with above stability criteria versus the drag coefficient, C_5. First one notices that during the present measuring campaign which falls into the winter months, the majority of data are for unstable values. For small RI(5-0)-values (- 0.1 < RI(5-0) < 0.02) the data present themselves with a reasonable spread. An average C_5-values of $C_5 \simeq 1.30 \times 10^{-3}$ (corresponding: $C_{10} \simeq 1.15 \times 10^{-3}$) can be taken; this values being slightly higher for positive RI(5-0) (stable) and slightly lower for negative RI(5-0) values (unstable). For RI(5-0) values smaller than - 0.1 the spread of the data is considerable and thus no conclusion can be drawn from them.

ACKNOWLEDGEMENT

This work is partially sponsored by the Swiss National Scientific Foundation (FNSRS) under its special program "Fundamental problems of the water cycle in Switzerland".

SYMBOLS

ρ	air density
$V(u,v,w)$	velocity vector
q	specific humidity
Θ	potential temperature
c_p	specific heat at constant pressure
'	indicating turbulent fluctuations
‾	" mean value
y	" height of observation
s (subscript)	" water surface
a	" air
C_y	drag coefficient, with respect to the observation height y (i.e.: C_{10}, C_5)
u_*	friction velocity

312

k	Karman's constant
$S_M(y/L)$	stability function
T	absolute temperature
Ri	gradient Richardson Number
R_b	Bulk Richardson Number
g	gravitational acceleration
Y_o	roughness length
a	Charnock's constant
ν	kinematic viscosity

REFERENCES

Boullery, B., 1977. Etude expérimentale du coefficient de frottement pour un fetch court et en régime de vent faible. Bull. Dir. Etudes et Rech. Electricité de France, No 1, Série A.

Brocks, K. and Krügermeyer, L., 1970. The hydrodynamic roughness of the sea surface. Studies Physical Oceanography, Paper 5.

Donelan, M.A., Birch, K.N., and Beesley, D.C., 1974: Generalized Profiles of Wind Speed, Temperature and Humidity. Proc. 17th Conf. Great Lakes Res., 1974.

Donelan, M.A., 1977. Are Aquatic Micrometeorologists delivering the goods or is the over-water drag coefficient far from constant? Report Series No 43, Symposium on Modeling Transport Mechanisms in Oceans and Lakes. CCIW, Burlington, Ontario 6-8 Oct. 1975.

Graf, W.H., Perrinjaquet, C., Bauer, S.W., Prost, J.-P. and Girod, H., 1979. Measuring on Lake Geneva. In: Hydrodynamics of Lakes, ed. W.H. Graf and C.H. Mortimer, Elsevier Scientific Publishing Company, Amsterdam.

Kraus, E.B., 1972. Atmosphere-Ocean Interaction. Oxford Monographs in Meteorology, Claredon Press, Oxford.

Neumann, G. and Pierson, W., 1966. Principles of Physical Oceanography. Prentice Hall Inter. Inc., N.J.

Plate, E.J., 1971. Aerodynamic Characteristics of Atmospheric Boundary Layers. U.S. Atomic Energy Commission, TID-25465.

Pond, S., 1972. The Exchanges of Momentum, Heat and Moisture at the Ocean-Atmosphere Interface. In: Numerical Models of Ocean Circulation, Nat. Academy of Sci. Washington, Publ. of year 1975.

Prost, J.-P., Bauer, S.W., Graf, W.H. and Girod, H., 1977. Campagne de mesure des courants dans le Léman. Bull. Techn. Suisse Romande, Vol. 103, No 19.

Schlichting, H., 1968. Boundary Layer Theory. McGraw Hill, New York.

Sethuraman, S. and Raynor, G., 1975. Surface drag Coefficient Dependence on the Aerodynamic Roughness of the Sea. J. Geophys. Res., 80:4983-4988.

Stewart, R.W., 1974. The Air-Sea Momentum Exchange. Boundary-Layer Meteorology 6:151-167.

Tennekes, H. and Lumley, J., 1972. A First Course in Turbulence. MIT-Press, Cambridge.

Webb, E.K., 1965. Aerial Microclimate. Agricultural Meteorology, Meteorological Monographs 6:27-58, Boston, American Meteorological Society.

Wu, J., 1969. Wind Stress and Surface Roughness at Air-Sea Interface. J. Geophys. Res., 74:444-455.

EXPERIENCES FROM THE ESTIMATION OF EVAPORATION FROM A SHALLOW LAKE

F. NEUWIRTH

Zentralanstalt für Meteorologie und Geodynamik, Wien (Austria)

ABSTRACT

During the International Hydrological Decade the Central Institute for Meteorology has carried out hydrometeorological field experiments at Lake Neusiedl,
in particular to estimate the evaporation of that lake by different methods.
    The very different behavior of evaporation from the Class-A-pan in contrast
to that from the lake during typical weather situations is evident. It is
possible to estimate evaporation from the lake satisfactorily by empirical
evaporation formulae, if the empirical constants are evaluated carefully by
comparison with the results gained by the heat budget method. It is also shown
that for practical purposes evaporation from the lake can be estimated by
empirical formulae using long-term means of the data. By correlation analysis
the different influences of the single meteorological elements on the complex
quantity evaporation are examined.

INTRODUCTION

The Central Institute for Meteorology has carried out intensive hydrometeo-

rological field experiments within the framework of IHD at Lake Neusiedl in the

period 1966-1974 (Mahringer, 1966; Mahringer et al., 1968; Dobesch et al., 1974;

Austrian National Committee for IHD, 1974).

Lake Neusiedl (in Hungarian Ferto) is the only steppe-lake in Central Europe.

It has an average area of approximately 320 km^2 at an elevation of 115 m above

sea level. The predominant part of this area is Austrian territory, the rest

Hungarian. Its water depth varies from 30 to a maximum of 200 cm. Lake Neusiedl

has only little surface inflow, the discharge takes place through a man-controlled

canal, which is situated in Hungary. Therefore, the water balance is first of all

dominated by groundwater inflow, precipitation and evaporation.

The most interesting matter of our investigation was the evaluation of the

water and heat budget of the lake, the main goal being the exact determination

of evaporation.

314

For that purpose several meteorological stations in the area of the lake have been established (Fig. 1). The most interesting and important station was the station in the middle of the free water surface. This station could be kept working only during ice-free conditions (April till November). It was surrounded by at least 4 km of free water surface in all directions.

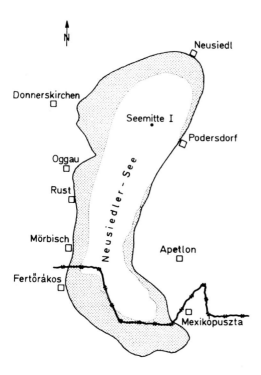

Fig. 1. Hydrometeorological stations in the area of Lake Neusiedl

At the main stations the evaporation was determined by means of a) evaporation pans, b) empirical evaporation formulae, c) heat budget method and d) aerodynamic profile method. For practical applications and, respectively, to get evaporation values for longer periods (years), the two last-mentioned methods proved too extensive as to the necessary measuring equipment. Therefore, primarily experiences and results gained with the first two methods are presented in this paper.

ESTIMATION OF EVAPORATION BY EVAPORATION PANS

The pecularities and difficulties of evaporation pans are well known (WMO,1966; Hounam, 1973; Neuwirth, 1973a).

During our investigations Class-A-pans and GGI-3000 pans were used, in accordance with the recommendations of WMO (WMO, 1966). Additionally, a floating GGI-3000 pan was kept close to the midlake station with the aid of a triangular raft (one side 7 m, the other two 10 m) (Neuwirth, 1973b).

Table I informs on the obtained coefficients to evaluate the evaporation of the lake from measured evaporation in Class-A-pans for monthly sums.

TABLE I

Monthly pan coefficients for the Class-A-pan at the midlake station, May to October 1967 to 1969

Year							
1967	0.70	0.70	0.70	0.71	0.75	0.68	0.71
1968	0.75	0.77	0.73	0.77	0.81	0.82	0.78
1969	0.80	0.77	0.68	0.61	0.59	0.61	0.67
Average	0.75	0.75	0.70	0.70	0.72	0.70	0.72

For estimating evaporation from measured values of pan evaporation, pans floating in the lake are recommended, because by this arrangement good agreement between the temperature regime in the pan and that of the lake is obtained. Incorrect values were, however, exposed, when wind-driven waves disturbed the evaporation mechanism.

How much evaporation of the lake during certain weather situations differs from evaporation of Class-A-pans is shown by Fig. 2 with the aid of four typical weather situations (Neuwirth, 1973b). Fig. 2a reveals the differences during a situation before the passage of a front with strong and dry winds from south. Under these conditions the evaporation from Class-A-pan is higher than that of the lake, because of the heavy overheating of the pan. During northwest-weather (Fig. 2b) after the passage of a cold front, the evaporation of the lake throughout the day is higher than that of the pan, since the lake attains higher temperatures than the pan because of its higher heat capacity. During the light winds of high pressure conditions (Fig. 2c) the evaporation of the Class-A-pan is higher than that of the lake, but due to the low wind speeds the evaporation values are generally small. Fig. 2d shows the evaporation features during the passage of a cold front, which occurred between 14^h and 15^h of the day in question. Evaporation from the pan in this hour is increasing rapidly, conditioned by the still high saturation deficit and the onset of strong winds. However, in the following period the evaporation from the pan is lower than that of the lake.

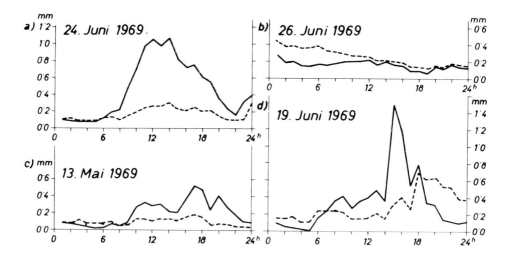

Fig. 2. Daily variation of Class-A-pan (————) and of Lake Neusiedl (————)
during certain weather situations.

EMPIRICAL EVAPORATION FORMULAE

Empirical evaporation formulae for a free water surface are generally used in
the form

$$V = f(u) (E_0 - e_z) \qquad (1)$$

where V means evaporation, $f(u)$ a function of wind speed u, E_0 saturation-vapour
pressure at the temperature of the evaporating water surface, e_z the vapour pressure
of air at height z above the water surface and $(E_0 - e_z)$ the saturation deficit.
We took the wind function $f(u)$ as $(a + bu^c)$, where a, b and c are empirically
estimated constants. The exponent c has been taken either 1 or has been estimated
by turbulence number after Sutton from measurements of the wind speed profile
(Richter, 1969). The constants a and b have been obtained by comparison with the
evaporation results estimated by the heat budget method and the aerodynamic profile
method (Neuwirth, 1974). The quite good linear relationship between $V/(E_0 - e_z)$
and u^c is shown in Fig. 3.

From these relationships for daily values of evaporation, the constants were
determined as a = 0.13 and b = 0.028 for c = 1, and a = 0.07 and b = 0.047 for
c = 0.85, with the wind speed being measured at a height of 3 m in km/h and the
vapour-pressure in mb.

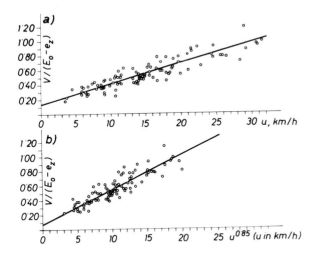

Fig. 3. Relationship between the daily means of V/(E$_o$ - e$_z$) and a) wind speed u
and b) u$^{0.85}$, midlake station, May to October 1969

The results obtained by means of the empirical evaporation formulae in comparison
with the results estimated by the heat budget method are summarized in Table II.

By simply dividing the constants a and b by 24 it was possible to estimate
hourly values of evaporation by means of empirical evaporation formulae. The results obtained in this manner were in surprisingly good agreement with the results
obtained from the much more exact aerodynamic profile method (Dobesch, 1974)

TABLE II

Correlation coefficients between the five-day (r$_5$) and daily (r$_1$) sums of evaporation estimated by empirical evaporation formulae (V$_1$, V$_3$) and estimated by the heat
budget method (V) in the midlake station, May till October 1967-1969

Year	r$_1$(V/V$_1$)	r$_5$(V/V$_1$)	r$_1$(V/V$_3$)	r$_5$(V/V$_3$)
1967	0.86	0.91	0.85	0.92
1968	0.94	0.98	0.93	0.98
1969	0.88	0.96	0.87	0.95

This is probably caused by the high frequency of neutral stratification of the
air above the lake (Dobesch, 1973).

By means of empirical evaporation formulae the annual evaporation of the lake
has been estimated (Fig. 4). Because of the low heat capacity of the water body of

the shallow lake, the early maximum of evaporation at the beginning of July is typical - in contrast to deep lakes, where the maximum of evaporation occurs at the end of July or in August. The rapid increase of evaporation at the beginning of March after ice breaking is also characteristic.

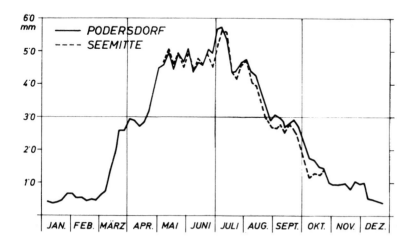

Fig. 4. Mean evaporation of Lake Neusiedl on the shore in Podersdorf (————) and in midlake (— — — —), 1968-1969

Wind function f(u)

Kahlig (Kahlig, 1973) has found by means of dimension analysis that, in otherwise constant conditions the constants b and c in (1) cannot be chosen independently from each other. On the basis of our existing voluminous data material the validity of these assumptions has been verified.

Starting from different c-values and using the constants a and b, obtained by regression analysis (Table III), the daily values of evaporation were estimated. The ascertained monthly sums are shown in comparison with the results estimated by the heat budget method. For practical purposes it is sufficient to use the simplest case, that is the linear form, for the wind function (c = 1).

Günneberg (Günneberg, 1976) has compared our empirical formula with the linear wind function to other formulae known from literature. He ascertained that our formula is in quite good agreement with the others.

TABLE III

Monthly evaporation sums, estimated by empirical evaporation formulae
($V = (a+bu^c)(E_o-e_z)$) with variable c and estimated by the heat budget method in
the midlake station, May till October 1969, in mm.

c	May	Jun.	Jul.	Aug.	Sept.	Oct.	May-Oct.
1.00	157.3	133.6	144.2	109.5	80.6	44.6	669.8
0.85	151.8	130.9	141.2	108.9	80.1	43.7	652.9
0.75	161.3	134.9	147.2	113.9	84.9	45.8	688.0
0.50	152.7	122.1	141.2	111.1	84.5	44.4	656.0
	171.8	143.6	152.5	107.7	77.6	50.5	703.7

ESTIMATION OF EVAPORATION USING LONG-TERM MEANS

For application in climatology and hydrological engineering evaporation is
often estimated from monthly averages of the data by means of empirical evaporation formulae. Using our data material, it was possible to examine which errors
are found by using long-term means (Neuwirth, 1978). Doing this, we have taken
data from 360 days and have carried out the following types of averaging
(t = time of averaging = 2, 3, 4, ... 90, 180 days):

$$V_1 = \sum_1^t (a_1 + b_1 u_1)(E_o - e_z)_1 \tag{2}$$

$$V_2 = t(a_1 + b_1 \bar{u}^t)\overline{(E_o - e_z)}^t \tag{3}$$

$$V_3 = (a_t + b_t \bar{u}^t)\overline{(E_o - e_z)}^t \tag{4}$$

$$V_4 = t(a_1 + b_1 \bar{u}^t (E_o - e_z(\bar{T}^t, \overline{RF}^t, \bar{T}_w^t)) \tag{5}$$

$$V_5 = \sum_1^t (a_2 + b_2 u_1)(E_H - e_z)_1 \tag{6}$$

$$V_6 = t(a_2 + b_2 \bar{u}^t)\overline{(E_H - e_z)}^t \tag{7}$$

$$V_7 = t(a_2 + b_2 \bar{u}^t)(E_H - e_z(\bar{T}^t, \overline{RF}^t)) \tag{8}$$

Hence V_1 represents the evaporation summed up from daily values, V_2 the evaporation estimated by use of the averages of u and E_o - e_z with unchanged empirical
constants, V_3 the same as V_2 but with modified constants for the actual t, V_4
evaporation by use of the saturation deficit, determined from the averages of T,
RF and T_w (T = air temperature, RF = relative humidity, T_w = water temperature),
V_5 the evaporation summed up from daily values by use of the saturation deficit
of the air, V_6 and V_7 the same as V_2 and V_4, gained however, from the saturation
deficit of the air.

In Fig. 5 it is shown that by use of the long-term averages of the saturation
deficit, evaporation is over-estimated (V_2, V_6), whereas by use of the saturation
deficit, calculated by taking the averages of T, RF and T_w, evaporation is underestimated. This is in conformity with the situation in oceans after Laevestu

320

(Laevestu, 1965). Nevertheless, if evaporation is estimated by monthly averages, the differences in relation to evaporation summed up from daily values are small. It also seems possible to estimate the evaporation of a lake by use of the saturation deficit of the air (V_5), if the empirical constants are determined carefully.

DEPENDENCE OF EVAPORATION OF THE LAKE ON DIFFERENT METEOROLOGICAL ELEMENTS

It is also interesting to what extent the different meteorological elements influence the complex element evaporation taken collectively and singularly. It was attempted to evaluate these influences by means of correlation analysis (Neuwirth, 1975).

Starting from the simple two-dimensional correlation-coefficient, the multiple correlation-coefficients with increasing numbers of independent variables are summarized in Table IV.

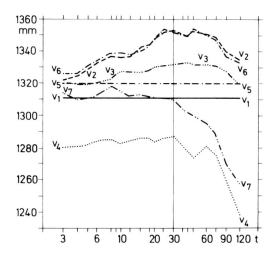

Fig. 5. Dependence of evaporation sums on time of averaging t

It is shown that in any case the multiple correlation coefficients rise, if the number of the independent variables which were taken into consideration increases. According to the amount of the increase it is possible to judge the importance of the respective element. The eminent influence of wind speed is shown in any case by a distinct rise of the r-values. Furthermore, it is seen that the dependence of evaporation on both wind speed and saturation deficit is remarkably high. The net radiation seems not to have a direct, particular influence on the variation of evaporation.

TABLE IV

Two dimensional correlation-coefficients ($\bar{r}$) and multiple correlation coefficients (r) between evaporation (V) and the single meteorological elements (T_w water temperature, u wind speed, T air temperature, R relative humidity, S net radiation, E saturation deficit), for daily and hourly values

$\bar{r}_{VT_S}$	0.50	0.09	$\bar{r}_{VT_S}$	0.50	0.09
$r_{V(T_S,u)}$	0.75	0.65	$r_{V'(T_S,T)}$	0.52	0.09
$r_{V(T_S,u,T)}$	0.77	0.67	$r_{V(T_S,T,R)}$	0.66	0.52
$r_{V(T_S,u,T,R)}$	0.84	0.86	$r_{V(T_S,T,R,S)}$	0.68	0.52
$r_{V(T_S,u,T,R,S)}$	0.85	0.86	$r_{V(T_S,T,R,S,E)}$	0.68	0.52
$r_{V(T_S,u,T,R,S,E)}$	0.87	0.91	$r_{V(T_S,T,R,S,E,u)}$	0.87	0.91
$\bar{r}_{Vu}$	0.49	0.51	$\bar{r}_{VS}$	0.57	0.13
$r_{V(u,E)}$	0.79	0.84	$r_{V(S,T)}$	0.57	0.13
$r_{V(u,E,T_S)}$	0.82	0.85	$r_{V(S,T,R)}$	0.62	0.43
$r_{V(u,E,T_S,T)}$	0.83	0.86	$r_{V(S,T,R,T_S)}$	0.68	0.52
$r_{V(u,E,T_S,T,R)}$	0.85	0.91	$r_{V(S,T,R,T_S,u)}$	0.87	0.90
$r_{V(u,E,T_S,T,R,S)}$	0.87	0.91	$r_{V(S,T,R,T_S,u,E)}$	0.87	0.91

By calculating the partial correlation-coefficients, it is possible to estimate the influence of a single, meteorological element on evaporation (Table V).

TABLE V

Two dimensional correlation-coefficients (r) and partial correlation-coefficients (ρ) between evaporation (V) and the single meteorological elements (analogous to Table IV). (NS = not significant with significance level 5%)

r_{Vu}	0.49	0.51	r_{VE}	0.57	0.37
$\rho_{Vu.E}$	0.67	0.81	$\rho_{VE.u}$	0.71	0.77
$\rho_{Vu.(E,T_S)}$	0.72	0.81	$\rho_{VE.(u,T_S)}$	0.41	0.60
$\rho_{Vu.(E,T_S,T)}$	0.72	0.82	$\rho_{VE.(u,T_S,R)}$	NS	0.48
$\rho_{Vu.(E,T_S,T,R)}$	0.73	0.87	$\rho_{VE.(u,T_S,R,T)}$	NS	-0.39
$\rho_{Vu.(E,T_S,T,R,S)}$	0.73	0.88	$\rho_{VE.(u,T_S,R,T,S)}$	NS	-0.40
r_{VT_S}	0.50	0.09	r_{VT}	0.40	NS
$\rho_{VT_S.u}$	0.70	0.65	$\rho_{VT.u}$	0.65	0.43
$\rho_{VT_S.(u,T)}$	0.55	0.55	$\rho_{VT.(u,R)}$	0.46	0.17

$\rho_{VT_S.(u,T,R)}$	0.61	0.80	$\rho_{VT.(u,R,S)}$	NS	0.18
$\rho_{VT_S.(u,T,R,S)}$	0.59	0.80	$\rho_{VT.(u,R,S,T_S)}$	-0.41	-0.67
$\rho_{VT_S.(u,T,R,S,E)}$	0.38	0.71	$\rho_{VT.(u,R,S,T_S,E)}$	-0.33	-0.93
r_{VR}	-0.52	-0.36	r_{VS}	0.57	0.13
$\rho_{VR.u}$	-0.55	-0.49	$\rho_{VS.T}$	0.38	NS
$\rho_{VR.(u,T)}$	-0.44	-0.31	$\rho_{VS.(T,T_S)}$	0.42	0.15
$\rho_{VR.(u,T,T_S)}$	-0.52	-0.73	$\rho_{VS.(T,T_S,R)}$	NS	NS
$\rho_{VR.(u,T,T_S,S)}$	-0.38	-0.72	$\rho_{VS.(T,T_S,R,u)}$	0.28	-0.15
$\rho_{VR.(u,T,T_S,S,E)}$	NS	-0.57	$\rho_{VS.(T,T_S,R,u,E)}$	0.30	-0.15

The first group in Table V confirms the dominating influence of wind speed: If the influence of the other five variables is eliminated, the highest correlation-coefficients are obtained. The second group deals with the influence of the saturation-deficit. The highest values are obtained, if only wind speed is taken into consideration additional to the saturation-deficit. In the third group it is attempted to find out the influence of surface water temperature: The highest values are reached for $\rho_{VT_S(u,T,R)}$. The fourth group deals with air temperature. The ρ-values are first slightly positive, by additional consideration of T_S, however, they reach high negative values. The explanation of this unexpected result is probably that the highest evaporation occurs during advection of cold air-masses across the lake, while the water is still warm. In the fifth group the relative humidity is examined: Without exception only negative values appear. The greatest dependence of evaporation on RF is shown by taking u, T and T_S into account. In the last group the net-radiation is considered. Although the radiation is to be considered as the motor of the complete system, no direct statistical dependence occurs.

REFERENCES

Austrian National Committee for the International Hydrological Decade, 1974.
    IHD-Activities in Austria 1965-1974. Report to International Conference on the
    Result of the IHD 2.-14.September 1974, Paris.
Dobesch, H., 1973. Das Wind-, Temperatur- und Feuchteprofil über einer freien
    Wasserfläche. Arch.Met.Geoph.Biokl., Ser.A,22:47-70.
Dobesch, H., 1974. Die numerische Bestimmung der Transporte fühlbarer und laten-
    ter Wärme mittels verschiedener Methoden über einer freien Wasserfläche.Arch.
    Met.Geoph.Biokl.,Ser.A,23:263-284.
Dobesch, H. und Neuwirth, F., 1974. Übersicht über die Ergebnisse aus den hydro-
    meteorologischen Untersuchungen des Neusiedler Sees im Rahmen der Internatio-
    nalen Hydrologischen Dekade 1966-1974. Wetter und Leben, 26:151-156.
Günneberg, F., 1976. Abkühlungsvorgänge in Gewässern. Deutsche Gewässerkundliche
    Mitteilungen, 20:151-161.
Hounam, C.E., 1973. Comparison between pan and lake evaporation. WMO Technical
    Note, No. 126.

Kahlig, P., 1973. Zur theoretischen Begründung einiger empirischer Verdunstungsformeln. Arch.Met.Geoph.Biokl., Ser.A, 22:409-424.

Laevastu, T., 1965. Daily Heat Exchange in the North Pacific and Its Relation to
Weather and Its Oceanographic Consequences. Soc.Scient.Fennicae, Op. Physica-
Mathematica, 31:1-53.

Mahringer, W., 1966. Über die Einrichtungen meteorologischer Stationen zur Bestimmung der Verdunstung des Neusiedlersees. Wetter und Leben, 18:223-229.

Mahringer, W. und Motschka, O., 1968. Meteorologische Untersuchungen am Neusiedlersee im Jahre 1967 im Rahmen der Internationalen Hydrologischen Dekade.
Wetter und Leben, 20:159-163.

Neuwirth, F., 1973a. Die Bestimmung der Verdunstung aus einer Class-A-Wanne durch
empirische Verdunstungsformeln.Arch.Met.Geoph.Biokl., Ser.A, 22:97-118.

Neuwirth, F., 1973b. Experiences with evaporation pans at a shallow stepplake in
Austria. Proceedings of the Int.Symp. on the Hydrology of Lakes. IAHS Publication No. 109:290-297.

Neuwirth, F., 1974. Über die Brauchbarkeit empirischer Verdunstungsformeln dargestellt am Beispiel des Neusiedlersees nach Beobachtungen in Seemitte und in
Ufernähe. Arch.Met.Geoph.Biokl., Ser.B, 22:233-246.

Neuwirth, F., 1975. Die Abhängigkeit der Verdunstung einer freien Wasserfläche
(Neusiedlersee) von meteorologischen Einzelelementen. Arch.Met.Geoph.Biokl.,
Ser.A, 24:53-67.

Neuwirth, F., 1978. Die Bestimmung der Verdunstung einer freien Wasserfläche aus
längerfristigen Mittelwerten. Arch.Met.Geoph.Biokl., Ser.B, 25:337-344.

Richter, D., 1969. Ein Beitrag zur Bestimmung der Verdunstung von freien Wasser-
flächen, dargestellt am Beispiel des Stechlinsees. Abh.d.MHD d. DDR, XI,Nr.88.

WMO, 1966. Measurement and Estimation of Evaporation and Evapotranspiration.
Technical Note, No. 83.

THE DAILY CYCLE OF THE WATER TEMPERATURE OF A SHALLOW LAKE

G. TETZLAFF

Institut für Meteorologie und Klimatologie der Universität Hannover

(Federal Republic of Germany)

ABSTRACT

The surface heat balance is applied to a lake's surface. The net heat flux through the surface determines the temperature response of the water. Assuming advective conditions and the formation of an inversion above the lake the water temperature is got as a result. Only the meteorological data of the surroundings upwind the well-mixed lake and its depth are needed to get solutions. An equilibrium temperature with no heat flux through the surface is defined. Applied to daily cycles of the surface temperature of lakes in the arid zones of the trades generally one harmonic is sufficient to describe the water temperature. This was shown by comparison of computed values with surface temperature measurements taken from a satellite (NIMBUS 4).

INTRODUCTION

The water surface temperature plays a key role in the description of the heat fluxes through the air-water interface. An analytic solution using a well-mixed lake's hydrological data and the meteorological data of the surrounding land surfaces assuming advective conditions is presented giving the daily cycle of the water surface temperature. The consideration of the heat budget of the water surface is the basis of the concept following as mainly derived by Edinger et alii (1968) and Fraedrich (1974). The evaporation occurs at the water surface but is described in terms of the conditions met at an inversion as it is nearly always formed above water surfaces under advective conditions. Underneath the inversion the lake's properties and above the inversion the upwind land properties are represented (Fraedrich, 1974). It has to be assumed that the vertical heat fluxes along a trajectory across the lake are constant. The equilibrium vertical heat fluxes then are dependent on the properties of the advected air masses and the water temperature. A minimum width of the lake is required to allow the formation of the inversion (Fraedrich, 1974). The water mass of the lake is assumed to be almost constant with no mass exchanges except for the evaporation. The heat flux through the ground of the lake is neglected.

THE EQUATIONS

The equation for the surface heat budget describes the heat sources or sinks for the lake. It is applied here in the form of equation (1).

$$S = (Q_R - A) - (H + LE) \tag{1}$$

with S the net heat flux through the water surface, $(Q_R - A)$ the surface radiation budget, H the vertical flux of sensible heat and LE the vertical flux of latent heat. Solar radiation and atmospheric counterradiation have to be determined by measurements or by empirical formula. Surface albedo and emissivity have to be available. The equilibrium case is given with no heat flux through the water surface (S=0). The fluxes of latent and sensible heat are parameterised by bulk formula.

$$LE = - L \alpha (q_S - q_a) \tag{2}$$

$$H = - c_p \alpha (T_S - T_a) \tag{3}$$

with L the evaporation energy, α a transfer coefficient depending on the wind speed u, $(q_S - q_a)$ the mixing ratio difference between the lake surface and the atmosphere above the inversion, $(T_S - T_a)$ the temperature between the water surface and the air.

It is assumed that α depends linearly on u (equation 4).

$$\alpha = \rho c u \tag{4}$$

The drag coefficient c contained is not always readily available. Under the conditions found here a value in the magnitude of 10^{-3} is a good approach (Hasse, 1968)

The longwave outgoing radiation A is described by Stefan-Boltzmann's law with $\Delta = 273$ K. Hence the heat balance equation transforms into equation 5.

$$S = Q_R - \varepsilon \sigma \Delta^4 - 4 \varepsilon \sigma \Delta^3 T_S - 6 \varepsilon \sigma \Delta^2 T_S^2 - L \rho u c (q_S - q_a)$$
$$- \rho u c (T_S - T_a) \tag{5}$$

To reduce the number of variables the water vapour pressure curve is used in the form of equation 6.

$$(e_S - e_d) = \delta (T_S - T_d) \tag{6}$$

Taking equation 6 in the case of S=0 or $T_S = T_e$ (surface temperature for equilibrium conditions) and subtracting it from the equation for $S \neq 0$ one gets equation 7 using the Bowen ratio with the constant C_1.

$$S = 4 \varepsilon \sigma \Delta^3 (T_e - T_S) + 6 \varepsilon \sigma \Delta^2 (T_e^2 - T_S^2) + L \rho ((C_1 + \delta) T_e$$
$$- (C_1 + \delta) T_S) c u \, 0.623 / p \tag{7}$$

Neglecting all small terms the presentation of the heat flux through the water surface is found to be:

$$S = M (T_e - T_S)$$

$$M = (4 \varepsilon \sigma \Delta^3 + L \rho u c (C_1 + \delta) 0.623 / p) \tag{8}$$

The heat transfer coefficient M depends on the time, because u and δ do so as well. The temperatures T_S and T_e are time dependent too.

The heat flux through the surface S can also be expressed in terms of the water temperature (equation 9).

$$\rho_w c_w h \frac{\partial T_S}{\partial t} = M (T_e - T_S) \tag{9}$$

This equation can give the description of all types of temperature variations including daily cycles provided some simplifications may be applied. If M and T_e are assumed to be constant with time the temperature difference ($T_e - T_S$) decreases with time exponentially (Keijman, 1974). In the case considered here, arid zones of the trades, a Fourier analysis of the equilibrium temperature exhibited the dominance of the first harmonic wave. The contributions of the other harmonics are smaller than about 1 K in general. Therefore, the equilibrium temperature may be represented by equation 10.

$$T_e (t) = T_{me} + T_i \sin (2 \pi \omega t + \phi_1) \tag{10}$$

Considering on the other hand all parameters used in the heat budget equation the equilibrium temperature results as follows in equation 11.

$$T_e = \frac{Q_R - \varepsilon \sigma \Delta^4}{M} + \frac{M - 4 \varepsilon \sigma \Delta^3}{M (C_1 + \delta)} (C_1 T_a + \delta T_d) \tag{11}$$

Generally in the arid zones M may be regarded as a single harmonic wave with a very small amplitude. A sensitivity analysis showed that M may even be treated as a constant, because the influence on the surface temperature is negegible. However, inserting it as a harmonic wave would not alter the structure of the solution of equation 9.

APPLICATION

Lake Chad is the example selected for further consideration. The air flow across the lake is almost uniform in winter due to the steadiness of the African trades. Some surface data of the lake are available from satellite observations (NIMBUS 4) allowing to test the results.

According to the sinusoidal forcing exerted by the equilibrium temperature the solution for the surface temperature is got in the form of equation 12.

$$T_S (t) = T_{mS} + T_u \sin (2 \pi \omega t + \phi_2) \tag{12}$$

Relations between T_e and T_s may be used to determine the amplitudes of both temperatures. The phase lag between T_e and T_s is obtained for some cycles from observations. It is found to be very uniform and close to $\pi / 2$.

Comparaisons between the computed and the observed surface temperature values are represented in table 1. Examples for the data of the daily cycle of most of the parameters are given in the figures 1 and 2. All the data refer to Lake Chad in winter time.

TABLE I

Comparaison of computed (T_s) and observed surface temperature values

	local time	T_s (°C)	T_{Sat} (°C)
15.12.1970	11h 17	14.5	15.3
27.12.1970	11h 02	15.2	15.6
2. 2.1971	11h 17	16.9	17.2
7. 2.1971	11h 03	17.9	18.6
18. 2.1971	11h 32	22.4	22.7
25. 2.1971	11h 33	23.4	23.4

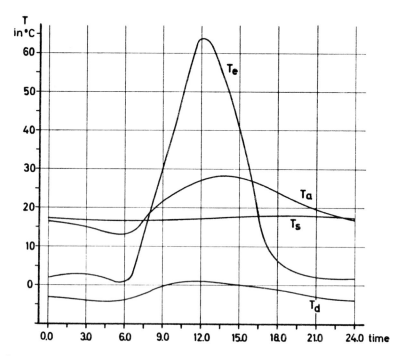

Fig. 1. Air temperature T_a and dewpoint temperature T_d of advected air upwind Lake Chad and water surface temperature T_s and equilibrium temperature T_e of Lake Chad for the 2nd of February 1971.

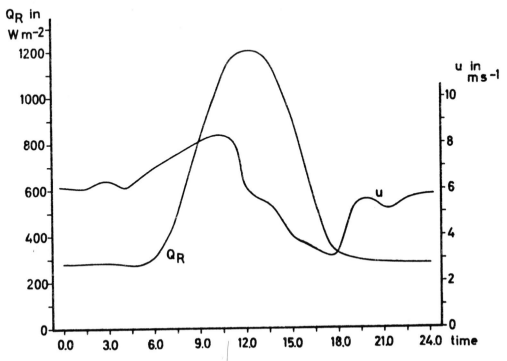

Fig. 2. Wind speed u and radiative gain of the surface of Lake Chad for the 2nd of February 1971.

The close coincidence in the results presented should not imply a similar accuracy. The errors produced by the assumptions and the satellite are at least in the order of magnitude of 1 K.

LIST OF SYMBOLS

A	long wave radiative losses of the surface
c	drag coefficient
c_w	specific heat of water
C_1	constant
e_s	water vapour pressure at the surface
e_d	water vapour pressure in the atmosphere
h	depth of the lake
H	flux of sensible heat
L	evaporation energy
LE	flux of latent heat
M	heat transfer coefficient
p	air pressure

q_S	mixing ratio at T_S
q_a	mixing ratio at T_a
Q_R	incoming radiation
S	heat exchange through the surface
T_a	air temperature
T_d	dew point temperature
T_e	equilibrium temperature
T_i	amplitude of T_e
T_{me}	average of T_e
T_{mS}	average of T_S
T_{Sat}	observed satellite temperature
T_u	amplitude of T_S
t	time
u	wind velocity
α	transfer coefficient
δ	slope of vapour pressure curve
ε	emissivity
ρ	density of air
ρ_w	density of water
σ	Stefan-Boltzman-constant
ω	frequency
ϕ	phase lag

REFERENCES

Edinger, J.E., Duttweiler, D.E., Geyer, J.C., 1968. The response of water temperatures to meteorological conditions. Water Resources Res., Vol. 4, No. 5: 1137-1143.

Eggers, K.A. and Tetzlaff, G.. A simple model for the description of the heat balance of a shallow lake with application Lake Chad. Boundary Layer, in press.

Fraedrich, K., 1974. Further studies on the equilibrium evaporation of a lake under convective conditions, unpubl. manuscript.

Hasse, L., 1968. Zur Bestimmung der vertikalen Transporte von Impuls und fühlbarer Wärme in der wassernahen Luftschicht über See. Hamburger Geophys. Einzelschriften, 11.

Keijman, J.Q., 1974. The estimation of the energy balance of a lake from simple weather data. Boundary Layer, 7:399-407.

Tetzlaff, G., Eggers, K.A., Roth, R., 1977. Wasserhaushaltskomponenten von zwei Inlandseen in trockener Umgebung. Annalen d. Meteorol., NF 12: 131-133.

A MODEL FOR THE PREDICTION OF REAERATION COEFFICIENT IN LAKES FROM WIND VELOCITY

M. SIVAKUMAR and A. HERZOG

Department of Civil Engineering, University of Newcastle, New South Wales 2308,
   Australia.

ABSTRACT

Sivakumar, M. and Herzog, A., 1978. A model for the prediction of reaeration
   coefficient in lakes from wind velocity.

Wind over lakes and ponds induces water circulation and also affects the reaeration
of water and the process of diffusion of dissolved oxygen. A modification of the
eddy cell method of mass transfer is presented which permit the calculation of the
oxygen transfer coefficient from the given wind velocity. It is suggested that a
linear relationship exist between the reaeration coefficient and the wind shear
velocity. This relationship is similar to that which exists between the water shear
velocity and the reaeration coefficient in streams and rivers.
   The proposed model attempts to clarify the basic physical processes at the air-
water interface. The model gave realistic predictions when used with observed data
published by other researchers.

INTRODUCTION

The oxygen transfer at the air-water interface and the parameter which controls
it, is of particular interest in determining the mass transfer rates. Wind action
over polluted water bodies induces turbulence at the zone of the interface which
increases the rate of oxygen absorption. The transfer of oxygen at the air-water
interface is characterized by the oxygen transfer coefficient (K_L) or by the reaeration coefficient (K_2). The effect of wind on the reaeration in natural streams and
rivers has been studied by Mattingly (1977) in open channel flow under laboratory
conditions. He demonstrated that the effect of the wind can produce more than one
order of magnitude increases in the reaeration coefficient.

There is little information available as to what extent the wind action affects
the reaeration of lakes. Work by Banks (1975) gave an insight of the dependency of
the oxygen transfer coefficient and of the turbulent diffusion coefficient on wind
speed. He postulated that the oxygen transfer coefficient may be linearly related
to the wind velocity.

Several models have been developed to represent the aeration of water for various
mixing conditions. Apparently, Holley (1973) is the first person who treated the
reaeration problem as a diffusion model and introduced the region of steep gradient

332

at the air-water interface as an "oxygen boundary layer". The model presented in this paper makes use of the boundary layer concept in surface film at the air-water interface. In this work, the eddy cell theory as applied by Brtko and Kabel (1976) is modified by making use of the turbulence surface film concept. This produced a relatively simple model for the prediction of the reaeration coefficient from readily measurable parameters. The model indicates a definite linear correlation between the wind shear velocity and the reaeration coefficient.

BACKGROUND WORK

One of the controversial and earliest known theories of gas absorption process is the film theory proposed by Whitman (1923) and Lewis and Whitman (1924). They assumed that there exists a stagnant film adjacent to the free liquid surface through which mass is transferred by molecular diffusion. Since oxygen has low solubility in water, the concentration distribution at the air-water interface will be as shown in figure 1.

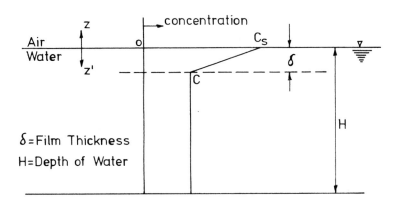

Fig. 1. Sketch of surface film.

However, the assumption of stagnant film at the free surface in a turbulent liquid has not been accepted. Since then various theories have been proposed by Higbie (1935), Danckwerts (1951), Dobbins (1964), Lamont and Scott (1970) and Holley (1973). Holley assumed turbulent conditions and developed a diffusion model for the transport of oxygen from the free surface into the body of water. The transport equation for diffusion in the z' direction as shown in figure 1 is given by Bird et al. (1960)

$$F = D_{TC} \frac{\partial C}{\partial z'}$$ (1)

where F is the amount of oxygen transferred per unit area per unit time, D_{TC} is a diffusion coefficient and C is the concentration of oxygen with turbulent fluctuation averaged out. Holley referred D_{TC} as $D_m + D_t$ where the subscripts m and t refer to molecular and turbulent contribution to diffusion. From the definition of oxygen transfer coefficient.

$$F = K_L(C_S - C) \tag{2}$$

where C_S is the saturation concentration at the surface. From equations (1) and (2) Holley obtained the relationship,

$$K_L = D_{TC}/\delta \tag{3}$$

where δ is the thickness of the turbulent surface film. Two important assumptions are made in deriving the above simplified equation. One is that in equation (1), for the concentrations and transport rates, the effect of turbulent fluctuations has been averaged and the second is the assumption of a linear concentration distribution through the turbulent film.

Lamont and Scott (1970) considered an eddy cell model for the hydrodynamic behaviour of a turbulent liquid near the surface. It related the observed mass transfer behaviour directly to the state of the turbulent field. The model assumes that the very small scale turbulent motions are the controlling factors in effective mass transfer. The eddies as shown in figure 2 travel towards the surface and are reflected back into the bulk of the liquid, thereby the mass is transferred by molecular diffusion very near the surface. Since the smallest scales are predominantly viscous, the motions are idealized as square viscous eddy cells as shown

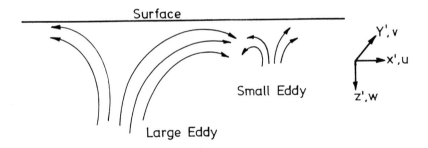

Fig. 2. Representation of eddies.

in figure 3. Lamont and Scott (1970) assumed that a sinusoidal shearing motion of amplitude A exists at a distance 'a' below the free surface. The motion is treated as time steady in the analytical solution of the flow and it is assumed that the diffusion equations are applicable in the eddy cell. The final result of the solution is (Lamont and Scott, 1970)

$$\frac{k'_\ell a}{D_m} = 0.445 \, N_{Pe}^{1/2} \tag{4}$$

334

where k_ℓ' is the mass transfer coefficient of an idealized eddy cell, D_m is the molecular diffusivity and N_{Pe} $(= \frac{aA}{D_m})$ is the Peclet Number. In order to determine

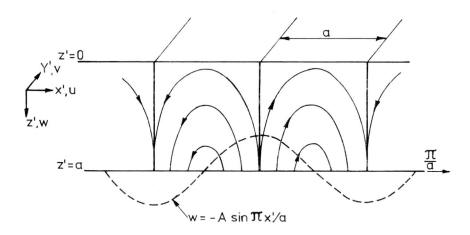

Fig. 3. Idealized Viscous Eddy Cell (After Lamont and Scott, 1970).

the overall mass transfer coefficient, it is necessary to add up the contributions of eddies of all sizes. They used the Kovasznay energy spectrum (Hinze, 1959),

$$E(k) = 0.45\varepsilon^{2/3}k^{-5/3}[1 - \frac{0.6\nu \, k^{4/3}}{\varepsilon^{1/3}}]^2 \tag{5}$$

to determine the turbulent energy distribution over the various wave numbers k $(= \pi/a)$. In equation (5), $E(k)$ represents the three dimensional energy spectrum, ε is the rate of energy dissipation and ν is the kinematic viscosity of fluid. By assuming that the amplitude of the sinsoidal shearing motion A is proportional to $\sqrt{kE(k)}$ and integrating over the wave numbers in the dissipation range, the following equation was obtained (Lamont and Scott, 1970).

$$K_L = 0.40 \, (\nu/D_m)^{-1/2}(\varepsilon\nu)^{1/4} \tag{6}$$

REAERATION AND WIND SHEAR VELOCITY

To calculate mass transfer using equation (6), the energy dissipation which is defined by equation (7) should be known.

$$\varepsilon = \nu \overline{(\frac{\partial u_i}{\partial x_j} + \frac{\partial u_j}{\partial x_i}) \frac{\partial u_j}{\partial x_i}} \tag{7}$$

where u_i and u_j are the turbulent fluctuations in the x_i and x_j directions respectively. To calculate ε, careful measurements of the profiles of the turbulent velocity fluctuations near the fluid surface are necessary. These are too cumbersome. However, for hydrostatically neutral flow in the atmosphere the energy dissipation is equal to the rate of mechanical energy production: (see Pasquill, 1963)

$$\varepsilon = u_*^2 \frac{\partial U(z)}{\partial z} \tag{8}$$

where u_* is the friction velocity at the surface in the air and $U(z)$ is the wind velocity at a reference height z. For this type of flow over a water surface, the wind velocity distribution is given by

$$U(z) = \frac{u_*}{\kappa} \ln(z/z_{oa}) \tag{9}$$

where κ is the universal von Karman constant and z_{oa} is the roughness height in air. In addition, Shemdin (1972) experimentally demonstrated that under neutral conditions there exists a logarithmic velocity profile near the water body. This was previously observed by Bye (1967) in ocean drifts. This velocity profile is given by

$$U_w(o) - U_w(z') = \frac{w_*}{\kappa} \ln(z'/z_{ow}') \tag{10}$$

where $U_w(o)$ is the surface drift velocity, $U_w(z')$ is the velocity at some depth z' below the fluid surface, w_* is the friction velocity in water and z_{ow}' is the roughness height in water. To determine an expression for the energy dissipation, Brtko and Kabel (1976) assumed that under neutral conditions in the liquid, the rate of energy dissipation is analogous to equation (8) which gives,

$$\varepsilon = - w_*^2 \frac{\partial U_w(z')}{\partial z'} \tag{11}$$

substitution of equation (10) into equation (11) results,

$$\varepsilon = \frac{w_*^3}{\kappa z'} \tag{12}$$

which is similar to the relation for energy dissipation rate in water bodies as given by Phillips (1966). By assuming,

$$\tau_a = \rho_a u_*^2 = \tau_w = \rho_w w_*^2 \tag{13}$$

where τ is the shear stress at the surface, ρ is the fluid density and the subscripts a and w refers to air and water respectively. Now, equation (12) could be written as,

$$\varepsilon = \frac{u_*^3}{\kappa z'} (\frac{\rho_a}{\rho_w})^{3/2} \tag{14}$$

Brtko and Kabel used a lengthy procedure to determine the reference depth z' even though it is referred later as the depth at which the concentration of oxygen (in the case of oxygen transfer) is measured. The authors suggest herein that it is reasonable to assume that in the case of atmospheric oxygen transfer, the reference depth z' below which the concentration of oxygen is constant, is equal to the thickness of the turbulent surface film δ. Thus, equation (14) becomes

$$\varepsilon = \frac{u_*^3}{\kappa\delta} \left(\frac{\rho_a}{\rho_w}\right)^{3/2} \tag{15}$$

Substitution of equations (15) and (3) into equation (6) gives an expression for the oxygen transfer coefficient under neutral conditions as,

$$K_L = 0.40 \frac{(\nu/D_m)^{-2/3}}{(\nu/D_{TC})^{-1/3}} \left(\frac{\rho_a}{\rho_w}\right)^{1/2} u_* \tag{16}$$

Using the relation $K_2 = K_L H$, the expression for reaeration coefficient will be

$$K_2 = 0.40 \frac{(\nu/D_m)^{-2/3}}{(\nu/D_{TC})^{-1/3}} \left(\frac{\rho_a}{\rho_w}\right)^{1/2} \frac{u_*}{H} \tag{17}$$

where H is the depth of water.

If we assume that D_{TC} is constant under certain mixing conditions, we will get,

$$K_2 = \text{const.} \frac{u_*}{H} \tag{18}$$

which is precisely the same form that Thackston and Krenkel (1969) have presented for the relationship of K_2 and u_* in natural streams.

Now, to relate K_2 with the free stream velocity $U(z)$ (usually z = 10m under field conditions), the definition of shear stress is useful. It is of the form,

$$\tau_a = \rho_a C_D U(10) \tag{19}$$

where C_D is the drag coefficient. From equation (13) and (19), the following expression is obtained for the wind shear velocity,

$$u_* = \sqrt{C_D} \, U(10) \tag{20}$$

Substituting equation (20) into equation (17) gives,

$$K_2 = 0.40 \frac{(\nu/D_m)^{-2/3}}{(\nu/D_{TC})^{-1/3}} \left(\frac{\rho_a}{\rho_w}\right)^{1/2} \sqrt{C_D} \, \frac{U(10)}{H} \tag{21}$$

If C_D is considered constant, this result indicates that the reaeration coefficient is directly proportional to wind velocity provided D_{TC} is a constant. This is exactly the same relation as postulated by Banks (1975).

COMPARISON WITH OTHER DATA

Liss (1973) has performed wind tunnel experiments for oxygen absorption under laboratory conditions. The depth of water used was 30 cm and the wind speed was

TABLE 1

Liss' experimental results compared with predicted values

U_{10}, m/s	u_*, cm/s	Oxygen Transfer Coefficient K_L, cm/h		
		Liss	Brtko & Kabel	Eq. 16
1.6	5.8	1.04	4.75	1.26
2.3	12.1	1.45	8.20	2.63
3.3	17.3	1.92	10.75	3.75
4.2	19.0	2.96	11.53	4.12
5.0	33.5	4.59	17.62	7.27
6.0	31.1	7.72	16.70	6.75
8.2	47.3	11.17	22.77	10.26

measured at a height of 10cm above the water surface with wind speeds varying from 1.6m/s to 8.2m/s. Field studies have been carried out by the Thames Survey Committee (1964) on reaeration rates in the Thames Estuary. Based on this field data,

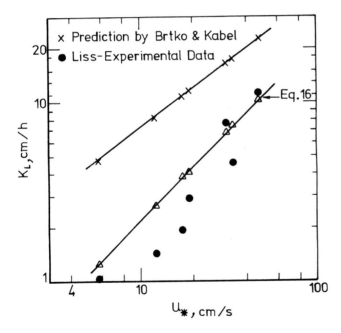

Fig. 4. Predicted and Experimental values of oxygen transfer coefficient for various values of wind shear velocity.

Banks (1975) deduced the following relationship for the effect of wind on oxygen transfer coefficient as,

338

$$K_L = 1.22 \, U \qquad\qquad (22)$$

in which K_L in centimeters per hour and U is in meters per sec. In order to verify the model proposed by the authors the above data were used. Brtko and Kabel (1976) found their predicted values high when compared with data obtained by Liss. Table 1 shows a comparison of the oxygen transfer coefficient values measured by Liss with values predicted by Brtko and Kabel (1976) and by the authors using equation (16).

It should be noted that in the calculation of eddy cell models the physical properties were taken as at 20°C and the diffusion coefficient D_{TC} is assumed to be equal to 0.5 sq.cm. per sec. (see Liu and Perez, 1971, p. 931). It can be observed from figure 4 that equation (16) gives closer agreement with the experimental values of Liss than the predicted values of Brtko and Kabel (1976).

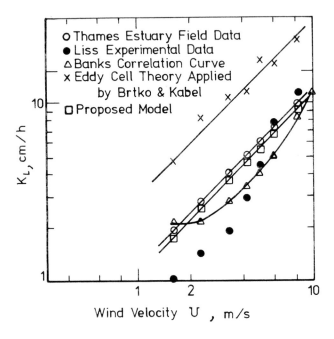

Fig. 5. Comparison of predicted oxygen transfer coefficients with data from other studies.

Recently, Banks (1977) analysed the results of studies conducted by Downing and Truesdale (1955) and Hindley and Miner (1972) and established the correlation line,

$$K_L = 0.36 \, (8.43 \, U^{1/2} - 3.67 \, U + 0.43 \, U^2) \qquad\qquad (23)$$

where U is the wind velocity in meters per sec. and K_L is the oxygen transfer coefficient due to wind action in centimeters per hour. Figure 5 compares the predicted oxygen transfer coefficient for various velocities with the results of all the previously mentioned studies. The Thames Survey Committee (1964) field data is in good agreement with the proposed model equation (16). By assuming a value of $C_D = 0.0030$, it can be shown that the equation (21) can be reduced to,

$$K_L = 1.19 \ U(10) \tag{24}$$

which is similar to equation (22).

When observing figure (4) and (5), the oxygen transfer coefficient seems to correlate better with wind shear velocity, than with the free stream wind velocity. This may be due to the fact that the drag coefficient need not be constant and as several investigators Wilson (1960), Hidy and Plate (1966), and Wu (1968) suggested that C_D may itself be a function of wind velocity.

CONCLUSION

Several assumptions have been made in deriving equation (16). The drastic one being that the diffusion coefficient in the turbulent surface film is assumed to be a constant for all mixing conditions. Although the surface turbulent film may be physically unrealistic, the model nevertheless gave satisfactory prediction within the range of wind velocities considered. There are several limitations to this model. In applying equation (17) to calculate K_2 in shallow lakes, the wind shear velocity should be known. In order to obtain the wind shear velocity, the assumed logarithmic velocity distribution should be correct. The above distribution in both water and air will be valid only if neutral conditions prevail in the atmosphere which may not be always true. Another limitation is the assumption made in deriving the eddy cell model that the free liquid surface remains flat with no wave formation which is possible only at very low wind speeds.

The model predicts oxygen transfer coefficients from first principles. Having made certain assumptions and applied limitations, good agreement was reached with oxygen transfer coefficients calculated from data measured by others. The relationship presented in equation (21) could be used to measure reaeration or oxygen transfer coefficient in shallow water bodies for low wind speeds. It is also applicable to calculate the amount of atmospheric pollutant transfer into water bodies.

It is believed that the diffusion coefficient D_{TC} may depend on mixing conditions and as assumed in this paper, it may be equal to a value in between the molecular diffusion and the turbulent diffusion. In the case of shallow lakes, the mixing and turbulence at the surface is caused by the action of wind and work is continuing to find the effect of D_{TC} on wind velocity.

REFERENCES

Banks, R.B., 1975. Some features of wind action on shallow lakes. J. Environ. Eng. Div., Am. Soc. Civ. Eng., 101:813-827.

Banks, R.B., 1977. Effect of wind and rain on surface reaeration. J. Environ. Eng. Div., Am. Soc. Civ. Eng., 103:489-504.

Bird, R.B., Stewart, W.E. and Lightfoot, E.N., 1960. Transport Phenomena. A Wiley International Edition, New York, 780 pp.

Brtko, W.J. and Kabel, R.L., 1976. Pollutant transfer into water bodies. Water, Air and Soil Pollut., 6:71-95.

Bye, J.A.T., 1966. The wave-drift current. J. Mar. Res., 25:95-102.

Danckwertz, P.V., 1950. Significance of liquid film coefficients in gas absorptions. Ind. Eng. Chem., 43:1460-1467.

Dobbins, W.E., 1964. BOD and oxygen relationship in streams. J. Sanit. Eng. Div., Am. Soc. Civ. Eng., 90:53-78.

Downing, A.L. and Truesdale, G.A., 1955. Some factors affecting the rate of solution of oxygen in water. J. Appl. Chem., 5:570-581.

Hidy, G.M. and Plate, E.J., 1966. Wind action on water standing in a laboratory channel. J. Fluid Mech., 26:651-687.

Higbie, R., 1935. The rate of absorption of pure gas into a still liquid during short period of exposure. Trans. Am. Inst. Chem. Eng., 31:365-389.

Hindley, P.D. and Miner, R.M., 1972. Evaluating water surface heat exchange coefficients. J. Hydraul. Div., Am. Soc. Civ. Eng., 98:1411-1426.

Hinze, J.O., 1959. Turbulence. McGraw-Hill Book Co. Inc., New York, 586pp.

Holley, E.R., 1973. Diffusion and boundary layer concepts in aeration through liquid surfaces. Water Res., 7:559-575.

Lamont, J.C. and Scott, D.S., 1970. An eddy cell model of mass transfer into the surface of a turbulent liquid. Am. Inst. Chem. Eng. J., 16:513-519.

Lewis, W.K. and Whitman, W.G., 1924. Principles of gas absorption. Ind. Eng. Chem., 16:1215-1219.

Liss, P.S., 1973. Processes of gas exchange across an air-water interface. Deep Sea Res., 20:221-238.

Liu, H. and Perez, H.J., 1971. Wind-induced circulation in shallow water. J. Hydraul. Div., Am. Soc. Civ. Eng., 97:923-935.

Mattingly, G.E., 1977. Experimental study of wind effects on reaeration. J. Hydraul. Div., Am. Soc. Civ. Eng., 103:311-323.

Pasquill, F., 1963. The determination of eddy diffusivity from measurements of turbulent energy. Ibid., 89:95-106.

Phillips, O.M., 1966. The Dynamics of the Upper Ocean. Cambridge University Press, Great Britain, 261 pp.

Shemdin, O.H., 1972. Wind generated current and phase speed of wind waves. J. Geophys. Res., 2:411-419.

Thackston, E.L. and Krenkel, P.A., 1969. Reaeration prediction in natural streams. J. Sanit. Eng. Div., Am. Soc. Civ. Eng., 95:65-94.

Thames Survey Committee and the Water Pollution Research Laboratory, 1964. Effects of polluting discharges on the Thames estuary. Water Pollut. Res. Tech. Pap. No. 11, Her Majesty's Stationery Office, London, pp. 357-358.

Wilson, B.W., 1960. Note on surface wind stress over water at low and high wind speeds. J. Geophys. Res., 65:3377-3382.

Wu, J., 1968. Laboratory studies of wind-wave interactions. J. Fluid Mech., 34:91-111.

EFFECTS OF BOUNDARY LAYERS ON MIXING IN SMALL LAKES

Niels-Erik Ottesen Hansen

Institute of Hydrodynamics and Hydraulic Engineering, The Technical University
of Denmark, DK 2800 Lyngby (Denmark).
Danish Hydraulic Institute, Horsholm, Denmark

ABSTRACT

Ottesen Hansen, N.-E., 1978. Effects of boundary layers on mixing in small lakes.

An analysis of lee effects and boundary layer effects on the mixing in two
layered lakes is presented. Especially small lakes can be exposed to these effects
resulting in decreased rates of mixing compared with greater lakes.
   The surface wind shear stress may be very unevenly distributed over the surface of the lake due to lee effects. Typically in the lee of trees, rocks, hills
etc. it will remain zero over a length of 6 times the height of the sheltering
feature and over a further distance of 7 times the height, it will grow to its
fully developed value. In front of lee giving features the corresponding length
is 2 times the height.
   It is shown that winddriven flows in lakes have character of surface boundary
layer over lengths of 15-30 times the depth of the upper layer depending on the
surface shear stress distribution and it is further shown that the mixing between
the different layers in these areas is negligible. Analytical expressions for
rates of mixing are presented as functions of Richardson Numbers, sheltering effects and fetch length to depth ratios. They are found to be in reasonable agreement with measurements.
   Finally mixing in lakes dominated by through-flow is considered.

INTRODUCTION

   In the following the term small lakes is used for lakes in which the flow is

governed by the topography of the surrounding areas or by the shore topography.

The windfield over such lakes is normally rather uneven, because it is influ-

enced by lee-effects from the surroundings, and it consists for a considerable

part of growing boundary layers instead of fully developed turbulent flow. The

same feature will be present in the lake-flow itself in which growing boundary

layers may play an important role. Schematically the problem for wind-driven

flow is shown in Fig. 1. It appears that there has to be a certain distance to

the lake-shore before the turbulence is fully developed. Apart from affecting

the normal wind-driven circulation, this will, for a stratified lake, affect the

342

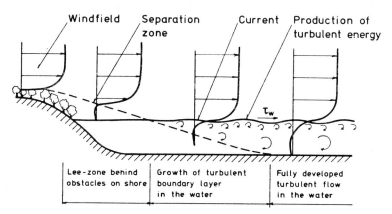

Fig. 1. The development of a Flow Field in a Lake. τ_w is the wind shear stress on the surface of the lake.

mixing between the different layers, which in areas with boundary layer flow will be substantially lower than in regions with fully developed turbulence. The reason for this is naturally that all turbulence is dissipated in the upper part of the upper layer leaving the lower part virtually non-turbulent with the result that only a negligible amount is active in the mixing process.

Now how important are these phenomena for the mixing in stratified lakes? As an example one of the greater Danish lakes - Lake Esrum - is considered, see Fig. 2.

The lake may probably with international eyes be considered rather small as the surface area only is 17 km². It is surrounded by forest covered hills reaching elevations 30-80 metres above the lake surface. The trees are typically 10-20 metres high. This means that the lake surface is in lee from winds and especially from the western winds, which are the predominant winds in Denmark. To get a first rough estimate of the boundary effects some numbers have to be assigned to the growth rate of the boundary layers. Considering first the wind, a distance of approximately 6 times the height to the top of the trees will pass before the wind flow attaches itself to the lake surface (Etheridge and Kemp, 1977) which in this example means that approximately 200-300 m of the lake surface outside the wind side shore is in lee. At the point of attachment the wind shear stress further is zero and it takes a length of approximately 7 times the height to the tree tops before the shear stress attains its final value (Bradshaw and Wong, 1972) which means that the final value first is reached approximately 500 m from the wind-side shore. Of course this will heavily influence the flow in the lake, because the lake is not even 2 km wide. Further a large part of the flow will be boundary layer flow. Typically the depth of a surface boundary layer increases 1:15 to 1:25 with distance before the flow is fully developed. A typical depth

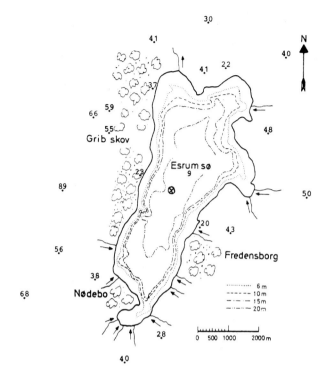

Fig. 2. Lake Esrum. All numbers are the altitude in metres above mean sea level.

for the thermocline in Lake Esrum in the summer is 10-15 metres implying a boundary layer flow over a distance of 250 m - 350 m which is a considerable part of the lake width. Adding the wind lee-effect and the boundary layer effects it is realized that more than half the lake surface is dominated by these effects, making calculations on application of existing models for lake flow rather difficult in this case.

The features in wind driven flows are present too in situations with strong through flow which may occur in ice-covered stratified lakes, see Fig. 3. A boundary layer is formed at the inflowing river and it increases depth with approximately 1:70 to 1:100 with distance i.e. it may cover a large part of the length of the lake.

For the moment the various models for turbulent flows are not so advanced that they can be used on the afore mentioned flows, so instead the problems are analysed with a simple analytical model for the turbulent energy budget. In many practical cases such an approach is sufficient, because the hydraulic calculations usually are input to biological estimates which for the moment are rather crude.

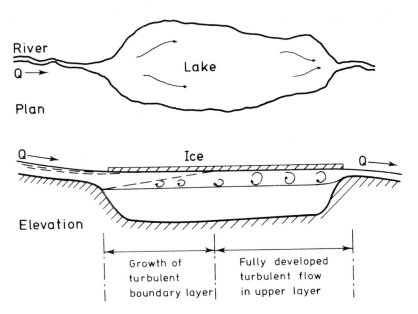

Fig. 3. Flow Field in a lake with through-flow.

MIXING IN FULLY DEVELOPED TURBULENT STRATIFIED FLOW

For later being able to compare the mixing in fully developed turbulent flow
with that in boundary layer flow a short review of the former is presented. The
approach is based on the budget equation for turbulent energy as described by
(Pedersen, 1976, 1977 and 1978 or Ottesen Hansen, 1975). The approach is limited
in the respect that it only applies to situations in which one of the layers is
turbulent and the adjacent layers non-turbulent (Tabel 1), but fortunately
these are the more commen situations in lake hydraulics. The basic assumption is
that a relatively constant fraction of the available turbulent energy is transferred to the entrained fluid. The assumption is not obvious, but experiments and
measurements in nature confirm it. To deduct the necessary relations the analytical
expressions for the contributions to the turbulent energy budget have to be considered. The reader is referred to Table 1 for the notation in the following calculations.

The amount of turbulent energy transferred to the entrained fluid consists of
two parts:

1. The rate of gain in potential energy per area unit

$$\frac{1}{2}\xi\rho g\overline{\Delta}yv_E \tag{1}$$

2. The rate of gain in turbulent kinetic energy per area unit

$$(\frac{1}{q} \int_0^Y u\bar{e} \, dx_3 - e_i)v_E \tag{2}$$

in which

x_3 = vertical coordinate

$\bar{}$ = time average

$'$ = turbulent fluctuation

v_j = velocity component in j direction

u = horizontal velocity

v_E = rate of entrainment

$q = \int_0^Y u \, dx_3$ = rate of flow per unit width

y = depth of turbulent layer

ξ = a constant depending on the density distribution ($=1$ for uniform and $2/3$ for triangular distribution)

g = gravitational acceleration

ρ = density of the turbulent layer

ρ_0 = the density of the stagnant layer

$\bar{\Delta} = (\rho_0 - \rho)/\rho_0$

$\bar{e} = \frac{1}{2}\rho\overline{v_k' v_k'}$ = the turbulent energy per unit mass

e_i = the turbulent energy per unit mass at the interface

In Eq. (1) the following parameters can be identified:

$\frac{1}{2}\xi y$ = average movement of the entraining fluid into the turbulent layer,

$\rho\bar{\Delta}$ = the density deficit of the entraining mass,

and in Eq. (2) the following parameter is identified

$\frac{1}{q} \int_0^Y u\bar{e} \, dx_3$ = average turbulent kinetic energy in the turbulent layer weighed with the distribution of velocity,

which means that Ex. (2) simply states that the gain in turbulent kinetic energy of the entrained mass is the difference in turbulence level between the turbulent layer and the interface times the volume flux of the entrained fluid.

The gain in energy for the entraining mass has to be taken from the turbulent layer. The sources for the presence of turbulence are the following:

Production of turbulent energy in the volume Ω

$$\int_\Omega (-\tau\frac{\partial u}{\partial x_3}) \, d\Omega = \text{PROD} \tag{3}$$

Storing or removal of turbulent energy by advection

$$- q\frac{\partial}{\partial x_j} (\frac{1}{q} \int_0^Y v_j \bar{e} \, dx_3) = \text{STORE} \tag{4}$$

in which

τ = horizontal shear stress (Reynolds Stress)

Ω = the volume considered.

The ratio between the sink terms, Eqs. (1) and (2), and the source terms, Eqs. (3) and (4), is a measure of the efficiency of the transfer mechanism for turbulent energy to the entraining fluid and is by (Pedersen, 1976) denoted the Bulk Flux Richardson Number R_f^T

$$R_f^T = \frac{v_E[\frac{1}{2} \xi \rho \overline{\Delta} g y + \frac{1}{q} \int_0^Y \overline{ue} \, dx_3 - e_i]}{PROD + STORE}$$ (5)

This efficiency of course depends on the distance between the interface and the main generating center for turbulent energy. If the distance is large a large proportion of the energy is dissipated before it reaches the interface and can be active in the mixing process, so in this case R_f^T is small. This is the case in winddriven flows. On the other hand R_f^T is larger when the distance is small, as for instance for internally generated turbulence. For fully developed turbulent flow over the layer depth the magnitude of R_f^T is only weakly depending on how the turbulence is generated. The typical range is:

$$0.05 \leq R_f^T \leq 0.2$$ (6)

in which the lower limit is valid for turbulence generated far from the interface and the upper limit is valid for turbulence generated close to the interface. R_f^T is constant for a particular flow situation which means that as soon as the flow type is identified R_f^T can be determined from tables as Table 1 or the literature – see (Pedersen, 1977, 1978). With R_f^T known Eq. (5) can be used to determine the rate of entrainment v_E. The equation, however, is in the present form impractical, because the different terms are not expressed by the usual hydraulic flow parameters as depth, velocity, or frictional coefficients. In Table 1 expressions are given for the parameters together with the final results for the entrainment. To express this several parameters have been used and they are listed in the following

τ_w = wind shear stress

V = average velocity in the turbulent layer

$U = \sqrt{\alpha} V$

$\alpha = (1/V^3 y) \int_0^Y u^3 \, dx_3$ = velocity distribution coefficient

u_i = horizontal velocity in the interface

τ_i = interfacial shear stress

τ_b = bottom shear stress

$u_f = \sqrt{\tau_w/\rho}$ = the frictional velocity

$F_\Delta^2 = U^2/g\overline{\Delta}y$

$R_i^* = g\overline{\Delta}y/u_f^2$

For more details of the entrainment functions the reader is referred to (Pedersen, 1977, 1978 or Ottesen Hansen, 1975). In Fig. 4 the expressions in Table 1 are compared with experiments.

Table 1. Expressions for entrainment the v_E in different types of flow.

	Wind driven circulation	Heavy turbulent bottom layer	Lighter turbulent upper layer
$\int_\Omega \tau \frac{\partial u}{\partial x_3} d\Omega$	$\rho A u_f^2$; $A \sim 30$; $u_f = \sqrt{\frac{\tau_w}{\rho}}$	$V\tau(1-\beta)$; $\beta = \frac{u_i}{V}\frac{\tau_i}{\tau_i + \tau_b}$	$\rho g q F_\Delta^2 \alpha \sqrt{\alpha}\left[\frac{f}{2}\left(1-\frac{u_i}{U}\right) + \frac{v_E}{U}\frac{1}{2}\left(1-\frac{u_i}{U}\right)^2\right]$
$\cdot\frac{1}{q}\frac{\partial}{\partial x_j}\left(\frac{1}{q}\int_0^y \overline{u_j e}\, dx_3\right)$	~ 0	~ 0	~ 0
$\frac{1}{q}\int_0^y \overline{ue}\, dx_3 - e_i$	$\rho B u_f^2$; $B \sim 7$	Not known	$B\tfrac{1}{2}\rho U^2$; $B \simeq 0.13$
R_f^T	0.05	$0.05-0.13*$	0.13
ξ	$0.5-1$	$0.5-1$	$0.5-1$
Entrainment rate v_E (general expression)	$\frac{v_E}{u_f} \simeq \frac{3}{R_i^* + 15}$	Not known	$\frac{v_E}{U} = 2\left(\frac{u_\tau}{U}\right)^2\left(1-\frac{u_i}{U}\right)$; $\frac{u_i}{U} \simeq 0.5$; $\left(\frac{u_\tau}{U}\right)^2 \simeq \frac{f}{2}$ $\frac{v_E}{U} = \dfrac{R_f^T F_\Delta^2}{1 + F_\Delta^2\left[B\left(1-\left(\frac{u_i}{U}\right)^2\right) - R_f^T\left(1-\frac{u_i}{U}\right)^2\right]}$
v_E for small F_Δ (large R_i^*)	$\frac{v_E}{u_f} \simeq \frac{3}{R_i^*}$	$\frac{v_E}{U} = 0.05-0.13\frac{f}{2}F_\Delta^{2*}$	$\frac{v_E}{U} = 0.13\frac{f}{2}F_\Delta^2$; $\frac{f}{2} \simeq 5\times10^{-4}$
v_E for large F_Δ (small R_i^*)	$\frac{v_E}{u_f} \simeq 0.2$	$\frac{v_E}{U} = f$; $f \simeq 0.075$	$\frac{v_E}{U} = f$; $f \simeq 0.075$

*The lower limit is valid for externally generated turbulence, the upper limit for internally generated turbulence (Pedersen, 1977, 1978).

348

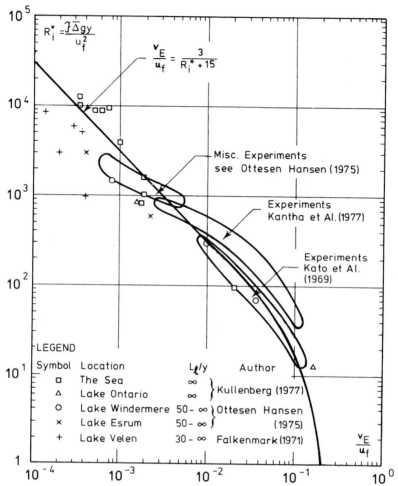

Fig. 4. Calculated and measured entrainment rates v_E in lakes with fully developed turbulence in the upper layer. L_ℓ is the wind fetch length across the lake surface.

ENTRAINMENT IN WIND-DRIVEN BOUNDARY LAYER FLOWS

From Fig. 4 it appears that the measured rates of entrainment may have considerably lower values than found by the theory for fully developed turbulent flow. This is of course due to the formation of boundary layers. To analyze the problem the steady state equation of momentum is considered.

$$v_j \frac{\partial v_1}{\partial x_j} = - g \bar{\Delta} \frac{\partial y}{\partial x_i} + \frac{1}{\rho} \frac{\partial \tau_1}{\partial x_3}$$

(7)

(All the parameters are defined in the previous chapter or in Fig. 5). In the first stage of the boundary layer flow or in flows with very deep thermoclines the pressure term (first term on the right hand side) is small, and Eq. (7) is reduced to

$$v_j \frac{\partial v_1}{\partial x_j} = \frac{1}{\rho} \frac{\partial \tau_1}{\partial x_3} \tag{8}$$

A solution for constant wind shear stress τ_w has been found (Larnæs, 1976)

Boundary layer growth: $\quad \delta = 0.011 \, x_1 \tag{9}$

Shear stress distribution: $\dfrac{\tau}{\tau_w} = \exp\{-0.32 \, \eta^2\} \tag{10}$

Velocity distribution: $\quad \dfrac{u}{u_f} = 11.5(1 - 2N(0.8 \, \eta)), \quad \eta > 0.34 \tag{11}$

in which $\quad\quad\quad\quad \dfrac{u}{u_f} = 6.4 - 2.45 \, \ln\eta, \quad\quad \eta < 0.34$

$$\eta = \frac{x_3}{\delta} \tag{12}$$

and $\quad\quad\quad\quad N(u) = \dfrac{1}{\sqrt{2\pi}} \displaystyle\int_0^u \exp\{-x^2/2\}dx \tag{13}$

u_f is the surface velocity $u_f = \sqrt{\tau_w/\rho}$.

The velocity distribution in the solution is unidirectional, resulting in a net drift of water in the direction of the flow. Of course volume has to be preserved in a lake, so a compensating flow will be induced either as an opposite drift or as a large scale lateral circulation. However, the velocities associated with this drift or circulation will be small because they tend to be uniformly distributed over the depth of the upper layer and will therefore not influence the growth of the boundary layer in the beginning. When the boundary layer on the other hand attains a magnitude comparable with the layer depth the influence of this feature will be felt.

Another important effect for surface boundary layer growth is the longitudinal distribution of surface shear stress. In Table 2 approximate solutions are shown for different conditions.

The velocity and shear stress distributions are not dependent on the longitudinal variation in surface shear stress.

From the expressions of the boundary layer thickness in Table II and the shear stress distribution in Eq. (10) it appears that the transition from surface boundary layer flow to fully developed flow takes place approximately when $\delta = y/3$ (the fully developed flowed is characterized by an almost linear variation of shear stress from surface to interface). Therefore a measure for the length of the boundary layer flow will be the distance from the point of zero boundary layer depth to the point at which $\delta = y/3$. This distance is denoted λ. By means of

TABLE II

Growth of Surface Boundary Layer Depth δ for different situations or variations in surface shear stress.

	Ideal Two-dimensional situation (no compensating drift)	Surface Boundary Layer Growth in Lakes
τ_w constant	$\delta = 0.011\, x_1$	$\dfrac{\delta}{y} = 0.33[1-\sqrt{1 - \dfrac{1}{15}\dfrac{x_1}{y}}\,]$
$\tau_w \sim x_1$	$\delta = 0.0055\, x_1$	$\dfrac{\delta}{y} = 0.33[1-\sqrt{1 - \dfrac{1}{30}\dfrac{x_1}{y}}\,]$
$\tau_w = \tau_{w_0}(1-\exp[-x_1/L])$:the fully developed surface shear stress	$\delta = 0.011\,\dfrac{x_1-L(1-\exp[-x_1/L])}{1 - \exp[-x_1/L]}$	$\dfrac{\delta}{y} = 0.33[1- \sqrt{1 - \dfrac{1}{15y}\dfrac{x_1-L(1-\exp[-x_1/L])}{1 - \exp[-x_1/L]}}$

$\sim$ means proportional with and L is a length scale describing the increase in surface shear stress.

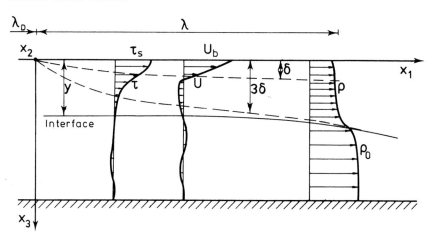

Fig. 5. Definitions of parameters in boundary layer flow. λ_D is the distance from shore.

table II λ can be approximately calculated when pressure gradients are neglected. The results for λ are to be considered as length scales for the development of the boundary layers due to the rather crude methods applied. However, the theory is not that refined that more accuracy is needed. The results are shown in Table III

TABLE III

The length scale for the development of the surface boundary layer in a lake as function of the depth of the upper layer y.

	Ideal Two-dimensional situation (no compensating drift)	Surface Boundary Layer Growth in Lakes
τ_w constant	$\lambda = 30y$	$\lambda = 15y$
$\tau_w \sim x_1$	$\lambda = 60y$	$\lambda = 30y$
$\tau_w = \tau_{w_0} (1-\exp[-x_1/L])$	$\lambda = (30y + L)(1-\exp[-\lambda/L])$	*$\lambda = (15y + L)(1-\exp[-\lambda/L])$

*) This equation can within an error of 3% be approximated with $\lambda = 15y(2-\exp[-0.055L/y])$.

From Table III it appears that the boundary layer zone in lakes will vary between 15-30 times the depth of the upper layer depending on the longitudinal variation of the wind shear stress. The mixing between the upper and lower layer in this zone must be considerably reduced compared with the fully developed turbulent flow because a greater part of the turbulent energy is dissipated before it reaches the interface and can be active in the mixing. As a reasonable working assumption the conditions for turbulent energy and boyancy exchange down to the depth 3δ are identical to the exchange in fully developed flow. The entrainment v_E through an interface is governed by an expression of the following type (Ottesen Hansen, 1975)

$$\frac{v_E}{u_{f,interface}} \sim \frac{\rho e_i}{g\rho \Delta \ell} \tag{14}$$

in which ℓ is a turbulent length scale (in this context proportional with the depth of the upper layer). The entrainment $v_{E\delta}$ through the interface below a surface boundary layer is therefore related to the entrainment in fully developed flow v_E by

$$\frac{v_{E\delta}}{v_E} \simeq \frac{(e_i u_f) \text{ boundary layer}}{(e_i u_f) \text{ fully developed}} \simeq [\exp(-0.32(\eta^2-9))]^{3/2} \tag{15}$$

in which the expression for the distribution of shear stress - Eq.10 - has been applied. From Eq. 15 the average entrainment per unit length $< v_{E\delta} >$ in a boundary layer is found

$$< v_{E\delta} > = \frac{1}{\lambda} \int_0^\lambda v_{E\delta} \, dx_1 \sim 0.01 \cdot v_E \tag{16}$$

which is sufficiently small to be neglected in practical applications. An average
rate of entrainment over a certain distance from the start of the boundary layer
$< v_E >$ can be defined as

$$< v_E > = \frac{1}{L_f} \{ \int_0^\lambda v_{E\delta} \, dx_1 + \int_\lambda^{L_f} v_E \, dx_1 \} \qquad (17)$$

in which L_f is the length over which the wind shear stress acts. This expression
is shown in Fig. 6 as function of the length scale L for the development of the
lake surface shear stress.

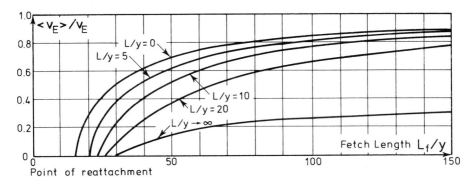

Fig. 6 . The length averaged entrainment rate in lakes with boundary layer flow
compared with the rate of entrainment in fully developed turbulence as function
of the fetch length.

From Fig. 6 it appears that the rate of entrainment in small lakes with limited
fetch length is heavily dependent on the surface shear stress distribution. This
means that lee-effects etc. for a lake have to be carefully studied before any
calculation is undertaken. Further, the expression for entrainment in fully developed
turbulent flow in the upper layer cannot always be used. Instead a family of curves
as shown in Fig. 8 has to be applied.

THE WIND SHEAR STRESS DISTRIBUTION ON A LAKE SURFACE

From the preceding section it appears that The rates of entrainment are rather
dependent on the distribution of surface shear stress, so shelter and lee-effects
from the surrounding countryside play an important role. For the moment the methods
for estimating these effects are rather crude and are more rules of thumb . When
greater accuracy is necessary, model tests or field measurements are applied. In
Fig. 7 the results of tests, which can be used as rules of thumb , are given. The
tests considered are flow over steps - a flow which is similar to the flow behind

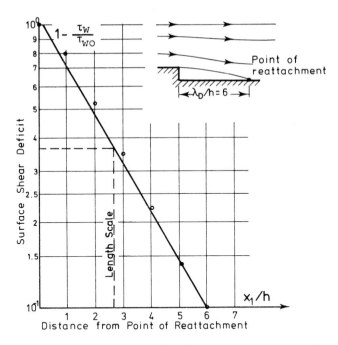

Fig. 7. The growth of wind shear stress τ_{wo} from the point of reattachment of the flow after a step or a sheltering feature. τ_{wo} is the final value of the shear stress (Bradshaw and Wong, 1972).

hills, hedges etc. (Bradshaw and Wong, 1972). It appears that the distance from the point of separation to the point of reattachment is approximately 6 times the height of the lee-giving feature. Further it appears that after the flow has re-attached itself to the lower boundary, the surface shear stress will approach its final value τ_{wo} exponentially. The length scale for this growth is approximately 2.6 times the height.

The results can be applied together with Table III and Fig. 6 in calculating the average entrainment across the interface. In Fig. 8 the entrainment function for deep lakes with steep shore and bottom topography are shown.

The down-wind side of the lake surface may be exposed to shelter too if the shore topography is dominated by steep brinks or by high trees. This area will usually be rather small only covering 1-2 times the height of the obstacle (Hjorth, 1975). The effect on the entrainment is usually small because it acts on lake areas too shallow to be stratified.

COMPARISON WITH MEASUREMENTS

During the years of 1974, 1975 and 1976 an extensive program of measurements were carried out in Lake Esrum, Denmark; water, temperatures, wind velocity and

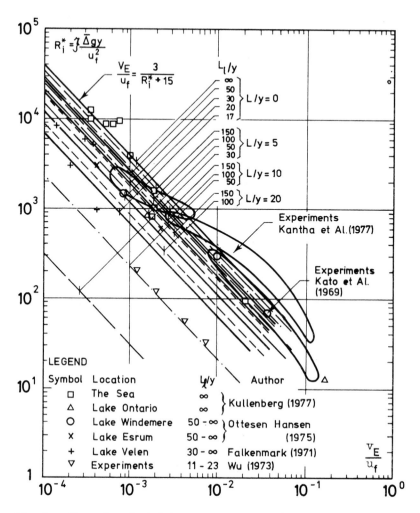

Fig. 8. The rate of wind induced entrainment as function of Richardson Number, the ratio of windfetch to depth of upper layer L_ℓ/y and the ratio of length scale for surface shear stress growth to depth of upper layer L/y ($L_\ell = \lambda_D + L_f$)

direction, evaporation, solar radiation, cloudiness, precipitation and lumidity. In Fig. 9 the isopleth diagram for the summer 1976 is shown and the position of the interface is drawn. Based on the observations of wind speed and direction and of water temperatures through the summer the erosion of the interface is calculated by means of the expressions shown in Figs. 6, 7 and 8. The result is shown in Fig. 9. It appears that the presented theory overshoots a little, but the agreement is satisfactory considering that no constants or expression have been changed to fit this particular lake.

BOUNDARY LAYER EFFECTS IN LAKES WITH THROUGH FLOW

The problem with growing boundary layers in cases with through flow - as shown in Fig. 3 has allready been analyzed (Pedersen, 1972, 1978 ; Pedersen and Ottesen Hansen, 1974). The results of these analyses are that the entrainment functions presented in Table for fully developed through flow can be used for boundary layers too, when the depth of the flowing layer in these equations is replaced by the boundary layer thickness δ. δ is in this context the displacement thickness of the boundary layer. Hence the general formula for the rate of entrainment $v_{E\delta}$ across the interface in a growing interfacial boundary layer approximately is equal to

$$\frac{v_{E\delta}}{u_f} \simeq \frac{f}{2} \frac{R_f^T \ \mathbb{F}^2_{\Delta\delta}}{1 + \frac{1}{2}R_f^T \cdot \mathbb{F}^2_{\Delta\delta}} \tag{17}$$

in which

$$\mathbb{F}_{\Delta\delta} = \frac{u^2}{g\Delta\delta} \tag{18}$$

$$\frac{f}{2} \simeq 0.005 \tag{19}$$

$$\delta \simeq \frac{1}{70} \cdot x_1 \tag{20}$$

Eqs. 17-20 indicate that mixing in the boundary layer is rather large; but it is of little consequence for the rest of the free flow because the mixing is kept inside the boundary layer.

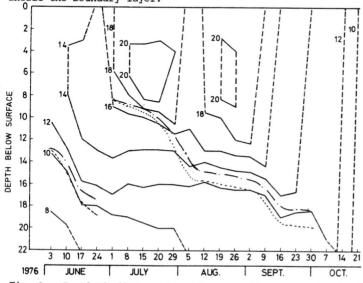

Fig. 9. Isopleth diagram for Lake Esrum the summer 1976. The measurements are compared with theoretical calculations. ———·———Interface position, measured. ----··············· Interface position, calculated.

356

ACKNOWLEDGEMENTS

The writer wishes to thank the Danish Hydraulic Institute for making the field measurements in Lake Esrum available.

REFERENCES

Andersson, S.Å., 1977. Heat Balance in Lakes (in Danish). Report 77-1. The Laboratory of Sanitary Engineering, The Technical University of Denmark.

Bradshaw, P. and Wong, F.Y.F., 1972. The Reattachment and Relaxation of a Turbulent Shear Layer. Journal of Fluid Mechanics, 52, p. 113.

Etheridge, D.W. and Kemp, P.H., 1978. Measurements of Turbulent Flow Downstream of a Rearward-facing Step. Journal of Fluid Mechanics, 86, Part 3:545-566.

Falkenmark, M., 1971. Dynamic Studies in Lake Velen. International Hydrological Decade Sweden, Report 31. Swedish Nature and Science Research Council.

Hjorth, P., 1975. Studies of the nature of local scour. Bulletin series A No. 46. Lund University, Sweden.

Kantha, L.H., Phillips, O.M., and Azad, R.S., 1977. On Turbulent Entrainment at a Stable Density Interface. Journal of Fluid Mech., 79, Part 4:753-769.

Kato, H., and Phillips, O.M., 1969. On the Penetration of a Turbulent Layer into Stratified Fluid. Journal of Fluid Mech., 37, Part 4:643-655.

Kline, S.J. et. al., 1968. Proceedings. Computation of Turbulent Boundary Layers. 1968 AFOSR-IFP-Stanford Conference. Stanford University.

Kullenberg, G., 1977. Entrainment Velocity in Natural Stratified Vertical Shear Flow. Estuarine and Coastal Marine Science 5:329-338.

Larnæs, G., 1976. Formations of Wind Waves. Series Paper No. 10. Institute of Hydrodynamics and Hydraulic Engineering. The Technical University of Denmark.

Ottesen Hansen, N.-E., 1975. Entrainment in Two-layered Flows. Series Paper No. 7. Institute of Hydrodynamics and Hydraulic Engineering. Technical University of Denmark.

Ottesen Hansen, N.-E., 1975. Effect of Wind Stress on Stratified Deep Lake. A.S.C.E. Vol. 101 No. HY 8:1037-1051.

Ottesen Hansen, N.-E., 1978. Mixing Processes in Lakes. Nordic Hydrology,1978,9: 57-77.

Pedersen, Fl.Bo, 1972. The Friction Factor for a Two-layer Stratified Flow, Immiscible and Miscible Fluids. Progress Report 27:3-13, Dec. 1972. Institute of Hydrodynamics and Hydraulic Engineering. The Technical University of Denmark.

Pedersen, Fl.Bo, 1974. Entrainment in Two-layered Flows. Progress Report 33:23-26. August 1974. Institute of Hydrodynamics and Hydraulic Engineering. The Technical University of Denmark.

Pedersen, Fl.Bo, 1976. The Flux Richardson Number and the Entrainment Function. Progress Report 39:23-28, August 1976. Institute of Hydrodynamics and Hydraulic Engineering. The Technical University of Denmark.

Pedersen, Fl.Bo, 1977. The Bulk Flux Richardson Number Applied on Turbulent Entrainment at a Stable Density Interface. Progress Report 43:11-16, August 1977. Institute of Hydrodynamics and Hydraulic Engineering. The Technical University of Denmark.

Pedersen, Fl.Bo, 1978. The Entrainment Function for Gradually Varying Two-layered Stratified Flow. Part 2. Progress Report 45:13-22, April 1978. Institute of Hydrodynamics and Hydraulic Engineering. The Technical University of Denmark.

Svensson, U., 1978. Examination of the Summer Stratification. Nordic Hydrology, 9, 1978:105-120.

Wu, J., 1973. Wind-induced Turbulent Entrainment Across a Stable Density Interface. Journal of Fluid Mechanics. 61, Part 2:275-287.

SUBJECT INDEX